STUDIES IN ENGLISH LITERATURE

Volume XXXIV

ENGLISH LITERARY PERIODICALS

AND THE CLIMATE OF OPINION DURING THE SEVEN YEARS' WAR

by

ROBERT DONALD SPECTOR

Long Island University

1966

MOUTON & CO.

THE HAGUE · PARIS

Printed in The Netherlands by Mouton & Co., Printers, The Hague

For Eleanor
whose patience, courage,
faith, and love I have
drawn upon for my strength

CONTENTS

INTRODUCTION

Within recent years an increased scholarly interest in periodical literature has been apparent, and yet the subject is so vast and the possibilities of investigation so varied, that each new effort in research seems like an act of pioneering. Bibliographers have naturally led the way, and certainly any worker in eighteenth-century periodicals must be grateful for their topographical aids. He must acknowledge, as well, the few studies of individual magazines, journals, and reviews that enable him to make his own way in areas that are largely uncharted. For the scholarly editions, the general histories, and biographical data that illuminate his path, he must express his appreciation.

Yet finally he comes to confront the darkness. If he chooses to describe English literary periodicals and the climate of opinion, 1756-1763, he discovers that of the thirty-nine periodicals that he has decided to discuss, the majority are no more than bibliographical entries. Others that have received the attention of scholars are often neglected for the period in which he is making his study or have been considered from what, for him, is a restricted point of view. Even before he can examine their form and content, he must in some instances record their existence beyond their listing in bibliographies.

What he is attempting, therefore, is a primary account of the periodicals during those years which roughly coincide with the Seven Years' War. His main concern is to present to a reader interested in a particular periodical what its writers had to offer on subjects of major importance – whether these comments arose directly from the events of the war or emerged from the general climate of opinion. At the very least, his research should offer a clearer vision of a periodical's position on a specific subject; at its best, it may suggest the range of conservative and liberal opinion for these years both in and outside the periodicals viewed. Yet there are by-ways that he must first investigate because they have previously escaped notice. He has received considerable assistance from those researchers who have uncovered information regarding authorship and editorial techniques in some of his periodicals; but he misses most of all, and must provide for himself, a demonstration of how the characteristics of a periodical type affected its treatment of material.

Perhaps, too, because the area is relatively unexplored by comparison with the well-defined highroads of literature in the middle of the century, he is sometimes even compelled to justify his venture. It is not difficult to do. To be sure, he is working in the undergrowth of literature and is caught up in the tangle of non-literary material, but the lower branches can be as fruitful for the examination of a literary historian as the major works are for the critic. Moreover, what the one discovers, the other frequently needs. It would be useless for anyone to argue that the periodicals themselves were an aesthetic achievement, but they are, perhaps, the most suitable background against which the creative effort in any era may be brought into focus.

For whatever light this particular study sheds on periodical literature from 1756-1763, the researcher must express his indebtedness to those who have helped in various ways. The printed sources are dutifully acknowledged in the bibliography. But there is personal appreciation to Professors Lewis Knapp, Richmond P. Bond, Ray C. Longtin, George Nobbe (deceased), and Elliott S. M. Gatner for the aid that they have given, and to Mrs. Betty Skalecki for her struggles in typing the manuscript. To the university and college libraries of Long Island, Columbia, Trinity, Yale, Texas, and Tulane, and to the staffs at the New York Public and Engineering Society Libraries, there are obligations for patience and courtesies too numerous to specify. Long Island University has contributed generously in money and time. From the very beginning, Professors James L. Clifford, Howard Schless, Allen T. Hazen, and Peter Gay of Columbia have seen him through his dark and muddled moments. For his wife no words are needed to express his gratitude.

NOTE ON THE TEXT

In quotations from the eighteenth-century periodicals, typographical changes have been made consistent with modern use of italics and capitalization.

I

FIGHTING THE WAR

Throughout the Seven Years' War, from which England emerged as the world's foremost commercial empire, English literary periodicals both recorded and influenced the "spectacle of British civilization . . .".[1] Essay-journals like the *World* and *Connoisseur* commented on taste and conduct, while political essay-journals like the *Test, Con-Test, Monitor, Briton,* and *North Briton* tried to mold public opinion on both domestic and international policies. In the pages of the *Annual Register, Gentleman's, London,* and a host of minor magazines, original articles, correspondence, summaries and extracts from important publications presented a variety of views on subjects ranging from Biblical exegesis to corn prices. And, finally, the two literary reviews, the *Critical* and *Monthly,* passed judgment upon pamphlets and books concerned with matters as trivial as the circulating library novels and as important as the negotations for the Peace of Paris.

But a study of the periodicals reveals more than the climate of

---

[1] R. P. Bond, editor, *Studies in the Early English Periodical* (Chapel Hill, 1957), p. 45. Although Bond stresses the importance of the periodicals as sources for the historian, a study of the contents of these serials provides an index to their political, social, religious, scientific, and literary opinions, as well as an illustration of the varied techniques of the periodical types. – One of the periodical writers (*Universal Museum*, I, January, 1762, p. 25) calls attention to the importance of these journalistic records: "Periodical papers form the truest pictures of the manners and principles of the times; we should consult them to discover the reigning foibles and fashions; and (if I may be allowed the expression) the spirit of the people." – In all quotations from the periodicals, capitalization and typography have been regularized according to modern standards. However, the original spelling and punctuation have been retained.

opinion; an investigation of their comments indicates the differences in the characteristics of the periodicals themselves. Those non-political essay-journals in the *Spectator* tradition failed to survive because, at least in part, they did not appeal to the public's hunger for political and military news, and even the competent and established *World* and *Connoisseur* did not endure beyond the first year of the war.[2] On the other hand, political essay-journals, using Swift's *Examiner* as model and source, often came into existence to serve a particular cause, and when the need had been met the periodicals vanished. But whatever the differences between the two types of essay-journals, they expressed opinions more frankly and frequently than the magazines, whose main function was to provide weekly or monthly journalistic coverage and whose eclectic methods of borrowing from important publications tended to balance arguments on major public issues. Like the magazines, the reviews played a journalistic role, but the journalism was combined with editorial comment as strong as the opinions expressed in the essay-journals. Both the *Monthly* and *Critical* attempted to report on all publications as they appeared, and the reviewers' judgments required candid opinions on a variety of subjects.

The chief subject, however, for almost all the periodicals was the war itself, which, in these early years from 1756-1760, provided incidents and issues that commanded public attention. In 1756 Admiral Byng's failure to support the garrison that defended the island of Minorca raised the question of ministerial responsibility and led to the fall of the Newcastle administration. Then, after he had gained political control in the following year, William Pitt introduced measures that called for a national militia and a German alliance, both of which challenged the political *status*

[2] G. P. Winship, Jr., "The Printing History of the *World*", in Bond, pp. 190, 195 n. 14, relates the termination of publication to plans for volume editions. Essay-journals did not run long, and no doubt when the decision to terminate publication was made, the editors considered plans for publication in reprint volumes. Nevertheless, this explanation does not altogether account for the particular time of termination. After 1756 the only non-political essay-journals that were attempted during the war were Goldsmith's *Bee* and *Busy-Body*, 1759, which were of short duration. Johnson's *Idler* (1758-1760) appeared as a feature in the *Universal Chronicle*.

quo. At the same time, he had assumed the burden of planning military operations, so that the unsuccessful Rochefort expedition and Lord Sackville's part in limiting the victory at Minden brought under consideration Pitt's own responsibility as a war minister. In their response to these events, the periodical writers indicated their own attitudes as well as the climate of opinion effected by the fortunes of the war. Here, in its disastrous beginning, as in its victorious climax after 1760, the Seven Years' War brought forth comments that revealed the editorial political sympathies of periodicals whose comments obviously contributed to the making of public opinion itself.

Once officially under way, the war immediately produced these events that stirred public interest, but when Great Britain formally declared war on France in May, 1756, not even the head of the British ministry, the Duke of Newcastle, recognized the significance of the struggle "in which the main lines of the British Empire were finally laid down . . .".[3] Unofficially, England and France had been engaged in a commercial conflict since 1754,[4] but the dispute that had originated over trade rights in the Ohio Valley now became a world war in which the old balance of European power was replaced by a set of strange new alliances.[5] Austria, Britain's erstwhile ally, joined with France and Russia to oppose Frederick the Great's Prussia, which had united in a Protestant triumvirate with England and its Hanoverian protectorate. From the point of view of the English, after its meager beginnings over American colonial possessions, the Seven Years' War finally developed into a war for conquest, and the area of battle included not only America and Europe, but Asia and Africa as well.

[3] J. S. Corbett, *England in the Seven Years' War* (London, 1907), I, pp. 7, 15. The quotation is from p. 7. O. A. Sherrard, *Lord Chatham: Pitt and the Seven Years' War* (London, 1955), pp. 14-15, is correct when he says that the war for a colonial empire was the creation rather than the object of the conflict. See, also, B. Williams, *The Whig Supremacy, 1714-1760* (Oxford, 1942), p. 327.
[4] Corbett, I, pp. 14-15.
[5] For the steps leading up to the actual outbreak of the war and for the circumstances of the alliances, see H. Butterfield, *Man on His Past* (Cambridge, 1955), pp. 142 ff.

Newcastle's inability to comprehend the importance of the war was only one indication of the confusion that characterized the early military operations, and despite Britain's ultimate triumph, the first years of fighting almost destroyed the nation. Within three months, Oswego had fallen to the French in America, and the reports from the Black Hole of Calcutta had thrown the English nation into despair.[6] Yet the greatest disgrace for the English was in the very action that marked the beginning of the war – Admiral Byng's failure at Minorca and the fall of the gallant military garrison that was quartered there. Byng had been sent to defend the fortress. He had engaged the French fleet with some success, but then he had failed to follow up his advantage and had finally left the garrison to defend itself against the enemy. Not even the heroism of the Minorcan troops could nullify the rage of the public for whom Byng's conduct was a challenge to British honor and courage.

No single event better illustrates the climate of despair and hysteria that characterized the English nation during the opening stages of the war. When news of the fall of Minorca first reached England, the populace was infuriated, and Byng was relieved by Hawke and brought home under arrest. He was accused of having delayed on his journey to the battle, having refused to carry through with his attack, and having permitted the outpost to fall when a defense was possible.

Whatever the merits of the case against Byng, political factors actually determined his sentence.[7] Byng's military failure threatened the continuation of the Duke of Newcastle's administration, and the ministry acted to protect its political life.[8] Seeking to

---

[6] Sherrard, p. 120.

[7] Corbett, I, pp. 132-133; A. S. Turberville, *English Men and Manners in the Eighteenth Century* (Oxford, 1926), pp. 232-233. On pp. 104, 111-112, and 115, Corbett describes the selection of Byng as poor, ascribes the failure to the government, and evaluates the moral failings and military credits of the admiral. In a recent study of the Byng episode, Dudley Pope (*At Twelve Mr. Byng Was Shot*, Philadelphia and New York, 1962) has described the extent to which Byng's trial and execution were an act of "judicial murder", intended to provide a defense for the ministry.

[8] L. H. Gipson, *The British Empire before the American Revolution*

eschew responsibility for the catastrophe, the duke enlisted the aid of a horde of pamphleteers who directed a public attack on the negligence and cowardice of the admiral.[9] While Byng's official letters were released in a form prejudicial to his defense,[10] naval officers of his court-martial board – some of them Members of Parliament – were reminded that their actions would affect their future preferment,[11] and the king himself was induced to pledge that he would deal speedily and severely with the culprit Byng.[12]

For Newcastle, the Byng case had ominous significance. The duke's personal reputation was involved, his control over the military was threatened, and his ability to conduct the war was challenged.[13]

Whatever the actual responsibility of Newcastle's ministry, Pitt – who had forewarned the nation of the fall of Minorca –[14] was now in a position to wrest the power of government from the hands of the old Whig aristocracy. He had the support of the London mob, the livery companies, the leading merchants, army and navy men, many of the clergy, and even Leicester House.[15] In the vanguard of the attack on the Newcastle

(Caldwell, 1936-56), VII, pp. 10-11, describes the mob violence directed against Newcastle as well as Byng. G. Nobbe, *The North Briton* (New York, 1939), p. 23, rightly asserts that the fall of Minorca was responsible for ending Newcastle's ministry.

[9] Sherrard, p. 115.

[10] Sherrard, p. 117. *Cf.*, Tobias Smollett, *The History of England from the Revolution in 1688 to the Death of George II* (Philadelphia, 1828), II, pp. 189-190; Horace Walpole, *Memoirs of the Reign of King George the Second* (London, 1846), II, p. 247.

[11] R. Pares, *King George III and the Politicians* (Oxford, 1953), pp. 20-21; Dr. A. Carlyle, *Autobiography* (London, 1860), p. 302.

[12] Sherrard, p. 118.

[13] Turberville, *Men and Manners*, pp. 232-233, describes Newcastle's bitterness because Byng had the audacity to lay the blame on civil authority. L. B. Namier, *The Structure of Politics at the Accession of George III* (London, 1929), I, pp. 37, 42-43, shows the relationship between military affairs and parliament and the concern that Newcastle had for military patronage.

[14] Sherrard, p. 118. See, also, Erich Eyck, *Pitt versus Fox, Father and Son, 1735-1806*. Translated by Eric Northcott (London, 1950), p. 72.

[15] Gipson, VII, p. 11.

ministry was the City of London, where Pitt was especially popular.[16]

Not surprisingly, the Newcastle ministry fell, but so successful were its efforts in defaming Byng that the admiral – in accordance with a law untempered by mercy – was condemned to death.[17] Despite Pitt's mild attempt on Byng's behalf – which cost the new minister some of his popularity –[18] the admiral was executed to satisfy the appetites of the London mob.

Throughout the Byng controversy, which started in May, 1756, and continued after his death in March, 1757, the periodicals played an important role in both shaping and recording public opinion. The literary reviews offered commentary on the myriad publications evaluating the merits of Byng's case, assessing the responsibility of Newcastle's administration, and stirring the populace before and after the investigation. At the same time, the magazines, functioning journalistically, narrated the details, presented the evidence, offered the opinions of correspondents, and less frequently editorialized on the events. But the sharpest and most direct opinions came from the essay-journals, at least from the *Test, Con-Test,* and *Monitor,* which either actively supported or opposed the Newcastle administration.

Both the *Test* and *Con-Test* owed their existence to the ministerial struggle. The allegiance of the former was to Henry Fox, Secretary of State in Newcastle's ministry,[19] and the essay-journal made its first appearance at the time of Newcastle's fall in order to challenge Pitt's first administration.[20] Attempting to undermine Pitt's investigation of the previous ministry's responsibility

[16] Eyck, p. 73. See, also, W. L. Dorn, *Competition for Empire, 1740-1763* (New York, 1940), p. 347.

[17] Namier, I, p. 73, offers evidence that without political pressure the admirals would never have rendered the same judgment on Byng.

[18] Eyck, pp. 78-79 and Gipson, VII, p. 23.

[19] The attack on the handling of the admiralty by Pitt's administration was part of the *Test's* (#16, February 26, 1757, p. 87) defense of Fox's ability during the Newcastle administration.

[20] N. Drake, *Essays ... Illustrative of the Rambler, Adventurer, and Idler* (London, 1809-1810), II, p. 345, says that the *Test* was published in support of the ministry; however, the essay-journal first appeared after Newcastle's fall. It did continue during the months between Pitt's first and second ministries.

for the failure at Minorca, Arthur Murphy, chief editor of the *Test*,[21] was determined to prove that the verdict of the court-martial was itself sufficient evidence of the admiral's guilt: [22]

If it did not appear to the Court-Martial that he [Byng] was guilty of cowardice, disaffection, or neglect, upon what motives could they find him guilty within that article [Article XII, under which Byng was convicted]? Surely their decision upon those three criminal causes of mis-conduct might have been very preemptory; and if he is only guilty of an error in judgment, it is apprehended the martial law does not prescribe death, for what the best admiral in England may be liable to. Without censuring a solemn act of the legislature, without complaining of the severity of that article, it is, I think, very apparent, that they might (if it was their opinion) have done justice to the prisoner and their country. It is no hardship upon the gentlemen of the navy, that the law prescribes death for cowardice, disaffection, or neglect of duty; it should prescribe it, and they who call for an alternative, are not animated with a true heroic fortitude and a zeal for the honour of their country. When an admiral under sailing orders, and a fair wind courting him out, can stop to call for an alternative in case he should be delinquent in any of the above particulars, I may perhaps deserve to be absurd for my singularity, but I own I have no very sanguine hopes of success from his expedition.

Despite the insistence of Fox's supporters that Byng's conviction under Article XII meant that the admiral had been guilty of cowardice, disaffection, and negligence,[23] the decision of the court-martial, which recommended mercy, clearly left the impression that Byng's judgment rather than honor had been wanting.[24] In order to protect the reputation of Newcastle's ministry, which could not have been responsible for suspecting the honor of the Byng family but should have known the capacity of its admiral's judgment, one writer in the *Test* defined *negligence* as an instance

---

[21] For the authorship of the *Test* and *Con-Test* see Drake, II, p. 345 and J. Nichols, *Literary Anecdotes of the Eighteenth Century* (London, 1812-1816), IV, p. 97. During the later *Briton* and *North Briton controversy*, the author of the *Briton* was described as having been the author of the *Test* (*Political Controversy*, I, p. 135). The confusion probably arose because Murphy was editor of the *Auditor*, ally of the *Briton*.

[22] *Test*, #14 (February 12, 1757), pp. 75-76.

[23] *Test*, #16 (February 26, 1757), p. 86; #18 (March 12, 1757), p. 98.

[24] Sherrard, pp. 164-165.

"when a commander actually engaged does not execute with vigor and dispatch what the exigence, his duty, and a sense of honour should immediately urge him to perform without hesitation or delay . . .".[25]

For Newcastle's supporters, Byng had to be guilty, because if he was not personally responsible, then the ministry had to be.[26] They described attempts to save Byng's life as politically motivated plots; [27] deplored efforts "to make royal justice look like cruelty"; [28] and argued the justice of the sentence on the basis of its popularity.[29] In using the argument of popular support, they were ridiculing Pitt, whose rise to power was ascribed to the clamor of the mob, but, actually, Murphy's writers were more concerned with royal prerogative than with the voice of the people, since Newcastle's strength came from the support of George II; [30] and when Pitt's first ministry had fallen and the Byng episode had ceased to bear public approval, they did not hesitate to condemn the "giddy multitude" that could be swayed by demagogic control.[31]

On the Byng issue, the writers in the *Con-Test* could not afford to attack the public, not even when they were defending Pitt's unpopular efforts to gain mercy for the admiral. Owen Ruffhead, the shrewd political writer who, under the political guidance of Sir Philip Francis, edited the *Con-Test*,[32] sought to condemn the public behavior without alienating the popular support upon which Pitt's power depended. To achieve this feat, Ruffhead's staff turned upon the devious tactics that the Newcastle administration had used to mislead the people, and while emphasizing

---

[25] *Test*, #16 (February 26, 1757), p. 86.
[26] Sherrard, p. 163.
[27] *Test*, #20 (March 26, 1757), p. 113; #21 (April 2, 1757), pp. 119-120.
[28] Quotation is from #21 (April 2, 1757), p. 120; also see #23 (April 16, 1757), p. 128.
[29] *Test*, #17 (March 5, 1757), p. 96.
[30] Murphy, as editor of the *Test*, was arguing for a cause that he was to defend again later as editor of the *Auditor* when it opposed Wilkes and the *North Briton* on the matter of the royal prerogative of King George III.
[31] *Test*, #26 (May 7, 1757), pp. 148-149.
[32] B. C. Nangle, *The Monthly Review, Indexes of Contributors and Articles* (Oxford, 1934), p. ix, lists Ruffhead on the *Monthly*'s staff.

the unscrupulous practices of the ousted ministry, expressed their faith in the public's ability to perceive the truth when all the facts were made available.[33] In the case of Admiral Byng, one writer remarked, it was not surprising that the multitude had been unable to judge accurately "a man, of whose guilt it would be difficult for men of the best penetration to form a perfect judgment".[34]

Instead of exonerating Byng,[35] the essays in the *Con-Test* were concentrated upon the failure of the Newcastle administration,[36] and, without directly challenging the decision of the court-martial, admonished the intemperance of the sentence.[37] According to these supporters of Pitt, the old ministry to preserve itself had created an atmosphere in which no just verdict could be rendered,[38] and they deplored the part that the former ministers had played in vindictively thwarting merciful efforts to save the admiral's life.[39]

In their desire to place the burden of responsibility for the fall of Minorca on the Newcastle administration, the writers in the *Con-Test* were motivated by both political and economic considerations. Ruffhead's staff sought to demonstrate that the inexperience of Pitt's ministry was no hindrance to its handling of naval affairs, and, in fact, there was virtue in the Treasurer of the Navy's not being personally involved with the naval hierarchy, since such involvement brought with it corruption.[40] But of even greater importance was their admission that the struggle between Pitt and the old Whig aristocracy was a battle for trade interests in which the new minister represented the City of London and its merchants, who were challenging the vested commercial powers for control of contracts and investments.[41]

Commercial interests brought a third essay-journal, the *Moni-*

---

[33] *Con-Test*, #16 (March 5, 1757), p. 92.
[34] *Con-Test*, #15 (February 26, 1757), p. 86.
[35] *Con-Test*, #16 (March 5, 1757), p. 94.
[36] *Con-Test*, #1 (November 23, 1756), pp. 1-2; #18 (March 19, 1757), pp. 107-108; #21 (April 9, 1757), p. 123; #36 (July 23, 1757), p. 213.
[37] *Con-Test*, #14 (February 19, 1757), pp. 82-83.
[38] *Con-Test*, #18 (March 19, 1757), p. 105.
[39] *Con-Test*, #15 (February 26, 1757), p. 90.
[40] *Con-Test*, #5 (December 18, 1756), pp. 27-28.
[41] *Con-Test*, #18 (March 19, 1757), pp. 107-108.

tor, to the political side of the *Con-Test*. Representing the city trade groups,[42] the *Monitor* emphasized economics rather than politics, and found in Pitt a spokesman for the merchant class of the metropolis, which opposed Newcastle and the Whig aristocrats. Even the *persona* used by the essay-journal represented commercial rather than political commitments. Unlike the eidolons of the *Test* and *Con-Test*, Mr. Monitor, who after all was "The British Freeholder", bore no resemblance to a politician. When he spoke, it was with the voice of the irate citizen rather than the political persuader. As a citizen of London, who had been among those demanding the immediate trial and punishment of Byng,[43] Mr. Monitor refused to dismiss the admiral's responsibility: [44]

Should it be said, that there was a great deal of injustice in the popular clamour, lampooning and burning of Byng: and that his crime was magnified with great art to draw off the public attention from the administration, no-body will deny it. But this ought not to be a bar against justice. His arrest was just: his imprisonment was just: and it will be both unjust to those, who found him guilty, and to the public weal, should any future commander in chief, instead of attempting all in his power to execute his instructions, call their practicality in question, desert the service of his king and country, and not be obliged to render an account of his conduct.

Yet, as the quotation indicates, the *Monitor*'s economic commitments led to political involvement, for Alderman Beckford, who controlled it, was greatly concerned with the culpability of the Newcastle administration, which represented his commercial opposition.[45] Even before the fall of Minorca, a writer in the *Monitor* had accused the ministry of unpreparedness which would lead

---

[42]   The *Monitor* began publication in 1755. It "was William Beckford's paper, conducted by [John] Entick and speaking for the City groups who were interested in the Seven Years' War". (N. S. Jucker, editor, *The Jenkinson Papers, 1760-1766*, London, 1949, p. 211.) See further material on the authorship of the *Monitor* in Chapter III.

[43]   Sherrard, p. 118, describes the conduct of the City of London in the Byng case.

[44]   *Monitor*, #118 (October 22, 1757), p. 717; see also II (August 7, 1756), p. 4 and II (March 12, 1757), pp. 333 ff.

[45]   L. S. Sutherland, *The East India Company in Eighteenth-Century Politics* (Oxford, 1952), p. 31.

to disaster,[46] and once the debacle had occurred, the administration was castigated for failure to meet the crisis and to give the public the facts.[47] While they maintained the tone of the irate citizen by using epistolary devices, the writers in the *Monitor* also availed themselves of historical analogy and irony to arouse the public. For them, it was the duty of the citizens – the merchants of London – to direct the actions of the government, and as one writer later declared, it was the obligation of a free press to a-waken the eyes of the people to such corruption as the ministry's during the Byng affair.[48]

As well equipped as the essay-journals were to speak out directly on the events of the war as they occurred, comment on these matters was limited mainly to those papers that had a specific political or economic interest. Aside from cursory remarks in the *Crab-Tree* [49] and *Old Maid*,[50] the writers in other essay-journals were silent on Byng and the fall of Minorca. In an age when the public was vitally interested in the serious affairs of state,[51] it is not surprising that even the *Connoisseur* and *World*,[52] which had been in existence before the war but which tended to ignore the important occurrences for the sake of mildly ironic social com-

---

[46]   *Monitor*, I (May 15, 1756), pp. 400-403.
[47]   *Monitor*, I (July 10, 1756), pp. 466-468; I (July 17, 1756), p. 473; I (July 31, 1756), pp. 492 ff.; II (August 7, 1756), pp. 4-5; II (August 14, 1756), pp. 19-21; II (August 21, 1756), p. 43; II (August 28, 1756), p. 53; II (May 7, 1757), pp. 407 ff.
[48]   *Monitor*, II (April 2, 1757), p. 368.
[49]   *Crab-Tree*, #14 (July 26, 1757), pp. 80-81. W. Graham, *English Literary Periodicals* (New York, 1930), pp. 130-131, describes the essay-journal as propaganda, but as such it was ineffective. See Chapter II.
[50]   *Old Maid*, #35 (July 10, 1756), pp. 284-286; #36 (July 17, 1756), p. 297.
[51]   H. J. Laski, *Political Thought in England: Locke to Bentham* (London, 1950), pp. 112-113, describes the change that was taking place during the Seven Years' War. Certainly, the reliance of Pitt and Wilkes on the emotions of the populace brought the public closer to the political and military events than even the Queen Anne's War had done.
[52]   For the authorship and publication details of both journals, see Graham, pp. 128-130. The *World* was Robert Dodsley's publication and ran from 1753-1756. Among its authors were Edward Moore, Lord Chesterfield, and Horace Walpole. The *Connoisseur*, which ran from January, 1754-September, 1756, was largely the work of George Colman and Bonnell Thornton. Sources for identification of authors of individual essays will be given at the appropriate place in the notes.

mentary, should pass quickly from the scene. Although their *personae* were not intended to evoke laughter, like Mary Singleton of the *Old Maid* and Nicholas Babble of the *Prater,* the *World* and *Connoisseur* had associated too long with light criticism of manners to adopt a serious political tone.[53]

For the magazines the problem was different, if, indeed, there was a problem at all. The war demanded more attention to politics and economics,[54] but preying upon popular works for their material, the magazines were less likely to offer a unified editorial point of view than to present a conglomeration of contemporary opinion. Relying on an appeal to topical interest and attempting to satisfy the public taste for weekly or monthly journalism, the editors suggested their own sympathies only through infrequent editorials or in the emphasis of their selection of articles and correspondence.

Nothing of the heat generated by the essay-journals was produced by the two major magazines. Neither the *Gentleman's* nor the *London* was so deeply committed politically that the Byng case could provide an issue for frenetic squabbling about the responsibility of the ministry as compared to the personal guilt of Byng.[55] For the most part, the magazines merely followed the development of the issues and reported to the public.

---

[53] Graham, pp. 128-129, notes Johnson's criticism of both journals for wanting substance.

[54] C. L. Carlson, *The First Magazine. A History of the Gentleman's Magazine* (Providence, 1938), p. 107.

[55] The *Gentleman's Magazine* had begun publication under Edward Cave in 1731, but at this time and until 1760, the periodical was being conducted by his nephew, Richard Cave, together with David Henry (Nichols, *Literary Anecdotes,* V, p. 58). Carlson, p. viii, describes the significance of the magazine's parliamentary news reports as " a protest against arbitrary government". At the same time, both Carlson, pp. 55 and 201, and Nichols, *Literary Anecdotes,* V, p. 18, remark on the lack of political bias in the nominally Whig periodical. – The *London Magazine,* which commenced publication in 1732, remained a close rival and imitator of the *Gentleman's* throughout the existence of the former, until 1785 (Graham, pp. 161-162). Both magazines appealed to the London independent commercial class and were influenced by its interests. – D. J. Greene ("Johnson's Contributions to the *Literary Magazine*", *RES,* 1956, VII, pp. 374-375) has pointed out the difficulty of distinguishing original material from the unidentified extracts, abstracts, and direct quotations in the magazines.

The *Gentleman's* began its report in June, 1756, by presenting the observations of a sea officer.[56] Consistent with the general national reaction, the account was wholly unfavorable to Byng. But when news of Blakeney's gallant defense of the island reached England, Byng's conduct suffered even more from comparison, and again the widespread public response was reflected in the pages of the magazine.[57] Yet the editors printed without comment two accounts of Byng's trial,[58] presented his defense objectively,[59] and balanced Dr. John Shebbeare's attack on him and the ministry with a refutation of the charges.[60]

To be sure, there were suggestions of editorial opinion that regarded Byng as guilty of cowardice. In a review of the decision of the court-martial, a contributor to the magazine argued strongly that the verdict itself was evidence of Byng's misconduct,[61] and the editors' own notes on the summary of the trial emphatically condemned the admiral: [62]

. . . the admiral when the French rear first made sail and run, did not, nor could know, that any part of our fleet, except the *Intrepid*, could not pursue, being at too great a distance from the van to judge of the damage it had received; and by the rear of the French making sail, had more reason to think, that their van was disabled or beaten, than that ours was unfit for the pursuit; the conclusion therefore from these premises is obvious.

But even these were balanced by opposing opinions,[63] and the

---

[56]   *Gentleman's Magazine*, XXVI (June, 1756), p. 313.
[57]   *Gentleman's Magazine*, XXVI (July, 1756), pp. 322, 351, 356, 358; XXVI (August, 1756), pp. 400, 402; XXVI (September, 1756), pp. 412, 424-427; XXVII (January, 1757), pp. 9-17.
[58]   *Gentleman's Magazine*, XXVI (Supplement, 1756), pp. 599-602; XXVII (January, 1757), pp. 30-32.
[59]   *Gentleman's Magazine*, XXVI (October, 1756), pp. 479 ff.
[60]   *Gentleman's Magazine*, XXVI (August, 1756), pp. 387-390; XXVI (November, 1756), pp. 529 ff.
[61]   *Gentleman's Magazine*, XXVII (February, 1757), pp. 69-71.
[62]   *Gentleman's Magazine*, XXVII (March, 1757), p. 102. See, also, XXVII (February, 1757), p. 84 and XXVII (April, 1757), pp. 154-155.
[63]   *Gentleman's Magazine*, XXVII (January, 1757), p. 44; XXVII (March, 1757), p. 134; XXVII (April, 1757), p. 176.

result is an impression of straight reporting which may be contrasted with the heavily biased comments in the essay-journals.

In the *London,* the other major magazine, at the time of the incident the pattern was virtually the same. With the early reports of Byng's failure, the poetry in the *London* repeated the outraged popular reaction,[64] but then the periodical settled down to straight reporting, indicating the editors' desire to appease the readers' curiosity rather than to pass judgment on the admiral.[65] During the Byng proceedings, the only charges that the *London* offered which implicated the ministry were two reprints – one from the *London Evening Post* and another from the *Monitor,*[66] and nothing in the magazine expressed a belief in the justice of the court's decision until May, 1758, at which time the writer of the *London's* parliamentary history noted that any leniency in the sentence would have been construed as ministerial responsibility.[67]

Yet in the *London's* later accounts of the episode, when the editors sought to celebrate Pitt's achievement in saving the nation, the attitude toward the Newcastle ministry's part in the loss of Minorca suddenly changed. Now, whatever his guilt, Byng was depicted as bearing the burden of the administration's failure.[68] To save their positions, according to accounts in the magazine, the ministers had conspired to sacrifice Byng,[69] who had made the mistake of complaining about neglect or misconduct in the administration.[70] Unwilling to take a stand when two Whig factions were struggling for power, the editors of the *London* were clearly in the camp of the victor once the struggle was over.

[64] *London,* XXV (July, 1756), p. 352; XXV (August, 1756), pp. 394-395; XXV (September, 1756), pp. 445-446.
[65] *London,* XXV (October, 1756), pp. 483-486; XXV (Appendix, 1756), p. 634; XXVI (February, 1757), pp. 51-56; XXVI (March, 1757), pp. 134 ff.; XXVI (April, 1757), p. 184.
[66] *London,* XXV (November, 1756), p. 536; XXVI (July, 1757), pp. 338-343.
[67] *London,* XXVII, p. 226.
[68] *London,* XXIX (January, 1760), pp. 18-19; XXIX (February, 1760), p. 59.
[69] *London,* XXIX (January, 1760), pp. 22-24; XXIX (October, 1760), pp. 518-524.
[70] *London,* XXIX (November, 1760), pp. 574-575.

In the minor magazines the emphasis was again on keeping the public informed, but an occasional note indicated editorial judgment. The *General Magazine of Arts and Sciences* alone, of the four magazines publishing material on the Byng case, was content with merely chronicling the events,[71] while the *Literary* and *Universal Magazines* and the *Universal Visiter* printed comment that suggested their editorial sympathies.

Of these three, the *Literary* was most decisive in its editorial attitude toward Byng's responsibility for the fall of Minorca. Despite their journalistic presentation of the trial,[72] the editors – before and after the court-martial – emphasized the view that the admiral was being sacrificed for the sake of the ministry.[73] Johnson and other writers insisted that justice was being defied by ministerial efforts to have the public judge before the legal procedure was under way. In both their own comments and in their

---

[71] *General Magazine of Arts and Sciences*, Pt. V (December, 1756), pp. 457-458; Pt. V (January, 1757), pp. 472 ff.; Pt. V (February, 1757), pp. 488 ff., 493; Pt. V (March, 1757), pp. 506 ff. The *General Magazine of Arts and Sciences*, which began in 1755, was composed of five parts, of which Part V was published as *Miscellaneous Correspondence*, by Benjamin Martin. The *Miscellaneous Correspondence*, which included Essays, Poetry, Remarkable Occurrences in the Month, Book Catalogue, and Stock Prices, was the least interesting portion of the periodical. Other sections, particularly those on science and religion, are important for this study. – Comments on Byng which appeared in the *Grand Magazine*, I (April, 1758), p. 196; *Royal Magazine*, I (July, 1759), p. 46; *Weekly Magazine*, #8 (June 3, 1758), pp. 225-226; *Imperial Magazine*, III (June, 1762), p. 286; and *Universal Museum*, I (August, 1762), pp. 434-435, all came well after the event had taken place and have no bearing on this discussion.
[72] *Literary*, II (January-February, 1757), pp. 39-44; (February-March, 1757), pp. 81 ff.
[73] Greene, pp. 390-391, correctly terms the *Literary* a political magazine, opposed to the Newcastle administration, and favoring the landed Whig aristocracy and state trading monopolies. Johnson, who was largely responsible for the early numbers of the magazine, opposed Pitt and the free trading independent business interests of London and Bristol. When the *Literary* showed a change in policy favoring Pitt, Greene suggests, it brought about Johnson's break with the magazine (Greene, p. 392). – Identification of Johnson's contributions (unless otherwise stated) is from E. A. Bloom, *Samuel Johnson in Grub Street* (Providence, 1957), pp. 263 ff. Where the attributions are not clearly made in the text, they will appear after the reference in the notes.

selection of material, the editors left no doubt that the Whig oligarchy had acted to protect itself.[74]

The *Universal Magazine*,[75] like the *Literary*, printed without comment accounts of the court-martial and opinions on Byng's guilt.[76] However, the material in the *Universal* was neither as extensive nor decisive as that in the *Literary*. Reacting to the shock of the incident, the editors printed a parody of the Byng affair which concluded that the admiral should be punished for cowardice, and they supported the charge by including a brief newspaper account that condemned Byng.[77] Then, in the poetry section for the following month, they offered a mock answer from the admiral to his friends which ironically branded him a traitor.[78] By October, the magazine gave extracts from pamphlets concerning the Byng case and published a letter demanding that they be printed so that neither Byng nor any other Englishman might be deprived of the right to defend himself.[79]

While the balanced pattern is also observable in the *Universal Visiter*,[80] the few opinions expressed in the magazine attributed the failure to ministerial irresponsibility. A letter to the magazine questioned the sufficiency of ships and efficiency in responding

---

[74] *Literary Magazine*, I (September-October, 1756), pp. 299-300 (Johnson); I (October-November, 1756), pp. 336 ff. (Johnson); II (January-February, 1757), p. 7; II (March-April, 1757), pp. 116 ff., 153.

[75] The *Universal Magazine* commenced publication in 1747 and continued through the century. Despite its commercial success, it was no more than an imitation of the major magazines. Graham, p. 168, inaccurately describes it as having "little in common with the *Gentleman's* and *London*". However, he is correct in his comment that it was "a 'popular' magazine in the modern sense". Its editor was Percival Stockdale.

[76] *Universal Magazine*, XX (January, 1757), p. 37; XX (February, 1757), pp. 78 ff. and 82 ff.

[77] *Universal Magazine*, XVIII (Supplement, 1756), p. 329.

[78] *Universal Magazine*, XIX (July, 1756), p. 41.

[79] *Universal Magazine*, XIX, p. 172.

[80] *Universal Visiter*, #6 (June, 1756), pp. 267, 288-289; #7 (July, 1756), pp. 336-337, 340. The magazine, conducted by Christopher Smart and Richard Rolt, included the work of Johnson, Percy, and Garrick (Graham, pp. 174-175). Its impression of originality may be attributed to its short run, since the magazines, except the *London*, began publication with a high percentage of original material, but shifted the balance after the first few numbers.

to the emergency, two points implicating the ministry; [81] and the printing of the full text of Byng's letter to the Admiralty was a challenge to the motives of the ministry in suppressing those passages involving ministerial responsibility.[82]

It is clear from their response to the Byng incident that neither the minor nor major magazines had strong political commitments at the outset of the war. While the magazines generally were sympathetic to the trade interests, the question of allegiance to particular interests by uncommitted periodicals had not yet arisen. Pitt's later emergence to full power in the name of the City trade groups was to bring to his side the majority of the magazines, but here where the conflict between two elements of the Whig party had not yet been clearly defined, partisanship was also limited. Indeed, for magazines like the *Literary*, different opinions among the staff on such matters as the Byng case made a strong position not only difficult but unusual. Perhaps Carlson overstates his conclusion that "in a sense, [the magazines] are the most lifeless of eighteenth century documents",[83] but on political matters, it is true that this lack of commitment made the magazines the least interesting periodicals for those concerned with partisan politics.

While the *Annual Register,* in many respects, was like a magazine, it had many advantages over the monthly and weekly serials, not the least of which was the fact that Burke, its editor, had time to view events with some historical perspective.[84] For the Byng case, along with the other occurrences early in the war, Burke had ample time to consider the facts, since the *Annual Register* made its first appearance in 1759.

Burke's account of the Byng incident was mature and unmarked by recriminations. Recognizing the ministry's responsibility, he also noted the general hysteria of the nation, the common fear of

---

[81] *Universal Visiter*, #7 (July, 1756), pp. 327-328.
[82] *Universal Visiter*, #10 (October, 1756), pp. 467 ff.
[83] Carlson, p. 107. He sees the lack of political commitment as the major cause for the magazines' blandness.
[84] Actually, the *Annual Register* published its first number, for 1758, in 1759, and the periodical is not very important for this early period. Consequently, details of its publication will be found in Chapter III, which deals with the later period.

invasion. He neither minimized the administration's inability to act nor its failure to proceed with proper strength. With a sympathetic tone, he summarized the meaning of the court-martial: [85]

Our affairs were in such a condition that we were driven to the expedient of a court martial to revive the British spirit, and to the unfortunate necessity of shedding the blood of an Admiral, a person of a noble family, as a sacrifice to the discipline of our navy.

Finally, as though reminding the nation that aroused public opinion was not easily abated, Burke stressed the fact that the sacrifice of Byng had not prevented the people from turning upon the ministry.[86]

Neither the tone nor the relative impartiality of the *Annual Register* was to be expected in the treatment of the Byng case by the *Critical* and *Monthly Review*.[87] They were committed to direct comment on the myriad publications put forth by the ministerial and anti-ministerial writers, and both reviews had editors with decided political opinions. Indeed, Smollett himself led the *Critical*'s attempt to make political capital of the Newcastle administration's failure,[88] and even the conservative distrust, which

85   *Annual Register*, I (1758), p. 5.
86   *Annual Register*, I (1758), p. 9.
87   Graham, p. 213, presents the standard view that the *Critical* represented Tory and Church opposition to the *Monthly*. However, as this study should show, Graham's view is an oversimplification. Despite Nangle's contention (p. xi) that Ralph Griffiths, publisher of the *Monthly* from its inception in 1749, did not dictate policy to reviewers, Nangle also asserts that, in general, the reviewers shared the publisher's views. Actually, the *Monthly*'s views on politics and religion are too uniform to be accidental, just as those in the *Critical*, begun in 1756 by Archibald Hamilton and Tobias Smollett, are too consistent in their point of view to be a result of chance. Norman Oakes' recent unpublished Columbia dissertation, using later evidence, demonstrates the care with which Griffiths selected reviewers who shared his own opinions. However, the terms *Tory* and *Whig* are not precise enough to indicate the differences between the two reviews.
88   Although D. Roper, "Smollett's 'Four Gentlemen': The First Contributors to the *Critical Review*", *RES*, X (1959), p. 39, describes Smollett's criticism of the Whig administration as "more moderate and judicial in tone than we should perhaps expect", it suited the editor's purpose to play the role of judge when the facts themselves condemned his opponents either for their planning of the battle or their choice of Byng.

he shared with Burke, of stirring up the passions of the populace was used in Smollett's attack on the Whigs.[89]

Actually, three things stand out in the *Critical*'s comments on Byng, Minorca, and the Newcastle ministry. First, after the general uproar in which the review shared, the articles in the *Critical* compared the extent of Byng's responsibility with the culpability of the administration which was, after all, composed of Smollett's political opponents. Secondly, as a part of the *Critical*'s continuing war with the minions of Grub Street, the reviewers abhorred the scurrilous publications which were raised by the Byng case and dumped upon the market without regard for justice or decency. And finally, and perhaps most importantly, there were Smollett's characteristic dislike of the mob and fear of public fervor.

After the initial shock, Smollett joined the anti-ministerial writers in their attacks and viewed Byng as a scapegoat sacrificed for the failures of the administration.[90] In fact, an unidentified reviewer went even further and noted that Byng's loss and the fall of Minorca were not a single event, and that the outpost was doomed by the inadequacy of the ministry's preparations.[91] Willing to concede the admiral's deficiencies, a later article – consonant with the decision of the court-martial – attributed his failure to an error of commission rather than to an act of cowardice.[92]

In all, the tragic consequences of the Byng expedition, his trial, and his execution provided a carrion for the pamphlet publishers

---

[89] All identifications, unless otherwise noted, are drawn from Roper's article. Where attributions are not made in the text, they appear in the notes.

[90] Such writers as John Shebbeare (*A Fourth Letter to the People of England*, London, 1756, p. 108) viewed the ministry as at least responsible for the selection of the officer to head the expedition. In Tobias Smollett's own history of England, he attempted to show that the ministry had made a poor choice in Byng and that Byng was innocent. The argument led Smollett into a palpable contradiction (see my article in *N&Q*, II, 1955, pp. 66-67). For the views in the *Critical*, see II (August, 1756), p. 35; II (October, 1756), pp. 257, 285-286. All were by Smollett.

[91] *Critical*, II (October, 1756), p. 281.

[92] *Critical*, III (February, 1757), p. 185.

and scribblers to pick over.[93] The spectacle provided a chance for
the *Critical* reviewers to raise their Juvenalian voice, to decry the
political blockheads and scoundrels, to berate the immorality and
insensitivity of the ghoulish booksellers and their hacks. Angered
by the lack of decency and taste, Smollett and his staff scorned
what they called illiterate efforts,[94] patched-together accounts,[95]
and the merciless resurrection of the admiral's ghost.[96]

But of even greater concern to Smollett was the manner in
which the public had been deliberately aroused and the way in
which popular indignation had been exploited to divert the attack
from the ministry to the admiral. Most strenuously, the reviewers
objected to the way in which the prejudices and clamors of the
public had been played upon by an administration for which
Smollett had little love.[97] For the review, whose editor feared that
a people once stirred up would not know when to subside,[98] the
Byng case was an object lesson in the danger of heeding the popular voice in government.

To stress political principles, however, is to ignore the important part that practical politics played in shaping the opinions of
the periodical writers. Until the open division between Pitt and
his Tory supporters over the making of the peace, the reviewers
on the Tory *Critical* could take the side of the Whig minister
whose views on Minorca and Newcastle coincided with those of
the Tory Earl of Bute, tutor and adviser to the future George III.[99]
The matter was less simple for Griffiths on the *Monthly*, who was
not yet in a position to decide between the two Whig factions:
Pitt, the spokesman for the London independent trade interests;
Newcastle, representative of the Whig aristocracy.

Apart from having to choose between allies, the reviews, unlike

---

[93]   From June, 1756, to September, 1757, at least twenty-three reviews on
the subject of Byng were recorded in the *Critical*.

[94]   *Critical*, II (October, 1756), p. 284 (Derrick).

[95]   *Critical*, II (October, 1756), pp. 278-279 (Smollett).

[96]   *Critical*, III (March, 1757), p. 286.

[97]   *Critical*, II (August, 1756), p. 35 (Smollett); II (October, 1756), pp. 251-
252 (Smollett), pp. 285-286 (Smollett); III (March, 1757), p. 283.

[98]   *Cf.*, Smollett, *History of England*, II, pp. 189-190.

[99]   R. Sedgwick, "Letters from William Pitt to Lord Bute, 1755-1758", in
Essays Presented to Sir Lewis Namier (London, 1956), pp. 121-122. Sedg-

the magazines, easily maintained a coherent point of view toward politics. Here there were no problems arising from either eclecticism or differences among the staff writers. The files of the *Monthly* disclose that Griffiths frequently assigned one writer to comment on all publications concerned with a particular subject.[100] In the treatment of the Byng case, the reviewer generally was James Ralph, a Whig pamphleteer as early as 1739, when he was associated with Fielding and the *Champion*.

Like the *Critical* reviewers, Ralph deplored the scurrility of the Grub Street pamphleteers,[101] but while he cautioned against pre-judging the case,[102] he also took advantage of the occasion to argue that it was the privilege of every free nation to have an open discussion of public affairs.[103] Such discussion, of course, was in accord with Pitt's promises during his first ministry, and Ralph's demands for a complete investigation were no more than the City of London had been advocating.[104] Yet when the final decision on Byng had been made, the reviewer argued against continued controversy, which would serve only to widen the rift between the Whig factions: [105]

The subject of this pamphlet [on the justice of the court-martial verdict] has been so long and eagerly discussed, that the world has reason to be weary of it — Some believe justice has been done: others that a sacrifice has been made. Either way, controversy ought to be at an end: for as on the one hand, the Admiral has suffered all he was liable to; so on the other, life can never be restored: craft can

---

wick's article shows the close relationship between Pitt and Bute throughout this early period of the war.
[100] All identifications, unless otherwise noted, are from Nangle. Where the names of reviewers are not included in the text, they appear in the notes.
[101] *Monthly Review*, XV (October, 1756), p. 422 (Ralph); XV (Supplement, 1756), p. 676 (Ralph); XVI (March, 1757), p. 284; XVI (April, 1757), pp. 347-348 (Ralph).
[102] *Monthly Review*, XV (October, 1756), p. 422; XV (November, 1756), pp. 517-518.
[103] *Monthly Review*, XV (October, 1756), p. 408.
[104] *Monthly Review*, XV (November, 1756), pp. 518-521, 526, 527 ff.
[105] *Monthly Review*, XVI (April, 1757), p. 348. See, also, Ralph's review in XVI (February, 1757), p. 177 and XVI (April, 1757), pp. 360-361; XVI (May, 1757), p. 457 (Goldsmith).

never be made to forego its purpose, nor faction its violence; and those who seek for truth in the midst of prejudice and animosity, will hardly be able to find it. Peace to the ashes of Admiral Byng then, for the sake of the public peace, – and let posterity do the rest.

Although the total effect of his words seems comparable with that of the *Critical,* Ralph's emphasis, as a full study of the *Monthly* shows, was upon reconciling the old Whig families and the City trade interests, while the *Critical,* like the Tory Country Gentlemen, supported Pitt in the hope that he could break the power of the Whig aristocrats.

Indeed, on his assumption of full responsibility for the ministry in July, 1757, Pitt needed all the help he could get. The measures he was called upon to take were embarrassing in the face of his earlier commitments, and his success seems little short of a political as well as a military miracle. Despite his earlier attacks upon the formation of a militia and upon the German alliance,[106] he now found both essential to his strategy.[107] But only after a struggle that lasted for the next two years was he able to convince the nation of the wisdom of his policy.

The militia was the easier matter to handle – at least politically.[108] While Newcastle's supporters could attack Pitt's change in

[106]   Gipson, VII, p. 10.
[107]   Gipson, VII, pp. 3-5, 7-9, who is severe in his criticism of what he terms Pitt's *opportunism,* acknowledges (VII, pp. 128, 132) the military realities that forced Pitt's reversal of attitudes. In much the same way as Gipson, Eyck, pp. 71-72, 79-80, concludes that Pitt could not retain the attitudes he had held while in the opposition once he became responsible for the conduct of the war. At the same time, Corbett, I, p. 291, insists that the reversal of Pitt's attitude toward sending troops to Germany was consistent with his early military plans for using the German war as a diversionary measure. From a political point of view, Sedgwick, "Letters from William Pitt to Lord Bute", p. 108, seems most accurate when he notes that Pitt's actions, which were eventually to lead to a rupture between Pitt and his Tory supporters, was only another example that a minister could not retain power without yielding his connections with the heir-apparent.
[108]   Sherrard, pp. 95-97, shows the confusion that existed politically on the issue of a militia. Within the Whig party there was a conflict produced by traditional approval of a militia as opposed to a standing army and the demonstrated success of continental standing armies (see C. Robbins, *The Eighteenth-Century Commonwealthman,* Cambridge, Mass., 1959, pp. 293,

policy, they could not oppose the measure, since the plan had originally been conceived during the Newcastle administration.[109] At the same time, Pitt was able to placate his isolationist Tory supporters by insisting that the troops used for home defense would rid the nation of the Hessian and Hanoverian mercenaries who had been needed for the task.[110] The one remaining problem was convincing the public, for Newcastle's earlier use of a militia had outraged the people, and Pitt's measure itself now brought riots when enforcement began.[111] Although the popular opposition prevented full effectiveness of the civilian military force, Pitt was successful, and the militia was an important step in his military moves. No opposition could deny the contribution that the militia made to England's victories in 1758 and 1759.[112]

Pitt's reversal in his attitude toward the German alliance proved politically more difficult than his militia bill.[113] Here his *volte-face* allowed the opposition, which had consistently favored the Ger-

---

382). While the Tories traditionally opposed a militia, they regarded it as a means of breaking the ties with Hanover, an occurrence which would appeal to their isolationism (see D. Greene, *The Politics of Samuel Johnson*, New Haven, Conn., 1960, p. 7). Of course, Pitt was working without regard for the individual party preferences. His London connections were Tories as well as Whigs, and the Tories, at least, were apolitical (Sherrard, pp. 148-149). Pitt managed to gain the support of the various Whig factions (Sherrard, p. 152), and his position depended mainly on results. At the same time, his ability to gain passage of a militia bill was a result of watering down the original version (Sherrard, p. 174).

[109] Corbett, I, p. 88, points out that Pitt's own earlier opposition to the government complicated his job when in office.

[110] Sherrard, p. 177 and K. G. Feiling, *The Second Tory Party, 1714-1832* (London, 1938), p. 64.

[111] Corbett, I, p. 223. Sherrard, p. 226, notes that the public attitude was a result of Newcastle's earlier deceit, when he shipped conscripted soldiers to America, although he had promised that they would not leave the country. Newcastle, in his opposition to Pitt, was delighted by the difficulties of enforcing the Militia Act (Sherrard, p. 276).

[112] J. Fortescue, "The Army", in *Johnson's England* (Oxford, 1933), edited by A. S. Turberville, I, pp. 79-80.

[113] Corbett, I, pp. 155-156, points out that Pitt had become known as the foremost opponent of the continental connections, but that the minister now found it essential for his strategy, which his critics did not understand. Gipson, VII, pp. 21-22, also notes the relationship between Pitt's change in attitude toward the German measures and his war policy, but Gipson describes his move as the greatest about-face in Pitt's career.

man connection, to make political use of his sending troops and
aid to Prussia. However, the major problem for Pitt was satisfying
his Tory friends,[114] and by limiting his moves, Pitt convinced Bute
and Leicester House that the change was wrought through necessity. The nation itself, which had objected to the German alliance
and to the defense of the king's Hanoverian connections, was
swayed primarily by the military successes of the King of Prussia,
who was taking on the figure of a popular hero.[115] Although Pitt,
at the time of the peace negotiations, was to hear more from the
Tories about his change of heart on Prussia, for the moment he
managed to take bold political and military measures without
alienating the support of the nation.

As with the Byng case, comment in most of the essay-journals
virtually ignored both the German alliance and the militia. Apart
from a remark in the *Crab-Tree,* in July, 1757,[116] objecting to the
support of Hanover and ridiculing the idea of a Protestant War,[117]
only the writers in the politically engaged *Test* and *Con-Test* and
the commercially committed *Monitor* wrote frankly about issues
that commanded the attention of the nation.

Indeed, even the arguments in the *Test* and *Con-Test* all but
ignored the militia. Despite his later opposition to Pitt's militia,
Newcastle had used the force earlier for his own advantage, so
that writers in the *Test* could afford only to touch upon the issue

---

[114] Corbett, I, p. 241 and Sedgwick, "Letters from William Pitt to Lord
Bute", pp. 116 ff., 128-129, 153-154, 165-166, present a clear picture of
Pitt's ability to convince the Tories that he was their man, while he used
their political support to further his military aims. Finally, of course, the
Bute-Pitt relationship broke on the matter of the German connections.
Smollett, *History of England,* II, p. 238, is a typical attack by the Tories
on Pitt's reversal on German measures. Smollett's attack came, of course,
after the peace negotiations had separated Pitt from his Tory supporters.
In a bit of doggerel printed by the *Grand Magazine* (II, February, 1759,
p. 99), Pitt's ability to convince even the Tories on Hanoverian aid, German subsidies, and paid troops abroad was depicted as a measure of his
political success.
[115] Corbett, I, pp. 285-286.
[116] *Crab-Tree,* #12 (July 12, 1757), p. 71.
[117] *Busy Body,* #8 (October 25, 1759), p. 45, in a fictional dream, describes the difference between men fighting for their homeland and those
fighting for pay.

as a basis for an attack on Pitt.[118] At the same time, those in the *Con-Test* merely ascribed the need for a militia to the demands for preservation,[119] since the chance to ignore Pitt's change of heart was welcome to an editor whose periodical was appealing to a public less than enthusiastic about the measure.

Actually, Fox's supporters in the *Test* should have remained silent about Pitt's *volte-face* on the German connections, too, for the Newcastle ministry had been a staunch defender of the king's Hanoverian interests. However, the editors could not forego the advantage of describing Pitt's change of heart when he assumed the responsibility for the ministry. Perhaps, too, the fact that Arthur Murphy − at the end of the war in charge of the anti-German *Auditor* − was chief editor accounts for his writers' eagerness to attack Pitt on his continental measures.

Whatever the reason, the essays in the *Test* attempted to make political capital of Pitt's contradictory attitude toward Hanoverian troops and Prussian subsidies from one session of parliament to the next.[120] While reminding Pitt that he had been brought to power because of his opposition to those very measures that he now proposed,[121] the writers ignored the fact that an attack on the German alliance was no credit to the defunct Newcastle administration and that an accusation which charged Pitt with ignoring Britain's proper interest in America for the sake of continental connections was equally an attack on Newcastle's ministry.[122] At the same time, by linking support of Germany to the Toryism of Pitt's ministry,[123] the writers intentionally distorted the historical fact of Leicester House's opposition to George II's Hanoverian ties.

For Ruffhead in the *Con-Test,* the German alliance presented the problem of explaining the sincerity of Pitt. Whether by design or accident, Pitt's supporters struck upon an essential truth of his

---

[118] *Test,* #3 (November 27, 1756), pp. 10, 12.
[119] *Con-Test,* #11 (January 29, 1757), pp. 62-63.
[120] *Test,* #1 (November 6, 1756), p. 4; #3 (November 27, 1756), p. 11; #15 (February 19, 1757), p. 81.
[121] *Test,* #10 (January 15, 1757), pp. 51, 53.
[122] *Test,* #5 (December 11, 1756), p. 23 and #17 (March 5, 1757), p. 92.
[123] *Test,* #13 (February 5, 1757), pp. 69-70.

seemingly pragmatic policies. In its very first number, the editor laid the groundwork for all future arguments in defense of Pitt's apparently contradictory behavior: [124]

But, even with regard to measures, it may become justifiable in him vehemently to oppose the same expedients at one time, which he vigorously promoted at another. The fluctuating state of the political system will not admit of invariable rules of policy.

The statement was an unconscious prophecy of Pitt's future conduct of the war, but not even Pitt's City supporters could realize that his use of the German alliance would one day be responsible for the extension of Great Britain's commercial empire or that his pragmatic policy with regard to Germany was but an instance of the adjustment of his practices to his vision.[125] Without this realization, the ministerial writers nevertheless appreciated both the power and the glory of Pitt's negotiations with Germany. The essay-writers recognized that he had been personally responsible for making palatable to the nation the unpopular measures of protecting "the King's German dominions, attacked in an English quarrel".[126] At the same time, they attributed Britain's success in preventing a French invasion to the wisdom of Pitt's aid to the King of Prussia.[127]

Although the writers in the *Monitor* did not share these opinions on German involvements, these supporters of Pitt agreed on the need for a militia. But while the brief comments on the subject in the *Test* and *Con-Test* represented no more than the editors' political attachments, the remarks in the *Monitor* were also an indication of a philosophy of government. Like the Whigs of the Revolution, Beckford's writers feared a strong military that could be used as an instrument of despotic power,[128] but also like those earlier Whigs they believed in the efficacy of a domestic military force entrusted to people who had something for which they were

---

[124] See footnote 113 on page 35. *Con-Test*, #1 (November 23, 1756), p. 3.
[125] *Con-Test*, #36 (July 23, 1757), pp. 211 ff., is a response to the *Monitor*'s opposition to the German alliance.
[126] *Con-Test*, #27 (May 21, 1757), p. 161.
[127] *Con-Test*, #28 (May 28, 1757), pp. 163-164.
[128] *Monitor*, I (January 24, 1756), pp. 217 ff.

willing to fight.[129] Before Pitt had even come to power, writers in the *Monitor* were arguing for a militia, particularly as a means of keeping the nation free from foreign entanglements and from the employment of Hessian and Hanoverian mercenaries. One essayist's words anticipated the argument that Pitt later used to convince the Tories, a fact which indicates the basis for Pitt's success in being able to gain Tory support while representing City trade interests: [130]

Should it not be considered, before such measures [i.e., engaging foreign soldiers for home defense] are resolved upon, that to fetch troops at a vast expense from distant nations into an island of faithful and brave people, is both needless, hazardous, disgustful, and a burthen too heavy to be added to the other incumbrances of a war? to invite over a military force, trained up in beggary, and in republican, or in despotic principles, into a land of plenty and liberty is dangerous to the constitution?

For Beckford's staff the militia remained an argument against foreign connections, even after Pitt had engaged on a policy committed to the continuance of German alliances and subsidies.[131] While insisting on a well-regulated militia, the journalists left no doubt that the people – those with a stake in government – should bear the responsibility for their own security: [132]

In every well governed state, which proposes to maintain a just poise between tyranny and licentiousness, the subject is, by his original contract, obliged to support the government in the pursuit of such measures, as shall be necessary for protecting their own property and privileges, and for strengthening the crown against all foreign and domestic foes . . .

On the matter of a militia, the writers in the *Monitor* could readily support Pitt's policies, which accorded with their own principles, but that the minister's change in attitude toward German connections later strained that relationship will be obvious upon exami-

[129] *Monitor*, I (May 29, 1756), p. 418.
[130] *Monitor*, I (March 13, 1756), p. 297.
[131] *Monitor*, I (April 24, 1756), p. 369 and II (September 11, 1756), p. 69, show the *Monitor*'s early attitude; and #215 (September 1, 1759), pp. 1296-1297 and #244 (March 22, 1760), p. 1471, show that the attitude remained the same.
[132] *Monitor*, II (January 29, 1757), p. 269.

nation of the journalists' pronouncements. The particular appeal
of the militia for these Whig writers, as for the Tories, was that
such a force negated the need for the foreign alliance; only the
final realization that the foreign war was important to commerce
could alter their view of the German treaties. Yet even during the
peace negotiations, while arguing for the extension of the trade
empire, the writers in the *Monitor* refused to give credit to the
German alliance, which had made the victory possible.

Certainly throughout the early stages of the war, these Whig
journalists, like Beckford himself, did not grasp the significance
of Pitt's German policy. Despite their desire for a revolutionary
extension of trade, they did not recognize the need for an international realignment of power. From the outset, they were opposed to the continental and Hanoverian ties even when necessary for Britain's defense,[133] and, according to the writers, the
continental battle was unrelated to the American conflict and
hence unimportant for Britain's interests.[134] Even when they
praised Pitt's contribution to the vast commercial victories, the
journalists stressed the control he had kept over foreign aid,[135]
and, although giving grudging tribute to the King of Prussia, emphasized the monarch's self-interest and the weakness of France.[136]

What is remarkable about the commentators in all these journals is their inability to see how the minister in every facet of his
conduct of the war was departing from tradition. Pitt was leading
England into the position of world leadership, and yet foe and
friend alike were slow to realize the extent of the change that was
taking place.[137] If the journalists that were closest to the political

---

[133] *Monitor*, dedication to Volume I; I (January 17, 1756), pp. 214-215;
I (January 24, 1756), p. 217; II (November 6, 1756), pp. 148-149.

[134] *Monitor*, II (March 19, 1757), p. 341; #106 (July 30, 1757), p. 635;
#136 (February 25, 1758), pp. 824-825; #160 (August 12, 1758), pp. 966 ff.;
#162 (August 26, 1758), pp. 977 ff.; #163 (September 2, 1758), pp. 983 ff.

[135] *Monitor*, #176 (December 2, 1758), p. 1066.

[136] *Monitor*, #127 (December 24, 1757), p. 772; #139 (March 18, 1758),
pp. 843-844; #164 (September 9, 1758), pp. 989 ff.

[137] J. H. Plumb, *England in the Eighteenth Century* (London, 1950), p.
113, points out that even as late as 1760 Pitt had to convince so eminent
a City tradesman as Alderman Beckford of the value of the conquests in
the West Indies.

maneuvering were unable to discern the direction of Pitt's policies, then certainly the writers in the general magazines were not likely to perceive it.

Indeed, in the major magazines, the issues of German treaties and the militia were kept apart. Perhaps the main reason for the approval of the German measures was the popular figure of Frederick the Great, who made interesting news for a reading public that could find some hope in the military successes of the Prussian forces. With their Whig affiliations, the editors of both magazines were easily convinced of the necessity for a national militia.

Commentary in the *Gentleman's Magazine* on the King of Prussia's exploits had a story-book quality. In their preface to the 1756 volume,[138] the editors contrasted the heroism of the small Prussian nation and its monarch with the English and their military disgraces. Then, in the December number,[139] the magazine offered a visual and word portrait of Frederick which extolled his genius and character, and even when his military successes had somewhat diminished, the editors and contributors continued to praise him in his struggle against incredible odds.[140] It was not to be expected that those who expressed such admiration for Britain's ally should begrudge credit to him in effecting Britain's later military victories. Indeed, one writer in the *Gentleman's* scorned a pamphlet attacking Pitt's alliance with Frederick and remarked: [141]

... we are told, notwithstanding the protection of our own trade, the destruction of that of France, the ruin of her navy, and destruction of her harbours, the expedition against Cape Breton, and our success in Africa, that they [the ministry] have done nothing, or worse.

Despite the generally indecisive comments on most subjects in the magazines, the statements in the *Gentleman's* on both the German alliance and the militia were decisive. Particularly in selecting letters, the editors seemed concerned with showing the impor-

---

138 *Gentleman's Magazine*, XXVI.
139 *Gentleman's Magazine*, XXVI, p. 855.
140 *Gentleman's Magazine*, XXVII (1757), Preface; XXVII (May, 1757), p. 228; XXVII (October, 1757), p. 472; XXVII (December, 1757), p. 566; XXVII (Supplement, 1757), pp. 592-593.
141 *Gentleman's Magazine*, XXVIII (August, 1758), pp. 378-379.

tance of the militia to the trade and commercial interests of the nation.[142] There was no question about needing the militia; indeed, the only quibbles were concerned with proper representation and training on Sundays.[143]

While neither so quick nor so sanguine as the editors of the *Gentleman's* to approve the German treaties and the militia bill, the men who conducted the *London* supported Pitt's efforts in both. That the minister had captured the support of both magazines is readily apparent in their lack of comment on his reversal of opinion on the German measures. To the militia bill, the writers in the *London* had no objections other than those of the methods of implementation. In its "History of the Last Session of Parliament", the magazine noted that the public had not been properly informed on the measure and that opposition could be expected on that account.[144] At the same time, the article expressed distrust of the features of the bill that made substitutions possible, thus enabling the least reliable part of the population to be entrusted with the defense against France and the preservation of the liberties and privileges of the nation.[145] Despite an insistence on the importance of a militia,[146] the writers continued to be disturbed about possible abuses of the act and stressed the responsibilities incumbent upon the nobility and landed gentry.[147]

On the continental measures, the editors were less enthusiastic than their rivals. Their direct comment, as well as the poetry and extracts they selected, lauded the stature of the Protestant ally, Frederick, both in victory and defeat,[148] but even their praise of

142 *Gentleman's Magazine*, XXVI (June, 1756), pp. 294-295; XXVII (November, 1757), pp. 509-512.
143 *Gentleman's Magazine*, XXVI (September, 1756), pp. 432-433; XXVI (October, 1756), pp. 457-460; XXVII (March, 1757), pp. 131-133; XXVII (September, 1757), pp. 391-392; XXVII (November, 1757), pp. 509-512.
144 *London*, XXVI (December, 1757), p. 579.
145 *London*, XXVI (December, 1757), p. 580.
146 *London*, XXVII (September, 1758), pp. 458-461.
147 *London*, XXVII (October, 1758), p. 500; XXVII (December, 1758), pp. 609-610.
148 *London*, XXVI (1757), Preface; XXVI (October, 1757), p. 477; XXVI (November, 1757), p. 567; XXVI (December, 1757), pp. 576, 609, 614-615; XXVII (January, 1758), p. 44; XXVIII (1759), Preface.

Frederick suggested that the continental fighting took something away from the importance of Britain's true interest – the American war.[149] Nevertheless, if they failed to see the direction of Pitt's policy, at least they were aware of what Prussia's victories had meant to England during that nation's most forlorn hours. Granting the justification of Frederick's war with Austria, the editors expressed their gratitude for his aid and insisted that England must follow his lead and support his cause: [150]

His virtues deserve it, and his wisdom will improve it If we oooond hlm, as our own interest, nay, our preservation seems to require, we have every thing to expect from his valour and prudence. Let not murmuring at past miscarriages divert our attention from the main point; we are not so far gone in effeminacy and sloath, but we have got some men, who are willing and able to retrieve the nation's honour. Let us emulate the king of Prussia. . . .

Some of the contradiction in the *London*'s statements on the German alliance was apparently the result of the eclectic borrowing practiced by all the magazines. Under such circumstances, that there was contradiction is no surprise; what is a surprise was the direct support expressed in both major magazines for Pitt's ministry. In some measure, their overall attitudes indicate the speed with which Pitt was winning over the nation, and the popularity of the magazines suggests the influence that they had upon public opinion.

Of the minor magazines that offered comment on both the militia and Germany, only the *Literary* presents a coherent and developed point of view, actually anticipating the demands for the new trade empire that was to emerge from the Seven Years' War. Johnson's own isolationist views on the militia were those of a Tory Country Gentleman,[151] which coincided with the City trade groups' desire to place the defense of the nation in the hands of those who had something for which to fight.[152] But for another, more expansionist writer in the magazine, the militia was impor-

---

[149] *London*, XXVI (October, 1757), pp. 474-475; XXVII (August, 1758), pp. 390, 407.
[150] *London*, XXVII (January, 1758), p. 4.
[151] Greene, *The Politics of Samuel Johnson*, pp. 157-158.
[152] *Literary Magazine*, I (June-July, 1756), p. 121.

tant not only for "our glory abroad, our security at home, and our very being as a nation", but also to "secure our liberties, properties, and religion".[153] Unafraid that the new military force would lead to tyranny, he insisted that the need for provisions, stimulated by the militia, would lower prices and extend British goods to a world market.[154]

In much the same way, a later writer in the magazine argued that the German alliance was necessary for the security of England in a new balance of powers which he related to the advances of British commerce: ". . . in the event of the success of the four great Crowns in alliance, viz, Austria, France, Russia and Sweden, a new system of power and property must take place in Europe." [155] Nor was he reluctant to effect the necessary changes, since "systems of power are no other than combinations of interests; and every fluctuation of interest introduces an alteration of system".[156]

Not surprisingly, therefore, the comment in the magazine voiced whole-hearted approval of Frederick. His abilities were celebrated in poetry,[157] and even in Johnson's "Memoirs of the King of Prussia", Frederick's every action was described as an illustration of "consummate wisdom".[158] His conduct in victory and defeat was lauded,[159] and his war against Vienna, Saxony, and Russia was described as defensive action.[160] Later, Frederick himself was classified simply as the greatest of epic heroes.[161]

Nothing comparable to this manner of expression on both the militia and Germany appeared in the other minor magazines. De-

---

[153] *Literary Magazine*, II (March-April, 1757), pp. 147-148.
[154] *Literary Magazine*, II (March-April, 1757), p. 148.
[155] *Literary Magazine*, III (February, 1758), p. 53.
[156] *Literary*, III (February, 1758), p. 53.
[157] *Literary*, II (November-December, 1757), p. 543; III (February, 1758), pp. 85-86.
[158] *Literary*, I (September-October, 1756), p. 318. See also I (October-November, 1756), pp. 327 ff.; I (November-December, 1756), pp. 383 ff.; I (December-January, 1757), pp. 439 ff. See Greene, *The Politics of Samuel Johnson*, pp. 172-173.
[159] *Literary*, II (July-August, 1757), p. 359.
[160] *Literary*, II (July-August, 1757), pp. 359-360.
[161] *Literary*, III (January, 1758), p. 40.

spite partisan attacks on the bill, writers in the *Universal Maga-zine* argued the necessity of a well-regulated militia,[162] and re-peated the popular praise for the King of Prussia.[163] However, there is nothing of real importance on either issue in the maga-zine. At the same time, an article in the *Universal Visiter* argued the need for a militia,[164] but the editors took no notice of the Ger-man alliance.

In the other minor magazines, in 1758, there were interesting statements about the German treaties,[165] The comments in the *Grand* are of importance because they show that as late as 1758 – when the magazine first appeared – the full intention of Pitt's war for empire was not completely understood even in periodicals favorable to the independent London trade interests. As the edi-tors of the *Grand* were later forced to admit,[166] their policies in 1758 were opposed to the German alliance. Despite their personal praise of Frederick,[167] inescapable in a magazine whose eclecticism pillaged the popular publications, the writers in the *Grand* dis-trusted England's new ally and the king's Hanoverian connections. Although balanced by recognition of the country's need for help, their comments opposed England's participation in what the writers regarded as a quixotic continental war.[168]

While articles in the *Weekly Magazine* also praised the Prussian king, they expressed no strong opinions on the German treaties. Instead, the editors presented both sides of the argument,[169] and

[162] *Universal Magazine*, XXI (September, 1757), p. 124.
[163] *Universal Magazine*, XXI (August, 1757), p. 77; XXI (Supplement, 1757), p. 321; XXIII (September, 1758), p. 137; XXIII (December, 1758), p. 306; XXIII (Supplement, 1758), p. 363.
[164] *Universal Visiter*, #4 (April, 1756), pp. 166 ff.
[165] Even the *Spiritual Magazine*, I, p. 1, printed a poem lauding Frederick.
[166] See Chapter III. The *Grand*'s later argument was that England could not afford aid to Prussia early in the war, but the tremendous triumphs made it possible for Britain to extend help when the conquests provided the means.
[167] *Grand*, I (January, 1758), p. 42; I (February, 1758), p. 97; I (March, 1758), pp. 114, 149; I (July, 1758), pp. 347-349; II (1759), Preface, pp. iii-iv; II (January, 1759), p. 31.
[168] *Grand*, I (February, 1758), pp. 53-54, 59-60, 73-75; I (March, 1758), pp. 127-128; I (August, 1758), p. 377.
[169] *Weekly Magazine*, #4 (May 6, 1758), pp. 106 ff.; #9 (June 10, 1758), pp. 271 ff.; #13 (July 8, 1758), pp. 392 ff.

Frederick's conduct was praised more to depict the contrast with the behavior of the British nobility than to celebrate his achievement.[170]

In the *Annual Register,* Burke was virtually silent on the militia,[171] but gave mature consideration to the German alliance in his "History of the War". Writing well after the events – prior to the final peace negotiations – he could present the most balanced view of the continental war: [172]

As France persisted in her attachment to the enemies of his Prussian majesty, Great Britain entered into still closer engagements with that monarch, the lustre of whose virtues, set off by his late wonderful successes, quite turned our eyes from the objections which were raised against the consistency of that alliance with our interests. How far it is consistent with them, is, I think, a much more difficult point to settle, than the adherents to either party seem willing to allow. But it ought to be considered, that the circumstances of the war, hardly admitted of any other choice; it had been the height of madness to have been on ill terms with his Prussian majesty at that time: and it was impossible to have kept good terms with him, without being on very bad ones with Vienna.

Notwithstanding his historical perspective and his praise for the Hanoverian military victories after Russia and Sweden had withdrawn from the war,[173] Burke either did not understand the war strategy of Pitt or did not approve alliances that threatened the pre-war *status quo.* He described the involvement in the continental war as a diversion from American fighting and depicted the Prussian treaty as an attempt solely to put at rest the affairs of Germany.[174] Neither point penetrated to the core of Pitt's policy which was turning the battle for the defense of the empire into

[170]   *Weekly Magazine,* #1 (April 15, 1758), pp. 4-6; #2 (April 22, 1758), p. 39; #13 (July 8, 1758), p. 389. General comments on Frederick's greatness appeared in the *General Magazine of Arts and Sciences,* II, Pt. V (December, 1757), pp. 709-710 and II (January, 1758), pp. 718-719; *Royal Female Magazine,* I (January, 1760), p. 35; *British Magazine,* I (July, 1760), p. 439.
[171]   For two such comments, see *Annual Register,* II (1759), p. 115 and IV, Pt. I (1761), p. 83.
[172]   *Annual Register,* I (1758), p. 39.
[173]   *Annual Register,* I (1758), p. 26.
[174]   *Annual Register,* I (1758), pp. 5-6.

a struggle for the conquest of empire. Despite his particular praise for Frederick,[175] Burke either did not understand the significance of the alliance or – as his later attitude toward the peace suggests – feared the rapid change that was taking place in the realignment of power.

The aroused public interest on Germany and the militia brought forth a multitude of publications which the *Critical* and *Monthly* were obliged to review, and in their comments the reviewers indicated their political sympathies. In their attitude toward both Germany and the militia, writers in the *Critical* closely followed the line of Leicester House and the Earl of Bute. Although the reviewers' antagonism toward George II's continental alliances seems more obviously derived from Smollett's political affiliations, the proposals for a militia were actually just as dependent upon an opposition to the king's policies. Smollett's writers, like the Tory Country Gentlemen, favored a militia rather than a standing army which would place military control in the hands of George II.[176] At the same time, the writers, including Smollett, insisted upon the necessity of a militia to weaken the ties between the king and his continental allies by keeping foreign mercenaries out of England.[177]

On the question of Germany, of all the periodical writers, the *Critical* reviewers were most outspoken in opposition to the alliance. Despite their approval of Frederick as a personality and their conservative distrust of raising a public alarm,[178] they agreed with opponents of the German subsidies.[179] Unwilling to see a shift in the European balance of power,[180] Smollett himself rejected all arguments based on the mercantile advantages to be gained

[175] *Annual Register,* I (1758), pp. 18, 21, 235-237; II (1759), pp. 3-4, 28-29, 278-281.
[176] *Critical,* II (September, 1756), p. 188 (Samuel Derrick); III (February, 1757), pp. 179-180, 180-182.
[177] *Critical,* II (September, 1756), pp. 121 ff. (Smollett); II (December, 1756), pp. 471-472 (Smollett); III (January, 1757), p. 83; IV (October, 1757), pp. 369-370.
[178] *Critical,* I (January-February, 1756), p. 89 (Smollett); VI (July, 1758), pp. 81-83; VI (November, 1758), p. 438.
[179] *Critical,* I (January-February, 1756), p. 88 (Smollett).
[180] *Critical,* I (April, 1756), p. 259 (Smollett).

by continental measures,[181] and, commenting on the treaties protecting Hanover, he insisted that they were designed without regard for British interests and that a European defense alliance
would ultimately bankrupt the nation.[182] Not even the support that
they were otherwise willing to give to Pitt's administration could
cause the reviewers to approve his *volte-face* on continental measures; [183] for like the Leicester House opposition to George II's
foreign policy, the writers in the *Critical* looked ahead to a time
when Prussia would forsake its English allies.[184]

While Ralph on the rival *Monthly* agreed with the reviewers in
the *Critical* on the need for a militia, he was equally concerned
with the importance of keeping the militia in check. Unlike the
writers in the *Critical*, he was not disturbed by possible abuses by
George II, but rather by the prospect of any king's usurping the
powers of the constitution.[185] Recollecting that Charles I, with the
advantages of a militia, could have governed without parliament,[186]
Ralph, nevertheless, supported a militia as a lesser danger than a
standing army.[187] Whatever doubts Ruffhead expressed about the
ability of men of property to serve as soldiers, he did not contradict the need.[188]

Regarding Britain's continental alliances, Ralph and other political writers in the *Monthly* had no qualms. Ralph himself declared that Frederick had been justified in his attack on Saxony
and his activities had greatly benefited the British.[189] At the same
time, Owen Ruffhead and John Berkenhout, the latter a former
Prussian officer, placed Frederick's character above all description and his talents beyond all comparison.[190]

[181]   *Critical*, I (January-February, 1756), p. 89; I (April, 1756), pp. 259-260.
[182]   *Critical*, I (April, 1756), pp. 263-264.
[183]   *Critical*, VI (August, 1758), pp. 170-171.
[184]   *Critical*, V (February, 1758), p. 101.
[185]   *Monthly*, XVI (January, 1757), pp. 90, 93-94; XVI (April, 1757), pp.
356-357.
[186]   *Monthly*, XV (October, 1756), p. 415.
[187]   *Monthly*, XV (Supplement, 1756), p. 674.
[188]   *Monthly*, XVI (January, 1757), p. 79; XVII (Supplement, 1757), pp.
601-602.
[189]   *Monthly*, XV (December, 1756), p. 651; XVI (March, 1757), p. 280.
[190]   *Monthly*, XVII (October, 1757), p. 360 (Berkenhout); XVII (December, 1757), p. 567 (Ruffhead); XVIII (May, 1758), pp. 489-490 (Ruffhead).

From the extensive comments in all the periodicals, it is clear
that whatever qualms the writers had about either the German
alliance or the formation of a militia, they were (with the exception of those in the *Test*) giving maximum support to Pitt in his
efforts to lead the country out of despair. As the references to the
periodicals indicate, discussion of the militia program and continental measures continued throughout these years of the war, and,
at the same time, Pitt had the responsibility for planning the nation's military manoeuvres. In his first brief ministry, he had raised
the nation's hopes by displaying a willingness to take action, and
with his assumption of full power in July, 1757,[191] the public
waited expectantly for his next military move. A great victory
would have roused the nation, which stirred to the rumors of plans
to invade the French coast, but instead the expectations were
frustrated when the military forces failed to make a landing at
Rochefort. Even if it was a military success, as some historians
have suggested,[192] this so-called secret expedition left the nation
dejected, for a diversionary action was not what the English public
had anticipated.

The true importance of the Rochefort expedition lay in the
public opinion of the failure and Pitt. The demands for an investigation give evidence of the way in which people had learned to
expect explanations from their leaders,[193] and their desire to fix
the responsibility for failure on the king or his military forces
attests to the supreme popularity that Pitt had achieved within a
short time of his assumption of full power.[194]

Pitt's prestige is obvious from the absence of opposition essay-

[191]   Pitt's ministry with Legge was ousted in April, 1757, but Pitt returned
to power in mid-June.
[192]   Corbett, I, pp. 209, 227-228, 245; Gipson, VII, pp. 123-124; Sherrard,
pp. 221-222, all see its success as a diversionary measure. Only Gipson
does not indicate that it was the major purpose of the attack.
[193]   Sherrard, pp. 238-240, describes the public outrage and the analogy
with Byng. Sherrard also describes Pitt's refusal to make Mordaunt another
Byng, but notes the minister's use of the occasion to convince the nation
of the need for civil control of the military.
[194]   Sherrard, p. 239, notes that the general view was that the failure had
been part of a scheme to get the French to relax their efforts against
Hanover, but the plot was not attributed to Pitt.

journals. No anti-ministerial periodicals of any kind gained prominence as a result of Rochefort, and those already in existence unanimously supported him. Of the essay-journals, only the *Monitor* remained in late 1757, and, despite their opposition to some of Pitt's continental measures,[195] the editors certainly regarded him as a national hero and refused to hold him responsible for the failure of the Rochefort expedition. In their demands for an investigation, the writers in the *Monitor* insisted on the public right to get at the truth and equated public with the City of London.[196] At the same time, by distinguishing between those afraid of an investigation and those who demanded it, they placed themselves squarely on the side of Pitt,[197] and when dissatisfied with the decision of the court-martial, warned: [198]

The government, which denied a just satisfaction to the subject, has always provoked the people to exact it by force, and to extend their resentment against those, who, entrenched in power, dared them by their partiality and arbitrary proceedings, to stand up in defense of their property, rights, and privileges.

By "those entrenched in power" and by those who cloaked the Rochefort affair in mystery, the writers in the *Monitor* meant the old Whig oligarchy, which was suspected of plotting against the success of the expedition in order to undermine Pitt's war plans.[199] Indeed, the investigation actually made clear that the failure of the engagement was directly attributable to the land officers, so that neither Pitt nor the members of the old administration were responsible.[200]

While the magazine writers, of course, were less outspoken than those in the *Monitor,* they, too, made apparent their faith in Pitt and their belief in the public right to investigate, which must

---

[195] Sherrard notes that the move was designed as diversionary and not as a continental measure, which would account for the *Monitor*'s view.
[196] *Monitor,* #120 (November 5, 1757), pp. 728-729; #121 (November 12, 1757), pp. 733-734.
[197] *Monitor,* #120 (November 5, 1757), pp. 728-729.
[198] *Monitor,* #125 (December 10, 1757), p. 759.
[199] Sherrard, p. 239.
[200] Corbett, I, p. 232.

certainly be related to the popular approval of Pitt as the "Great Commoner". At the same time, the magazines maintained their journalistic function in reporting the event and the subsequent trial proceedings.[201]

On the responsibility for the failure at Rochefort, the writers apparently had no doubt. The earliest comment in the *Gentleman's* argued that the plan was not only feasible but astute, making the best possible use of naval power and having the advantage of surprise.[202] In the same number, the editors reprinted statements from other periodicals, all of which demanded justice and suggested the failure of the military men, and in a footnote, the editors concluded that Pitt had already exonerated himself before the nation.[203] Finally, their report of the court-martial proceedings questioned the defense of the generals and linked the charges against General Mordaunt with those against Byng, implying that both men had disgraced the nation.[204]

Although the comments on Rochefort in the *London* began with a demand for an inquiry and an insistence upon withholding judgment until all the facts had been gathered, the writer, at the same time, expressed his faith in the ministry.[205] Like the editors of the *Gentleman's*,[206] those of the *London* printed a letter the next month, November, 1757, supporting Pitt and urging him not to become despondent.[207] Then, after one writer had raised the question, in February, 1758, of the practicability of Pitt's plan and intimated that Pitt's critics must demonstrate its impractica-

[201] See *Gentleman's Magazine*, XXVII (November, 1757), pp. 491-492; XXVII (December, 1757), pp. 535 ff.; *London Magazine*, XXVI (October, 1757), pp. 467-468; XXVI (Supplement, 1757), pp. 647-653; XXVII (January, 1758), pp. 13 ff., 18 ff., 37 f.; *Grand Magazine*, I (January, 1758), pp. 26-31.
[202] Corbett, I, pp. 209, 214-215, offers judgments of Pitt's strategy which accord with the views expressed by the *Gentleman's*. *Gentleman's*, XXVII (October, 1757), p. 441.
[203] *Gentleman's*, XXVII (October, 1757), pp. 456 ff.
[204] *Gentleman's*, XXVII (November, 1757), pp. 504-506; XXVII (Supplement, 1757), pp. 581-584.
[205] *London*, XXVI (October, 1757), pp. 504-505.
[206] *Gentleman's*, XXVII (November, 1757), pp. 504-506.
[207] *London*, XXVI, pp. 547-548.

bility,[208] another writer indicated his dissatisfaction with those responses that attempted to exonerate the military.[209]

The three minor magazines that offered comment on Rochefort all supported Pitt and attributed the failure to the conductors of the expedition. An extract from a pamphlet defending the planning of the attack drew praise in the *Grand Magazine*,[210] which later gave further support to the ministry in an article lauding Pitt's fortitude in continuing after the major disappointment.[211] In a more direct manner, one writer in the *Literary Magazine* assailed the military's failure to take advantage of its superiority in position and numbers, and insisted that the conduct of the British soldiers and sailors justified an inquiry.[212] Then, in the next number, an article repeated the call for an investigation and scored the degeneracy of the English fighting spirit.[213] After the court-martial proceedings, the magazine's writers had no doubt about the military's disgraceful behavior and characterized Mordaunt's defense as the ludicrous argument that his discretionary powers permitted him "to lay aside the attempt, *to make the attempt*".[214] Although the *Weekly Magazine* printed only one comment of importance,[215] its support of Pitt was apparent. His ministry's courageous behavior was contrasted with that of Newcastle's administration in the case of Byng, and, according to the writers, the current conduct of the military men hardly demonstrated their fortitude as they hurried to absolve themselves in the public press. As the author described the attempted apologies and self-exculpations, Pitt's stature rose merely by contrast.

While the weight of magazine opinion favoring Pitt is impressive, perhaps nothing better describes the extent of the periodical writers' allegiance to the minister at this time than the complete

[208] *London*, XXVII, pp. 89-90.
[209] *London*, XXVII (May, 1758), pp. 219-220.
[210] *Grand Magazine*, I (January, 1758), p. 31.
[211] *Grand Magazine*, I (May, 1758), pp. 222-224.
[212] *Literary Magazine*, II (September-October, 1757), pp. 414 ff.
[213] *Literary Magazine*, II (October-November, 1757), pp. 457 ff.
[214] *Literary Magazine*, III (January, 1758), p. 14. See, also II (November-December, 1757), pp. 510 ff., 515 ff.
[215] *Weekly Magazine*, #9 (June 10, 1758), pp. 275-276.

agreement in the two reviews. For, in spite of frequent and harsh opposition, the reviewers, in this instance, had no argument about the responsibility for the unsuccessful landing expedition. Those on the *Critical* took advantage of the occasion to designate Pitt as "the most venerable character of the age" and to lament attacks upon him as "invidious and unjust . . .".[216] Decrying the "wretched or contemptible" productions of Grub Street,[217] the reviewers defended Pitt against attempts to justify the generals at his expense and lauded efforts to substantiate the adequacy of his planning.[218] In their comments on the court-martial, the writers in the *Critical* rejected Mordaunt's defense and cited Admiral Hawke's testimony as evidence of the misconduct of the generals.[219] At the same time, the reviewers accused the old administration, and especially Fox, of political deceit in trying to discredit Pitt's conduct of the war,[220] adding that the minister did not require the aid of pamphleteers to vindicate him since the deficiences were not his own.[221]

Despite basic political disagreement, the arguments in the *Monthly* were not distinguishable from those in the *Critical*. One reviewer scoffed at the effort to denounce Pitt for the planning and conduct of the expedition,[222] and, like writers in the *Critical,* Owen Ruffhead, now Griffiths' chief political writer, denounced the Grub Street attempts to capitalize on the military setback.[223] Again like his rivals on the *Critical,* Ruffhead denied the need for Pitt's vindication by a pamphleteer [224] and expressed dissatisfaction with the court-martial decision.[225] In every respect, there is nothing to choose between the *Monthly*'s and *Critical*'s support of Pitt's conduct in the Rochefort affair.

Only in one small matter does there seem to have been a vari-

[216] *Critical,* IV (October, 1757), p. 371.
[217] *Critical,* IV (November, 1757), p. 468; see, also, IV (December, 1757), pp. 551-552.
[218] *Critical,* V (January, 1758), pp. 83 and 83-85.
[219] *Critical,* V (January, 1758), pp. 86-87.
[220] *Critical,* V (January, 1758), p. 83; V (February, 1758), p. 165.
[221] *Critical,* V (April, 1758), pp. 354-355, 355-360.
[222] *Monthly,* XVII (October, 1757), p. 379.
[223] *Monthly,* XVII (December, 1757), pp. 558-560 (Ruffhead and Leman).
[224] *Monthly,* XVIII (March, 1758), p. 266.
[225] *Monthly,* XVIII (January, 1758), pp. 89-93.

ance in the reviews' treatment of the expedition,[226] and that concerned the culpability of Admiral Knowles. Here the matter was
not directly related to Pitt, and the disparity of their views was as
much a part of their commercial rivalry as a difference in their
political opinions. A board of inquiry had implied that Knowles'
lack of either judgment or courage had been responsible for the
British failure to attack Fort Fouras as part of the Rochefort plan.
When the admiral rushed into print with his own defense, it was
unacceptable to Smollett, and the *Critical's* article on the pamphlet was caustic enough to evoke a libel suit.[227] To be sure, the
reviewer's language would have angered even a temperate man,
but Knowles' response also left something to be desired in the
way of gentlemanliness. By guaranteeing Smollett a gentleman's
satisfaction, Knowles lured him into professing authorship of the
article, but the admiral's choice of weapons proved to be a lawsuit
which ended with Smollett's imprisonment.

Whether the comments in the *Critical* were the result of his
honest convictions or simply the extension of his earlier argument
with the admiral,[228] Smollett's court defense insisted that truth
was not libelous – an advanced theory of journalistic practice,
which was not challenged by the decision. The judgment of the
court proved only that the editor was guilty of "written censure
upon public men for their conduct as such, or upon the laws, or
upon the institutions of the country".[229]

Journalistic truth seems not to have been the concern of
Griffiths in this instance, for both the timing and tone of the

[226]   Parts of Knowles' defense appeared in the *Grand*, I (May, 1758), pp.
241-243, and *Weekly Magazine*, #7 (May 27, 1758), pp. 206-213. In the
London, XXVII (May, 1758), pp. 219-220, a letter on the pamphlet found
it disappointing in its failure to answer the questions posed by the inquiry,
and the *Literary* published without comment an extract in May (III, pp.
205 ff.), but also printed a letter in June in which Knowles' pamphlet was
described as another failure to add clarity to the facts about the expedition (III, pp. 261 ff.).
[227]   *Critical Review*, V (May, 1758), pp. 438-439.
[228]   L. Knapp, *Tobias Smollett* (Princeton, 1949), pp. 36-37, describes
Smollett's possible earlier association with Knowles, and (pp. 213-214, 230-
233) also discusses the review and the case.
[229]   For the best discussion of the legal issues of the case, see A. Parker,
"Tobias Smollett and the Law", *SP*, XXXIX (1942), pp. 545-558.

Monthly's article suggest that he was using the review to attack the *Critical*. The question of Pitt's responsibility for Rochefort was not involved in Knowles' defense, for the issue lay between the minister and the land officers of the expedition, so that the review could exonerate Knowles without attacking Pitt. Benjamin Dawson's article in the *Monthly* appeared a month after the *Critical*'s, when the libel action already had begun, and its language indicates that an oblique attack on the *Critical* was intended: [230]

... it must give every one, who looks farther than to such pieces of politics as are commonly retailed, a sensible pleasure to find the Admiral willing to satisfy, by an open unreserved explication of his behaviour, the doubts of well-meaning persons; and (were it possible by any thing to do it) to stop, by a deduction of undeniable facts, the mouth of slander itself.

Regardless of Knowles' actual character or his responsibility,[231] the *Monthly*'s comments on his pamphlet seem aimed at the *Critical* as does the judgment in the *Gentleman's Magazine*. Publishing an extract from the pamphlet, in the same month as the *Critical*'s article, the editors of the magazine declared: "These answers to the several charges that have been brought against Adm. Knowles are extracted from the account lately published by himself . . ., authenticated by certificates and affidavits, which cannot be doubted." [232]

But Knowles' pamphlet was only a side-issue of controversy for the periodical writers in comparison to their general agreement that Pitt's ministry was not responsible for whatever disappointments the secret expedition had wrought. The faith the writers placed in Pitt was rewarded, for, whatever the disappointments of Rochefort, it was the last major failure for the British during Pitt's administration. Indeed, the turn of battle had already come in India with Clive's victories after the disaster of Calcutta; and in 1758 the capture of Louisburg and Cape Breton, together with the triumph at Cherbourg, forecast the glorious military achievements of 1759.

[230] *Monthly Review*, XVIII (June, 1758), p. 621.
[231] Knapp, p. 233, n. 47, gives an unfavorable view of Knowles' character.
[232] *Gentleman's Magazine*, XXVIII (May, 1758), p. 203.

Yet even in the midst of victory, there was to be one last reminder of the catastrophes of 1756 and 1757. At Minden, in
August, 1757, Lord George Sackville was responsible for the failure of Prince Ferdinand to complete a rout of the French forces,
and despite the important contribution of the British infantry to
the triumph,[233] the English nation had to bear the shame of
Sackville's conduct.[234] The analogy between Sackville and Byng
was inescapable, but the public reaction was not equal in fervor to
the tumult at the beginning of the war, and although Sackville
had been a personal favorite of Pitt,[235] no one held the ministry
responsible for the conduct of the commander.

The contrast between the cases of Sackville and Byng is a measure of the change in the climate of opinion that had taken place
in England between 1756 and 1759. Despite the efforts of the
Grub Street pamphleteers to make the most of the scandal,[236] the
periodicals indicate the less hysterical atmosphere at the time of
Sackville's disgrace. Although public resentment of Sackville's
behavior is reflected in most of the periodicals, there was a greater
willingness to let the facts determine the outcome of his trial, and
the blasts at the ministry which characterized the reaction to
Byng's failure were not repeated in the attacks on Sackville. Pitt
had led the nation out of despair; he had wrought unity out of
chaos; and nobody was willing to suggest that the minister was in
any way responsible for the conduct of the military commander.

Of the essay-journals included in this study, only the *Monitor*

---

[233]   Sherrard, p. 323.

[234]   Corbett, II, p. 30, describes Sackville's conduct as "cowardice". Gipson, VIII, pp. 34-35, calls the charges against Lord George "well-grounded";
and Sherrard, p. 323, says the conduct of Sackville "robbed [the English
infantry] of its full fruits . . .".

[235]   L. Marlow, *Sackville of Drayton* (London, 1948), p. 110, in a very
biased account of the episode, numbers Pitt among Sackville's enemies.
However, Sherrard, p. 323, is correct when he notes that although Sackville was a favorite of both Pitt and Bute, the minister could not forgive
Sackville's failure. Pitt's formerly high opinion of him is shown throughout
the letters of the minister to Bute (see Sedgwick, "Letters from William
Pitt to Lord Bute").

[236]   Marlow, chapters VI and VII, shows the extent of the Grub Street
attacks, but as the references to the periodicals will indicate, the temper of
the nation had changed under Pitt's successful leadership.

had anything to say on the subject of Sackville.[237] While articles in the *Monitor* now firmly supported Pitt,[238] and did not accuse him of being responsible for Sackville's misconduct, they used the occasion to make an argument for a new social structure. In their condemnation of a system in which the principles of the Court "taught that places were made for men, and not men for places",[239] lay the implication that the independent free men of England must be given an opportunity to display their individual talents without hindrance.

The same principle governed the *Monitor's* comment on the public's right to a full knowledge of Sackville's behavior, for the writer, although insisting that the journal would not yield to irresponsible clamor, warned: [240]

But it is the right of an injured people; a people, whose money, whose blood, and their national interest are concerned in every act and deed of their general, to canvass his conduct, and to force him to answer for those particulars, whereby they apprehend themselves to be injured.

Although Beckford's writers obviously had no doubt about Sackville's guilt,[241] they insisted that he would receive a fair trial. Unlike the Byng case, in which Sackville had played the role of one of the admiral's defamers,[242] this time there would be no pressure by men in power. This ministry did not have to act in self-defense and would not, therefore, make a public sacrifice if Sackville were indeed innocent.[243]

To say that the comments in the magazines were more moderate than those in the *Monitor* would be an understatement. The customary balance of political opinion in the major magazines was virtually undisturbed by the Sackville incident. In the *Gentleman's* material pertaining to Sackville was presented mainly as

[237] Both the *Bee* and *Busy Body* were being published at this time, but neither offered comment on Sackville. However, the *Busy Body*, #12 (November 3, 1759), pp. 69-70, acclaimed Pitt's successful government and his achievement of political unity.

[238] *Monitor*, #228 (December 1, 1759), pp. 1373-1374.

[239] *Monitor*, #216 (September 8, 1759), p. 1305.

[240] *Monitor*, #216 (September 8, 1759), p. 1302.

[241] *Monitor*, #216 (September 8, 1759), p. 1303.

[242] *Monitor*, #216 (September 8, 1759), p. 1302.

[243] *Monitor*, #219 (September 29, 1759), p. 1320

news.[244] If their comments at the end of their account of the trial suggested that the failure of witnesses to offer opinions implied a belief in Sackville's guilt,[245] the editors of the *Gentleman's* balanced this by a favorable treatment of an apology printed in his defense and by an objection to tasteless attacks on him.[246]

Much the same treatment was accorded to Sackville in the *London Magazine.* By presenting the facts to the public, the editors felt they were performing their proper journalistic function.[247] While they printed a letter defending him and another expressing outrage at the libelous assaults that threatened proper justice,[248] the editors' intention, even when comparing the incident to the trial of Byng, was more concerned with the unfairness of Grub Street than with passing judgment on the commander.[249]

For the minor magazines, too, the Sackville affair provoked no strong opinions on his innocence or guilt. The primary function was journalistic,[250] and comments in both the *Grand* and *Royal* displayed the wariness that the furor over Byng had induced in the periodicals. The *Grand,* published by Griffiths, used the incident to ridicule the political affiliations of the *Critical Review,* which, according to a writer in the *Grand,* protected Sackville because he was a favorite of the Tory Earl of Bute.[251] However, an article in the *Grand* itself warned: [252]

[244] *Gentleman's,* XXIX (September, 1759), pp. 416 ff.; XXX (March, 1760), pp. 136-143.

[245] *Gentleman's,* XXX (April, 1760), p. 189.

[246] *Gentleman's,* XXX (July, 1760), pp. 338-339.

[247] *London,* XXVIII (September, 1759), pp. 479-480; XXIX (April, 1760), pp. 171-184.

[248] *London,* XXVIII (August, 1759), p. 406; XXVIII (September, 1759), p. 491.

[249] *London,* XXVIII (September, 1759), pp. 511-512; XXVIII (October, 1759), p. 575.

[250] *General Magazine of Arts and Sciences,* III, Pt. V (April, 1760), pp. 394 ff. and III, Pt. V (May, 1760), pp. 409 ff.; *Universal Magazine,* XXV (September, 1759), pp. 156-158; XXVI (April, 1760), pp. 204 ff., and XXVI (May, 1760), pp. 245 ff.; *Grand Magazine,* II (September, 1759), pp. 505-506; II (October, 1759), pp. 561-563; II (November, 1759), pp. 617-618; III (April, 1760), pp. 198-204; *Royal Magazine,* I (September, 1759), pp. 115-116 and II (April, 1760), pp. 189-214.

[251] *Grand,* II (September, 1759), pp. 486-487.

[252] *Grand,* II (August, 1759), p. 434.

. . . we must suspend our judgment [of Sackville] till we are acquainted with the merits of his own defense: and happily for the supposed delinquent, the nation seems disposed to hear him with candour and impartiality.

In the same way, a writer in the *Royal* related the Sackville and Byng cases in order to insist on a judgment relevant to the facts.[253]

With the Sackville case, Burke's *Annual Register* did not enjoy any great time advantage over the magazines, for its comments followed shortly after the event. In his collection of state papers, the editor offered pertinent material without criticism,[254] but in his history of the war, he condemned the public in terms that closely followed the logic in his later argument in favor of a doctrine of prescription: [255]

The public as usual judged definitively upon the first charge. They never pardon a general whose error it is to fall short. In vain they are prayed to suspend their judgment, and to wait for a full discussion; the matter is already decided; they have a fact against an officer, and they look upon all reasoning in his favour, not so much as a defence of his conduct, as the exertion of eloquence and artifice to palliate a neglect of duty.

Yet his admonishments about hasty judgments did not prevent Burke from offering his own opinions of Sackville, which were certainly not unfavorable.[256]

While the comments in the *Annual Register*, like those in the *Monitor*, suggest the political tension underlying the surface unity, those in the two reviews clearly foreshadowed the eruption that was to take place with the coming attempts to end the war. As the writer in the *Grand Magazine* had indicated, the *Critical* was firmly on the side of Sackville. Unwilling to involve Pitt's administration in the controversy because the minister was still a

---

[253] *Royal*, I (August, 1759), pp. 92-93.
[254] *Annual Register*, II (1759), pp. 267-272.
[255] *Annual Register*, II (1759), p. 19.
[256] In a letter to Robert Dodsley in September, 1759, Burke himself described the reaction to the Sackville incident: "However there does not seem to be the same violence nor the same artifice against him that was used against Byng." (T. W. Copeland, editor, *The Correspondence of Edmund Burke*, Chicago, 1958, I. p. 128.) *Annual Register*, II (1759), p. 20; III, Pt. I (1760), p. 178.

favorite of Smollett, the *Critical* reviewers, nevertheless, were sympathetic to Sackville. The time had not yet arrived when Smollett, editor of the *Critical,* was employed for Bute in the controversy with Pitt's supporters, but already the ties between Pitt and the Tories were being strained, and the review's defense of Sackville, who was a favorite of Bute, forecast the political alignment of the reviews and essay-journals during the peace negotiations.

In its attack on the *Critical,* the *Grand* had not been disinterested, for Griffiths, the publisher of the *Grand,* was also the publisher of the *Monthly,* which was openly engaged with the *Critical* in a controversy over Sackville. In its very first comment on Sackville, the writer in the *Critical* abused Griffiths for seizing every opportunity to make capital of the nobleman's disgrace, and accused the publisher of distorting the facts and jumping to conclusions.[257] Again, in an article on a pamphlet published by Griffiths, the *Critical's* reviewer repeated the charge that Griffiths acted from mercenary causes, and the writer added a pyrrhonistic dread of arousing "the rage and indignation of the people".[258]

But the *Critical* reviewers did not limit their attack on Grub Street to Griffiths. One deplored the lack of "genuine concern" of the pamphleteers,[259] and another condemned their wantonness: [260]

If a nobleman's character and life were not at stake, it would be diverting enough to see the sons of Grub-street thus divided upon a subject which neither side understands, and in which none of them are in any other way interested than as the sale of their performances is concerned.

Yet what is more important about their own treatment of the Sackville case is that, after having noted the baselessness of the charges against Sackville,[261] in all their subsequent reports the reviewers never uttered a word of condemnation upon his conduct.

In contrast, Ruffhead in the *Monthly* found no words in de-

[257] *Critical,* VIII (August, 1759), pp. 160-161.
[258] *Critical,* VIII (November, 1759), pp. 410-411.
[259] *Critical,* VIII (October, 1759), p. 326.
[260] *Critical,* VIII (September, 1759), p. 256.
[261] *Critical,* VIII (August, 1759), p. 161.

fense of Sackville and had only praise for attacks on his conduct.[262] Despite his insistence that "it does not become us to anticipate the opinions of the public in an affair which will shortly be determined in a course of legal examination", Ruffhead could not accept Sackville's arguments on his own behalf.[263] The writer attacked the weaknesses of Sackville's self-justification and criticized his apparent attempt to suppress the evidence.[264] Finally, when Sackville had been convicted, Ruffhead condemned what he described as the officer's brazen attempts to flout the sentence of his lenient judges and to ignore the irreparable damage that he had done his country.[265]

Pitt's ability to remain above criticism in the periodicals throughout this controversy indicates how successful his efforts had been in unifying the nation. Politics had become a subdued issue during his conduct of the war, and the periodical writers in 1759 suppressed their political emotions for the sake of the country and its popular minister. But now the war was about to move into its second stage – a struggle not to protect but to extend the empire – and with the death of George II in 1760, the domestic quiet, ironically enough, was to be broken by the national debates on peace.

[262] *Monthly Review*, XXI (October, 1759), pp. 361-364; XXI (December, 1759), pp. 530-531.
[263] *Monthly Review*, XXI (August, 1759), pp. 174-175.
[264] *Monthly Review*, XXI (September, 1759), pp. 266, 268-269.
[265] *Monthly Review*, XXII (May, 1760), p. 437.

II

THE CLIMATE OF DEFEAT

The impact of England's military defeats came close to shattering the national spirit. Not until 1758 did the gloom that had descended upon the nation after the fall of Minorca show any real signs of dispersing, and only with the complete conquest of Canada in 1759 did an air of optimism return. In these early years of the war, the periodical writers' comments on politics, mankind, and the age frequently reflected the general pessimism, although those writers who catered to the interests of the increasing power of the City merchants and "the thickening strata of the professional classes" demanded an increased voice in government for them and sometimes looked hopefully to the future.[1]

But there was no uniformity of opinion, pessimistic or optimistic; differences existed according to periodical types, political allegiance, and philosophies of government. The writers in the apolitical essay-journals expressed a characteristic distrust of social change and virtually ignored the political controversy, while those in the *Test, Con-Test,* and *Monitor* subordinated all other interests to political and economic considerations. In the magazines, where the opinions were frequently culled from books and pamphlets that lamented the military disasters, the comments often echoed the cries of despair, but sometimes included a note drawn from the political sympathies of the staff of the magazine itself. For the two literary reviews, opinion depended chiefly upon their editors' political attachments and theories of government.

To be sure, comment was not restricted to the periodicals, and

[1]   J. H. Plumb, *The First Four Georges* (London, 1956), pp. 98-99.

PN 5124. P4

SP 31 e

epravity of the times, the impious disdain for the rown's *Estimate of the* its enormous popularity, nood of the public,[2] and , the *Estimate* provides he varied views in the

?itt, Brown attacked the were the main source of ed the evils of the age, ; perversion of national irruption of taste.[6] But k on the degeneracy of nan is innately weak: led, is always defective its effects."[7] Out of his icient for the improve- e was gradually devel- argued for a govern- strated necessity and of the great for its n people", Brown re- ich warned against the

..ought in the 18th Century (London, popularity of Brown's work.

...urate when he notes that the middle class was exempt from Brown's indictment. Actually, the middle class is the focal point of Brown's attack. See, also, Robbins, p. 309.

[4] Brown, I, pp. 22, 173, 216-217. The edition of Brown's work used in this study is the second (London, 1757-1758).

[5] Brown, I, pp. 42-43, 49, 58-59, 86.

[6] Brown, I, pp. 35-38, 47-48; II, p. 73.

[7] Brown, II, p. 38.

[8] Brown, I, pp. 157, 160; II, pp. 95-96.

[9] Brown, I, pp. 77, 102-104, 108, 136 ff., 204 ff.; II, pp. 26-27, 33, 105, 189-190.

[10] Brown, I, p. 25; II, p. 49.

[11] Brown, II, pp. 106 ff., 194-195.

Although the *Estimate* appealed to a public that was intent upon both self-castigation and a desire to find leadership out of the
morass, those periodical writers who commented on the work, for
a variety of reasons, were generally unfavorable in their criticism.
Certainly, not the least cause of their dissatisfaction was Brown's
attack on the weekly and monthly publications,[12] but even some
of the writers in those periodicals whose editorial opinions did not
differ considerably from his estimate of mankind, his denigration
of the age, and even his ideas on government attacked his im-
periousness, conceit, and superficiality.[13]

Yet some of the individual comments also revealed the particular attitudes of the writers and editors of the periodicals. While
those of the *Literary Magazine* rejected Brown's arguments because they attacked commerce,[14] Burke in the *Annual Register,*
writers in the *Grand* and *Weekly* objected to his emphasis on the
decadence of this particular age. According to them, selfishness
was actually the ruling passion of mankind in all ages.[15] On the
other hand, those in the *Gentleman's* and *London Magazine,* who
approved of the *Estimate,* were less concerned with Brown's ideas
than the effect they would have in lifting the public spirit that
had sunk beneath the pressures of military disaster,[16] while the
writers in the *Universal* based their approval on the consistency
of Brown's view with their own estimate of mankind.[17] But per-

[12]   *Critical Review,* III (April, 1757), p. 346; *Monthly Review,* XVI (May,
1757), p. 430 (Rose); XVI (June, 1757), p. 522 (Griffiths); XVIII (April,
1758), pp. 354 ff. (Ruffhead); XVIII (June, 1758), p. 558 (Ruffhead); *Literary Magazine,* II (March-April, 1757), p. 128.
[13]   *Critical Review,* V (April, 1758), p. 284; V (June, 1758), pp. 501-507;
Weekly Magazine, #9 (June 10, 1758), pp. 262 ff.; #12 (July 1, 1758), pp.
381 ff.; *Annual Register,* I (1758), p. 446.
[14]   *Literary Magazine,* II (March-April, 1757), pp. 128, 131-134.
[15]   *Annual Register,* I (1758), pp. 445-446; *Grand Magazine,* I (January,
1758), pp. 36-37; *Weekly Magazine,* #8 (June 3, 1758), p. 246.
[16]   *Gentleman's Magazine,* XXVII (April, 1757), pp. 166-168; XXVIII
(April, 1758), pp. 174-177; XXVIII (May, 1758), pp. 211 ff.; XXVIII
(June, 1758), pp. 249-251; *London Magazine,* XXVI (April, 1757), pp. 155-
157; XXVI (May, 1757), pp. 233-236; XXVII (April, 1758), pp. 186-187;
XXVII (June, 1758), p. 268.
[17]   *Universal Magazine,* XX (April, 1757), p. 158; XX (May, 1757), pp.
205 ff.; XXII (April, 1758), pp. 177 ff.; XXII (May, 1758), pp. 254-257;
XXIII (July, 1758), pp. 10 ff.

haps the most important comment in the periodicals was a *Critical* reviewer's pyrrhonistic disapproval of a work that threatened, through its popular appeal, to arouse the public to revolutionary fervor.[18] Unlike the writers in the *Gentleman's* and *London*, he deplored the appeal to mass emotions. He felt that the effect of Brown's *Estimate* was comparable to that of the infamous Dr. John Shebbeare, whose letters to the people of England added fuel to the inflammatory spirit of rebellion. Even more than he disapproved of the aid such work gave to the enemy, the reviewer dreaded its domestic danger.

Whatever the periodical writers thought about Brown's work, they were similarly engaged in evaluating the times, examining mankind, and theorizing on both the nature of government and politics. Indeed, the extent of a periodical's appeal depended upon its treatment of these subjects. By condemning public concern for the news, the writers in the apolitical essay-journals in effect were discouraging those London groups whose interest in events was related to a desire for a wider franchise in government,[19] while essayists in the *Test, Con-Test*, and *Monitor* gained attention because they propagandized for causes that involved these questions of political power. At the same time, the magazines indicate the intense public concern for the occurrences of the war by emphasizing political and military articles and presenting background material on Minorca, Guadeloupe, and Martinique, when those places became the scene of battle.[20] And the pamphlets and books that were evoked by the military struggle produced a journalistic

---

[18] *Critical Review*, V (April, 1758), pp. 313-314, 319.

[19] For the attack on the public's interest in the news, see *Centinel*, #22 (June 2, 1757), p. 127; *Prater*, #22 (August 7, 1756), pp. 127 ff.; *Connoisseur*, #134 (August 19, 1756), p. 209; *Busy Body*, #1 (October 9, 1759), p. 6; #6 (October 20, 1759), pp. 31 ff.; #7 (October 22, 1759), pp. 38-39; #8 (October 25, 1759), pp. 43-44; *Bee*, #4 (October 27, 1759), pp. 86-87. In the *Busy Body*, #8, p. 44, a particular attack is made on the *Monitor* for catering to the news-hungry.

For frivolous treatment of the war, see *Prater*, #7 (April 24, 1756), pp. 37-38; *Connoisseur*, #110 (March 4, 1756), p. 87; #137 (September 9, 1756), p. 226; *World*, #183 (July 1, 1756), p. 263; #205 (December 2, 1756), p. 380.

[20] For the shift in emphasis to political and military articles by the magazines, see Carlson, p. 107.

rather than literary effect in the reviews of the *Critical* and *Monthly*.

Of the four essay-journals that ceased publication in 1756, three – the *Connoisseur, Prater,* and *Old Maid* – presented opinions that were mainly conventional disapproval of fashionable manners and dress,[21] but even here the criticism sometimes went deeper than superficial cynicism and expressed a conservative distrust of man's nature. In an essay heavily scored by the customary ironic tones of these essay-journals, one writer in the *Old Maid* suddenly shifted to a straightforward commentary on man's passion for glory and warned of the attendant dangers: [22]

That this passion may sometimes be productive of ill I readily allow; and the same may be said of every principle which actuates the mind of man: even religion, the sweet, the mild, the amiable source of virtue, sometimes degenerates into the darkest superstition, and produces the most fatal effects: and the generous spirit of liberty carried to excess, gives birth to licentiousness and confusion. Such is the imperfect state of humanity.

With even greater stress upon the "depravity of human nature",[23] essayists in the *Connoisseur* described "the whole history of the world moral and political [as] but a Cyclopaedia of Nonsense",[24] and then provided an index through historical examples.[25] Like the writer in the *Prater,* who considered man's imperfections such

---

[21] *Connoisseur,* #112 (March 18, 1756), pp. 95-98; #118 (April 29, 1756), p. 131; #122 (May 27, 1756), p. 147; *Prater,* #2 (March 20, 1756), p. 7; #7 (April 24, 1756), pp. 37 ff.; *Old Maid,* #9 (January 10, 1756), pp. 63-68; #10 (January 17, 1756), pp. 72 ff.; #15 (February 21, 1756), p. 121. Where attributions of authorship in the *Connoisseur* are given, they are from Chalmers' edition (Boston, 1866) unless otherwise stated. – *Nicholas Babble* was the *persona* of the *Prater,* a periodical probably edited by Hugh Kelly (*CBEL,* II, p. 664). – *Mary Singleton* was the *persona* of the *Old Maid,* edited by Frances Moore Brooke, (*CBEL,* II, p. 664). J. R. Foster, *History of the Pre-Romantic Novel in England* (New York, 1949), p. 145, attributes the termination of the periodical to the fact that the editor had married. However, Foster gives the terminal date as April, 1756, but the essay-journal actually continued until July 24, 1756.
[22] *Old Maid,* #31 (June 12, 1756), p. 256.
[23] *Connoisseur,* #107 (February 12, 1756), p. 71.
[24] *Connoisseur,* #118 (April 29, 1756), p. 128.
[25] *Connoisseur,* pp. 128-132.

that nothing could change them and that they must be borne,[26] Colman, editor of the *Connoisseur,* attributed the failures of human conduct to the limited and partial view of mankind.[27]

The comments in the fourth essay-journal, the *World,* differed in two ways from the remarks in the other three. The writers in the *World,* though they have been criticized for their lack of seriousness,[28] were at once more confirmed in their low estimate of mankind and more conscious of the social changes that were taking place. While their supercilious tone was ineffectual for serious political commentary, the *World* journalists used irony effectively to denigrate man's capacity for happiness and benevolence.[29] Yet with more cynicism than irony, one of them remarked: [30]

I take it for granted that the most sensible and informed part of mankind, I mean people of fashion, pursue singly their own interests and pleasures; that they desire, as far as possible, to enjoy them exclusively, and to avail themselves of the simplicity, the ignorance, and the prejudices of the vulgar, who have neither the same strength of mind, nor the same advantages of education.

Although Chesterfield and the editor might scoff at the notion that human nature was now worse than it had ever been before,[31] or ridicule the cliches about contemporary degeneracy,[32] the essays in the *World* itself often commented upon the decay of taste and learning in what they called a Shopkeeper's Age.[33] By ascribing the decline in taste and morals to the liberalism of the English Constitution,[34] by ridiculing the current false notions of

[26] *Prater,* #14 (June 12, 1756), p. 79.
[27] *Connoisseur,* #101 (January 1, 1756), pp. 38-39.
[28] Drake, II, pp. 258-259. J. H. Caskey, *The Life and Works of Edward Moore* (New Haven, 1927), pp. 142-143, describes the journal's emphasis on the details of high life. – Identifications of authors, unless otherwise stated, are from Chalmers' edition (Boston, 1866).
[29] *World,* #167 (March 11, 1756), p. 173 (J. Tilson); #170 (April 1, 1756), pp. 189 ff. (Hamilton Boyle).
[30] *World,* #189 (August 12, 1756), p. 297.
[31] Caskey, p. 137. *World,* #197 (October 7, 1756), p. 340 (Chesterfield).
[32] Caskey, p. 144. *World,* #165 (February 26, 1756), p. 161; #192 (September 2, 1756), p. 314 (Moore).
[33] *World,* #160 (January 22, 1756), pp. 133 ff. (Horace Walpole); #165 (February 26, 1756), pp. 160 ff.
[34] *World,* #171 (April 8, 1756), p. 195.

honor,[35] the "epidemic madness for theatrical employments",[36] and the state of servant-master relationships,[37] these writers in the *World* displayed a conventional bias against the *nouveaux riches* or City merchant class, which was setting the patterns for society.

Clearly, the remarks in the *World*, like those in the *Prater, Old Maid*, and *Connoisseur*, while reflecting some of the dismal atmosphere of a nation in defeat, had no particular relation to the events of the war. What is more, despite the ministerial struggles that were taking place in 1756, these essay-journals were virtually devoid of political comment. The *Test* and *Con-Test*, however, which owed their existence in 1756 and 1757 to the political crisis produced by England's failure in the early fighting, were committed to a kind of political commentary that casts a strong light on the party-structure in these years.

The *Test – Con-Test* debate is as revealing of the party-structure or party-anarchy of the period as any other evidence that can be presented. Although both journals were nominally Whig, the *Test*, edited by Arthur Murphy, favored the Newcastle-Fox faction of the party, and Owen Ruffhead's *Con-Test*, politically guided by Philip Francis, supported Pitt and the City trade interests.[38] While national party organization in the modern sense was unknown during the Seven Years' War,[39] and certainly all major groups opposed the extremes of democratic government and despotism,[40] these political journalists themselves used party-names and advocated different forms of government.

The crucial issue for the writers in the *Test* was whether Pitt

[35] *World*, #161 (January 29, 1756), p. 144 (Earl of Orrery).
[36] *World*, #159 (January 15, 1756), p. 128 (J. G. Cooper).
[37] *World*, #157 (January 1, 1756), pp. 116 ff (Soame Jenyns).
[38] Feiling, p. 64, describes the split in the so-called Whig party. The *Test*'s attack on Alderman Beckford indicates the lack of unanimity even among the commercial interests. Beckford represented the rising political power of the City trade groups; Newcastle's administration represented the older, entrenched Whig families, an aristocracy that had developed after the Revolution of 1688.
[39] Namier, I, pp. vii, 181, 264-265; H. Butterfield, *George III and the Historians* (London, 1957), pp. 11-13.
[40] Laski, pp. 13, 15-16; B. N. Schilling, *Conservative England and the Case against Voltaire* (New York, 1950), pp. 71-73.

and his City supporters had the power to dictate to the king. Behind the journalistic demands for the preservation of the king's prerogative, of course, lay the more practical desire to restore control to Newcastle and Fox, whom George II looked upon favorably. But political and philosophical arguments merged when Murphy, describing his purpose in the final number, revealed the differences that existed within the Whig party: [41]

A paper war was not my business, however it might be the interest of the mercenaries of faction: to stand up for the prerogative of the crown, to detect false pretensions, to unmask mock patriotism, to oppose the democratic faction of a giddy populace, to recall men bewildered with temporary applause to the paths of reason, and to effectuate a coalition of parties; these were the laudable ends which the *Test*-writer had in view. . . .

The effect was to place the *Test* in opposition to the popular form of government which, its writers contended, had brought Pitt to power. Describing themselves as representatives of the old revolutionary Whigs,[42] they decried the spirit of party behind Pitt as a threat to the constitution.[43] Indeed, they presented Pitt's popular support as the irresponsible expression of the giddy voices of an intoxicated multitude,[44] incapable of reliable political judgment: [45]

The mechanism of government is too intricate and subtle, in all its various motions, for a common eye to perceive the nice dependencies and the secret springs, that give play to the complex machinery; and, in consequence, the generality of people, while the great political movements are passing before them, are full of undiscerning astonishment, and only gaze on in expectation of the event.

To the writers in the *Test,* the "generality of people" meant the

---

[41] *Test*, #35 (July 9, 1757), p. 203.
[42] *Test*, #1 (November 6, 1756), p. 2; #6 (December 18, 1756), pp. 27 ff.; #12 (January 29, 1757), pp. 60 ff.; #13 (February 5, 1757), p. 71; #32 (June 18, 1757), p. 182.
[43] *Test*, #1 (November 6, 1756), p. 2; #7 (December 25, 1756), p. 31.
[44] *Test*, #1 (November 6, 1756), p. 6; #2 (November 20, 1756), pp. 4-5; #19 (March 19, 1757), p. 103; #23 (April 16, 1757), pp. 128-129; #29 (May 28, 1757), pp. 163-164; #30 (June 4, 1757), pp. 169 ff.; #35 (July 9, 1757), p. 201. The second number of the *Test* repeated the pagination of the first.
[45] *Test*, #14 (February 12, 1757), p. 73.

City trade groups supporting Pitt. The essayists argued for senatorial rule,[46] but the senate was not to be one composed of representatives of the new commercial class. Instead, it was the "duty of the collective body of the British nobility, who should look upon themselves as the guardians of the constitution, to exert their most vigorous efforts for our preservation . . .".[47] At the same time, Murphy's writers clearly indicated that their concern for the king's prerogative was motivated by the favor that George II had shown to the Whig aristocracy whose wisdom had governed the nation during Newcastle's administration.[48]

At times, the differences between the arguments in the *Test* and *Con-Test* may seem over-subtle, but with careful study one can find that the views of the latter obviously were more concerned with representative government than with the interests of a few large and influential families. To be sure, this demand for representative government was hardly the expression of egalitarian principles. The Popular Whig party in the City was merely seeking to reform parliament "by a wider franchise and some redistribution of seats" according to the importance of independent trade interests rather than the monopolistic power of the Newcastle Whigs, who favored the large corporations.[49] Nevertheless, this constant agitation finally evolved into an effectual "formal opposition", an important part of the parliamentary process, and periodicals like the *Con-Test* were in large measure responsible for the change.[50]

The writers in the *Con-Test* distinguished between faction and man's right to protect the constitution and to join in action to defend it. In defending Pitt, they warned of the dangers of faction,[51]

[46]   *Test*, #24 (April 23, 1757), p. 133.
[47]   *Test*, #1 (November 6, 1756), p. 3.
[48]   *Test*, #1 (November 6, 1756), p. 3; #2 (November 20, 1756), p. 5; #3 (November 27, 1756), pp. 9-12; #26 (May 7, 1757), pp. 145-146; #33 (June 25, 1757), p. 188.
[49]   Robbins, pp. 9, 16, 228; Sutherland, pp. 30-31; Plumb, *The First Four Georges*, pp. 98-99.
[50]   Maccoby, p. 8.
[51]   *Con-Test*, #2 (November 30, 1756), p. 7; #4 (December 14, 1756), pp. 20-21; #6 (December 25, 1756), pp. 31-32; #9 (January 15, 1757), p. 48; #11 (January 29, 1757), p. 61.

but never relinquished the argument that the delegation of one's rights in a representative government did not imply their renunciation.[52]

Indeed, Ruffhead's staff went further and distinguished between political and natural rights, the latter apparently being the eternal privilege of revolution itself.[53] Although the populace might be slow to see its proper interests, it would not remain blind to truth,[54] and the people's participation was necessary to insure a wholesome government.[55] Throughout the controversy with the *Test,* the writers in the *Con-Test* insisted upon "the people's right of inspecting the conduct of state pilots, and, we say, that if, upon inspection, they find themselves injured, our constitution has chalked out a particular mode of application for redress".[56] By the people, the journalists made clear that they meant the men who had "a real interest, in the welfare of the kingdom and the honour of the crown" – not the mob or rabble, not the aristocratic Whig and Tory families, but the corporations, lord mayor, and court of aldermen of the City of London.[57] According to the arguments in the *Con-Test,* even the king's prerogative was dependent upon a properly representative parliament, and not upon the old Whig oligarchy.[58] In all of its political statements, the essay-journal supported a government in which the voices of Pitt's City mercantile supporters would be well represented.

While the important remarks in both the *Test* and *Con-Test* were concerned with politics, a few were directed as well to the nature of man and, of course, the character of the age. Together with the comments in the other essay-journals, they suggest that for the writers optimism and pessimism were economic and politi-

---

[52] *Con-Test,* #4 (December 14, 1756), p. 21; #23 (April 23, 1757), p. 137.

[53] *Con-Test,* #28 (May 28, 1757), p. 167.

[54] *Con-Test,* #20 (April 2, 1757), p. 119.

[55] *Con-Test,* #14 (February 19, 1757), pp. 79-80; #21 (April 9, 1757), pp. 124-125; #22 (April 16, 1757), p. 128.

[56] *Con-Test,* #5 (December 18, 1756), p. 30. See, also, #1 (November 23, 1756), pp. 4-5.

[57] *Con-Test,* #26 (May 14, 1757), pp. 154-155; #23 (April 23, 1757), p. 136.

[58] *Con-Test,* #1 (November 23, 1756), pp. 4-5; #24 (April 30, 1757), p. 139; #26 (May 14, 1757), pp. 151-153.

cal concepts rather than philosophical. Although acknowledging the sad state of the nation in November, 1756, the writer in the *Test* insisted that the experienced government of Newcastle, with the aid of the king, was competent to raise the level of both morale and morality.[59] With similar political interest, the writers in the *Con-Test* saw the degeneracy of the times as an illness and Pitt as the proper ministrant to the body politic.[60] Neither essay-journal could afford politically to accept the dismal situation as irremediable.

Although not directly engaged in the *Test – Con-Test* dispute, the writers in the *Monitor,* most outspoken of all these journalists, shared the political opinions of those in the *Con-Test.* Using dream allegories, historical analogies, and pseudo-travelogues, all of which forms they borrowed from the Whig and Tory journals that had engaged in political controversy earlier in the century, Beckford's writers argued that the whiggism of the London mercantilists was for the benefit of the entire nation.[61] The journalists evaluated government according to its appropriateness to City commercial interests,[62] and made property, taxes, and finances the key considerations in their political doctrines: [63]

In every well governed state, which proposes to maintain a just poise between tyranny and licentiousness, the subject is, by his original contract, obliged to support the government in the pursuit of such measures, as shall be found necessary for protecting their own property and privileges, and for strengthening the crown against all foreign and domestic foes: the government is by the same obligation engaged not to encroach upon the liberty of the subject, nor to misapply the public aid, nor to impose the necessary taxes in such a manner as to throw too great a burthen upon individuals, or which might be raised upon the whole community with greater satisfaction to the people and more advantage to the state.

[59]   *Test,* #1 (November 6, 1756), p. 2.
[60]   *Con-Test,* #12 (February 5, 1757), p. 70; #29 (June 4, 1757), p. 174; #31 (June 18, 1757), p. 186.
[61]   *Monitor,* I (April 17, 1756), pp. 347 ff.; II (1756-1757), Dedication;; II (April 9, 1757), pp. 371 ff.
[62]   *Monitor,* I (March 6, 1756), p. 280; II (September 11, 1756), p. 69; II (September 25, 1756), p. 88; #142 (April 8, 1758), pp. 859-860; #153 (June 24, 1758), pp. 927-928; #155 (July 8, 1758), pp. 938-939.
[63]   *Monitor,* II (January 29, 1757), p. 269.

Even in their analysis of national freedom, the writers in the *Monitor* used the protection of trade as a major premise.[64]

It was natural, therefore, that they advocated a representative government in which the London merchants would have a decisive voice.[65] In no other periodical was the demand so persistently made.[66] According to articles in the *Monitor,* which equated the merchant class with the people, laws were the prerogative of the people; [67] the public had a "right to demand . . ."; [68] power naturally and properly derived from the consent of the governed; [69] a sovereign must listen to the *vox populi*;[70] and ministerial conduct was accountable to the public.[71]

Despite their insistence that they disapproved of revolution,[72] many of the writers in the *Monitor* warned that to thwart the public's will was to invite rebellion,[73] for the power that raised the ruler was capable of pulling him down.[74] One writer, using historical analogy – a favorite device in the journal – recalled that an injured people had dragged Sejanus "through the streets with a hook in his nose . . .".[75] According to other commentators, the result of maladministration was revolution,[76] but kings "who placed their confidence on their people, and governed according

---

[64] *Monitor*, I (March 6, 1756), p. 286.
[65] *Monitor*, I (January 10, 1756), pp. 200-201; I (April 24, 1756), pp. 360-363.
[66] *Monitor*, #119 (October 29, 1757), p. 722; #143 (April 15, 1758), p. 863; #154 (July 1, 1758), pp. 929-930; #155 (July 8, 1758), pp. 936-937; #178 (December 16, 1758), pp. 1074-1075; #183 (January 20, 1759), p. 1105.
[67] *Monitor*, I (March 27, 1756), pp. 319-320.
[68] *Monitor*, II (September 4, 1756), p. 67.
[69] *Monitor*, II (January 15, 1757), p. 249; #147 (May 13, 1758), pp. 888-889.
[70] *Monitor*, II (January 22, 1757), p. 267; II (March 26, 1757), p. 351; #137 (March 4, 1758), p. 828; #154 (July 1, 1758), pp. 933-934; #165 (September 16, 1758), p. 999; #168 (October 7, 1758), pp. 1013-1014.
[71] *Monitor*, II (December 25, 1756), p. 217; II (February 4, 1757), p. 285.
[72] *Monitor*, II (January 15, 1757), pp. 240-241; II (July 2, 1757), p. 479; #133 (February 4, 1758), pp. 803-804.
[73] *Monitor*, I (May 8, 1756), pp. 387-389; II (August 14, 1756), pp. 13-14; II (November 27, 1756), p. 183; II (January 8, 1757), p. 237.
[74] *Monitor*, II (November 13, 1756), p. 163.
[75] *Monitor*, II (April 23, 1757), pp. 392-393.
[76] *Monitor*, II (May 28, 1757), pp. 436-437.

to the established laws of the land, were ever the most prosperous and happy . . .".[77] In reminding the king that monarchs who abused their power had been deposed and that man has a natural right that society's laws cannot take away,[78] Beckford's writers were serving notice that the new commercial interests would not be denied a voice in their own government.

As spokesmen for those interests, the writers in the *Monitor* refused to accept the picture of the age as degenerate,[79] but instead proclaimed their confidence in the English "people's" ability to rise to the necessary defense of the kingdom: [80]

. . . however differing in sentiment about other matters; they have always had wisdom to unite against the sappers of our constitution. And there is no reason to fear they will ever remit any part of that manly preserving zeal, which has overcome all opposition; or suffer themselves to be surprized into an election, which would convict them of supineness, levity, and disunion; and of doing a thing, which would dishonour the city, and discourage the whole kingdom, whose conduct is generally framed on the example of its metropolis.

Even in their least optimistic moments, the writers believed that the people of England – particularly the Londoners – could be saved and were worth saving,[81] and normally expressed complete confidence in progress when the representative of the independent commercial classes was guiding the nation.[82]

Alongside the comments in the *Monitor, Test,* and *Con-Test,* the remarks on politics and the state of the nation in four other essay-journals – the *Centinel,*[83] *Crab-Tree, Bee,* and *Busy Body* – seem scant. Both the *Centinel* and *Crab-Tree* appeared briefly in 1757. While Thomas Franklin denied that his *Centinel* had any

---

[77]   *Monitor*, II (September 11, 1756), p. 75.
[78]   *Monitor*, II (September 4, 1756), p. 55; #127 (December 24, 1757), pp. 767-768.
[79]   *Monitor*, I (March 13, 1756), pp. 291 ff.
[80]   *Monitor*, II (September 25, 1756), p. 96.
[81]   *Monitor*, II (February 19, 1757), pp. 307-308; II (June 18, 1757), pp. 460 ff.
[82]   *Monitor*, #152 (June 17, 1758), p. 919; #156 (July 15, 1758), pp. 941 ff.; #157 (July 22, 1758), pp. 948-952; #159 (August 5, 1758), pp. 960-961; #182 (January 13, 1759), p. 1097. Robbins, p. 271; Sutherland, pp. 30-31.
[83]   Thomas Franklin was editor of the *Centinel* (Graham, p. 132).

political affiliations,[84] he did insist that its job was to protect the nation at home.[85] At the same time, the writers in the *Crab-Tree*, in allegiance to Lord Halifax, indicated their opposition to a parliament composed of merchants.[86] The evidence, however, is insufficient to permit any conclusions about the extent of the political commitments of either essay-journal.

On the matter of politics, nothing of importance appeared in either the *Busy Body* or *Bee*, which were published in 1759.[87] The date itself is of some consequence because Oliver Goldsmith, whose connection with the *Busy Body* has been noted and who was responsible for the *Bee*,[88] published his *Enquiry into the Present State of Polite Learning in Europe* earlier in the same year, and the comments on man and society in both essay-journals were consistent with the pessimism of the *Enquiry*. In the *Busy Body*, man's benevolent nature became the subject for satire;[89] the effects of liberty were shown in the raucous behavior in the theatres;[90] the power of reason was declared to be a myth,[91] and the conduct of the public in an emergency was depicted scornfully.[92] The essays in the *Bee*, in much the same way, condemned the taste and morals of the times,[93] and commented caustically on mankind's reaction to justice and generosity:[94]

---

[84] *Centinel*, #3 (January 20, 1757), p. 14.
[85] The *Centinel*'s denial of its pro-ministerial position in favor of Pitt and Legge, made in the third number, was necessitated, according to the periodical, by misinterpretations of its remarks in the first number. *Centinel*, #1 (January 6, 1757), p. 1.
[86] *Crab-Tree*, #12 (July 12, 1757), p. 69; #13 (July 19, 1757), p. 74; #14 (July 26, 1757), p. 79.
[87] *CBEL*, II, p. 639.
[88] According to Graham, p. 132, the *Bee* began as a miscellany rather than an essay-journal, but moved closer to the latter form in its later numbers. While Graham is correct, the *Bee* differed from the magazines because it was always the work of Goldsmith himself.
[89] *Busy Body*, #2 (October 11, 1759), pp. 7-12.
[90] *Busy Body*, #4 (October 16, 1759), p. 21.
[91] *Busy Body*, #5 (October 18, 1759), pp. 25-27.
[92] *Busy Body*, #8 (October 25, 1759), p. 46.
[93] *Bee*, #2 (October 13, 1759), pp. 31-39; #4 (October 27, 1759), p. 109; #5 (November 3, 1759), p. 116.
[94] *Bee*, #3 (October 20, 1759), p. 74.

In this manner do men generally reason upon justice and generosity. The first is despised, though a virtue essential to the good of society; and the other attracts our esteem, which too frequently proceeds from an impetuosity of temper, rather directed by vanity than reason.

If skepticism of man's natural benevolence and human reason indicates conservatism, most of the writers in the essay-journals were conservative. Only those in the *Con-Test* and *Monitor,* advocates for the London commercial classes, presented an optimistic view, and their optimism was more economic and political than philosophical. Yet, without equating optimism and liberalism, it is still possible to note that they were closely related in the periodical writers' arguments for the extension of the franchise to the mercantilists and their allies in the City. At the same time, the pessimistic distrust, even when expressed in criticism of taste and manners, of giving voice to the independent trade interests plainly suggests political and economic conservatism.

The comments in the individual magazines were less onesided than those in the essay-journals. Drawn from the profusion of letters and publications that delighted in self-pitying denunciations of England's failure during the early fighting, the estimates in the magazines were often gloomy, but nevertheless were frequently sympathetic to London's independent commercial class. Perhaps the eclectic policy of the magazines explains the comments in the *Grand* which complained of man's inherent weakness and the degeneracy of the times, but, when discussing the question of the proper basis of government, stressed the importance of heeding the voice of that very public of which other writers in the magazine were suspicious.[95] But anonymity, which permitted an author to change his mind without public embarassment because of political expediency, was as responsible as eclecticism for contradictions in separate articles like those by Rolt in the *Universal Visiter* that charged the decadence of the age to commerce and trade, but demanded a greater share in government for the independent merchants and their supporters.[96]

[95] See the discussion of the *Grand* in the section on minor magazines later in this chapter.
[96] See the discussion of the *Universal Visiter* in the section on minor magazines later in this chapter.

Some of the confusion is apparent in the statements in the major magazines, the *Gentleman's* and *London,* but out of the weight of their opinions the two emerge as supporters of the London trade interests and defenders of the ability of the London merchants to rise from defeat. Despite the editors' conventional insistence on their impartiality,[97] the writers in the *Gentleman's* viewed government as a means of protection for the liberty and property of the individual.[98] In their concern for corn prices and representative government, they indicated their sympathy for the City tradesmen and their attendant laborers who were being forced to pay the prices demanded by the country interests. To be sure, the editors presented a few stray comments to balance the arguments in the poetry and articles,[99] but the weight lay heavily on the side of a government-controlled price.[100] To insure that such control was proper, however, one writer in the magazine insisted that the only proper regulation of abuse of governmental power was to give the people a responsible share in the government.[101] Although the editors gave voice, in their selection of poetry, to the lamentations for the low state of Britain's fortunes in the war, its general tone was one of neither despair nor defeat, but rather of hopeful determination.[102] Perhaps the writers in the magazine were no strong believers in man's beneficent nature,[103] but at least one expressed his faith in a nation whose charity was unrivalled.[104]

The pattern in the *London Magazine* was similar. While some

[97] *Gentleman's,* XXVI (December, 1756), pp. 571-572.
[98] *Gentleman's,* XXVII (Supplement, 1757), pp. 591-592.
[99] *Gentleman's,* XXVI (Supplement, 1756), pp. 608, 622-624, 625.
[100] *Gentleman's,* XXVI (October, 1756), p. 486; XXVI (November, 1756), p. 534; XXVI (December, 1756), pp. 557, 575-576; XXVII (January, 1757), p. 32; XXVII (February, 1757), pp. 71-73; XXVII (March, 1757), pp. 129-131; XXVII (October, 1757), p. 471; XXVIII (March, 1758), pp. 125-126; XXVIII (November, 1758), pp. 509-511.
[101] *Gentleman's,* XXVI (January, 1756), p. 19.
[102] *Gentleman's,* XXVI (August, 1756), p. 400.
[103] See, for example, XXVI (May, 1756), pp. 253-254, a book review of *A Vindication of Natural Society.* While the *Gentleman's* recognized the satire, the review commented seriously on the argument for a beneficent natural society.
[104] *Gentleman's,* XXVII (January, 1757), p. 7.

of the *London*'s correspondents berated the luxury, vice, and effeminacy of the times,[105] others insisted that virtue and tender
affections were not dead.[106] The latter saw the need to protect the
weaker members of society,[107] but attributed the decadence less to
man's innate baseness than to his economic circumstances: [108]

For luxury, by its constant, and natural consequences, leads a state
to destruction; it not only emasculates the minds, and debilitates the
bodies of the people, but deprives them of their industry, which is
the strength of every state; for no other people were ever at once
luxurious and industrious.

But the comments in the magazine were not those of despair, for,
as one writer put it, there was always hope of reform, particularly
during the time of war.[109]

While its practices led to the publication of comments on the
exorbitant price of corn which were both favorable and unfavorable to the control of distribution,[110] the *London*'s own editorial
remarks represented the independent trade interests of the City
that were arguing for a lower price.[111] For the editors of the *London*, such governmental, or rather parliamentary, regulation was
important for the proper working order of a state dedicated to the
cause of the independent London commercial class.[112] Accordingly, writers in the magazine argued that the public had a right to
know what was going on in parliament, so the people could act

---

[105] *London*, XXV (January, 1756), pp. 15-17; XXV (October, 1756), pp.
473-476; XXVI (December, 1757), p. 576. The attack on the degeneracy of
the age, appearing as early as 1756, suggests the background for Brown's
Estimate.

[106] *London*, XXVII (December, 1758), p. 633.

[107] *London*, XXVIII (March, 1759), pp. 136-139; XXVIII (October, 1759),
p. 523.

[108] *London*, XXVII (May, 1758), p. 223.

[109] *London*, XXVII (May, 1758), pp. 223-224.

[110] *London*, XXVI (September, 1757), pp. 419-420; XXVI (November,
1757), p. 567; XXVII (March, 1758), pp. 124, 126.

[111] *London*, XXVII (March, 1758), p. 126.

[112] When the *London* printed extracts from a pamphlet censuring Pitt for
challenging the king's prerogative, the magazine explained its action as an
instance of its impartiality (XXVI, May, 1757, p. 249). However, the *London*'s publication of an attack on court corruption for rejecting Pitt because of his virtues was offered without apologies (XXVI, June, 1757, p.
304).

wisely at election time.[113] The purpose of parliament itself was to regulate labor rates,[114] encourage the industrious and necessary laborers,[115] keep the lower classes from becoming the tools of an ambitious monarch,[116] and insure a representative government.[117]

Overall, the comments in the *London* suggest a favorable attitude toward a system in which the public voice could be heard, a system associated in the magazine with the logical outcome of the Glorious Revolution.[118] As one letter-writer to the magazine remarked – paraphrasing Sir William Temple – monarchy was the best form of government when, like a pyramid, it rested on the support of the people, whose opinions and interests were the primary concern of the king.[119]

Among the minor magazines, political sympathies, attitudes on the nature of man and the depravity of the age were less clear. Comments ranged from the conventional lamentations on the decline of manners and taste and morals in the *Weekly* and *Grand Magazine of Magazines*,[120] to the more extensive, if more confused, statements in the *Grand Magazine* and *Universal Visiter*. Of the minor magazines, the *Grand* had the most to say on these subjects, but its frequently contradictory statements reflected its eclectic policy. The contrast between the *Grand*'s apparently confused philosophy and the decidedly liberal comments in the *Monthly,* also published by Griffiths, is the difference between the magazines and the reviews.

---

[113] *London*, XXV (July, 1756), p. 331; XXVI (August, 1757), pp. 371 ff.
[114] *London*, XXVII (January, 1758), p. 11.
[115] *London*, XXVII (March, 1758), pp. 112-113; XXVIII (May, 1759), p. 236. Characteristically, the magazines were concerned with the lower classes only as they were important to the middle and upper classes (*Weekly*, #9, June 10, 1758, p. 258; *Universal Magazine*, XXI, September, 1757, p. 121 and XXI, November, 1757, p. 235; *Universal Visiter*, #9, September, 1756, pp. 416-417).
[116] *London*, XXVIII (April, 1759), pp. 178-179.
[117] *London*, XXVIII (May, 1759), pp. 236-238.
[118] *London*, XXVIII (November, 1759), pp. 581-582.
[119] *London*, XXVIII (September, 1759), p. 483.
[120] *Weekly Magazine*, #9 (June 10, 1758), pp. 257 ff.; #12 (July 1, 1758), pp. 353 ff.; *Grand Magazine of Magazines*, II (March, 1759), p. 184. *The General Magazine of Arts and Sciences*, which had much to offer on the age in connection with science and religion, had nothing to offer on this subject in relation to politics.

Although the *Grand* made its first appearance relatively late in
this period, and although comments shortly afterwards argued for
Pitt's hard peace because of England's glorious military victories,
its writers depicted the age as degenerate and their skeptical evaluations of man's vaunted reason were peculiarly characteristic of
the pessimism during the first years of the war rather than the
optimism that was beginning to return to the nation in 1759.
Whether attempting to rouse the public from its "state of shameful indolence, and abandoned profligacy",[121] or ironically praising the superiority of this age to past ages in the arts of peace,[122]
or scoring the tastelessness of modern times,[123] the comments in
the *Grand* were pessimistic in their appraisal of the age. But the
disapproval was not only for modern man. One writer, describing
the life of Sir Robert Walpole, berated the conduct not merely of
the minister and his opposition, but condemned human nature itself: [124]

Human nature sinks greatly in our esteem, when we reflect on the
inconsistencies and many shameless deviations of the greatest characters, when influenced by ambition, avarice, spleen, or any other
violent passion. If we adhere to the most celebrated partizans for a
few years together, we shall find ourselves adopting opinions, and pur-
suing measures absolutely contradictory; and that while we are blind-
ly following our leaders, they are only promoting their own interest,
to which they make their dearest friends subservient, if men of such
disposition can be thought capable of friendship.

Yet despite the cynical appraisal of politics in the *Grand* and the
lack of faith in the ability to arouse an informed public opinion,[125]
the strongest arguments in the magazine demanded a representative government devoted to the interests of more than the king
and a privileged few.[126] The writers found no attraction in a chain
of being that was used to encumber the vertical movement in so-

[121] *Grand*, I (March, 1758), p. 116.
[122] *Grand*, I (July, 1758), p. 360.
[123] *Grand*, II (January, 1759), p. 24.
[124] *Grand*, II (April, 1759), p. 197.
[125] *Grand*, I (February, 1758), pp. 68, 73; I (September, 1758), p. 450; I
(October, 1758), p. 514; II (June, 1759), pp. 298-299.
[126] *Grand*, I (January, 1758), pp. 1-15; I (April, 1758), p. 164; I (October,
1758), p. 519.

ciety; [127] instead, in an argument characteristic of Pitt's City supporters, they advocated the principles of the Glorious Revolution and demanded the broadest possible freedom for the individual.[128]

Coming earlier in the war than the comments in the *Grand*, those in the *Universal Visiter* were less numerous but equally pessimistic in their evaluation of man. Here there was political purpose as well as eclecticism that governed the comments not only on an estimate of mankind but on a concept of government. To be sure, the denunciation of vice, luxury, and corruption were affected by the specter of British military defeats that appeared to be leading the nation to doom.[129] But in the editors' selection of letters and essays which contrasted the nation's affluent degeneracy with its power in less opulent times, there is also the suggestion of a political point of view.[130] For the anti-commercial critics of the decadent age, the argument was simple, as Samuel Johnson described it: the old agricultural structure of English society had given way to the less dependable one of commerce, and a country reliant upon trade interests was doomed to the fluctuations and uncertainties of commercial power.[131] The result, as another writer concluded, was that a dependence upon trade led inevitably to the destruction of custom upon which stability depended.[132]

Such was the character of the magazines, however, that the *Universal Visiter*, despite these comments accusing commerce of debilitating the strength of the nation, could present politically expedient arguments that demanded a greater voice in the government for the independent commercial interests. Richard Rolt, writing anonymously, could harass the Newcastle administration by insisting that the monarch heed the voice of the governed, an argument shortly to be used by Pitt's advocates.[133] Yet, when the

[127] *Grand*, I (January, 1758), pp. 11-12; II (January, 1759), pp. 6-7.
[128] *Grand*, I (February, 1758), pp. 57-58; I (March, 1758), p. 119; I (November, 1758), p. 565.
[129] *Universal Visiter*, #8 (August, 1756), p. 351.
[130] *Universal Visiter*, #8 (August, 1756), pp. 355-356, 357, 365.
[131] *Universal Visiter*, #3 (March, 1756), pp. 112-115. For identification of Johnson as author, see Bloom, p. 270.
[132] *Universal Visiter*, #8 (August, 1756), pp. 353-354.
[133] *Universal Visiter*, #1 (January, 1756), pp. 15 ff., 22. The attribution to Rolt is made by C. E. Jones, "Christopher Smart, Richard Rolt, and the

London merchants were making the same demands, Rolt, like Johnson, denounced the effect of trade, in general, on the stability of the nation.[134]

Comments in three other magazines – the *Universal,* the *New Royal and Universal,* and *Literary* – were either too general in scope or too limited in number to be particularly revealing of editorial sentiments. At that, the articles in the *Universal* presented the unusual combination of independent trade interests [135] and a pessimistic appraisal of man.[136] Although those in the *New Royal and Universal* presented no such contradiction, neither did they offer much beyond the comment that keeping mankind in check was "an ill-natur'd office" [137] and the observation that [138]

They that laid the first foundations of the civil life did very well consider, that the reason of mankind was generally so slight and feeble, that it would not serve for a rein to hold them in from the ruin of one another; and therefore they judged it best to make use of their passions, which have always a greater power over them; and by imposing necessary cheats on their hopes and fears keep them within those limits, which no principles of reason or nature could do.

From the contradictions and limited comments in the *Literary Magazine,* it is equally difficult to determine the editorial position. Some of the difficulty may be attributed to the disagreement between Samuel Johnson and his publisher about Pitt's administration, for while Johnson disliked Newcastle and the Whig aris-

---

Universal Visiter", *Library,* XVIII (1937), p. 214. See, also, *Universal Visiter,* #9 (September, 1756), pp. 410 ff., at a time when factions within the Whig party were engaged in controversy.

[134] *Universal Visiter,* #6 (June, 1756), pp. 264-265. Identification of Rolt is from Jones, "Christopher Smart, Richard Rolt, and the *Universal Visiter*", p. 214.

[135] *Universal,* XVIII (February, 1756), p. 57; XVIII (April, 1756), p. 149. See, also, XVIII (February, 1756), p. 57; XVIII (April, 1756), p. 149. For the magazine's opinions that the war was a commercial necessity and that trade interests should determine the peace, see Chapter III.

[136] *Universal,* XX (Supplement, 1757), p. 308; XXIV (January, 1759), p. 4; XXV (August, 1759), pp. 70, 73-74.

[137] *New Royal and Universal* (November, 1759), p. 218.

[138] *New Royal and Universal* (October, 1759), p. 152. See, also (November, 1759), pp. 218-219. The account of the *New Royal and Universal* in this study is based on an incomplete run of the magazine.

tocracy, he did not approve of Pitt, whom other writers in the magazine favored.[139] However, Johnson himself, despite his skeptical views of mankind and his distrust of commercial expansion,[140] in his attack on Newcastle agreed with the new mercantilists that all Englishmen had a right to know what was happening in administrative affairs.[141] And when the rising corn prices, which were increasing the costs for tradesmen and affecting business and commerce in the City, represented a threat to the orderliness of the state, he insisted on an official investigation [142] When Johnson was not involved, the articles in the *Literary* were clearly pleading the cause of Pitt and the independent City trade interests. Internationally, writers in the magazine regarded the war itself as commercially important to Britain,[143] and domestically, they demanded a government that was at once representative of the City trade groups and conducive to individual liberty.[144] In these comments, at least, the writers in the *Literary Magazine* were on the side of the anti-Newcastle Whigs.

Perhaps that is the most significant general comment that can be made about the magazines. As a measure of public opinion during the Seven Years' War, they – with their tendency to conduct a public forum – reflect the subtle change that was taking

[139]   Greene, p. 391. See Chapter I, pp. 27-28.

[140]   For Johnson's skepticism, see his review of Soame Jenyns' *Free Enquiry into the Nature and Origin of Evil*, II (April-May, 1757), pp. 171 ff.; II (May-June, 1757), pp. 252 ff.; II (June-July, 1757), pp. 301 ff. Although Johnson attacked Jenyns' presumption, he agreed with the author's assertion that evil in government cannot be removed but its excesses must be checked. J. W. Krutch, *Samuel Johnson* (New York, 1944), pp. 163 ff., gives an admirable account of Johnson's appraisal. Greene, p. 391, describes Johnson's views as anti-commercialist, anti-imperialist, and anti-expansionist. In the comments cited above, Johnson was attacking the Newcastle administration, which was a characteristic practice in the early numbers of the magazine. – In a comment on the *Test* and *Con-Test* in the *Literary*, I (December-January, 1757), p. 461, the opposition to Newcastle and support of Pitt were clearly indicated.

[141]   *Literary*, I (July-August, 1756), pp. 161 ff. See Greene, p. 383. For the magazine's comment on corn prices, see II (November-December, 1757), pp. 518 ff.

[142]   *Literary*, I (October-November, 1756), p. 333. Greene, pp. 388-389, suggests Johnson's authorship of the article.

[143]   *Literary*, III (July, 1758), pp. 289-290.

[144]   *Literary*, II (November-December, 1757), pp. 505, 507.

place in the political atmosphere. The control of the Whig aristocracy, with its commercial interest in the monopolistic trading
companies, was slipping away. In its place the independent City
merchants were struggling for power. To be sure, magazines like
the *Universal Visiter* opposed all commercial interests and expansion of trade, but the great majority of the magazines supported
the Popular Whigs in their effort to gain control. Whether this
was one of the liberal impulses that Schilling has described as
modifying the extreme conservatism that had set in after the Glorious Revolution may be debatable,[145] but there is no question that
the periodicals catering to the new commercial interests were also
demanding international expansion of trade and domestic extension of the franchise.

The attitude was not characteristic of the comments in the
Annual Register. For Burke the war was being fought over commercial territory that neither the British nor French could properly claim,[146] and his support for Pitt, coming in 1759, was not in
the interest of City trade groups but rather in consideration for
the national harmony that the minister had achieved.[147] Indeed,
the comments on government itself reflected the ideas of Burke's
doctrine of prescription with its approval of a system that had
evolved out of need and therefore was the best that time and man
could offer.[148] While they did not approve of the change that
characterized a commercial age,[149] the articles in the *Annual
Register*, like those in the *Critical Review,* went further and professed a conservative attitude that followed the belief that man's
nature did not differ fundamentally from age to age.[150]

Although less oblique and more committed than those in the
magazines, the articles in the *Annual Register* were also less direct
than those in the *Critical* and *Monthly Review*, which shared the
sense of commitment of the political essay-journals. Smollett him-

---

145   Schilling, pp. 12-13.
146   *Annual Register*, I (1758), pp. 2-3.
147   *Annual Register*, I (1758), pp. 10-13, 28, 256 ff.; II (1759), pp. 7, 439-
443.
148   *Annual Register*, I (1758), pp. 10-13; II (1759), pp. 4, 274.
149   *Annual Register*, I (1758), p. 476.
150   *Annual Register*, I (1758), pp. 262-263.

self, expressing his disagreement with Joseph Warton's statements on Pope, set the tone for the review: [151]

We think the author of the essay mistaken, when he asserts . . . that the sciences cannot exist but in a republic. The assertion savours too much of a wild spirit of democratic enthusiasm, which some people have imbibed from the writings of the Greeks. – [Such reasoning] betrays its owner into all the absurdities of an over-heated imagination. – The sciences will always flourish where merit is encouraged; and this is more generally the case under an absolute monarchy, than in a republic, for reasons so obvious, that they need not be repeated

Only when the editor's reputation as an impartial historian was at stake did the *Critical* reviewers defend the Glorious Revolution.[152] Otherwise, they were neither friends to the parliamentary triumph of 1688,[153] nor, despite their high regard for Pitt, supporters of the trade interests.[154] Whether arguing from historical analogy or addressing themselves to contemporary politics, they demanded a conservative approach to government, an acceptance of the general *status quo*, rather than an unplanned change. They deplored the voices of faction and denounced political reforms that demonstrated a sharp break from the past.[155] Despite their opposition to Hume's religious views, the writers in the *Critical* welcomed his political conservatism,[156] even as they castigated the party spirit in Horace Walpole's *Catalogue of the Royal and Noble Authors of England.*[157]

While their condemnation of the age was no less severe than Brown's *Estimate*,[158] the reviewers' arguments for keeping mankind in check, recognizing man's limitations, and accepting

[151] *Critical Review*, I (April, 1756), p. 233.
[152] *Critical Review*, V (January, 1758), pp. 9-10; VI (September, 1758), pp. 228-234.
[153] *Critical Review*, V (April, 1758), p. 284.
[154] *Critical Review*, II (August, 1756), pp. 38-39 (Smollett).
[155] *Critical Review*, II (August, 1756), pp. 10-11 (Samuel Derrick); V (January, 1758), p. 1.
[156] *Critical Review*, VII (April, 1759), p. 292.
[157] *Critical Review*, VI (December, 1758), p. 483.
[158] *Critical Review*, I (March, 1756), p. 97 (Smollett); II (August, 1756), p. 48; II (September, 1756), p. 121 (Smollett); III (March, 1757), p. 238; IV (July, 1757), p. 46; VII (April, 1759), p. 375; VIII (October, 1759), pp. 271-272.

government because it is government are more important. The result was clearly expressed in Thomas Franklin's insistence on accepting the political order rather than risking a major change: [159]

... although it will very readily be granted, that every species of society, and every form of civil government is attended with many evils, and subject to inconveniences and abuse, it will yet, by no means follow, that total anarchy and confusion, which would be the inevitable consequences of (what he [the author of *A Vindication of Natural Society*] terms) *natural* society, are therefore eligible. The grievances and imperfections of which he so heavily complains, must always continue whilst men are men, unless he could persuade his friend [Bolingbroke] in the shades to send us one of his Utopian patriot kings to govern us, and a better rule than his *first philosophy* to regulate our moral conduct.

Without attempting to glorify either mankind or the public morals during the Seven Years' War,[160] the political writers on the *Monthly Review* took a position opposed to that of the *Critical* reviewers: [161] "We are far from believing that the nation is more vicious than formerly: that our freedom is in danger: or that we are tottering on the brink of ruin." Griffiths' writers, aware of man's vices,[162] nevertheless insisted that there is a universal tendency to happiness,[163] which could be achieved best if the new commercial groups, with a real stake in the government, were given control.[164]

Throughout their comments on government, the *Monthly* reviewers, led by Ralph and Ruffhead, emphasized the importance of commercial and trade interests.[165] They insisted that the government itself must act on behalf of the commercial classes, upon

---

[159] *Critical*, I (June, 1756), p. 426. In its comments on Burke's work, the *Critical*'s article failed to appreciate its satire. For further comment indicating Smollett's skepticism, see *Critical Review*, II (August, 1756), p. 44.
[160] *Monthly Review*, XV (September, 1756), p. 217 (Ward); XVII (October, 1757), p. 340 (Ruffhead).
[161] *Monthly*, XVIII (May, 1758), p. 465 (Ruffhead).
[162] *Monthly*, XV (September, 1756), p. 217 (Ward); XVII (July, 1757), p. 54 (Goldsmith).
[163] *Monthly*, XVI (April, 1757), pp. 302-303 (William Rose).
[164] *Monthly*, XV (September, 1756), p. 217 (Ward).
[165] *Monthly*, XIV (January, 1756), p. 37 (William Bewley); XIV (February, 1756), p. 81 (Rose); XVI (April, 1757), p. 349 (Ralph).

whose industry the happiness and security of the nation depended.[166] Not content merely to encourage government action for the improvement of trade,[167] the reviewers demanded a greater voice for the independent merchants in a free and active parliament.[168]

Ruffhead, despite his denial of party interests, attacked the Tories and approved the principles of the Glorious Revolution.[169] The beheading of Charles I was regarded with revulsion, but not out of respect for his government or admiration for kingship. Whatever their reservations about parliamentary government,[170] both Ruffhead and Ralph regarded the ultimate power as residing in the people, whom they identified with the City merchants. According to Ruffhead especially, Charles had been unfit to rule, and "upon any breach of kingly duty, the people can only revoke their trust [in the monarch], and transfer it to some more worthy object".[171]

These remarks on Charles I suggest the greatest difference between the *Monthly* and *Critical*: their editorial attitude toward change. Smollett's writers supported the *status quo* and exhibited a fear of disturbing the structure of society through tampering with its institutions. However, as in their laudatory comments on the success of the Romans,[172] Griffiths' reviewers argued for a government of checks and balances, a system in which change was not only desirable, but necessary, and an enlargement of territory that would add to the strength of the nation's commerce. In these opinions of the *Monthly*'s writers, lay the forecast of Pitt's objectives in the second phase of the Seven Years' War.

[166] *Monthly*, XIV (May, 1756), pp. 451-452 (Rose); XVI (April, 1757), p. 352 (Ralph); XVIII (March, 1758), p. 272 (Ruffhead).

[167] Demanding strong action to lower the corn prices, the *Monthly*, stressed the effect that the high price had on the nation's trade (XVI, February, 1757, p. 163; XVI, April, 1757, p. 352 [Ralph]).

[168] *Monthly*, XV (September, 1756), p. 233 (Ward); XV (October, 1756), p. 408 (Ralph); XVII (October, 1757), p. 291 (Ruffhead); XVII (November, 1757), p. 467 (Ralph).

[169] *Monthly*, XVIII (April, 1758), p. 305; XVIII (May, 1758), p. 543.

[170] *Monthly*, XVII (October, 1757), p. 291 (Ruffhead); XVII (November, 1757), p. 468 (Ralph).

[171] *Monthly*, XVIII (May, 1758), p. 401.

[172] *Monthly*, XV (July, 1756), pp. 1-2.

III

MAKING THE PEACE

Peace descended neither suddenly nor quietly upon England. Long before the actual signing of the Treaty of Paris in 1763, verbal warfare raged at home. Politicians and pamphleteers battled about the nation's obligations to its allies and its expectations of just and honorable terms from its enemies.

Indeed, from 1760 on, events were no less turbulent than they had been in the earlier years of defeat and disgrace. Conquests of Belleisle and Martinique stirred public opinion about the retention of the islands that was equal in clamor to the uproar that had accompanied Byng's failure at Minorca. Controversy flared anew about the advisability of war with Spain and then about the resignation of Pitt. With the fall of Havana, the new ministry of Bute, seeking a speedy settlement of the war, had to quell the demands of a nation exuberant with victory, and the temporary loss of Newfoundland forced the administration to try to quiet the public outrage at the sudden lapse of strength.

To all this the literary periodicals bear witness. The record of events and opinions is in their pages. How did their writers react and what were the positions they took? What, particularly, were their demands for a peace? The answers are only meaningful with some understanding of the character of the final stages of the war and of the fundamental differences in the attitudes of Pitt and Bute toward the peace.

Although peace talk was in the air in 1759, the struggle was far from over. With the capitulation of Montreal in September, 1760 – as Corbett has pointed out – the war moved from its primary to its secondary stage. The English had attained their original objective – the annexation of Canada – but their purpose now was to apply general pressure that would compel a favorable peace.[1]

It was Pitt's contention that the American victory had been made possible by the diversion of the French forces in the continental fighting.[2] One might well ask, why, if the main purpose had been accomplished, was Pitt unwilling to terminate the German alliance and bring the war to an end? To be sure, there were pressures enough demanding both. The severe financial crisis of 1759 had made many in the nation wary of continuing the fighting,[3] and the new king, George III, was bitterly opposed to the German connection.[4] Indeed, there was even good indication that the "man in the street", at least for a time, agreed with the fixed policy of Leicester House, which sought to end the German war.[5]

A pamphlet, Israel Mauduit's *Considerations on the Present German War*, had no small part in shaping this public opinion at the end of 1760.[6] Mauduit accused Frederick of using English aid for selfish purposes.[7] The writer appealed "to the insular national spirit".[8] Deliberately separating the continental fighting from the rest of the war, he aroused a public which was conscious of the monetary cost but not of the strategic importance of the European fighting.[9]

In actuality, as Corbett, an historian favorable to Pitt, has shown, England had no responsibility to continue the German subsidy after the danger had passed.[10] Nor was Frederick himself eager to continue the fighting, for the Prussian king believed that

---

[1] Corbett, II, pp. 119, 141.

[2] Gipson, VIII, pp. 7-8, 28-29, 289; C. W. Eldon, *England's Subsidy Policy toward the Continent during the Seven Years' War* (Philadelphia, 1938), p. 160.

[3] Namier, I, p. 67, quotes the Duke of Newcastle as commenting on "the impossibility of going on in this way". See, also, p. 211.

[4] Gipson, VIII, pp. 55-56; R. Sedgwick, editor, *Letters from George III to Lord Bute, 1756-1766* (London, 1939), p. 11.

[5] Feiling, p. 75.

[6] Gipson, VIII, p. 43.

[7] Israel Mauduit, *Considerations on the Present German War*, 3rd ed. (London, 1760), p. 47.

[8] Corbett, II, p. 145.

[9] Eldon, pp. 133-134.

[10] Corbett, II, pp. 337-338.

if England negotiated a separate peace with France, the latter would insist on Austria's agreeing to terms in order to keep the balance of power in Germany.[11] Why, then, did Pitt demand the continuation of aid to the continental allies and the prosecution of the war? The answer seems to rest primarily in the minister's connection with the independent London trade interests.

That Pitt represented this group is undeniable. Even after the negotiations were completed, "the Corporation of London was devoted to Pitt and refused to address the King on the Peace".[12] When Bute sought to sell his terms to the public, he was aware that he had to impress the antagonistic merchants of the City,[13] and even after his resignation, their hostility to the government remained and gave rise to serious faction.[14] The alignment of sides was clear. On the one hand, there was the alliance of Court and Country,[15] on the other, the City with the attendant mob that it controlled.[16] When their trade interests were involved, the Newcastle Whigs gave limited aid to the City merchants, but the old political aristocrats also kept close watch on the changes in the balance of power in hopes of capturing their lost control.

Pitt's relation to the London mercantile interests suggests the

[11] Corbett, II, pp. 141-142.
[12] Jucker, p. 145.
[13] Jucker, p. 69.
[14] Jucker, pp. 168, 246.
[15] Although Namier, I, pp. 8-9, is accurate in his assertion that Pitt's constituency lay in his appeal to the "country gentlemen", who were called "Tories" under George II, and that this group was in the opposition under George III, a significant change took place during the peace negotiations, when the Country Party felt its interests were with the Court (cf., Sedgwick, Letters from George III etc., pp. 208-209; Patriot, #2, June 26, 1762, pp. 9-10, and #5, July 17, 1762, pp. 28-29).
[16] G. M. Trevelyan, An Autobiography and Other Essays (London, 1949), p. 193. There were factions in the City trade interest. The Corporation of London and some of the smaller merchant groups were not always in agreement with such monopolies as the East India Company. However, the East India Company was "traditionally an ally of the Government in the City". See Sutherland, pp. 30, 92 ff. The quotation is from p. 104. – Greene, pp. 390-391, has described the divison in the Whig interests. Newcastle represented the landed Whig aristocracy and state trading monopolies, while Pitt was allied with the independent business interests of London and Bristol. Pitt's group was both less conservative in international affairs and more imperialistic or expansionist than Newcastle's Whigs.

importance of economic factors in his attitude toward the continental fighting. Among the minor points to be considered is the benefit the German war provided to many English merchants. "Subsidies to various German States, the commissariat of the British armies fighting in Germany and remittances of money for their use, opened a rich field for British merchants in the Dutch and Hamburg trade." The merchants had scurried after the contracts for supplying continental regiments, and such contracts naturally disappeared at the end of the war.[17]

But of far greater importance is the relation of Pitt's connections with the City trade interests to the object of the secondary phase of the war: compelling a favorable peace that would reduce the commercial power of the French empire. Pitt's terms of a favorable peace were clearly not those of Bute. Perhaps the difference has been described best by Gipson, who distinguishes between a war for the empire rather than a war for empire.[18]

That Bute preferred the former is evident in the policy he pursued at the accession of George III. Adverse critics of the minister have described him as seeking peace at any price and pressing for terms with greater urgency than the defeated enemy.[19] However, it is unnecessary to berate Bute in order to prove that he desired a peace for which he was willing to make concessions. The minister, after all, was serving the interests of a king whose primary concern was putting a speedy end to the war.[20]

At the same time, it is apparent that the administration's secretive and conciliatory methods were unlikely to please the London merchants who viewed the peace as an opportunity to replace French interests in a colonial empire. In order to achieve a speedy peace, Bute and the king were willing to bargain away the newly acquired territory that the mercantile interests coveted. George and his minister were fearful that the capture of Fort Royal would increase the public demands for compensation for the return of

[17] Namier, I, pp. 58-59, 65 n. 1. Quotation is from pp. 58-59.
[18] Gipson, VIII, p. 310.
[19] Corbett, II, p. 285; John Almon, *History of the Late Minority* (London, 1766), pp. 81 ff.
[20] J. Fortesque, editor, *Correspondence of King George the Third, from 1760 to December, 1783* (London, 1927-1928), p. xvi.

Martinique.[21] Bute worked desperately behind the scenes, negotiating covertly to defeat the opposition of his colleagues; [22] and
when a cabinet crisis arose because Grenville and Egremont insisted that Puerto Rico and Florida, at least, be retained for the
restoration of Havana, Bute was fully prepared to accept Florida
alone.[23] The king himself was willing to condemn Bedford, his
own ambassador, for failure to present terms acceptable to the
French, although the monarch recognized the duplicity of the
enemy's negotiations.[24] When France proved obstinate and rejected his conciliatory efforts, George floundered in despair.[25]

That Bute's peace was one of "moderation and compromise"
both his detractors and admirers are willing enough to admit.[26]
Yet such agreement does not indicate that they consider the peace
in the same terms. Those who regard Bute's efforts favorably
stress the acquisitions made by England: the settlement was one
"which secured the original objects of the war and satisfied the
reasonable ambitions of all Englishmen but those who lived by
war or war-mongering".[27] But for those who judge Bute's treaty
for what it might have been, the theme becomes: ". . . we were in
a position to extract still harder terms than we did. . . . Pitt would
have done so, and was minded by crushing the French navy, body
and soul, to put it out of her power ever to retaliate." [28] Thus the
issue was not whether England had gained by the peace, but
whether the nation might have gained more. When Wilkes declared that ". . . it was the damn'dest peace for the Opposition
that ever was made", what he meant, as all his later comments
indicate, was that the administration had a powerful showpiece

[21]   Sedgwick, *Letters from George III etc.*, p. 88.
[22]   Corbett, II, p. 351; Sedgwick, *Letters from George III etc.*, pp. 118, 121.
[23]   Sedgwick, *Letters from George III etc.*, pp. 142, 144-145.
[24]   Sedgwick, *Letters from George III etc.*, p. 178.
[25]   Sedgwick, *Letters from George III etc.*, p. 126.
[26]   For a view favorable to Bute, see Gipson, VIII, p. 313; for an opposed
view, see Corbett, II, p. 376.
[27]   R. Pares, *War and Trade in the West Indies* (Oxford, 1936), p. 610.
Sutherland, p. 92, expresses agreement with this view. Turberville, pp. 43-
44: ". . . a treaty which gave us Canada, Florida, and Senegal in West
Africa, is a notable landmark in British imperial development."
[28]   Corbett, II, p. 376.

for the public.[29] He was not unmindful that England, as even critics favorable to Bute acknowledge, had made great concessions to the enemy.[30]

What Pitt might have done had he remained in power must obviously remain forever conjecture. Yet it is apparent that in his conduct of the second phase of the war, he was pressing for a peace that would have made the battle a struggle for empire. He insisted on keeping the Newfoundland fisheries,[31] an acquisition that would have pushed France and her navy completely out of Canada, at the same time that it would have thwarted her rivalry for trade. His waiting for news of the surrender of Belleisle in order to force stronger terms upon the French indicates that he was unwilling to yield whatever he could possibly hold;[32] and his demand for war on Spain – an action popular with the City merchants seeking the rich prizes[33] – demonstrates his willingness to fight a commercial war.[34]

Nobbe has distinguished between the peace aims of Pitt and Bute. The former, he says, sought a treaty to "consolidate and ensure British gains"; the latter wanted terms that would "gratify the national spirit and at the same time be mild enough to prevent rejection by France".[35] The distinction seems fair enough, but requires some explanation of the ministers' purposes. For Pitt, indeed, once the war had begun and England had made her conquests at the expense of manpower and money, the nation was entitled to proper compensation, to be had through a hard peace that demanded as much of the conquest as would be advantageous

---

[29]   Nobbe, pp. 117-118, quotes Wilkes' remark which was made in private. Nobbe argues accurately that the preliminaries fairly quelled the parliamentary opposition. However, as the evidence in this study shows, the very points of attack cited by Nobbe remained a part of the journalistic controversy even after the signing of the treaty.

[30]   For such an admission, see Gipson, VIII, pp. 66-67.

[31]   Jucker, p. 9, n. 1.

[32]   Jucker, p. 1.

[33]   Corbett, II, p. 193.

[34]   Corbett, II, p. 254. J. S. Watson, *The Reign of George III, 1760-1815* (Oxford, 1960), p. 74, describes Pitt's aim in the war with Spain as an attempt to "open new areas for colonial conquest".

[35]   Nobbe, pp. 28-29.

to an expanding trade empire. His speech to the Commons lamented the treaty which he felt had yielded – especially from a commercial point of view – everything: [36]

France is chiefly, if not solely, to be dreaded by us in the light of a maritime and commercial power: and therefore by restoring to her all the valuable West India islands, and by our concessions in the Newfoundland fishery, we have given her the means of recovering her prodigious losses and of becoming once more formidable to us at sea.

Pitt spoke with the voice of the City trade interests,[37] but Bute's ears were not particularly sensitive to such arguments. For him England's main purpose had been the protection of her American possessions, and she needed no more than the soft peace that would ensure their safety, while making minor concessions to the demands of the merchants. Whatever other possessions England was able to retain seemed to Bute of less importance than a peace that would restore the old balance of power. He was certainly not concerned with the expansion of a commercial empire.

Throughout the negotiations and even after the final settlement, the periodical writers joined in the public debate on the issues. Their comments reveal not only their own position and the surrounding climate of opinion, but also the differences in the periodical types. Of all the writers, those in the essay-journals were the most outspoken. Not even the reviewers, whose critical function demanded direct comment, expressed their opinions as freely, for the use of the individual *persona* in the essay-journals gave them a degree of unity fairly impossible for the other periodicals to achieve.

Five essay-journals were concerned with the problem of the peace.[38] Indeed, four of them owed their very existence to the

[36] Quotation is from Plumb, p. 114.

[37] Plumb, p. 115.

[38] References to all the essay-journals, except the *Patriot*, during the peace negotiations are to the convenient collection called *Political Controversy*, edited by John Caesar Wilkes, commonly accepted as a pseudonym of John Wilkes. References to the *Monitor* outside the period are from separate editions of that journal. These journals have recently been discussed by Robert R. Rea in *The English Press in Politics, 1760-1774* (Lincoln, 1963), Chapter II.

conflict that the Bute ministry faced from the political opposition at home. Arthur Murphy and Tobias Smollett had been hired specifically to promulgate, through the *Auditor* and *Briton,* respectively, the virtues of the treaty negotiations and the merits of the minister himself. On the other side, John Wilkes and Charles Churchill responded in the *North Briton* with a virulent attack on the terms of the peace and a vehement denunciation of Bute. For a very brief time, the anti-ministerial forces received the support of the *Patriot,* a short-lived periodical, while the fifth of these essay-journals, the *Monitor,* which sided with the opposition to Bute, was neither a newcomer nor transient in the field.

The first of the four new essay-journals, the *Briton,* appeared on May 29, 1762. Bute relied on press propaganda to sway public opinion,[39] but in almost every way the *Briton* failed him. Instead, its editor became the object of ridicule, and while it apparently achieved little circulation, it raised fears of a government-controlled press.[40] Not only was the *Briton* unsuccessful in stemming the tide against Bute, but it positively raised the flood of anti-ministerial writings.[41]

That Smollett's effort was largely ineffective, there seems no doubt,[42] but the explanations advanced for his failure seem inadequate. Whitridge has described him as "an artist struggling in an unfamiliar medium",[43] and Nobbe has offered much the same criticism, adding that there were greater problems in defending a ministry than in attacking it, especially when the defense came from a Scotsman protecting a Scottish minister who did not always keep his hireling informed.[44] The comments of both scholars

---

[39] Nobbe, p. 31.

[40] Nobbe, pp. 32-34. John Almon noted that only 250 copies of the *Briton* were printed and that was probably in excess of the demand.

[41] D. Hannay, *Life of Tobias George Smollett* (London, 1887), p. 148.

[42] However, Nobbe, pp. 159-167, points out accurately that when the *Briton* and *Auditor* were dropped, the peace had already been made. He adds, though, that had they been successful, Bute probably would have continued them to popularize himself.

[43] A. Whitridge, *Tobias Smollett: a Study of His Miscellaneous Works* (New York, 1925), p. 87.

[44] Nobbe, pp. 32, 160-161. Whitridge, p. 65, also notes the lack of information given to Smollett.

seem incomplete rather than inaccurate. Why should an excellent satirist and an experienced participant in literary controversy have failed so miserably in a battle that required the very skills that he had formerly displayed? The answer lies less in the man and his personality than in the problems that he faced.[45] Those problems were more than is suggested by either Smollett's Scottish background or the customary difficulty of defending rather than attacking. The handicap was greater than the unmentioned fact that Smollett's connection with the *Critical Review* made him an easy target for the opposition.[46] The real liability lay in the peace that Smollett was asked to popularize and the ramifications of such an assignment.

To begin with, Smollett's partisanship required two reversals of attitude that must have weighed heavily on his political conscience, despite his sincere belief in the cause he was asked to defend. Firstly, making the peace demanded an attack on Pitt, who stood as a symbol of City trade interests. Although Knapp has insisted on Smollett's fairness and consistency in his overall estimation of Pitt,[47] the fact remains that Smollett himself felt called upon to explain publicly what appeared to be his defection.[48] Pitt was still the popular hero to the City, and Smollett could hardly expect to influence the followers of the fallen minister by labeling him blackguard, hypocrite, and deserter;[49] yet the demands of the peace required that Smollett make Pitt no less a target than Wilkes and Churchill.[50] But whatever appeal the attack on Pitt might have for the Whig aristocrats, whose support Smollett hoped to gain, the main opposition to Bute and the peace

---

[45]   Nobbe, p. 160, places the emphasis on a failure in Smollett's personality and ability. Rea, pp. 29-30.

[46]   For good examples, see *Political Controversy*, I, p. 34 and III, pp. 284-285.

[47]   Knapp, p. 245, and "Smollett and the Elder Pitt", *MLN*, LIX (1944), pp. 250-253.

[48]   Knapp, "Smollett and the Elder Pitt", pp. 254-255, quotes Smollett's letter to *The Gazetteer and London Daily Advertiser*, October 7, 1762. Here as in his change of attitude toward France, Smollett was consistent with his pyrrhonistic view of politics.

[49]   *Political Controversy*, I, pp. 24-27; II, pp. 256-257, 330 ff.

[50]   Whitridge, p. 75.

came from the independent City merchants and their followers, so that the *Briton* had no chance for London popularity.

Secondly, the decision to support the ministry of Bute in its efforts to make the peace depended on a reliance on French honesty, but faith in the honesty of the French was altogether inconsistent with Smollett's frequently expressed views. So virulent had been his acknowledged statements about the French that Lord Shelburne dared not recommend him later for a consulship at Nice for fear "the people wou'd rise upon him and stone him in the streets on his first appearance".[51] Yet in the *Briton*, Smollett had to respond to the charges of French treachery made in the *North Briton* by insisting that French despair made that nation dependable in its willingness to negotiate a peace.[52] But whatever debilitating effect these necessary changes in opinion might have had on Smollett's ability as a propagandist in the *Briton*, they were of less consequence to his failure than the extreme unpopularity of the cause that he had been asked to defend. True enough, defense generally is more difficult than opposition, but this particular defense was impossible under the circumstances that Smollett had to operate.

In the public eye (the City merchants and their supporters) the Bute ministry could do no right.[53] The administration was determined to bring about a quick end to the war,[54] but the fighting was still going on and had to be pursued diligently or explanations would be demanded by the opposition. Losses like that of Newfoundland gave Bute strong arguments for getting any peace that he could, but such losses brought a barrage of charges of incompetence. Victories like those of Martinique silenced the attack on his conduct of the war but lent strength to the most exorbitant demands for a victor's peace.[55] Smollett might argue that the peace terms were such that Pitt would have been happy to have them,

---

[51] E. C. Mossner and R. Klibansky, eds., *New Letters of David Hume* (London, 1955), p. 173.
[52] *Political Controversy*, I, pp. 399 ff.
[53] Sedgwick, *Letters from George III etc.*, p. 67, n. 2; Corbett, II, pp. 353-354.
[54] *Political Controversy*, III, p. 29.
[55] *Political Controversy*, I, pp. 101, 175-176, 178, 399 ff.; II, p. 27.

but such argument meant minimizing the importance of the conquests that he wanted to add to the credit of Bute; [56] or he might insist that the original purpose of the war had been achieved with the victory in America and that the negotiations were saving the country from ruin, but such insistence raised the question of the condition of the defeated enemies.[57]

Indeed, Smollett offered the great London public only a choice between two unattractive images of itself. At best it could regard itself as the dupe of private trade interests willing to continue the tremendous expenditures in manpower and money for the sake of personal benefits; [58] at worst it could see itself as a band of wild Goths whipped to a frenzy by promises of world plunder.[59] Billingsgate language might reasonably have been expected to arouse readers not subjectively involved in the attack, but the same readers might well have been expected to retreat from charges leveled at them and assign such comments to the paid infamy of a hired pen: [60]

One would imagine the people of this metropolis had eaten of the insane root, that takes the reason prisoner; or like those who have been bit by the tarantula, they have suffered from the stings of certain mischievous insects, which have the power of infusing such virulent poison in the wounds they give, as produces a temporary delirium, during which they act a thousand extravagances.

Perhaps Smollett was also hoping to appeal to those financiers and merchants who felt a personal need to restrain the "small man's radical point of view".[61] But whatever the reason, there was in everything he wrote a self-defeating acknowledgment that, despite his arguments, both Bute and the peace were unpopular. That the virtues of either were self-evident was denied by the need to publish a governmental paper to convince the public of their benefits. Do what he might, Smollett himself could not escape the

---

[56]   *Political Controversy*, I, pp. 368-369.
[57]   *Political Controversy*, II, pp. 293-294, 297.
[58]   *Political Controversy*, I, pp. 30, 366-367; II, pp. 173, 494-495.
[59]   *Political Controversy*, I, pp. 330-331.
[60]   *Political Controversy*, II, pp. 64-65; see also I, p. 218.
[61]   Watson, p. 50.

charge that he was being employed as a ministerial advocate.[62] He
was forced to scoff at the popular notion that the war was fought
as a crusade against Catholicism, and his arguments against retaining the conquests could only seem timid to an immoderate
public.[63] Neither the character of Bute nor the peace made
Smollett's task any easier.

It was quickly apparent that the *Briton* was unequal to the task
that the Bute ministry had assigned it, and Arthur Murphy was
called upon to provide support with the *Auditor,* which made its
first appearance on June, 10, 1762.[64] Murphy had two advantages
over Smollett: no earlier friendly association with Pitt and Wilkes
and access to better information about the treaty negotiations.[65]
Despite Murphy's willingness to use the first advantage freely in
castigating the opposition and attempting to split the Whig interests,[66] he counted strongly on the second to achieve his objective of making the peace palatable to the City trade interests. But
here, although he evidently knew what Bute intended to demand,
Murphy's arguments in the *Auditor* proved as ineffective as those
in the *Briton.*

Murphy had to demonstrate to his readers that there was no
connection between the war in Germany and the conquest of
Canada, for such a conclusion would mean that Britain had a
right to dissociate the two in the peace negotiations. The easiest
proof, according to the essays in the *Auditor,* was the fact that the
origin of the war in Germany was the French attack, not a British
diversionary move.[67] Whatever the questions about the accuracy
of this description of the events, the opposition found little difficulty in demolishing the reasoning. What if France had moved
foolishly, the critic asked; does that mean the English had no right

[62]   *Political Controversy,* I, pp. 40, 65-66, 175-176, 181; II, p. 50.
[63]   *Political Controversy,* I, pp. 64-65; II, p. 104.
[64]   Nobbe, p. 33.
[65]   Nobbe, pp. 160-161, notes Murphy's superiority in his sources of information. His view that Murphy "had even less conpunction [than Smol-
lett] about being personally abusive" seems accurate enough to me; although, like Whitridge, p. 62, I believe that Smollett overcame his com-
punction.
[66]   *Political Controversy,* I, pp. 82, 229-236, 381 ff.; III, pp. 107-108.
[67]   *Political Controversy,* I, pp. 5, 46; III, p. 159.

to use the mistake to their own advantage? And the question still remained: ". . . does it appear the least probable that we should have subdued our enemies in America, if they had turned their whole force that way?" [68] The point was not whether Pitt had intended that the German war be fought for American conquests, but whether the action actually had such an effect.[69]

But the German connection was a minor problem, for Murphy, like Smollett, sought also to convince the supporters of the City trade interests that yielding the conquests of empire was beneficial to commerce; and that despite the continued military victories of the British, the enemy was becoming increasingly more dangerous.

On the first point, the essays in the *Auditor* followed the policy of the administration, which insisted that England must give up part of the gain and choose what was best for the entire nation. Consistent with this argument, they attacked the faction that wanted the war fought for private benefit, and most vulnerable as profiteers were the stock-jobbers,[70] those investment capitalists operating on paper credit, who sought the extension of empire.[71]

Whatever the justification for these charges, Murphy did not come to terms with the question of why Britain could not retain all her conquests. To answer the question properly, he had two possible choices: to demonstrate either that part of the acquisition was not worth holding, or (as suggested by the second point above) that the nation had neither the power nor right to demand a hard peace. By minimizing the importance of Guadeloupe and Martinique, the ministerial writer attempted to prove that England was yielding little by returning them. He used the publication of *The Commercial Principles of the Late Negotiation* as a basis for criticizing the advocates for the retention of the sugar islands,

[68] *Political Controversy*, I, p. 6. The quotation comes from Wilkes' note in *Political Controversy*.
[69] *Political Controversy*, I, pp. 6-7.
[70] G. M. Trevelyan, *English Social History* (London, 1942), pp. 491-492, discusses the rise of the stock-jobbers and notes their Dutch connections. The origins of the group permitted Murphy to appeal to English provinciality in his attack.
[71] *Political Controversy*, I, pp. 307-310; II, pp. 3-4.

but his arguments resulted in quibbles that, if anything, weakened his position. In accusing the author of the pamphlet of dealing unfairly with his subject by considering the islands apart from the commercial connections that were responsible for the profit, Murphy played into the hands of the London merchants who argued that the conquest was consistent with the new trade empire.[72] Yet the details were unimportant, for whatever proof he might offer of the superiority of Canada and of the wonders of Florida,[73] the question remained, why yield any of them? [74]

Like Smollett, Murphy was unable to answer this question without abusing the ability of Bute to conduct the war. It was beside the point to argue that Pitt's 1761 negotiations were the basis for the preliminaries. Victories at Martinique and Havana had increased the public's demands. Let Murphy boast of those conquests, and the opposition quickly attributed the accomplishment to Pitt's ministry and insisted upon greater concessions from the enemy; let him argue that the loss of Newfoundland was a sign that the tide of battle could turn, and the anti-ministerial writers accused Bute of lacking the leadership of Pitt.[75] To Murphy's insistence that the object of the war had been America and that England had no right to these further conquests, the response was simple: England had as much right to them as France, who had, after all, taken them by conquest.[76] At the same time, there could be no peace without compensation for losses – such compensation, said the opposition, was the empire that English victory had bought so dearly.[77]

Of the three anti-ministerial essay-journals, the *Patriot* was certainly the least important. It survived only through five numbers, June 19-July 17, 1762, which were devoted to personal abuse of Bute and his followers and to praise for Pitt and his supporters.[78]

---

[72] *Political Controversy*, II, pp. 118-119.
[73] *Political Controversy*, II, pp. 155 ff., 193 ff.
[74] See also, *Political Controversy*, II, pp. 118, 160-161, 200, 357 ff., 361.
[75] *Political Controversy*, I, pp. 117-118, 159, 346, 459; II, pp. 8, 316 ff.
[76] *Political Controversy*, II, p. 318.
[77] *Political Controversy*, II, pp. 3-4, 47.
[78] *Patriot*, #1 (June 19, 1762), p. 2; #2 (June 26, 1762), pp. 9, 12; #3 (July 3, 1762), pp. 13 ff.; #4 (July 10, 1762), pp. 19 ff.; #5 (July 17, 1762), p. 25.

On the matter of the peace, writers in the essay-journal had nothing to say, and if the *Patriot* is worth noting at all, it is because they called attention to the political alignment which placed the interests of the City on one side and those of the Court and Country on the other.[79]

Although originally expected to have a run no longer than that of the *Patriot*, the *North Briton* proved so popular in the City that it outlasted both the *Auditor* and *Briton*.[80] The anti-administration essay-journal gave voice "to the powerful but inarticulate resentment of the commercial classes . . .". In its pages, the *North Briton* harassed the spokesmen for the ministry and embittered the Crown and its ministers,[81] until – out of desperation – the government made the regrettable error of censoring the periodical and prosecuting its editors.

Like its adversaries, the *Briton* and *Auditor,* the *North Briton* was a political organ,[82] which served the trade interests of the City, by emphasizing the ineptitude of the administration. Personal abuse of the minister took precedence over arguments about the peace. However, since the treaty had become the provenance of Bute, the writers in the *North Briton* found a convenient instrument for attacking him in his conduct of the war and his method of negotiating a peace.[83] Wilkes and Churchill had the tremendous advantage of the popular image of Pitt to hold before the public's eyes. Since Pitt could no longer be held responsible for actions in which he had no effective concern, whatever Bute did, they had only to insist that Pitt's administration had made

[79] *Patriot*, #2 (June 26, 1762), pp. 9-10; #5 (July 17, 1762), pp. 28-29.
[80] Nobbe, pp. vii-viii, says it was not expected to run beyond two or three numbers. The quotation is from these pages. See also p. 62.
[81] Nobbe, pp. 37, 121. However, Nobbe, p. 46, says, "Such outspoken comment on political events was a novelty in the eighteenth century"; the statement seems to ignore the same outspokenness in the *Monitor* and in the earlier *Test* and *Con-Test*. L. Hanson, *Government and the Press, 1695-1763* (Oxford, 1936), p. 72, puts it more accurately: "The *North Briton* in the trenchancy and depth of its criticism surpassed everything that had gone before."
[82] Nobbe, p. 3, notes the encouragement the journal received from Earl Temple.
[83] All identifications for authors in the *North Briton* are from Nobbe, p. [266].

possible the successes and would have prevented the failures. Let Martinique be captured, and the credit was Pitt's for the planning he had done.[84] Let Newfoundland be retaken by the French, and Wilkes gave solemn assurances that Pitt would neither have permitted it to fall in war nor be yielded in peace.[85]

According to Wilkes, Bute desired an immediate peace because he was unable to fight a successful war.[86] When the British forces made significant conquests under Bute's administration, the ministry's willingness to *negotiate* a peace became the target for the *North Briton*. The capture of Havana brought less praise than concern for how it would be used at the negotiations: [87]

The news of the reduction of the Havannah, which arrived last night, at the same time it gives me the sincerest pleasure, suggests to me some painful apprehensions with relation to the manner in which it is to be disposed of in case of a peace. Surely we can never think of immediately giving up what hath cost us so much blood, and gratify the insolent Spaniard with a sacrifice of so many brave fellows. If it is to be surrendered, which the people seem to take for granted, we certainly have a right to expect those articles, on which they grounded the present war, to be determined in our favour.

Wilkes' response to the conquest of Havana is only one example of the difficulty that the administration had in trying to press the advantage in war while attempting to conclude the peace. To the ministry's argument that its terms were no less demanding than Pitt's had been in 1761, Wilkes responded by noting that the former minister had been hampered by cabinet ministers unwilling to give the necessary support; and by citing the changes that had occurred since then, through the victories at Martinique and Havana and the turn of events in Germany.[88] Indeed, both Wilkes and Churchill contended that despite the less favorable circumstances, including Russia's presence in the war, the earlier negotiations had demanded more of the enemy than the terms that Bute was so anxious to settle for.[89]

---

[84] *Political Controversy*, I, pp. 108-109.
[85] *Political Controversy*, I, p. 111.
[86] *Political Controversy*, I, pp. 291-292.
[87] *Political Controversy*, I, pp. 453-454.
[88] *Political Controversy*, II, p. 338.
[89] *Political Controversy*, I, p. 75 (Churchill); III, pp. 113 ff. (Wilkes?).

In every way the *North Briton* was likely to have a more popular appeal than either the *Briton* or *Auditor*. The language used in the latter to subdue the public demands was subject to ridicule, especially when removed from context. To explain the difficulties in negotiating a popular peace, Smollett, in the *Briton,* had declared, "... among the other evil consequences of the war, I might reckon our extraordinary success". It was a simple matter for Wilkes and Churchill, in the *North Briton,* who after all could remind the public of the price that had been paid for such successes,[90] to note that the loss of Newfoundland must have made the ministerial advocates extremely happy and to show them how to eliminate the obstacles to peace.[91] And when Smollett ridiculed the public's demand that the French be made to compensate for the expenditures of war, Wilkes, using a letter from William Temple of Trowbridge, had the opportunity to comment on the interests that both sides represented: [92]

As the *Briton,* of Saturday the 11th instant, is an impudent libel on all the good people of England in general, as well as on the city of London in particular, representing all the nobility, gentry, merchants, tradesmen, yeomen, and all the commonality, as a seditious rabble, which despises all government, because they express a dislike to some measures relative to a peace; and as our constitution is reproached with being an *ochlocracy*, or mob-commonwealth, because it permits our people to murmur with impunity at the conduct they cannot approve (which by-the-bye is inculcating the vilest tyranny ever practised by the worst monsters of all the Roman emperors); pray indulge me in communicating to the public a few remarks upon so extraordinary a performance.

Wilkes could not but emerge from such argument as a champion of the public interest, and his prosecution only added to the impression. Actually, however, his approach to the peace was too concerned with politics and personalities to indicate what was the real object of the peace.[93] Only when called upon to argue for the values of specific conquests or to defend the position of a City

---

[90]   *Political Controversy*, II, pp. 304-305 (Churchill).
[91]   *Political Controversy*, I, pp. 109-113 (Wilkes).
[92]   *Political Controversy*, I, p. 484.
[93]   See, for example, *Political Controversy*, I, pp. 184 ff.

spokesman,[94] did the authors of the *North Briton* suggest, as they finally did in attacking the preliminaries, that the Bute ministry was attempting "to save what remains of our old empire, [rather] than to preserve what the late ministry conquered from the proud rivals of our trade and commerce".[95]

Although the essays in the *Monitor* – third of the anti-ministerial essay-journals – were personal enough in their methods for the Crown to engage in an aborted effort to prosecute the editors,[96] their emphasis was less political than commercial[97] From its outset, the *Monitor* was governed by City trade interests,[98] and as early as 1759, its writers had argued for a peace that would expand the English commercial empire.[99]

The words *trade, wealth, commerce,* and *property* figured most prominently in the *Monitor's* evaluation of the negotiations. While the authors of the *Auditor, Briton,* and *North Briton* concentrated on the virtues or vices of the Bute administration, the writers in the *Monitor* centered their attention on the causes and purpose of the war and considered the financial benefits of the peace. According to the essays in this journal, France had embarked on hostilities in an effort to capture England's colonial trade, and the effect of a French victory with Spanish aid would be to "engross the whole trade and wealth of the world".[100] As one writer put it, "dominion" was synonymous with "commerce" and

---

[94] *Political Controversy*, III, pp. 111, 259 ff.
[95] *Political Controversy*, I, p. 338.
[96] Nobbe, pp. 130-131, describes the action against the *Monitor* as a preparation for the attack on the *North Briton*. Almon, p. 60, recounts the ministry's decision not to follow through on the prosecution, with the result that the people involved brought successful damage suits against the government. For the contemporary report, see *Political Controversy*, II, pp. 192, 230, 247. Scott, one of the editors, broke from the others, and attempted to publish his own *Monitor*. He claimed that he was opposed to their favorable view of the German war and subsidy (*Political Controversy*, II, pp. 20, 60-61, 95).
[97] *Monitor*, #190 (March 10, 1759), pp. 1147-1148; also *Political Controversy*, I, pp. 134-135; III, pp. 53 ff.
[98] Drake, II, pp. 341-343. The *Monitor* was originally planned by Alderman Beckford.
[99] *Monitor*, #217 (September 15, 1759), pp. 1307 ff.
[100] *Political Controversy*, I, p. 17.

"tranquility" with "property".[101] The object of the peace, therefore, was clear. England had been brought into the conflict to protect her own possessions and to reduce the power of France: [102]

> But, if we sheath the sword before these grand points be gained, we shall do nothing: and if we restore those conquests we have made, or permit the family-compact [between France and Spain] to take effect, (which is no less than giving Spain, the Indies, the trade and wealth of the whole world to the House of Bourbon) we shall be so far from securing our own dominions and commerce, that we shall expose them to certain destruction.

For the writers on the *Monitor,* peace was desirable, but not so desirable that it was worth the yielding of advantages gained by war.[103] These anti-ministerial writers spelled out − as none of those on the other essay-journals did − the economic advantages to be gained from what they considered an honorable peace. They made it clear that the old order was changing and that in the new, "wealth and power are but different names for the same thing".[104] To yield the superiority achieved through military strength was to yield simultaneously naval and commercial advantages.[105] Speaking for the City of London, one writer warned: [106]

> What part soever we cede or restore out of our conquests, we diminish our trade and strength in proportion, and give so much trade and strength to our enemies. From these facts there follows this natural inference; *a prosperous war is much more advantageous to us, than a peace, that deprives us of that trade and strength*; which thrown into the scale of our natural enemy, shall recover him to a condition, in a short period, to dispute the sovereignty of the seas with us, and to worm us out of the best branches of our commerce.

Not surprisingly, another essay in the *Monitor* demanded the prosecution of the war until the enemy was willing to cede all. Justice, it asserted, gave sanction to Britain's claims. According to the law of nations, "Conquest conveys property"; and England had

101 *Political Controversy*, I, p. 21.
102 *Political Controversy*, I, p. 18; see, too, II, p. 134.
103 *Political Controversy*, I, pp. 22-23, 169-170, 437.
104 *Political Controversy*, I, p. 207.
105 *Political Controversy*, I, p. 172.
106 *Political Controversy*, I, p. 359.

the right to expect payment for the "equity of their cause, and for the injuries they have received".[107]

With the first indications of the terms of the peace, the writers in the *Monitor* displayed their dissatisfaction. Not content merely to ridicule the administration's arguments that a small, avaricious group of stock-jobbers was setting itself against the best interests of the nation;[108] and not satisfied to deprecate the ministry's contention that England's emergence as the world's greatest commercial power would antagonize even the nation's friends,[109] the authors in this journal offered a specific commentary on the details of the negotiations.[110] Once again their position rested solidly on the premise that trade and power were inseparable. Granting the rights to Newfoundland fisheries "would considerably diminish the profits of our own trade; [and] contribute vastly to the increases of the enemy's riches and naval power . . ."; retention of both Goree and Senegal was essential to Britain's African trade; the neutral islands were required for the safety of the West Indian sugar trade; Martinique and Guadeloupe were important to the French as both a nursery for seamen and a source of wealth; and Havana was the key to the power and wealth of the Spanish West Indies.[111]

In the arguments in the *Monitor* rest the main issues that were involved in the making of the peace. For the anti-ministerial forces, the war had been fought in the name of commercial power. France had been responsible for the outbreak of hostilities, but once England had been engaged, she had the right to take out of the fighting a trade empire that would change the balance of power as it had existed before the Seven Years' War. But for the ministerial advocates, repeating the arguments of Bute, England had been drawn into a war to protect her American possessions. A peace that restored the *status quo* was a peace well made.

On such matters as the making of the peace, the magazines, in

[107] *Political Controversy*, I, pp. 394-396.
[108] *Political Controversy*, I, p. 439.
[109] *Political Controversy*, II, p. 290.
[110] *Political Controversy*, I, pp. 323 ff., 436.
[111] *Political Controversy*, II, pp. 247 ff.; see, also, II, pp. 394-397, 472-473; III, pp. 16 ff.

general, offered a minimum of direct commentary. Unlike the editors of the essay-journals, those in the periodical miscellanies declared themselves for neither side. By pillaging generously from both ministerial and anti-ministerial publications, and by selecting letters from both sides, the editors tended to balance their arguments, and only by carefully weighing the comments and noting the occasional outspoken statement can one judge the political point of view in most of the magazines.

The *Gentleman's* and *London Magazine* failed to offer a definite view on the peace negotiations. From both of these major publications a general attitude emerges, but it is suggested obliquely by their editorial judgments in the excerpts and epitomes that they offered, or by the selection of letters that they published. Alongside the apparently favorable treatment of the City trade interests in the magazines' comments on man and the age, the attitude toward the making of the peace may seem incongruous. But the complexity of trade interests that Pitt's success had temporarily resolved reasserted itself with his resignation. Newcastle himself remained in Bute's ministry until May, 1762, and his arguments urging the terms of the peace lingered on,[112] while Fox, another Whig, served Bute's interests in order to secure a peerage.[113] With this political confusion it is not surprising that editors of periodicals that were generally favorable to the commercial demands of the Whigs but not committed to a particular faction should raise little objection to a peace that was generally regarded as a financial necessity.[114] Certainly, the editors of neither magazine expressed any strong approval of Bute's peace efforts nor condoned the expansionist desires of the London merchants or the continuation of the German subsidy.

This moderation probably speaks as well for the inability of the magazine, as a type, to take a strong stand on specific public issues as it does for the individual attitudes of the editors of the *Gentleman's* and *London*. Yet from the weight of its comments, the editors of the *Gentleman's* appear to have favored a settlement that

112   Watson, pp. 79, 83-84.
113   Watson, pp. 94-95.
114   Watson, p. 87.

retained Canada, restored Guadeloupe, and removed England from its continental connections. As early as September, 1758, an article considering the points to be settled before a conclusion of a peace declared that the major concern must be to set the proper limits in America and to take Britain out of its German entanglements.[115] In December, 1759, the editors approved of the arguments offered in *A Letter Addressed to Two Great Men*: America was the principal object of the war, Guadeloupe was unimportant, and Senegal and Goree were unnecessary.[116] Writers in the magazine were willing enough to yield conquests everywhere but in North America,[117] and one of them, in an account of *Remarks on the Letter Addressed to Two Great Men,* displayed little enthusiasm for keeping Guadeloupe, but urged, if possible, the permanent annexation of Canada.[118]

Yet even such mild comment was not characteristic of the magazine's treatment of selections from controversial pamphlets on the peace. Ordinarily, the abstracts, excerpts, or accounts of articles were published without editorial statement. The lead article giving an account of *Considerations on the Present German War* offered no opinion of the work,[119] although the editors were certainly interested in the subject. Not even a letter refuting the arguments of the *Consideration* and favoring the retention of Guadeloupe rather than Canada received a response from the editors, who had themselves expressed a contrary opinion.[120] Similar silent treatment was accorded to *Occasional Thoughts on the German War,*[121] and an answer to the work.[122] In the same way, *Considerations on the Present German Crisis* passed without comment,[123] as did a response to it.[124]

---

[115] *Gentleman's Magazine*, XXVIII (September, 1758), p. 430.
[116] *Gentleman's Magazine*, XXIX (December, 1759), pp. 585-592.
[117] *Gentleman's Magazine*, XXIX (Supplement, 1759), pp. 620-621.
[118] *Gentleman's Magazine*, XXX (January, 1760), pp. 24-27; XXX (May, 1760), pp. 207-211.
[119] *Gentleman's Magazine*, XXX (November, 1760), pp. 495-500.
[120] *Gentleman's Magazine*, XXX (December, 1760), pp. 577-579.
[121] *Gentleman's Magazine*, XXXI (December, 1761), pp. 575-579.
[122] *Gentleman's Magazine*, XXXI (Supplement, 1761), pp. 619-624.
[123] *Gentleman's Magazine*, XXXIII (May, 1763), pp. 211-212.
[124] *Gentleman's Magazine*, XXXIII (June, 1763), pp. 269-273.

As the letters replying to the above works indicate, the *Gentleman's Magazine's* policy on correspondence showed no strong bias. Yet some of these letters present an opinion closely parallel to what seems to have been the editorial opinion in the magazine. Arguments lamenting the greedy designs of those Britains who would continue the fighting until they conquered the world, or expressing satisfaction enough with Canada,[125] or insisting upon the protection of North American colonies,[126] or approving the peace itself,[127] were quite close to one of the few outspoken editorial statements on the peace, made after the remarkable victory over Spain. The writers in the *Gentleman's Magazine* were no strong advocates of the ministry,[128] but neither did they countenance what were described as the extravagant demands of the opposition trade interests. As one writer insisted, after having noted the difficulties that Bute's administration had in fighting the war and making the peace, any readers who consulted a map of North America indicating the acquisitions brought about by the peace "will easily discern how much more we have gained by the present treaty than we claimed as our right at the commencement of the war, and were then in possession of".[129] Despite the impartial policy so characteristic in a magazine that was primarily dependent upon borrowings, the editors of the *Gentleman's* seem to have favored a moderate attitude toward the extension of empire. If they were not particularly enthusiastic about Bute's achievement, neither were they concerned with extensively expanding English commercial interests into the farthest reaches of the French and Spanish colonial domains.

[125] *Gentleman's Magazine*, XXXI (February, 1761), pp. 71-72; XXXII (September, 1762), pp. 405-406.
[126] *Gentleman's Magazine*, XXXI (March, 1761), pp. 123-124; XXXI (November, 1761), p. 499.
[127] *Gentleman's Magazine*, XXXII (Supplement, 1762), pp. 605-606; XXXIII (April, 1763), pp. 189-190.
[128] For balanced views on Pitt, see *Gentleman's Magazine*, XXXI (October, 1761), pp. 460-468; XXXI (November, 1761), pp. 488, 513-520, 520-521, 528; XXXI (December, 1761), pp. 546-547, 580. For Bute, see XXXI (November, 1761), pp. 520-521; XXXIII (July, 1763), pp. 325-329; XXXIII (August, 1763), pp. 397-405.
[129] *Gentleman's Magazine*, XXXII (Supplement, 1762), p. 604.

Except in its "History of the Origin and Progress of the Present War" and its "History of the Last Session of Parliament", the editors of the *London,* like those on the *Gentleman's,* made few definite comments about the peace. Extracts from both sides of the controversy were published without editorial opinion,[130] and letters appeared both favoring and attacking what was the essentially moderate attitude of the writers in the magazine.[131] Most consistently, the writers argued for a peace that would keep the American conquests and terminate the German alliance. In one short catalogue review of a pamphlet on Canada, the writer in the *London* stressed the importance of that area and terms that would make it secure.[132] Another such article supported the arguments of the *Considerations on the Present German War,* Israel Mauduit's work which, with its anti-Prussian views, Bute later rewarded.[133]

Where the writers expressed themselves at greater length on the German war, their attitude remained unchanged. Their comments denounced the popular acclaim for Frederick and demanded that the needs for the protection of the Electorate of Hanover be met from the treasury of Hanover itself.[134] Germany, the writer declared in the magazine's history of the war, had drawn England into the continental fighting, but the alliance was foolish, and the author longed for a return to the former balance of power.[135] According to another writer, England's rightful business was with America, and the European war was without profit.[136] Simply stated, as another declared, the continental war was not England's war.[137]

---

[130] *London,* XXVIII (December, 1759), pp. 635-637; XXVIII (Appendix, 1759), p. 721; XXIX (January, 1760), p. 3; XXXI (June, 1762), pp. 291-296.

[131] *London,* XXIX (February, 1760), pp. 72 ff.; XXIX (December, 1760), pp. 619-622; XXX (January, 1761), pp. 5-7; XXX (February, 1761), pp. 78-80; XXX (July, 1761), pp. 339-342; XXX (August, 1761), p. 417; XXX (November, 1761), pp. 568-569; XXX (December, 1761), pp. 640-642; XXXI (January, 1762), pp. 15-16.

[132] *London,* XXVIII (October, 1759), p. 576.

[133] *London,* XXIX (December, 1760), p. 672. Almon, p. 13.

[134] *London,* XXX (November, 1761), pp. 575-576.

[135] *London,* XXIX (August, 1760), pp. 397-402.

[136] *London,* XXIX (September, 1760), p. 465.

[137] *London,* XXX (May, 1761), p. 238.

While the moderately anti-expansionist comments in the *London* suggest a clearer attitude toward the peace than those in the *Gentleman's*, they lack the definite pattern of the *Court Magazine*. Unlike most of the magazines, the *Court* offered a unified and consistent attitude on the negotiations, one that represented the trade interests of the City. Demanding a hard peace, an extension of the empire, and a rejection of the pre-war *status quo*, the arguments in the *Court* appeared mainly in a regular feature, "The Politician",[138] which gave them a consistency in their point of view.

The concern for trade dominated all other considerations in the *Court's* military analyses. Taking a stand in opposition to Pitt's call for a war with Spain, the writers in the magazine argued on behalf of the greater commercial value in continued peaceful negotiations with the Spaniards. Apparently the interests in the *Court* represented trade that would benefit less from the plunder of rich Spanish prizes than from the available markets and shipping opportunities already present in the established commerce. Those who sought the quick wealth of immediate acquisition stressed the backwardness of Spain as a nation and her unpreparedness as a foe. But a writer in the *Court* turned such arguments to his own advantage: [139]

... if from the neglect of their [the Spaniards'] marine, or backwardness to promote trade and commerce, they may appear less formidable as an enemy, it at the same time subjects them to stand in need of many necessary commodities from neighbouring kingdoms; which renders it more for the advantage of a commercial nation to cultivate and promote, by every probable means, a good understanding and harmony with them. – The English nation have long had an apparent advantage from trading with them: some of the principal articles they import from hence are woollen-cloth, stockings, Norwich-stuffs, hats, Manchester and Birmingham wares; most of which

---

[138] According to the *Bodleian-British-Union Catalogue of Periodicals*, the *Politician* exists as a separate periodical for 1762 in two volumes. However, the feature appeared regularly in the *Court* from the very first number of the magazine.

[139] *Court*, November, 1761, pp. 110-111. No volume number was given to the *Court* until January, 1763, which was marked Volume I.

are exported in English bottoms, and advance the interest of the public, as well as the emolument of individuals.

Before the declaration of war with Spain, therefore, the *Court* offered a variety of reasons against it. The articles in the magazine warned that the Spanish were being underrated, declared that their ports would pose a threat to Eastern shipping,[140] and cautioned that the Dutch awaited the opportunity of engrossing English trade.[141] Yet with the resignation of Pitt and the outbreak of hostilities with Spain, the writers refused to dwell on recriminations, but sought to gain the greatest commercial advantage possible in the altered situation and advised the immediate encouragement of trade with the new Portuguese allies.[142]

Whatever differences among commercial interests are suggested, in their attitude toward declaring war on Spain, the demands in the *Court* for a hard peace were uniformly consistent with those of the most outspoken advocates for the retention of a new colonial empire. Yet more important than the *Court* writers' agreement with the City opponents of Bute's peace negotiations is their ingenuous explanation of the magazine's policies. They measured the value of each new acquisition by the commercial benefits. With the conquest of Martinique, the articles in the *Court* stressed the island's many advantages to trade, ridiculed the opinion that eventually it would have to be restored, and belittled the fear that the French would be in a position to demand its return.[143] Recounting the recovery of Newfoundland, one writer underscored the commercial purpose of the war, an objective he did not want to see dimmed by a short-sighted view of the peace. England, he reminded his readers, was the victor and not the vanquished, and ". . . it will be our business to suffer no rivals in [the important fishery in Newfoundland], so profitable a branch of our commerce . . .".[144] Nor did the arguments in the *Court* contemplate bargaining away the advantages gained from Spain

---

140   *Court*, November, 1761, p. 111.
141   *Court*, December, 1761, p. 165.
142   *Court*, January, 1762, pp. 211-212; March, 1762, p. 307.
143   *Court*, April, 1762, p. 352.
144   *Court*, October, 1762, p. 652.

in the West Indies. After the conquest of Havana, a writer in the magazine made plain his opinion that the new England had a right to retain the trade empire that its military might had acquired.[145]

These reactions to the conquests were repeated in the *Court's* articles on the peace negotiations. Before the signing of the preliminaries, one writer in the magazine stated: [146]

As a commercial people, our first consideration must naturally turn upon our trade; and our business must be to limit the bounds of our enemies in the American world, so as to prevent any dangerous effects of a rivalship with our colonies, and to frustrate any intention they may have of engrossing the benefit of our traffick in that quarter.

Rather than return any of the French colonies, he preferred a continuation of the war,[147] and sensing the relaxation of Bute's demands, one commentator reaffirmed the warning that the nation expected England to take full advantage of its victory.[148]

Upon the publication of the preliminary articles of peace, the writers in the *Court* were outraged. They scoffed at the notion that Germany was draining England dry or that France could do anything but agree to the victor's terms, and once more reminded their readers that this had been a commercial war, to be satisfied only by a trade advantage.[149] Publishing the substance of a petition sent to the king by a large number of merchants trading with the conquered islands, the editors argued for the value of the conquests.[150]

Not even the signing of the definitive treaty quieted these angry voices. One writer, recognizing the futility of further argument, still could not refrain from commenting on a peace that he felt had betrayed the interests of the nation, a nation seeking to extend its commercial advantages. Terming the treaty ". . . absolute infatuation – or absolute –" (leaving the reader to fill in the blank),

[145]   *Court*, October, 1762, p. 653.
[146]   *Court*, September, 1762, p. 602.
[147]   *Court*, September, 1762, p. 603.
[148]   *Court*, November, 1762, pp. 698-700.
[149]   *Court*, December, 1762, pp. 739 ff.
[150]   *Court*, December, 1762, pp. 749 ff.

he bemoaned the acquiescence that had permitted France to continue as England's rival in trade.[151] For the writers in the *Court Magazine*, Bute's peace had been a conservative withdrawal before the prospect of a great commercial empire.

Although the analysis of the *Court* suggests that the editors of the magazines had it within their power to present a consistent attitude toward controversial political issues, the eclectic character of these periodicals made such unity a difficult task at best. None of the six other minor magazines to be considered in this chapter approached the consistency of the *Court* in dealing with the subject of the peace. Yet even in their seemingly balanced appraisals, these editors, both in their method of selection and occasional direct statements, revealed something of their attitudes.

Of the six magazines, four gave evidence of their editorial sympathy with the City trade interests. The comments in the *Imperial* were the least emphatic, but despite the editors' publication, without comment, of extracts from *Occasional Thoughts on the Present German War,* which opposed the continental alliance; [152] and despite the printing of an article disparaging the vulgar acclaim for the King of Prussia,[153] the majority of comments in the *Imperial* were generally favorable to Pitt and the London merchants.

In its own history of the war, a writer in the magazine justified Frederick's conduct by insisting that he had been involved in a war that was not of his own making.[154] As early as January, 1760, the *Imperial* published a long lead article expressing confidence in Pitt's ability to conduct peace negotiations as gloriously as he had directed the war, and, at the same time, the article stressed the commercial objectives of the conquests.[155] In both their selection of correspondence and poetry the editors offered the mercantile arguments for the retention of conquests, the denial of Canadian fishing rights to the French, and the justice of indemnification for

---

[151] *Court*, I (February, 1763), pp. 60-61.
[152] *Imperial*, III (January, 1762, pp. 22 ff.
[153] *Imperial*, I (January, 1760), pp. 12-13.
[154] *Imperial*, III (March, 1762), p. 105.
[155] *Imperial*, I, pp. 3 ff.

England's losses in money and manpower.[156] But perhaps more significant than any particular peace demands made in the *Imperial* was a proud comment on Britain's emergence as the foremost commercial and military power in the world: a determination that England must dominate world trade regardless of the opinions of other nations, enemy and friend alike.[157]

While the weight of such comment in the *Imperial* decidedly favored the advocates of a hard peace, it was not supported directly by many editorial statements. In this respect, the *Grand Magazine,* published from 1758 through 1760, was clearer in its attachment than the *Imperial.* Although the statements on the peace were limited to the earlier period of negotiation, and the magazine offered extracts that tended to balance each other,[158] its commitment, both in editorial and original essay, was obviously to the policies of Pitt.[159] Griffiths, publisher of the magazine, was of course, also the publisher and editor of the *Monthly Review,* which took a position opposed to the peace negotiations of Bute.

In its treatment of the continental alliance there is every indication that the magazine, had it continued, would have joined the anti-Bute forces. Not only did the editors approve of Pitt's reversal of policy by sending troops into Germany, but they offered justification for the apparent contradiction of their own earlier expressed attitudes. Citing their previous opposition in February and March, 1758, the editors of the *Grand* argued that what had been impossible then was now within the capabilities of the victorious English forces; [160] and in their publication of both letter and essay, they stressed England's obligation to a Prussia that had made possible the military conquests in America.[161] Having followed the line of Pitt's argument to this point, the *Grand Magazine* – like the *Monthly Review* – could hardly have defected.

[156]   *Imperial,* III (January, 1762), p. 27; III (May, 1762), pp. 251-252, 262; III (June, 1762), pp. 305-307, 307-308.
[157]   *Imperial,* III (June, 1762), pp. 305, 307-308.
[158]   *Grand,* II (December, 1759), p. 677; III (January, 1760), pp. 25 ff.; III (November, 1760), p. 545.
[159]   *Grand,* II (Dedication, 1759), pp. iii-iv; II (July, 1759), p. 374.
[160]   *Grand,* III (To the Public, 1760), pp. iii-iv.
[161]   *Grand,* II (December, 1759), p. 666; III (July, 1760), pp. 364-365.

Comments on the peace in the *Royal* were more numerous than those in either the *Imperial* or *Grand*. However, the amount of discussion – coming mainly in letters – gives little indication, until the end of 1761, of the magazine's own editorial views. If in January, 1760, the editors published a letter that objected to yielding Guadeloupe rather than Canada,[162] then in the next number they printed another which argued in favor of the retention of Canada,[163] and still another which demanded the restoration of neither conquest.[164]

The same non-committal attitude characterized the editors' treatment of the continental alliance,[165] but with the conflict between Bute and Pitt, they were more consistent in their choice of both poetry and letters favorable to the Whig minister.[166] At the same time, in their selection of articles and correspondence, the editors of the *Royal* advocated a vigorous pursuit of the war and an insistence that France meet the demands of the peace.[167] That the writers in the magazine spoke, if mildly, for the City trade interests is further suggested in the opinion that the proper government attitude toward commerce should be one of liberty and protection.[168] No wonder, then, that the *Royal* should display more partisanship when the champion of those interests was involved in a struggle with the administration.

The fourth of the magazines favorable to a mercantile peace was the *Universal*. Despite their balance of extracts and articles on the German war,[169] the editors in their limited statements indicated a sympathy with the trade interests by making commerce

---

162   *Royal*, II, pp. 24-25.
163   *Royal*, II, pp. 72-74.
164   *Royal*, II, pp. 87-88.
165   *Royal*, II (February, 1760), p. 93; IV (January, 1761), pp. 6-10.
166   *Royal*, V (October, 1761), pp. 171, 209; V (November, 1761), pp. 227, 234-236, 263; V (December, 1761), p. 313; see also, IX (September, 1763), pp. 118-119.
167   *Royal*, V (September, 1761), pp. 128-129; V (November, 1761), pp. 228-229, 245; VI (January, 1762), p. 3.
168   *Royal*, V (November, 1761), p. 233.
169   *Universal*, XXV (Supplement, 1759), pp. 351-359; XXVI (January, 1760), pp. 41-46; XXVI (March, 1760), pp. 120-123; XXVII (December, 1760), p. 300.

a grounds for patriotism. Not only did they present an illustration in which the gods offered the empire of the seas to Britain,[170] but in direct comment, they proclaimed that ". . . a tenacious regard to our commercial interests, both at home and abroad, will prove the great pillar of the state".[171] In more subtle ways, too, they were able to indicate their position. By saying nothing in praise of the peace, but by voicing a hope that it would be permanent; [172] by suggesting that the conquest of Havana would humble Spanish pride, "if a peace is not speedily concluded"; [173] and by noting that it was important to make a peace, but not at "the expense of safety"; [174] in extracts and directly, they aligned themselves with the London merchants who were demanding a continuation of the war until the enemy agreed to terms that would guarantee the expansion of the British commercial empire.

In the two remaining magazines – the *Universal Museum* and *British Magazine* – opinion was balanced in such a way that their editorial commitment is even more difficult to assess than it is in the magazines generally. The writers in the *Universal Museum*, which made its first appearance in January, 1762, deliberately sought to remain uncommitted, and, at times, succeeded in doing so even within a single article.[175] Their strong opposition to the German war, expressed in original articles and a history of the war,[176] was somewhat vitiated by praise for the King of Prussia and Pitt in the magazine's chronicle and correspondence.[177] Yet the attitude toward the continental connection is clear-cut by comparison with the editors' selection and comments on the peace. In an essay in May, 1762, the *Universal Museum* presented an argument for a hard peace negotiated from a position of

[170] *Universal*, XXX (January, 1762), p. 1.
[171] *Universal*, XXVIII (January, 1761), p. 6.
[172] *Universal*, XXXIII (July, 1763), pp. 1-2.
[173] *Universal*, XXXI (October, 1762), p. 169.
[174] *Universal*, XXIX (July, 1761), pp. 1 ff.
[175] *Universal Museum*, I (January, 1762), p. 26, states the position; for examples, I (January, 1762), pp. 16, 19 ff., 36-39.
[176] *Universal Museum*, I (January, 1762), pp. 35-36; I (February, 1762), pp. 76-77; I (April, 1762), pp. 213-214; I (September, 1762), p. 489.
[177] *Universal Museum*, II (February, 1763), p. 63; II (September, 1763), p. 484.

strength,[178] but later it published an approval of the Treaty of
Paris, terming it "an honourable and an advantageous one", and
declaring that its opponents who called "it a *bad* peace, only
mean, that it is *inadequate* to our success". If the comment suggests that the writer had expected more, his conclusion – that if
Pitt had done no better, he would have received wild applause –
makes clear that the commentator was perfectly satisfied.[179]

Even the remarks on empire published in the *Universal Museum*
offered no conclusive evidence of its editorial sympathies. When
the writer urged that England guarantee its commercial gains before sending troops to defend Portugal from a Spanish attack, he
took a position alongside the City trade interests.[180] Yet no
spokesman for that group would have suggested, as one writer in
the magazine did, that neither Britain nor France had a legitimate
claim to Nova Scotia.[181]

Equal balance in the comments of the *British Magazine* comes
as at least a moderate surprise. Although Smollett, one of the editors, worked for the Bute administration, the magazine was not
discernibly favorable to the Scottish minister. Indeed, its first
volume was dedicated to Pitt, and when he resigned, the comments
in the magazine, which reprinted John Brown's description of him
as an ideal minister, not only expressed their regret, but justified
his conduct.[182]

While Smollett's *Critical Review* and *Briton* were pleading
Bute's peace, the *British Magazine,* consistent with its claims of
impartiality,[183] balanced its presentation of views on the subject.
Commenting on the ruination of Rome through its conquests, one
writer in the magazine deliberately refused to make the usual
conservative analogy with modern Britain: [184]

---

178   *Universal Museum*, I, pp. 266-267.
179   *Universal Museum*, II (August, 1763), p. 417.
180   *Universal Museum*, I (April, 1762), p. 213.
181   *Universal Museum*, I (May, 1762), p. 277.
182   *British Magazine*, II (October, 1761), pp. 511 ff., 523 ff., 552-553; IV
(October, 1763), pp. 534-537.
183   *British Magazine*, IV (Advertisement, 1763), pp. 1-2.
184   *British Magazine*, III (May, 1762), p. 238.

No reflection is intended here against the British conquests; the author by no means thinking with some shallow politicians, that we have over-conquered ourselves. We are not engaged in an *unjust* war; therefore, in this as well as in every other respect, the two cases are entirely different. The end of our conquests is to bring our enemy to honourable and lasting terms of peace: to effect this, what means can be employed so easily and properly, as to pursue our conquests?

Although the Roman parallel *was* used later to ridicule the rage for conquest,[185] Smollett and Goldsmith continued throughout the controversy to balance favorable comments with attacks on the peace and to offer extracts from the very essay-journals with which Smollett's *Briton* was engaged in controversy.[186] It seems evident that if the editors intended to use the magazine for political purposes, then the character of such a publication proved inadequate for such designs. In their eclectic methods, the magazines tended to present balanced views on controversial subjects.

The same was true of a yearly publication like the *Annual Register*. But the once-a-year schedule and the use of a feature as well as much original material written by one man created a difference between the *Annual Register* and the magazines in their treatment of the peace.

In his "History of the Present War", the section containing the most pertinent comments on the peace negotiations, Burke declared, "We are historians, and not advocates".[187] His objectivity was considerably less than his boast, but the account of the proceedings was sufficiently impartial so that his *Annual Register* is now regarded as a reliable authority on events of his day.

Regarding the peace, Burke's tone and objectives were those of moderation. In compiling the history,[188] he attempted to present the varied views of the fundamental issues. He was aware of the basic commercial struggle that had motivated the warfare; [189] he

---

[185]   *British Magazine*, III (October, 1762), pp. 515-518.
[186]   *British Magazine*, III (June, 1762), pp. 295-299; IV (January, 1763), pp. 13-14, 16; IV (August, 1763), pp. 419-421.
[187]   *Annual Register*, IV, Pt. I (1761), p. 19.
[188]   J. C. Weston, Jr., "Burke's Authorship of the 'Historical Articles' in Dodsley's 'Annual Register'", *Papers of the Bibliographical Society of America*, LI (1957), p. 247.
[189]   *Annual Register*, II (1759), pp. 5, 11.

understood the significance of such conquests as that of Guadeloupe to the trade interests;[190] and he realized quite early what
difficulties England's alliance with Prussia would pose at the negotiations for peace.[191]

The *Annual Register* appeared at the beginning of the year
following that of its dateline,[192] by which time Burke was able to
evaluate each measure after it had been thoroughly debated or
even acted upon.[193] When, for example, he realistically observed
that France had rejected English and Prussian peace offers in
1760 because ". . . in her present condition she could scarcely
look for very favourable terms",[194] his observation came after the
French reaction was a matter of history. Yet Burke used the occasion to predict, accurately enough, that the peace would come
only with some moderation of the English demands and the sacrifice of some of the conquests.[195]

His prediction foreshadowed his own attitude toward a peace
settlement, an attitude consistent with his conservative tempera-
ment but also related to his support of Fox, who finally joined
Bute's administration.[196] Recognizing that the alternatives were a
peace which would restore the balance of the major powers or one
in which one side was completely broken, Burke advocated terms

---

[190] *Annual Register*, II (1759), pp. 12-14.
[191] *Annual Register, cf.*, II (1759), p. 45 and IV, Pt. I (1761), p. 21; V, Pt.
I (1762), p. 54.
[192] A comment in the book section of the *Annual Register*, I (1758), p. iv,
acknowledges the advantage that additional time gave for judgment. The
preface to 1761 (IV) carries an apology for the late appearance of the
volume in March, 1762. Thomas W. Copeland, *Our Eminent Friend Edmund Burke* (New Haven, 1949), p. 116, attributes the delay to the increased pressure of Burke's political life.
[193] *Annual Register*, III, Pt. I (1760), p. 55.
[194] *Annual Register*, III, Pt. I (1760), p. 3.
[195] *Annual Register*, III, Pt. I (1760), p. 5.
[196] In a letter to Charles O'Hara (30 October 1762), Burke wrote of
Bute's proposals for the peace: "I own I think it hard to form an idea of
a shameful peace, if this is not the most shameful that ever was made; and
with the least possibility of an excuse." However, Fox sought to get parliamentary approval for the preliminaries, and when the peace was made,
Burke did not attack the terms that his political colleague had supported
(*Burke Letters*, I, pp. 152, 154, n. 4 and 155, n. 1).

that would foster no issues or animosities for use in a later war.[197] Certainly, Burke was closer to the position of Bute, who sought "the restoration of the system of William III. – the old Triple Alliance which the war had upset",[198] than to the City trade interests, who demanded an extension of the empire most favorable to their commerce.

In his specific comments on the peace negotiations, Burke did not become outraged by demands for conquest – as, for example, the writers in the *Critical* did – but neither did he question the sincerity of France's willingness to make major concessions. He not only sympathetically portrayed the efforts of the ministry, "perplexed between the natural expectations of their country, and the reasonable expectation of their allies . . .", but was aware that "it must have fared ill with that administration, who should make a sacrifice of any of those objects on which the people had set their hearts".[199] However, Burke praised French "moderation" and called England's rejection less "than its [i.e., the French terms of peace] apparent fairness deserved".[200]

Despite Burke's insistence that he was non-partisan,[201] his comments on Pitt's resignation and the conduct of the king gave evidence of the writer's approval of the new ministry's peace efforts. Pitt's action was seen as precipitate, brought on by his desire for exorbitant power, and, according to Burke, the king's behavior was both gracious and wise. For Pitt's conduct of the war, Burke had the utmost praise, but "happy it had been for him, for his sovereign, and his country, if a temper less austere, and a disposition more practicable, more compliant, and conciliatory, had been joined to his other great virtues".[202] The resignation, because it had aroused faction, had been a disservice to the cause of peace.[203]

For the peace itself Burke had much praise and argued – contrary to the furor that was taking place in London – that the en-

197   *Annual Register*, IV, Pt. I (1761), p. 2.
198   *Corbett*, II, p. 287.
199   *Annual Register*, IV, Pt. I (1761), p. 6.
200   *Annual Register*, IV, Pt. I (1761), pp. 13-14, 19.
201   *Annual Register*, IV, Pt. I (1761), p. 47.
202   *Annual Register*, IV, Pt. I (1761), p. 47.
203   *Annual Register*, V, Pt. I (1762), p. 5.

tire country was weary of the war, tired of the expense in money and men. To be sure, even Newcastle was aware of the financial necessity to end the war, but Burke's argument was hardly popular: [204]

... it is grown into a sort of maxim, that nations greatly victorious, must cede something on a peace, the difficulty on our side was only what and how much we should retain. Not that there was a doubt, but whatever choice of acquisition could be made upon any rational principles, a great deal would still remain to give the fullest scope to every sentiment of equity and moderation.

More temperate in his language and methods than such ministerial advocates as Murphy in the *Auditor* and more objective than the reviewers in the *Critical*, Burke, nevertheless, was firm in his attitude toward the peace. He appreciated the administration's predicament in attempting to pursue a vigorous war and make a moderate peace and recognized that each loss was construed as incapacity and each success was turned to an argument for impossible treaty terms.[205] At the same time, his desire for a moderate peace caused him to contradict his earlier statement of Britain's obligations to its allies.[206]

Yet in his final assessments of the peace terms, Burke was indeed more moderate than the ministerial advocates; although hardly sympathetic to the demands of the City trade interests, he stressed the importance of the American conquests which had been retained but acknowledged that England had made major concessions in the West Indies.[207] His ultimate evaluation of the peace summarized what most certainly was the moderate conservative point of view: [208]

[The terms of the treaty are such] which nothing but adulation will assert to be free from defect, nor any thing but faction can deny to be productive of many very great and essential advantages to this kingdom.

---

[204]   *Annual Register*, V, Pt. I (1762), pp. 45-46.
[205]   *Annual Register*, V, Pt. I (1762), p. 47.
[206]   *Annual Register, cf.*, IV, Pt. I (1761), p. 6 and V, Pt. I (1762), p. 54.
[207]   *Annual Register*, V, Pt. I (1762), pp. 55-61.
[208]   *Annual Register*, V, Pt. I (1762), p. 62.

Because he himself wrote much of the pertinent comment in the *Annual Register*,[209] Burke was able to maintain a consistent attitude toward the peace. Close editorial supervision gave the *Critical* and *Monthly* the same advantage over the magazines, for despite the apparently free rein given to their writers in some areas, the reviews showed a remarkably consistent attitude in their opposing views of the peace.

Almost all of the comments pertaining to the peace which appeared in the *Critical* argued as consistently as possible in favor of the kind of terms for which Bute eventually settled. During the actual negotiations, Smollett, editor of the *Critical,* was one of Bute's chief propagandists, but the record of the *Critical* suggests that Smollett (as Whitridge and Hannay have indicated) [210] acted in good faith and genuinely believed in the cause. Indeed, earlier articles in the review offer sound enough reasons for Bute to have called upon Smollett for journalistic support of the ministry.[211]

Although Smollett's paid activity on behalf of Bute did not begin until May 29, 1762, a writer in the *Critical,* as early as December, 1760, had argued against the continuation of the German war, which he regarded as a financial and military catastrophe.[212] Lamenting the expenditure in money and manpower, he rejected

---

[209]   Weston, p. 247, says that Burke's editorship from 1758-1763 and his authorship of the historical articles have never been contested. According to Copeland, p. 118, "there is a high probability that any part of the magazine written before 1766 was written by Burke ...". Copeland also argues (p. 119) that the evidence suggests that Burke was also responsible for the entire book review section of the periodical. In this discussion of the *Annual Register*, only those comments that seem assuredly to have been Burke's have been attributed to him. Certainly, in the early years, Burke was responsible for planning, managing, writing, and compiling it single-handedly (Copeland, pp. 92-93). – For Burke's contract with Dodsley, see R. Straus, *Robert Dodsley* (London, 1910), pp. 257-258.

[210]   Hannay, pp. 146-147; Whitridge, p. 69. Both men are describing his work for the *Briton*, of course.

[211]   Whitridge, p. 60, ascribes Smollett's selection by Bute to the author's political sympathies as expressed in his *History of England*. No doubt Bute considered Smollett's political views as well as his journalistic style, but, as Nobbe, p. 32, notes, the work for the *Critical* was certainly one of his recommendations. The many attacks linking the *Critical* and *Briton* show that Smollett's adversaries related the two works.

[212]   *Critical*, X, p. 480.

Pitt's argument that the war in America was being won in Germany. As a later article on Smollett's own *Continuation of the Complete History of England* was to make clear, the reviewers looked upon the European alliance as a fatal entanglement in which England had become inextricably ensnared.[213]

But what must have convinced Bute that Smollett, beyond a doubt, was his man was the attitude toward a peace expressed in the *Critical*. Like Bute the reviewers displayed a willingness to return portions of the conquest that the City trade interests insisted must be retained. Regarding the demands for retention of all the conquest as a madness born of greed and an hysteria encouraged by mob intoxication, the writers readily found merit in arguments for the restoration of both Canada and the sugar islands.[214] In terms that could not fail to please Bute, the reviewers warned against excessive demands and cautioned that the extension of empire would only arouse the wrath and suspicions of Spain.

When Bute assumed major responsibility for government, the writers in the *Critical* continued to pursue a policy favorable to his administration. The real bar to peace, they insisted, was the rage for conquest, yet both England and France had much to gain from a sensible cessation of hostilities. The French, according to the reviewers, had demonstrated their willingness to co-operate by their voluntary surrender of the North American possessions (anti-ministerial writers pointed out that the French had little choice in the matter), but "the English people are become intoxicated with conquest, and woe be to any minister who should restore any of these conquests at a peace, except for a valuable consideration".[215]

After Smollett's connection with the Bute administration had begun, the reviewers continued their support of the administration's peace effort and the *Critical* became synonymous with the *Briton* in the eyes of Smollett's political opponents.[216] Formerly

---

[213] *Critical*, XII (October, 1761), p. 292; see, also, XI (January, 1761), pp. 78-79 and XII (December, 1761), pp. 473-474.
[214] *Critical*, XI (May, 1761), pp. 363 ff., 389-390.
[215] Quotation is from *Critical*, XII (November, 1761), p. 388; see, also, XIII (January, 1762), p. 72.
[216] *E.g., Patriot*, #5 (July 17, 1762), p. 28. *Critical Review*, XV (January,

admirers of Pitt,[217] the reviewers now distinguished between his successful prosecution of the war and what they deemed his failure to procure a peace.[218] Hopeful that Pitt would not interfere with Bute's negotiations, one writer in the *Critical,* in November, 1762, could speak of "his [Pitt's] generous unpensioned resignation"; [219] but a month later, disappointed by his intrusion (not to mention his pension), a *Critical* reviewer called his resignation "abrupt, precipitate, and passionate".[220]

The writers in the *Critical,* attempting to endorse the peace objectives of Bute's ministry, encountered the same difficulties as the editor did in the *Briton:* an ignorance of the precise terms of the negotiations. In October, 1762, one reviewer approved of a work in which the writer argued for the retention of the sugar islands. But the writer's attack on those people who were "too much elated with conquest to admit of any cession to a beaten, dispirited enemy" impressed the reviewer and was more important than his choice of retaining the West Indian rather than the Canadian conquest.[221] Since the Bute administration had not yet decided upon one or the other, the reviewers did not have to choose between them. But in April, 1763, when one writer praised the terms of the definitive treaty, the reviewer denied the importance of Guadeloupe and Martinique.[222] The earlier article had been concerned only with the willingness to part with some of the conquest, but now the reviewers, along with the administration, had to argue that the yielding of the French West Indies was *not* the sacrifice of British commercial interests that it was considered to be,[223] and that Bute's treaty, despite its concessions and limitations of empire, was a victory for national trade interests.

1763), pp. 68-69 and *Political Controversy,* III, pp. 284-285. – Although Nobbe, pp. 180-181, describes the *Critical's* review of the *North Briton* (XVI, October, 1763, pp. 277-285) as biased, the tone of the review seems remarkably restrained.

[217]   *Critical, e.g.,* XII (October, 1761), pp. 313-314.
[218]   *Critical,* XIV (September, 1762), p. 226.
[219]   *Critical,* XIV (November, 1762), p. 356.
[220]   *Critical,* XIV (December, 1762), p. 420.
[221]   Quotation is from *Critical,* XIV, p. 284; see, also, XIV, p. 293.
[222]   *Critical,* XV, pp. 278-279, 284.
[223]   Jucker, p. 251, shows the administration trying to justify its peace to

To measure the extent of these conciliatory peace terms, it is only necessary to compare them with the contrary demands made in the rival *Monthly Review*. Perhaps Paston and Nangle are correct in their assertions that the *Monthly* was untrammelled by party ties or uninfluenced by Griffiths's political sympathies,[224] but its attitude toward the peace hardly seems to justify their observations. The unguided uniformity of the *Monthly's* important comments would be as remarkable a coincidence as the *Critical's* equally strange conformity, without design, to the opinions of its editor.

The character of a literary review permitted the writers in the *Monthly*, like those in the *Critical*, to state directly their views on a judicious peace. Griffiths's reviewers, particularly Owen Ruffhead, shared the attitude of "The Politician" in the *Court Magazine*. With an eye toward the City commercial interests, the *Monthly* reviewers demanded a peace that would yield little if anything. Reviewing *A Letter Addressed to Two Great Men*, Ruffhead, after praising the author, commented specifically on the points of his argument. Ruffhead approved his desire to cede nothing in North America but objected to his willingness to permit French use of Cape Breton as a fishery. Accepting his demands for the retention of Senegal and Goree, the reviewer insisted on the equal importance of holding Guadeloupe in the interest of the sugar trade. Where the author displayed an inclination to negotiate, Ruffhead rigidly proclaimed a policy amounting to a demand for unconditional surrender. Expressing a desire for continental connections that would extend the empire, Ruffhead was equally insistent upon conceding nothing in the way of conquests to pay for such alliances.[225]

To justify the claims to an extension of empire, Ruffhead added to the general insistence that England had a right to those objects

---

the commercial interests by developing the territories it had acquired. The government could not convince the public that the restoration of the French West Indies was not a sacrifice.

[224] G. Paston, *Sidelights on the Georgian Period* (London, 1903), pp. 155-156. Nangle, p. xi.

[225] *Monthly*, XXII (January, 1760), pp. 50-53.

for which it had gone to war, the further demand that the nation was entitled "to receive some reasonable indemnification for the charges she has incurred in carrying it on".[226] Ruffhead recognized that France would not easily yield to such terms, but he rejected arguments for an immediate peace: [227]

Now certainly, in our circumstances, every delay is *necessary* which tends to perfecting an advantageous and lasting peace: and such a one cannot fail to be honourable. It would, indeed, be highly impolitic, in the wantonness of success, to insist on terms purely of parade and vain glory: but it would be more impolitic, to accelerate a peace on disadvantageous and ignominious conditions, from an unmanly dread of a reverse of fortune.

What conditions did the *Monthly* reviewers think honorable? Some answer is evident in the review's ironic treatment of a writer who thought it necessary to offer arguments for the retention of all of Canada. The review made it clear that Canada was no point to be discussed in the negotiations because England had a natural right to expect such cession as a matter of course rather than as a subject for debate.[228]

With the resignation of Pitt, the writers sensed a relaxation in the demands to be made of the enemy. Expressing his gratitude to the ousted minister, Ruffhead urged the same vigorous pursuit of Pitt's measures by the new administration.[229] Peace, Ruffhead later warned, was not the issue. If it wanted peace, England had no more to do than accede to the terms of a beaten enemy. What was at stake was the *kind* of peace, the victorious peace to which England was entitled.[230]

Unlike the writers in the *Court Magazine,* however, the *Monthly* reviewers accepted the peace once it had been made. There were no outstanding comments on the controversy that followed the Treaty of Paris. Only in a review of *The Case of Going to War, for the Sake of Procuring, Enlarging, or Securing of Trade, Considered in a New Light* did William Kenrick repeat Ruff-

[226] *Monthly*, XXII (January, 1760), p. 59.
[227] *Monthly*, XXII (March, 1760), p. 235.
[228] *Monthly*, XXV (September, 1761), p. 233.
[229] *Monthly*, XXV (November, 1761), pp. 369, 389.
[230] *Monthly*, XXVII (October, 1762), p. 310.

head's assertion that England was entitled to the most advantageous commercial terms to compensate for the expenses of a war
it had not sought. For the reviewer, trade was no excuse for going
to war, but was certainly an object once the sacrifices of men and
money had been made.[231]

The differences between the *Monthly* and *Critical,* while varying in degree from the differences between the ministerial and
anti-ministerial essay-journals, were drawn along the same lines.
Together with the comments in the magazines and annuals, those
in the reviews reveal two fundamental attitudes toward the peace:
the defenders of Bute's achievement were concerned primarily
with a return to the pre-war *status quo* or at least to the stability
of the old balance of power; the opposition to the minister looked
upon the treaty as a renunciation of England's right to a new world
empire.

[231] *Monthly,* XXVIII (March, 1763), pp. 212-215.

IV

THE CLIMATE OF VICTORY

Like the peace controversy itself, the climate of victory was tempestuous. From the opposition to Bute's treaty negotiations and tax policies, charges arose that George III, misled by corrupt ministers, was attempting to extend the royal prerogative. Bute, the king's favorite, was abused as a Scottish Jacobite whose treachery was subverting the English Constitution, and John Wilkes, idol of the London public, was hailed by his supporters as a champion of liberty and defender against the excise. Amid the conflict of personalities and the clash of economic interests, the more serious and deeper issues of natural and civil rights were objects of intense scrutiny.

Whether the Whig historians are right in depicting George III as a usurper of parliamentary power, or whether the Namier school is right in describing his actions as simple assertions of his proper privileges,[1] the controversy certainly provided an exercise

---

[1] Butterfield, *George III and the Historians*, presents the most comprehensive treatment of the subject of George III and the prerogative. Butterfield's summary of the situation seems most acceptable: "The men in the neighbourhood of Bute certainly seem to have imagined themselves to be collaborating in a new system, a comprehensive change of policy." (p. 225) According to Butterfield, their view was that they were engaged in restoring monarchial power from the usurpation of oligarchy (p. 225), and although, as Butterfield notes (p. 226), the Namier school disagrees with this description of George III's conduct, the view was one fostered by men who were close to the action. – For the Namier view, see Namier, I, p. 262; II, pp. 336, 380, 471; Sedgwick, *Letters from George III etc.*, pp. viii, xvi ff., and xlii; Gipson, VIII, pp. 52, 226; Pares, pp. 93, 100; Feiling, p. 69; Jucker, pp. 86-87; J. W. Wilkes, "British Politics Preceding the American Revolution", *HLQ*, XX (1957), p. 311. – For the view that the king was attempting to turn back the evolution of parliamentary government,

for popular political theorists at the end of the Seven Years' War. Pamphlets on the subject abounded; writers in the essay-journals dealt with it in terms that led to libel actions against both the *Monitor* and *North Briton*. Although the charges against the *Monitor* were dropped for lack of evidence,[2] and those against the *North Briton* were made specifically for its attack on the king's speech to parliament,[3] writers in both essay-journals were palpably challenging the monarch's right to govern without the specific consent of the people. The danger to the general *status quo* of government, particularly in Wilkes' arguments in the *North Briton*, was too apparent for the king and his ministers to ignore. But whatever the reasons for the legal action, John Wilkes had to invoke his parliamentary privileges to defend himself against prosecution for his share in the *North Briton,* and not even the representatives of the City trade interests, although seeking a greater voice themselves, would support him in his attack on a government opposed to the popular will.[4] Wilkes, discovering the limits of parliamentary immunity, turned to the London mob, and his use of the populace, like the methods employed by the Crown, foreshadowed the conduct involved in the French Revolution.

At stake in the Wilkes case was more than the immediate issue of whether George III had the right to choose his own ministers, or whether a member of parliament could publish scandalous libels against the king's selection of ministers. Not even the conflict

---

see Almon, pp. 27, 38-41, 55, 66-67, 69, 97; H. Walpole, *Memoirs of the Reign of King George the Third* (London, 1845), I, p. 15; Laski, p. 10; Corbett, II, p. 211; Trevelyan, *Autobiography*, pp. 189, 192-193; Turberville, *Men and Manners*, pp. 235-236; Nobbe, p. 25; E. H. Weatherly, editor, *The Correspondence of John Wilkes and Charles Churchill* (New York, 1954), pp. 10-11.
[2] See Chapter III, p. 105, n. 96.
[3] Sedgwick, *Letters from George III etc.*, p. 190, shows the king's determined effort to halt publication of the *North Briton*. See Jucker, p. 167. Pares, *George the Third and the Politicians*, p. 68, n. 1, notes that the king was probably incensed because of the periodical's insinuations about the relationship between Bute and the king's mother.
[4] Almon, pp. 138 ff., 175 ff., indicates the London merchants' use of the Wilkes case for their own purposes, but throughout the argument is concerned with the effect on the middle class. Wilkes's pleas for the lower class are virtually ignored.

between the London trade interests and Bute was as important as the principle that Wilkes was advocating – the principle that natural rights were civil rights.[5] To defend Wilkes without reservation actually meant to support the theory that upon the will of the people depended the existence of government.[6] Even in parliament Wilkes was denounced for his leveling principles, and his actions brought him the warning "not to set up the liberty of the people against the liberty of parliament".[7] Many of the periodical writers, it will be seen, expressed strong disapproval of Bute's imposition of a cider tax, but few of them indicated their support of Wilkes in his legal difficulties.

John Wilkes was a man whose opposition to the military, economic, and political policies of the early government of George III led him into a larger battle against the orthodox theory of English government. Despite William Pitt's title of the "Great Commoner", not even Pitt would support Wilkes, whose appeal was to more than the London trade interests.[8] Bernard Schilling is correct when he ascribes the opposition to Wilkes to a fear of his power to create popular enthusiasm,[9] and Harold Laski is equally accurate in asserting, "Wilkes was a sign that the populace was slowly awaking to a sense of its own power." [10] As Wilkes himself put it, he was fighting in the interests of both the middling and lower classes.[11] Such a battle could gain only the partial sup-

---

[5] Compare *A Complete Collection of the Genuine Papers, Letters, etc. in the Case of John Wilkes, Esq.* (Berlin, 1769), pp. 84-87, in which Wilkes relies on the public's judgment of government policy, with C. Parkin, *The Moral Basis of Burke's Political Thought* (Cambridge, 1956), pp. 21, 44-45, 47, which demonstrates Burke's opposition to this view of natural rights as being radical.

[6] Although Burke, for example, believed that the government of a tyrant could be superseded, he also insisted that the individual had yielded his freedom for civil society and could not restore his individual rights without, at the same time, destroying society itself (Parkin, pp. 27-29).

[7] Pares, *George the Third and the Politicians*, pp. 49-50.

[8] *Wilkes Papers*, pp. 119 ff., describes the split between him and Pitt.

[9] Schilling, pp. 130-131. Plumb, *The First Four Georges*, p. 103.

[10] Laski, p. 112. George Rude, *Wilkes and Liberty* (Oxford, 1962), has examined the political life of Wilkes and its importance to the development of British radicalism and later parliamentary reform. See pp. 17-36.

[11] *Wilkes Papers*, p. 92.

port of the London commercial classes. Seeking greater political voice for themselves, they could grant Wilkes' arguments against the excise and even against the broader powers of the king's prerogative when those powers threatened the economic independence of the middle class,[12] but in Wilkes' critical battle against the very standards of the existing government, his London supporters – as represented by the majority of magazines – remained virtually silent. While Wilkes in the *North Briton* was outspoken in his attack on the use of royal power, the writers in the magazines generally withdrew into reportorial objectivity in describing Wilkes' struggle against the Crown. Yet where Wilkes fought against the excise, in the interest of the City trade groups, the same magazines, through their publication of correspondence and selection of articles, clearly indicated support of his battle.

Whether Wilkes was the diabolical demagogue that his enemies accused him of being, or whether he was sincere in his revolutionary opposition to tyranny, as his admirers claimed,[13] seems less important than the theory of government that he advocated and – in this study – the reactions of the periodical writers to such governmental principles. Perhaps the best measure of Wilkes' theories is a comparison with the conservative arguments expressed by Edmund Burke on the difference between natural and civil rights. Where Wilkes placed the judgment of the body of the people above that of the ministers and parliament,[14] Burke insisted that "the people must be submissive to the legislature as to a superior wisdom".[15] Where Wilkes believed himself the political equal of any of the king's ministers,[16] Burke endorsed a natural aristocracy.[17] But perhaps the greatest difference between the theories of the two men lay in their attitude toward the methods

[12] When Wilkes was remanded to the Tower, the cry of the crowd was, "Wilkes for ever, and no excise!" (*Wilkes Papers*, p. 27).
[13] The editor's note to the *Wilkes Papers* (p. vii) reads: "a lasting monument of the resolute stand made for liberty against ministerial oppression and tyranny". However, Wilkes was frequently depicted in contemporary prints as the image of the devil himself.
[14] *Wilkes Papers*, p. 87.
[15] Parkin, p. 47.
[16] *Wilkes Papers*, p. 12.
[17] Parkin, pp. 34, 37.

of change in government. Wilkes' belief that natural rights extended into civil rights was the very point of Burke's later objections to the French Revolution.[18] According to Wilkes, the people surrendered none of their natural rights for the protection of government, and when the people wanted to make a change, the power was theirs,[19] but Burke regarded the civil rights of men to be the outgrowth and not the equal of natural rights. For Burke, the people who had yielded their individual voices in government could not then, through their own will, evoke a change in that government because of a temporary antagonism to its policy.[20]

While there is nothing as sophisticated or subtle as Burke's views in the periodical writers' reaction to the political controversy in which Wilkes was engaged, their response does reveal the political climate of opinion. It is necessary, however, to differentiate between immediate political considerations and fundamental political philosophy. As in the earlier period of the war, party differences were less distinct than group and personal allegiances,[21] and economic issues determined the political alignment. The City trade interests were opposed to the excise taxes established by Bute's administration,[22] and wanted a stronger voice in government to insure the commercial advantages gained by the war.[23] Naturally, writers in those periodicals that supported the City trade groups took a similar position, but on the immediate matter of Wilkes' opposition to the government, an opposition which demanded a recognition of the people's right to say by whom they might be governed, even these writers were reluctant to declare themselves. Wilkes was no longer merely Temple's journalist, but

[18]   *Wilkes Papers*, p. 90; Parkin, pp. 14-15, 21, 56. According to Parkin, p. 8, the difference between such attitudes as those expressed by Wilkes and Burke on the extension of natural rights into civil rights is the difference between radical and conservative thought. Burke did not regard the matter any differently in the early years of his political thought than he did at the time of the French Revolution (Parkin, p. 6).

[19]   *Wilkes Papers*, p. 90.

[20]   Parkin, pp. 11, 52, 56.

[21]   The general thesis has been well established by Namier in his description of English politics at the accession of George III.

[22]   Jucker, pp. 145, 168.

[23]   Sedgwick, *Letters from George III etc.*, p. 208.

sought instead the aid of those who were not borough owners and had no votes.[24] These were the very London radicals whom the wealthy City merchants wanted to keep in check.[25] At the same time, it was not difficult to convince the Country Gentlemen that Wilkes' intemperate action was an attempt to "enlist them in a factious plot of over mighty subjects",[26] and like the City tradesmen, they refused him their support.

When examined in the light of the evidence from the periodicals, Laski's comment on the English political climate at the end of the war seems at least exaggerated. According to Laski, "The basis of revolutionary doctrine was already present in England when, in 1762, Rousseau published his *Contrat Social*";[27] but apart from those in the *Monitor* and the *North Briton,* none of the periodical writers expressed political opinions that can be construed as radical. Even in their treatment of Rousseau's writings, they praised his literary talent but rejected his anti-institutionalism.[28] Rousseau's arguments were commonly described as

[24] Watson, p. 100.
[25] Watson, p. 50.
[26] Watson, p. 93.
[27] Laski, p. 125.
[28] J. H. Warner, "Eighteenth-Century English Reactions to the *Nouvelle Heloise*", *PMLA*, LII (1937), pp. 803-819, discusses the periodicals' reception of that particular work. Warner, p. 819, states that it was the only work by Rousseau to receive a predominantly favorable reception in England during the eighteenth century, but although he notes (pp. 814-815) that comments attacking its immoral influence did not appear in the early reviews and were not frequent until later, he acknowledges the *Critical*'s opposition and quotes from the *Monthly*, which though less severe was hardly favorable (p. 817). J. B. Heidler, *History, from 1700-1800, of English Criticism of Prose Fiction* (Urbana, Ill., 1928), pp. 100-101, considers the treatment of *The New Eloisa* (English translation of *La Nouvelle Heloise*) and *Emile* in both the *Monthly* and *Critical*, but offers no real comment on the reviews. E. Joliat, *Smollett et la France* (Paris, 1935), pp. 164-165, accurately describes the *Critical*'s treatment of Rousseau as appreciative of his literary genius but opposed to his paradoxes and unable to accept either his point of view or advice.

Actually, the following references to periodicals that offered comments on excerpts from Rousseau's writings or passed critical judgments reveal a fundamental agreement with the criticism of the *Critical: London Magazine:* XXX (March, 1761), pp. 135-138; XXX (April, 1761), pp. 171-173; XXXI (February, 1762), p. 69; XXXI (September, 1762), pp. 460-461; XXXII (December, 1763), p. 654.

dangerous, strange, and *singular,* and he was no less abused for his paradoxes and whimsy in the *Monthly* than in the *Critical Review.*

At the same time, particular arguments in the essay-journals, magazines, and reviews on politics and government reflect the same general caution.[29] Despite the many demands for extending the empire, the periodical writers were moderate in their argu-

---

Gentleman's Magazine: XXXI (January, 1761), pp. 34-35; XXXI (February, 1761), p. 62; XXXI (March, 1761), p. 110; XXXI (September, 1761), p. 395. – *British Magazine:* III (March, 1762), p. 158; III (November, 1762), p. 606; IV (August, 1763), pp. 409-411. – *Universal Museum:* I (January, 1762), pp. 46-47. – *Universal Magazine:* XXIX (August, 1761), p. 89; XXIX (September, 1761), p. 126. – *Annual Register,* V, Pt. II (1762), pp. 158-160, 225-237. – *Monthly Review:* XXIII (December, 1760), p. 492; XXIV (April, 1761), pp. 227-235; XXV (September, 1761), pp. 192-214; XXV (October, 1761), pp. 241-260; XXVI (May, 1762), pp. 331-342; XXVII (September, 1762), pp. 212-217; XXVII (October, 1762), pp. 261-265; XXVII (December, 1762), pp. 449-453; XXVIII (January, 1763), pp. 1-14; XXVIII (February, 1763), pp. 81-82; XXIX (December, 1763), pp. 382 ff. – *Critical Review:* VII (January, 1759), pp. 48-59; XI (January, 1761), pp. 65-66; XII (September, 1761), pp. 203-211; XIII (February, 1762), pp. 101 ff.; XIV (October, 1762), pp. 250 ff.; XIV (November, 1762), pp. 336-346; XIV (December, 1762), pp. 426-440; XV (January, 1763), pp. 21-34; XV (June, 1763), pp. 444-449; XVI (November, 1763), pp. 375-377. – The *Christian's Magazine,* IV (August, 1763), pp. 368-369, printed Rousseau's parallel between Jesus Christ and Socrates in *Emilius,* but it was that portion which most seemed to support Christian Revelation. This list includes only those references in which comments were made on Rousseau's work. Of these, only the *London's* and *Gentleman's'* may be described as decidedly favorable, and they passed no judgment on Rousseau's politics.

[29] *Cf.,* R. N. Stromberg, *Religious Liberalism in Eighteenth-Century England* (Oxford, 1954), pp. 123-124; " 'Liberalism' in this sense, viz. Whiggism in politics and a trend towards *laissez-faire* in economics, is the dominant philosophy in eighteenth-century England, and by and large a conservative one. For however radical English ideas seemed to European absolutists in this era, they were associated at home with a conservative oligarchy. Liberty and constitutional government were congenial to this ruling group; democracy and social equality were abhorrent. The 'masses' were barely beginning to push themselves on to the stage of history, and were in fact regarded by the new bourgeois potentates as peculiarly vicious. The humanitarian movement, along with the beginnings of a demand for political democracy, had to await the last quarter of the century for real growth. Until then, the England that inspired Voltaire and Montesquieu with its liberalism remained, on a modern view, sunk in complacency, amid social evils which cried for attention but received little."

ments for altering the structure of the state, and only in the *North Briton* and *Monitor* was the extension of royal authority directly challenged.

In terms that could lead only to attempts at censorship, John Wilkes and the *North Briton* argued the popular cause of opposition to the royal prerogative. So direct was the challenge to the king's authority through his ministers, that the action taken to silence the *North Briton,* after Number Forty-Five, is surprising only because it was so late in coming. Throughout its existence, the writers in the essay-journal maintained the attitude, expressed by Wilkes in one of its numbers, that "my only patron is the Public, to which I will ever make my appeal, and hold it sacred".[30] For William Temple in the *North Briton:* [31]

Government is a just execution of the laws, which were instituted by the people for their preservation: but if the people's implements, to whom they have trusted their execution of those laws, or any power for their preservation, should convert such execution to their destruc- tion, have they not a right to intermeddle? nay, have they not a right to resume the power they have delegated, and to punish their serv- ants who have abused it? If our King can do no wrong, his ministers may, and are accountable to the people for their conduct. This is the voice of Locke, the voice of our laws, the voice of reason; but we own not the voice of tyrants and their abettors, not the voice of the *Briton.* On the contrary, this wretch preaches up the doctrine, that some part of mankind, nay the mass, are born slaves, who ought implicitly to be submissive to the caprices of a few, who by accident, knavery, or cunning, shall wriggle themselves into power.

Clearly, Temple took the radical view that natural rights were not renounced for civil rights, and although speaking most particular- ly to the London trade interests,[32] he and Wilkes appealed to more than this limited group in advocating that the public be encour- aged to demand the subservience of the king's ministers to the will of both parliament and the people.[33] To be sure, the wealthy City

[30] *Political Controversy*, II, p. 36. References to the essay-journals are indicated by volume and page numbers in the collection called *Political Controversy*.
[31] *Political Controversy*, I, p. 486.
[32] *Political Controversy*, I, p. 484.
[33] *Political Controversy*, I, pp. 111, 114, 337.

trade groups appreciated Wilkes' opposition to the invasion of public rights through partial and prejudiced judges and illegal invasions of private homes,[34] but every small shopkeeper must have applauded Churchill's denunciation of the ministers' refusal to make the demands of the people known to the sovereign.[35]

Despite the lack of party organization, in the modern sense of the term, the *North Briton* was fighting a political battle in which Bute's advocates had given the names of *Whig* and *Tory* at least some meaning for the participants. These evil ministers, Wilkes argued, were "Tories turned courtiers"; [36] and he equated *Tory* and *Jacobite*,[37] which was as much as to say that the king's ministers were treasonous.[38] Using the irony characteristic in the political essay-journals, Wilkes complimented Dr. Johnson on having received the royal bounty for his attachment to the cause of liberty [39] – liberty in Tory terms, which Wilkes had described as slavery.[40] But without irony, a writer, perhaps Wilkes, in the *North Briton* depicted the Tory doctrine as a belief "that there is a *divine, hereditary*, indefeasible right in any family",[41] a principle opposed to the British Constitution.[42] At the same time, Wilkes lauded the Whigs as "those old and firm friends of the constitution .. .",[43] defenders of liberty,[44] and protectors of the nation.[45] For the arguments describing the Whigs as a faction committed to the destruction of public peace, the writer, probably Wilkes, in the *North Briton* had nothing but contempt.[46]

However, Wilkes' main attack was against the extension of the

---

[34]   *Political Controversy*, III, pp. 413-414 (Wilkes).
[35]   *Political Controversy*, I, pp. 74-75.
[36]   *Political Controversy*, II, p. 149.
[37]   *Political Controversy*, III, pp. 35-40.
[38]   For a discussion of these terms in the political controversy, see R. D. Spector, "Eighteenth-Century Political Controversy and Linguistics", *N&Q*, II (1955), pp. 387-389.
[39]   *Political Controversy*, I, p. 223.
[40]   *Political Controversy*, II, p. 149.
[41]   *Political Controversy*, III, p. 146.
[42]   *Cf., Wilkes Papers*, p. 116.
[43]   *Political Controversy*, II, p. 149.
[44]   *Political Controversy*, II, p. 33.
[45]   *Political Controversy*, II, p. 226; IV, p. 40.
[46]   *Political Controversy*, II, p. 414.

king's prerogative.[47] While he acknowledged the monarch's right to choose his ministers, Wilkes insisted that the privilege did not exempt the king from considering their prudence and fitness, and when his choice was unwise, it was the right of the people to raise an objection.[48] Even the talk about the independence and prerogative of the Crown Wilkes interpreted as advocacy of slavery.[49]

Ignoring threats of censorship and prosecution and defiant of the attempt to silence the *Monitor*,[50] the writers in the *North Briton* continued their opposition to the free use of the royal prerogative, until the forty-fifth number, Wilkes' attack on the king's speech to parliament, brought public prosecution. Actually, *North Briton* Number Forty-Five was no more seditious than earlier numbers; the tenor of Wilkes' arguments was in harmony with his frequently expressed views.[51] Indeed, he began with a declaration that the king's speech was traditionally considered as the speech of the minister,[52] so that an attack upon it was not intended to be an abuse of the sovereign. Nevertheless, Wilkes' clearly defined position on the limitations of the royal prerogative could hardly have met with the king's approval. According to Wilkes: [53]

The King of England is only the first magistrate of this country: but is invested by law with the whole executive power. He is, however, responsible to his people for the due execution of the royal function,

[47] *Political Controversy*, III, pp. 188-189.
[48] *Political Controversy*, II, pp. 31-32 (Wilkes), pp. 261-262 (Lloyd?).
[49] *Political Controversy*, II, pp. 479-480.
[50] *Political Controversy*, II, p. 262 (Lloyd), pp. 300-301 (Churchill).
[51] In the best discussion of the *North Briton*, Nobbe, p. 208, describes the "vehement denunciations of this last number of *The North Briton* to which men of all shades of political belief gave utterance in 1763". Although Nobbe says it is difficult for the modern reader to comprehend this reaction, his own comment which offers a quotation from Henry Fox provides the answer. "Such words [Nobbe says of the conclusion] led directly to what Henry Fox once called 'that nonsensical thing, undeserv'd popularity with the dregs of the people.' " It was this direct appeal to the people that was most obnoxious even to the members of parliament.
[52] Nobbe, p. 209, describes the attempt of the *North Briton* to distinguish between the sovereign and his ministers, but, as Nobbe indicates, the minister's sentiments were those of the king. *Wilkes Papers*, pp. 25-26. *Political Controversy*, IV, p. 72.
[53] *Political Controversy*, IV, p. 78.

in the choice of ministers, &c. equally with the meanest of his subjects in his particular duty.

No king who was concerned with demonstrating his authority
could afford to ignore the challenge of Wilkes' words, especially
when Wilkes made clear the implications of his argument by insisting that "the people too have their prerogative . . .".[54]

On the issue of the king's authority, Wilkes and the *North
Briton* were strongly supported by the writers in the *Monitor,* although the latter were committed primarily to the interests of the
middle class and were less emphatic than Wilkes in demanding the
rights of all classes.[55] For the *Monitor* opposition to the extension
of the royal prerogative was a major theme. While warning that
attempts to extend the king's powers had, in the past, invariably
led to his fall, the writers insisted that his duties were limited to
"creating the nobility, the confirming and executing the laws,
the pardoning criminals, and the coining of money . . .".[56] For
these journalists a king was best when he was "satisfied with his
original share in the political state of his dominions . . .",[57] and
they, like the Real Whigs,[58] regarded attempts to advance the
royal prerogative as encroachments upon the people's liberty.[59]
Although the writers in the *Monitor* stressed the particular rights
of the citizens of London, at least one insisted: [60]

But this is not their [the citizens of London's] right only: it is the
privilege of every Englishman. We are born free: and so long as we
exercise our freedom of thought and speech in a constitutional way,

[54] *Political Controversy*, IV, p. 78.
[55] Robbins, p. 228, declares that although these demands to improve the
constitution were considered radical at the time, the leveling and republican
direction taken by the Real Whigs was greatly exaggerated by their opponents. They were (p. 16) not egalitarian, although they stressed "to an
embarrassing degree the equality of man before God, or in a state of
nature".
[56] *Political Controversy*, III, p. 446.
[57] *Political Controversy*, III, p. 488.
[58] Robbins, p. 6, describes the aims of the Real Whigs as "a federal system in the British Isles, an amendment of parliament, a diminution of
ministerial prerogative, an increased toleration, and some modification of
mercantilist regulation".
[59] *Political Controversy*, III, pp. 448 ft.
[60] *Political Controversy*, I, p. 358.

no power can control that liberty. They that feel must also think: and who think themselves in danger, will cry out and endeavour to preserve themselves from the injury they dread.

Throughout these arguments for a balanced government, the emphasis was on the restriction of the royal prerogative [61] but, not content to present generalizations, Beckford's writers argued in terms of specific issues, particularly, the rights of property and the protection of commercial interests. The privilege of petitioning the king was especially important to the citizens of London; [62] taxation without consent was not to be tolerated; [63] and the increase of court dependents was the business of those merchants whose taxes would be necessary to support the king's favorites.[64]

In their attack on the king's favorites, the writers were, of course, opposing the government of Bute, who was unpopular with the City trade groups.[65] The anti-ministerial journalists clearly regarded the Scottish minister as responsible for George III's desire to extend the prerogative, an attempt which they considered tantamount to an infringement upon the people's rights. Using historical analogy, the device most commonly employed because of the security afforded by its indirection, the writers in the *Monitor* warned that absolute and arbitrary government was a frequent forerunner of revolution,[66] and describing the effect of the king's ministers upon the conduct of government, one declared: [67]

The constitution of a body politic, is in many respects, not unsimilar to that of the natural body: which may be neglected till it becomes so debauched in its inordinate desires, as to become incorrigible: till it grows so leprous, as to be eaten up by cancer in all its members; or in the head by the K—'s evil till one part violently opposes the good of the other: till a rancorous peccant humour gains the ascendant over the whole body: till its whole substance shall be exhausted; and till a fever tyrannizes, and destroys its vital parts.

[61] *Political Controversy*, III, pp. 247-248, 444.
[62] *Political Controversy*, IV, pp. 66-69.
[63] *Political Controversy*, IV, p. 70.
[64] *Political Controversy*, III, pp. 448 ff.
[65] *Political Controversy*, I, pp. 62, 133-134. Sutherland, p. 92; Jucker, p. 246.
[66] *Political Controversy*, I, pp. 60-61, 242 ff., 465; II, pp. 88 ff.; III, pp. 446 ff.
[67] *Political Controversy*, III, pp. 210-211.

As answer to the threat of royal tyranny, the journalists urged a parliament free from ministerial influences,[68] a parliament that would be representative of commercial and propertied interests.[69] The writers in the *Monitor* sought to check the power of the Crown through control of the public purse,[70] and insisted upon the responsibility of the ministry to keep the public informed.[71] But most importantly, the journalists, like the Whigs of the Glorious Revolution, opposed a standing army,[72] which they considered an instrument for enforcing arbitrary power and a threat to the people's liberty.[73]

The challenge of the *Monitor* and the *North Briton* to the Bute government was supported in the few numbers of the *Patriot,* whose writers obliquely criticized its opponents' arguments in favor of the royal prerogative. The articles in the *Patriot* ironically reminded the *Briton* that in its *proof* of the superiority of Bute to Pitt, the ministerial advocate had neglected to say "how much less likely a single m—ch is to be deceived, than a million of his subjects . . .".[74] At the same time, the *Patriot's* attack on Bute made the customary anti-ministerial charges of Scottish treachery,[75] and ironically reassured the minister that it was of no consequence that the voice of the people was raised against him.[76]

From the comments in the anti-ministerial essay-journals, it is apparent that, no matter how modern historians view the conflict between George III and Wilkes, the participants in the controversy regarded it as a struggle to determine the proper limits of the royal prerogative. As Herbert Butterfield has stated, the arguments of the spokesmen for Bute's administration were responsible for the terms of the controversy,[77] and the *Briton* and *Auditor*

---

[68]   *Political Controversy*, III, pp. 212, 216, 374.
[69]   *Monitor*, #243 (March 15, 1760), pp. 1464-1465. All other references to the *Monitor* in this chapter are to the *Political Controversy*.
[70]   *Political Controversy*, III, p. 488.
[71]   *Political Controversy*, I, p. 361.
[72]   Sherrard, pp. 95-97.
[73]   *Political Controversy*, III, pp. 288, 329 ff., 367, 405 ff.
[74]   *Patriot*, #3 (July 3, 1762), p. 13.
[75]   *Patriot*, #1 (June 19, 1762), pp. 3-4.
[76]   *Patriot*, #3 (July 3, 1762), p. 15.
[77]   Butterfield, *George III and the Historians*, pp. 225-226.

were the foremost advocates of the king's rights. Furthermore, the two periodicals were clearly responsible for casting the argument in political terms as a struggle between Whigs and Tories, although both essay-journals attempted to assert their impartial position.

Despite the lack of a modern party organization, the comments in the *Briton* indicate that a philosophy of party differences was manifest in the conflict about royal prerogative at the end of the Seven Years' War. Although he claimed that the Bute administration was neither Whig nor Tory,[78] Smollett ridiculed the Whig ministers who "have always been known to plume themselves with feathers they plucked from the prerogative; and have added to their own persons, that importance which they have filched from the crown".[79] The king's prerogative was "independent of men, and does not want the approbation of the Whigs, or any other faction", Smollett insisted, and the purpose of the Tories was to protect his independence.[80]

What purpose lay behind Smollett's arguments in the *Briton*? The *Briton* was still engaged in the task of making the peace acceptable to the opposition, and apparently Smollett hoped to gain the support of the Aristocratic Whigs by attacking the independent merchants and their City allies as a threat to the stability of the government on which the Whig lords depended for their trade interests. But Smollett's political philosophy was opposed to whiggism in general, and although he emphasized what he believed to be the leveling principles of the Popular Whigs, he never clearly distinguished between them and the Whig aristocracy. Moreover, anti-ministerial writers were quick to remark on his general assault on the principles of the Glorious Revolution, and in this matter of proper limitations on the royal prerogative, the Whig aristocrats had a real stake.

At the heart of the attitude expressed in the *Briton* was an opposition to popular government. Smollett objected particularly to Whig attempts "to widen the bottom of government, which was

---

[78] *Political Controversy*, III, p. 69.
[79] *Political Controversy*, III, p. 67.
[80] *Political Controversy*, II, p. 408. See, also, II, p. 451.

still farther widened by the late minister [Pitt], who thereby acquired the popularity he once boasted of in defiance of his fellow councellors".[81] In Smollett's opinion, the "popular principle" of whiggism in general was abhorrent to the country's natural inclination to monarchy,[82] and, in terms that were perhaps intended to drive a wedge between opposing trade groups, but unlikely to make the *Briton* effective in the City of London,[83] he scorned attempts to make "royalty itself a splendid phantom",[84] and ridiculed the clamor that came from "artisans, inferiour tradesmen, and the lower class of plebians, such as those who now presume to direct the wheels of government".[85]

In his opposition to the Whigs, Smollett expressed a skeptical distrust of political theories that threatened stability by tampering with the traditional order. For him the Whigs generally represented a sect of speculative philosophers opposed to all order and restraint, and to heed these theoretical legislators was to accept their very mistaken philanthropy which assumed: [86]

every individual to be equally free by nature, [and] draws this erroneous inference, that every individual has an equal right to intermeddle in the administration of public affairs; a principle subversive of all government, magistracy and subordination; a principle destructive to all industry and national quiet, as well as repugnant to every fundamental maxim of society.

Whatever attempt he made to defend the Bute ministry from the attack of the independent London trade interests,[87] Smollett argued in terms least likely to afford success. Bute's lack of popularity was in direct contrast with Pitt's powerful support by the City populace, and in order to convince that public of the error of its ways, Smollett was forced to deprecate the importance of whatever popular approval he was seeking for Bute's administration.[88]

[81]   *Political Controversy*, III, p. 68.
[82]   *Political Controversy*, III, p. 68.
[83]   The contemporary note by Wilkes in *Political Controversy*, III, p. 98, indicates the unpopular view taken by the *Briton*.
[84]   *Political Controversy*, III, p. 98.
[85]   *Political Controversy*, II, p. 139.
[86]   *Political Controversy*, I, pp. 330-331. See, also, III, p. 177.
[87]   *Political Controversy*, I, pp. 29-30.
[88]   *Political Controversy*, I, pp. 24-25, 28; III, p. 138.

The task was scarcely possible because it necessitated Smollett's vilification of Beckford, who was extremely popular in London.[89] At the same time, listening to themselves described as the "refuse of the vulgar" [90] and scandal-mongerers appeased only by the disgrace of their superiors,[91] the followers of Pitt were not likely to change their allegiance from him to the favorite of the *Briton*. Indeed, Smollett, perhaps to gain the support of the wealthy Whigs, seemed to scorn this very popularity: [92]

A wise man will scorn alike the censure and applause of the multitude; the first as an impotent attack which virtue must avoid, and innocence has no cause to fear; the last as a contemptible bubble, without solidity or duration.

Like the *Briton*, the *Auditor* depicted attempts to restrict the royal prerogative as evidence of a demagogic usurpation of proper authority. The *Auditor* used a variety of techniques – ranging from Swiftian irony to name-calling – in an endeavor to convince the public that George III was merely reasserting rights that the earlier Hanoverian kings had ignored because of their lack of acquaintance with the laws, manners, and customs of the nation.[93] If there was now a commotion in the nation, Murphy declared, the cause was a minister, Pitt, who had been so accustomed to his unlimited power that he resented a king who was unwilling to be made a pawn.[94] According to Murphy, appealing to the Whig Aristocrats, the king had no desire to strain the prerogative, but neither was he willing to be ruled by the mob.[95] Murphy, reporting an imaginary conversation in Brobdingnag, described George III as a man intent on restoring proper balance to the government by insisting on the rights of the Crown: [96]

[89] Nobbe, p. 181.
[90] *Political Controversy*, I, p. 105.
[91] *Political Controversy*, I, pp. 216, 250, 483.
[92] *Political Controversy*, I, p. 142.
[93] *Political Controversy*, I, pp. 78-79.
[94] *Political Controversy*, I, pp. 80-81.
[95] *Political Controversy*, I, p. 49.
[96] *Political Controversy*, I, p. 82. In another number (I, p. 194), the *Auditor* made the specific point that the birth of a child to the royal family meant that the nation would continue to "be ruled by kings *born and educated in this country*".

. . . the present king of Great Britain has endeavoured in the beginning of his reign to eradicate, on the one hand, the deep system of ministerial power, which had so long prevailed; and, on the other, to preserve the ballance of the constitution, by not throwing too much into the popular scale, but on the contrary by exerting the first rights of his crown, and the executive trusts vested in him by the laws. . . .

By insistence on the legality of the king's actions, Murphy set the stage for an attack upon the opposition. If the king's conduct was legal, then the arguments of his opponents were seditious. In Murphy's comments on the *North Briton,* the charge of sedition was made explicit.[97] He described anti-ministerial statements as "the daily and weekly libels which are issued forth against a ministry legally appointed by the sovereign power . . .",[98] and warned: [99]

. . . unless some proper steps are taken to render the authority of the state more respected, than has lately been the case, the liberty of this country will some time or other be endangered by the very love of liberty itself.

Yet Murphy like Smollett was confronted with the historical reality of the Whig aristocracy's purpose in the Glorious Revolution. Too optimistically, he apparently believed that he could convince them that their economic well-being, as well as their patriotic duty, called for their opposition to attacks on the prerogative. Pitt was described as a power-hungry militarist,[100] and the Whig attack on the prerogative was depicted as emanating from self-interest.[101] By tracing the history of the Whigs, Murphy sought to demonstrate that the party was destructive of liberty through its efforts to control the Crown by stirring up the populace.[102] The spirit of

---

[97]   *Political Controversy,* III, pp. 25, 27.
[98]   *Political Controversy,* I, pp. 375-376. See, also, *Political Controversy,* I, p. 116, in which Murphy charged that anti-ministerial writers were guilty of sedition since they "endeavoured to poison the minds of the people against the King, the Queen, and the most respectable branches of the royal family . . . ".
[99]   *Political Controversy,* I, p. 378.
[100]   *Political Controversy,* III, pp. 59-65, 106 ff.
[101]   *Political Controversy,* II, p. 485.
[102]   *Political Controversy,* II, pp. 307-311.

whiggism, he declared, was the spirit of discord and faction,[103] certain to disturb the public tranquility.[104]

Whatever hopes Murphy had of winning over the Whig lords, he had little chance of convincing the City merchants and their supporters of the merits of the king and Lord Bute's administration. To change the minds of his public, he had to make the people acknowledge that they were political incompetents who had been duped by special interests or that they were ungrateful wretches who were hungry for power, Neither choice was likely to be palatable. The attack on Beckford, probably calculated to ally the Old Whig representatives with the government, could not possibly have won acclaim in the City. Moreover, Murphy's assaults on "the clamours of an unthinking multitude",[105] "coffee-house statesmen, . . . Grub-street patriots",[106] and greedy tradesmen [107] could hardly have appeased the London radicals. Few people were likely to respond kindly to the charge that they were "never so happy as when you tell them they are ruined"; [108] nor to the ironic tones that described as ludicrous the strong mixture of popular government in the English Constitution which had created a state in which [109]

. . . every mechanic thinks he has a right to dictate the measures that ought to be pursued, and the men who ought to be entrusted with the conduct of affairs. A great number of heads must see more than one; the voice of the people is the voice of God; wisdom crieth out in the streets; and many more wise sayings might be alledged to assert the rights of the people.

While the opposition was advocating these very rights of all the people, Murphy was insisting that the general public needed a nursemaid: [110]

[103] *Political Controversy*, II, pp. 233-234.
[104] *Political Controversy*, I, p. 229.
[105] *Political Controversy*, II, p. 3.
[106] *Political Controversy*, II, p. 232.
[107] *Political Controversy*, I, p. 310.
[108] *Political Controversy*, I, p. 154.
[109] *Political Controversy*, I, pp. 81-82.
[110] *Political Controversy*, I, p. 192.

[It is] necessary for the *Auditor* to continue to watch over the understandings of the good people of England, who, it must be avowed, are such coarse feeders in politics, that the vilest provisions, if they happen to be seasoned highly with the palatable ingredients of a poisonous nature will ever go down with them, and hence the necessity of supplying them with wholesome fare, that they may not prey on garbage.

At the same time that Wilkes and the *North Briton* and the *Monitor* were appealing to the City to declare its rights, Murphy attempted to win by ridicule the disaffected populace. In no other paper is the tone of Murphy's argument better summarized than in the mock vision he employed to satirize the aspirations for political voice by the citizens of London: [111]

The same day a vote passed, *Nemine contradicente*, declaring the doctrine of kings, lords, and commons, absurd and erroneous, and directing for the future that the mob be deemed a 4th estate, to ballance and controul the prerogative, and to curb the authority of the nobles, who have hitherto sat judicially in the last resort; it being plain from the original contract that the dregs of mankind cannot resign their natural rights to any civil institution, which would be lese majesty of the people; and it was therefore resolved that the mobacracy be established in full force. . . .

Hearing the words of Wilkes, the general public might not think the idea so ridiculous as Murphy imagined. Whatever role Smollett and Murphy played in the success of Bute's efforts to achieve parliamentary approval of the peace, the minister's decision not to continue to use their periodicals to combat Wilkes' propaganda testifies to their ineffectiveness in bringing about ministerial popularity.[112]

For the writers in the essay-journals the primary issue, apart from the making of the peace, was the royal prerogative, and although the matter of the excise on cider and perry would have interested them,[113] it came after the peace, too late to play an important part in their political controversy. On the other hand,

[111]   *Political Controversy*, I, p. 48.
[112]   Nobbe, p. 167.
[113]   See, for example, the *Briton*, July 18, 1762 (*Political Controversy*, I, p. 30), which describes the "coalition of the sugar and malt distillery, under the figures of the *Monitor* and *North Briton* . . .".

in the magazines, the excise tax was more prominent than the quarrel about the king's privileges. The magazine editors were more willing to risk comments on the tax, whose economic effect on the City merchants was immediately apparent,[114] than upon the matter of the prerogative. To be sure, the methods of collecting the excise raised questions of constitutional liberties,[115] but the implications of Wilkes' challenge to the Crown were more radical, especially since he had invoked the power of the mob. Consequently, the magazines generally presented strong opinions about the excise but retreated into journalistic objectivity on Wilkes *vs.* Rex.

Both major magazines proved cautious in their treatment of the Wilkes case, although the editors of the *Gentleman's* were interested both in an expanded empire and a stronger middle class. While their selection of letters and comments on trade favored the London commercial interests,[116] the editors took no firm stand on either the king's prerogative or the case of Wilkes. Indeed, the articles in the magazine, while generally sympathetic to trade, were indisposed to challenge any administration. If their writers argued vaguely for the importance of civil liberties,[117] with the opportunity for specific comment at the time of Pitt's resignation, the editors were careful to present a balance of opinion. They declared, in a headnote to charges against Pitt, that he had been victimized because of his great popularity, and they even questioned a theory of government that forced the people to accept the new ministry.[118] Sympathizing with the public clamor that arose after Pitt's forced resignation, the editors argued, in a note: [119]

. . . when upright ministers are in power, and wise measures are pursued, the people of England ever did and ever will be pleased. But when corrupt ministers prevail, and the nation's honour is made a sacrifice to their venality, the people of England will murmur.

[114] Jucker, pp. 145, 168.
[115] Watson, pp. 91-92.
[116] *Gentleman's Magazine*, XXX (January, 1760), pp. 23-24; XXX (December, 1760), p. 550; XXXIII (September, 1763), pp. 446-447.
[117] *Gentleman's Magazine*, XXX (October, 1760), p. 453; XXXII (December, 1762), pp. 557-559.
[118] *Gentleman's*, XXXI (December, 1761), p. 580.
[119] *Gentleman's*, XXXI (December, 1761), pp. 579-580.

Again, in an article called "Serious and Seasonable Queries", the magazine published an attack on Bute which accused the king of suffering his great esteem to decay because of his attachment to a corrupt minister.[120]

Yet, a month later, the *Gentleman's* published a piece called "Circumstances Attending the Late Resignation", in which Pitt was abused as a rabble rouser and demagogue,[121] and when Bute himself was under attack in June, the magazine reprinted a poem from the *London Chronicle* in which the Scottish minister was defended against the assaults of malice and envy.[122] Finally, at the time of Bute's resignation, the *Gentleman's* published a letter depicting the opposition as an ungrateful multitude and the king as a martyr who had yielded his rights for the sake of freedom. The letter-writer warned: [123]

The turbulance of free states is a common theme of declamation, and seems a defect, in some degree, inseparable from liberty. I am afraid that this country has now given an instance of this disposition, which may lead future ministers, and future sovereigns, to views of government very different from those of the late Minister, and the present King.

In their selection of material on Pitt and Bute, the editors of the *Gentleman's* indicate the fundamentally indecisive political position taken by most of the magazines. Despite their sympathies toward the commercial interests and their overwhelming opposition to the excise,[124] the editors presented the arguments of both the government and the opposition, and where literary merit was involved, the selection and comment were apparently without bias.[125]

[120] *Gentleman's*, XXXI (November, 1761), pp. 520-521.
[121] *Gentleman's*, XXXI (December, 1761), pp. 546-547.
[122] *Gentleman's*, XXXII (June, 1762), p. 288.
[123] *Gentleman's*, XXXIII (April, 1763), pp. 189-190. See, also, XXXIII (August, 1763), pp. 397-405.
[124] Comments on the excise called it an affront to the dignity of free-born Englishmen, labeled it subversive of civil liberty, and described it as a source of tremendous discontent. See *Gentleman's*, XXXIII (March, 1763), p. 104; XXXIII (April, 1763), pp. 164 ff.; XXXIII (June, 1763), pp. 300 ff.; XXXIII (August, 1763), pp. 387-388; XXXIII (September, 1763), pp. 446-448.
[125] For example, the magazine published *A Letter from the Cocoa-Tree to the Country-Gentlemen* and *An Address to the Cocoa-Tree by a Whig,*

For the Wilkes case itself, the editors chose the security of reportorial treatment, and insisted that they acted from impartiality and a desire not to meddle "where private characters are concerned".[126] Publishing an attack on the government's action against the *North Briton*,[127] the editors were careful to include a response in the same number.[128] Only in a dedicatory poem to the 1763 volume, did they indicate, through ironic praise of Wilkes' flight to the continent, that, for all their sympathy to the City trade interests, they were no believers in the kind of opposition presented by the *North Briton*.

The same moderation marked the political comments in the *London Magazine*. While the *London*, particularly in its parliamentary history, favored an economic policy which protected both the small City trade interests and the laboring poor,[129] its editors were no advocates of leveling principles. According to the writers in the *London*, restraint of monopolies, high prices, and general taxation – especially the excise – was essential to the financial and political well-being of a commercial state,[130] and their political

---

opposed political essays, and described them as excellent pamphlets of their kind (*Gentleman's*, XXXII, Supplement, 1762, pp. 620-625.) – The *Gentleman's* treated Charles Churchill's poetry without indication of political consideration (XXXI, April, 1761, p. 190; XXXI, June, 1761, p. 286; XXXII, March, 1762, p. 139; XXXIII, November, 1763, p. 560; XXXIII, December, 1763, p. 610).

[126] For the magazine's treatment of the Wilkes episode, see *Gentleman's*, XXXIII (May, 1763), pp. 239-243; XXXIII (September, 1763), pp. 424, 449; XXXIII (October, 1763), pp. 475-476; XXXIII (November, 1763), pp. 525-527. Although it asserted (XXXIII, October, 1763, p. 476). that it would not pursue the matter except for the public interest, in reporting the proceedings (XXXIII, November, 1763, p. 527), the *Gentleman's* declared that the decision against privilege in the case would have the beneficial effect of bringing a halt to seditious writings.

[127] *Gentleman's*, XXXIII (July, 1763), pp. 325-329.
[128] *Gentleman's*, XXXIII (July, 1763), pp. 352-353.
[129] *London*, XXIX (January, 1760), p. 13; XXIX (February, 1760), pp. 67, 84-85; XXIX (May, 1760), p. 238; XXIX (October, 1760), p. 507; XXIX (December, 1760), p. 628; XXX (May, 1761), p. 233; XXX (December, 1761), p. 630; XXXI (January, 1762), pp. 9 ff.; XXXI (August, 1762), pp. 409-411.
[130] *London*, XXIX (October, 1760), p. 507; XXIX (December, 1760), p. 628; XXX (May, 1761), p. 233; XXX (December, 1761), p. 630; XXXI (August, 1762), pp. 410-411.

remarks were concerned with the maintenance of a government dedicated to keeping the balance of power.

In its correspondence, articles, and history of parliament, the *London* presented the view that England's security depended upon a balanced government. The writers in the magazine, which published a letter describing the importance of the public information service provided by its articles on parliament,[131] celebrated the virtues of the British senate [132] but insisted upon the need to keep that body free from corruption or, more than even an absolute monarch, it would be destructive of the citizens' liberty.[133] While some writers expressed fears of the extremes of republicanism and popular rule,[134] others were not less frightened by the specter of royal authoritarianism,[135] especially when supported by military power.[136] According to writers in the magazine, parliament, no less than the Court, must be subservient to the Constitution.[137] While selected letters were fearful of both unanimity and discord,[138] the articles in the *London* espoused a theory of constitutional government not unlike Burke's: [139]

[Constitutional changes, with public consent, are permissible, but] great changes in a state being delicate and very dangerous affairs, and ... frequent changes being in their own nature prejudiced, a people ought to be very circumspect in doing it, and never be inclined to make innovations without the most pressing reasons, or an absolute necessity.

In every way, the comments in the articles and letters published by the *London* show the moderate conservatism of a periodical

---

[131]   *London*, XXX (October, 1761), p. 511.
[132]   *London*, XXXI (May, 1762), p. 241.
[133]   *London*, XXX (January, 1761), pp. 9, 14.
[134]   *London*, XXIX (January, 1760), pp. 10-11; XXXII (January, 1763), p. 13; XXXII (April, 1763), p. 182.
[135]   *London*, XXIX (January, 1760), pp. 32-34; XXIX (August, 1760), pp. 412-415; XXXI (March, 1762), p. 125.
[136]   *London*, XXIX (November, 1760), p. 570; XXX (October, 1761), p. 518.
[137]   *London*, XXIX (August, 1760), p. 412; XXX (June, 1761), p. 290.
[138]   *London*, XXX (November, 1761), p. 567; XXX I (July, 1762), pp. 372 ff.
[139]   *London*, XXIX (September, 1760), p. 455. See, also, XXIX (September, 1760), p. 455; XXXII (October, 1763), p. 521.

which generally favored the commercial classes. While asking for more representative government than the writers in the *Critical Review, Auditor,* or *Briton* desired, those in the magazine, like many so-called Whig politicians, were not inclined to follow the demands being made by Wilkes and the *North Briton.* If the editors published a political dictionary which ridiculed the language used by Bute's supporters to defame the opposition,[140] they also printed a letter that praised the king's restraint in his use of the prerogative.[141] No foe to Scottish participation in English politics,[142] the editors nevertheless reprinted the *North Briton's* attack on the Scottish ministry.[143]

The same moderation characterized the *London's* treatment of the participants and events in the Wilkes case.[144] Arguing their impartiality,[145] the editors presented an objective account of the struggle between Wilkes and the Crown,[146] and in their comment on the legal battle over the *North Briton* censured both the ministerial and anti-ministerial advocates.[147]

From the minor magazines, too, Wilkes drew little support. Only the editors of the *Universal* expressed their sympathy with his cause. Their earlier sentiments had been only mildly favorable

---

[140] *London,* XXXII (June, 1763), p. 287; XXXII (July, 1763), pp. 378-379.

[141] *London,* XXX (March, 1761), pp. 117-118.

[142] *London,* XXIX (December, 1760), pp. 671-672; XXX (April, 1761), p. 177.

[143] *London,* XXXII (January, 1763), pp. 3-6. Although the *London* also reprinted another excerpt from the *North Briton* in February, 1763 (XXXII, pp. 88-90), in June, 1762 (XXXI, pp. 291-296), the magazine began a review of the political debates, which continued into the next number (pp. 375-380), and deplored the spirit of party and faction in all the essay-journals (pp. 291, 380). The *London* objected specifically to the anti-Scot views (p. 378).

[144] The *London's* treatment of Churchill and Hogarth presented virtually no opinion (XXXI, September, 1762, p. 463; XXXII, July, 1763, pp. 386-387; XXXII, August, 1763, p. 440; XXXII, November, 1763, pp. 614-615).

[145] *London Magazine,* XXXII (October, 1763), p. 549.

[146] *London Magazine,* XXXII (May, 1763), pp. 261-266; XXXII (September, 1763), pp. 499-500; XXXII (October, 1763), pp. 516, 549; XXXII (December, 1763), p. 627.

[147] *London Magazine,* XXXII (1763), Preface.

to the City trade interests, but now, at the end of the war, their account was obviously weighted against Bute's administration. Although they warned against civil discord [148] and writers in the magazine still maintained doubts about the beneficence of mankind,[149] the editors' selection of articles, letters, and poetry indicated an antagonism to Bute's policies. In particular the comments in the *Universal* were opposed to Bute's Cider Tax,[150] but the opposition extended to the minister's political battle against Wilkes and the *North Briton*. Despite an editorial disclaimer of partiality [151] and emphasis upon factual reporting,[152] writers in the magazine defended Wilkes and assailed Bute. Particularly in their selection of poetry, the editors presented Wilkes as a champion against oppression and a martyr for the popular cause,[153] while Bute was portrayed as a treacherous Stuart, whose resignation would prove a blessing to the nation.[154] But the attack on Bute's policies was not limited to the magazine's poetry. In a long communication from "Tacitus Britannicus", Wilkes' opposition to a throne surrounded by corruption was compared with the righteous indignation of the Whigs against the earlier Stuart kings,[155] and in both that communication and an article on political debate, the

[148]   *Universal Magazine*, XXX (January, 1762), pp. 1 ff.

[149]   *Universal Magazine*, XXVI (February, 1760), pp. 66 ff.; XXVII (July, 1760), p. 5; XXVIII (January, 1761), pp. 44 ff.; XXXIII (July, 1763), pp. 3-5; XXXI (July, 1762), p. 6.

[150]   After publishing an abstract from the Cider Act (XXXII, April, 1763, pp. 185-187), the *Universal* printed an extract from the *North Briton*, which anticipated the excise and attacked it, and two letters that severely criticized the act (pp. 187-189). Such treatment is to be contrasted with that of the *British Magazine*, which did not attack the Cider Tax and printed the abstract without comment. See, also, *Universal*, XXXII (April, 1763), p. 214; XXXII (June, 1763), pp. 327 ff.; XXXIII (August, 1763), pp. 93 ff.

[151]   *Universal Magazine*, XXX (June, 1762), p. 322.

[152]   The magazine offered no particular comment on Churchill's work, but published an attack on Hogarth (*Universal*, XXXI, September, 1762, p. 155; XXXIII, November, 1763, pp. 262-265; XXXIII, December, 1763, pp. 323-324; XXXIII, Supplement, 1763, pp. 374-376, 379-380).

[153]   *Universal*, XXXIII (August, 1763), p. 102; XXXIII (December, 1763), p. 325.

[154]   *Universal*, XXXII (April, 1763), p. 214; XXXIII (September, 1763), p. 155.

[155]   *Universal*, XXXIII (July, 1763), pp. 34 ff.

administration was admonished to explain its conduct to the public at large.[156]

Wilkes might also have received the support of the *Grand Magazine*, but that publication was defunct before he challenged the king's prerogative. However, in two letters, the *Grand Magazine*, as early as 1760, presented arguments that foreshadowed the political controversy of 1762-1763, and both statements were similar to the pronouncements later made by the *North Briton*. One, a letter on the king's speech to parliament, had the effect of reminding the monarch of his obligations. According to the letter-writer, the British Constitution, Magna Charta, and the Bill of Rights commanded the sovereign to speak without dissimulation to his people.[157] And, although the editors insisted that they acted to bring moderation to the public,[158] another letter advanced arguments that were more radical than any of the declarations of Wilkes: [159]

In considerations of public concern, the concern is that of the majority; whose emolument is to be regarded, rather than that of the minority.

If the former are slighted and despised by the latter, under the terms, *mob, rabble,* and *headstrong multitude*; why are they so, but because these latter have engrossed their property from them? and moreover, made them beasts of burden; by riding them in the characters of those genteel professions which exact compliance, and command reverence. . . .

No such radical statements were made in the *Universal Museum, Royal,* or *Court*. Although the editors of the three expressed their sympathies for the London commercial classes, none would condone Wilkes' conduct. Insistent upon their impartiality in recording the political debate,[160] the editors of the *Universal Museum* did report the details of the Wilkes case without editorial com-

---

[156] *Universal*, XXXIII (July, 1763), p. 35; XXXIII (September, 1763), pp. 155 ff.
[157] *Grand Magazine*, III (November, 1760), pp. 557-558.
[158] *Grand Magazine*, III (1760), p. iii.
[159] *Grand Magazine*, III (March, 1760), p. 123.
[160] *Universal Museum*, I (January, 1762), p. 26; I (July, 1762), pp. 379-380; II (September, 1763), pp. 486-487.

ment,[161] and gave no strong indication of a preference for Bute or Pitt,[162] other than to object to the popular applause upon which Pitt's power rested [163] and to the slanders used by the anti-ministerial writers in their attack on Bute.[164] Although the editors presented balanced comments on the Cider Act,[165] the disapproval of the age,[166] denigration of human nature,[167] and opposition to clamor by those out of office [168] expressed in the magazine could scarcely have made it a partisan of Wilkes' cause.

While writers in both the *Royal* and *Court* were more sympathetic in their treatment of City trade interests, they were, like those in the *Universal Museum*, disinclined to accept the arguments of Wilkes. For the writers in the *Royal Magazine*, whose sentiments on the peace were mildly in favor of the commercial spokesmen,[169] the Wilkes case was a challenge to the nation's stability. Despite their publication of arguments against the excise,[170] the editors, in their choice of articles, were advocates neither of the king's prerogative nor parliamentary control,[171] but sought instead to achieve a practical balance consistent with man's mixed nature, which was capable of both great good and much

---

[161]   *Universal Museum*, II (May, 1763), pp. 261-264; II (September, 1763), pp. 481-482, 501-502; II (December, 1763), pp. 647-659. The magazine's treatment of Churchill and Hogarth was impartial; although Churchill's poetry received high praise (II, December, 1763, p. 629), his meanness was denounced and his attack on Johnson deplored (I, March, 1762, pp. 168-169). See, also, II (August, 1763), pp. 435-436; II (November, 1763), p. 607; II (December, 1763), pp. 657-658.

[162]   *Universal Museum*, II (October, 1763), pp. 515-517.

[163]   *Universal Museum*, I (April, 1762), pp. 213-214; I (July, 1762), pp. 358-361.

[164]   *Universal Museum*, I (July, 1762), pp. 358-361.

[165]   *Universal Museum*, II (April, 1763), pp. 210 ff.; II (November, 1763), pp. 601-602.

[166]   *Universal Museum*, II (September, 1763), p. 459.

[167]   *Universal Museum*, II (June, 1763), p. 312.

[168]   *Universal Museum*, I (June, 1762), p. 329.

[169]   Comments in the magazine favored Pitt *(Royal*, V, October, 1761, p. 171; V, November, 1761, p. 227), expressed Whig sentiments (VIII, May, 1763, pp. 258-259), and stressed the government's responsibility to commerce (V, November, 1761, p. 233).

[170]   *Royal*, VIII (March, 1763), pp. 148-149; VIII (April, 1763), pp. 195-196; IX (November, 1763), pp. 262-263.

[171]   *Royal*, V (October, 1761), pp. 185-186; V (November, 1761), p. 227.

evil.[172] For such a view, Wilkes' conduct was a clear danger, and while the magazine's treatment of the political conflict was mainly reportorial, its brief editorial comments and selection of material indicated a distrust of the emotions and political activities aroused by both the *North Briton* and the attack on the ministry.[173]

In the same way, the *Court Magazine,* whose regular feature, "The Politician", strongly supported the London commercial group's peace demands, did not defend Wilkes' attack upon the royal prerogative. In miscellaneous articles, in letters, and in "The Politician" itself, the *Court* presented arguments that questioned the propriety of parliamentary resolutions, praised the king's efforts toward political harmony, and insisted upon his constitutional right to choose his own ministers.[174] While the editors published without comment accounts of Wilkes' legal struggle with the Crown,[175] the stress on the king's prerogative was clearly a rebuke to the *North Briton.*

However, in other comments, the writers in the *Court* indicated no predilection for the many abuses of privilege by the aristocracy. "The Politician" scorned despotism, court cabals, and royal favoritism,[176] and the editors devoted a lead article to an attack on the Cider Act, which they regarded as an infringement on individual freedom.[177] In other ways, too, the *Court's* articles, in their scathing remarks about the unlimited powers of justices and the ridiculous notion that noble birth was a sanction for ill-conduct,[178] suggested a disapproval of unlicensed power by an aristocracy.

[172]   *Royal,* II (March, 1760), p. 139; VII (July, 1762), p. 1; VIII (February, 1763), pp. 59-60; VIII (June, 1763), p. 305; IX (August, 1763), p. 63; IX (November, 1763), pp. 251-253.
[173]   *Royal,* VIII (May, 1763), pp. 258-259, 259 ff.; IX (July, 1763), pp. 4-7; IX (December, 1763), pp. 325 ff. The magazine's presentation of Churchill and Hogarth material was impartial (VII, September, 1762, p. 152; IX, July, 1763, p. 47; IX, December, 1763, pp. 321-322).
[174]   *Court,* June, 1762, p. 467; I (January, 1763), p. 25; II (September, 1763), p. 415; II (October, 1763), p. 479.
[175]   *Court,* I (May, 1763), pp. 240-252; II (July, 1763), pp. 350-356; II (September, 1763), pp. 437-439, 439 ff.
[176]   *Court,* February, 1762, p. 254.
[177]   *Court,* II (December, 1763), p. 553.
[178]   *Court,* February, 1762, p. 266; September, 1762, p. 599; II (July, 1763), p. 336; II (December, 1763), p. 596.

Perhaps the discrepancy between its articles on the rights of the Crown and the *Court*'s editorial support of the London trade interests is best explained by a comment in "The Politician", in December, 1761, which compared the body politic and the body natural and concluded, ". . . the least disorder in either demands a cool and temperate regimen, whereas too hasty a method in treating it, very frequently produces an inflammation that greatly endangers the constitution of both . . ":[179] If the articles in the *Court* did not favor Wilkes' attack on the Crown, perhaps the reason was simply the writers' fear of the civil dissension that the challenge aroused. The arguments in the *Briton* and *Auditor* had insisted that trade benefited most from internal harmony, an attitude not restricted to the conservative defenders of Bute's administration.[180]

The conservative defense of Bute was no more outspoken in the magazines than were the attacks on the minister. The very nature of the magazines did not lend itself to such outright partisanship, and even the *British Magazine,* of which Smollett was an editor, dealt rather obliquely with the political crisis. In selecting articles and poetry, which had been favorable to Pitt before Smollett's commitment to Bute's administration,[181] the editors remained sympathetic to Pitt at the time of his resignation.[182] However, after the Great Commoner had attacked Bute's ministry, the magazine published a long allegorical letter denouncing both Pitt and his supporters,[183] but even then the editors did not take a strong political stand. In its direct treatment of the Wilkes case, too, the magazine, with one exception, presented the issues with reportorial objectivity,[184] and only in the publication of one letter was there

---

[179]   *Court*, pp. 165-166.
[180]   The political sympathies of the *Court* have, of course, been discussed in the preceding chapter. However, for particular praise of Pitt, see November, 1761, pp. 128-129. The *Court*'s depiction of the nation's virtues (March, 1762, p. 307) is balanced by less favorable comments in April, 1762, pp. 343 ff. and July, 1763, II, pp. 340 ff.
[181]   *British Magazine*, I (March, 1760), p. 136.
[182]   *British Magazine*, II (October, 1761), pp. 524-525, 552-553.
[183]   *British Magazine*, IV (October, 1763), pp. 534-537.
[184]   *British Magazine*, IV (May, 1763), pp. 245-255; IV (September, 1763), pp. 470-472, 492-493; IV (December, 1763), pp. 638-642.

any indication of unfavorable editorial opinion of Wilkes' conduct.[185]

But if the editors of the *British Magazine* were cautious in expressing their political opinions, they were not reluctant to present their views on government. The comments they selected clearly regarded the times as degenerate,[186] but more than that they considered mankind to be weak and unreliable.[187] Looking upon earthly happiness as a delusion, the writers warned that "in our present state of probation, man should aspire to no higher happiness than an exemption from pain".[188]

In keeping with its articles extolling the chain of being,[189] the editors of the *British Magazine* indicated, by editorial comment and selection, a preference for a conservative social and political order and their opposition to the demands of the London commercial classes.[190] Accordingly, education should have as its objective the maintenance of class distinctions; [191] government by election was a source of evil; [192] and monarchy was the soundest system.[193] Warning that party strife could lead only to civil war,[194] the edi-

---

[185] *British Magazine*, IV (November, 1763), pp. 588-589. In the magazine's treatment of Churchill and Hogarth, the poet's subject matter was berated, although the poetry was praised (II, March, 1761, p. 161; IV, February, 1763, p. 98; IV, August, 1763, pp. 433-434).

[186] *British Magazine*, I (May, 1760), p. 139; II (March, 1761), pp. 130-131.

[187] *British Magazine*, II (December, 1761), pp. 638 ff.; IV (May, 1763), p. 236.

[188] *British Magazine*, II (January, 1761), p. 25.

[189] *British Magazine*, II (December, 1761), p. 640; IV (May, 1763), p. 236.

[190] Even on the matter of the excise, the editors of the *British Magazine* were not sympathetic to the London commercial classes. The absence of critical comment in the magazine's presentation of the facts of the excise was in itself indicative of the editors' attitude. When, for example, the *Universal* printed the abstract of the Cider Act, it was followed by an excerpt from a work that sharply opposed the tax. Nothing of the sort appeared in the *British Magazine* (IV, April, 1763, pp. 173-176; IV, June, 1763, pp. 315-317).

[191] *British Magazine*, II (March, 1761), p. 143; IV (March, 1763), p. 111.

[192] *British Magazine*, IV (February, 1763), p. 93.

[193] *British Magazine*, III (August, 1762), p. 412.

[194] *British Magazine*, IV (January, 1763), p. 23.

tors themselves regarded suspiciously even the public's interest in the conduct of their superiors.[195]

Both women's magazines also presented opinions that strongly favored a conservative social and political order. During the Wilkes controversy, the *Lady's Museum*, edited by Charlotte Lennox and perhaps Hugh Kelly,[196] was no longer being published, but its few earlier comments on society and government were consistent with those on feminine education, and the radical arguments of Wilkes could hardly have found a favorable reception in its pages.[197] Without altogether rejecting women's capacity to learn, its articles limited their necessary training to providing helpmates to husbands whose inherent intelligence was considerably greater than that of the weaker sex.[198] One writer, in particular, cautioned against educating women beyond their class, thereby breaking the natural links in the social chain of being.[199]

It is doubtful, however, that the *Royal Female Magazine* would have refused comfort to Wilkes, for Robert Lloyd, its editor,[200] was a member of the triumvirate on the *North Briton*. Yet despite Lloyd's association with Wilkes and Churchill, the opinions in the magazine, like those in the *Lady's Museum*, which also ran only in 1760, argued against a new social order. The writers in the *Royal Female,* and apparently Lloyd himself, had no more liberal views on feminine education than those expressed by its rival.[201] As for direct political comment, nothing in the *Lady's Museum*

---

[195]   *British Magazine*, IV (1763), Advertisement.
[196]   *CBEL*, II, p. 678. B. M. Stearns, "Early English Periodicals for Ladies", *PMLA*, XLVIII (1933), p. 59, describes the *Lady's Museum* as "the last of the essay-periodicals for women . . .", but actually its form is that of the magazines.
[197]   See, for example, the comment in *Lady's Museum*, I (1760), #2, pp. 134-135, which characterized public beneficence as a guise for self-interest.
[198]   *Lady's Museum*, I (1760), #1, pp. 9-11, #2, pp. 130-131, and #4, p. 295. Such comments should be contrasted with those more liberal statements on female education in the *General Magazine of Arts and Sciences*. The *General Magazine* offered no specific comments on government and will be discussed chiefly in its connection with science.
[199]   *Lady's Museum*, I (1760), #3, p. 183.
[200]   *CBEL*, II, p. 678.
[201]   *Royal Female Magazine*, I (1760), Dedication, and p. vi; I (January, 1760), pp. 1-2.

was more conservative than that in the *Royal Female* which contrasted the best-regulated state with the immorality bred by such a government as the mob-controlled democracy of Athens.[202]

If the writers in magazines, some of which advocated a great change in England's international position, were generally reluctant to support Wilkes in his challenge to the monarchy, then certainly his conduct could not be approved by Burke in the *Annual Register,* whose overall opinions were moderate. Burke expressed a faith in the English institutions that had evolved through "the wisdom of the ages",[203] and regarded the extinguishing of party and party-spirit as essential to the maintenance of civil order.[204] Unwilling to do anything to disturb those institutions that contributed to "the freedom, ease, and quiet of society",[205] Burke offered nothing on the excise which threatened political disruption.[206] The happiness of the state depended on a balanced social order,[207] and comments in the *Annual Register* extolled the English Constitution as the natural instrument for achieving political happiness.[208]

For Wilkes, then, there could have been little sympathy in the *Annual Register* since he represented a threat to the methods of gradual change in the governmental system. While insisting that he was unwilling to pass judgment on the *North Briton* controversy, Burke chose an account which he described as the best that had appeared,[209] an assertion that committed him to the views expressed in his "Chronicle". Those views were most unfavorable to Wilkes and his cause. Wilkes' personal conduct was depicted as questionable at best, and scandalous at worst,[210] and the opinion of the decision concerning Wilkes' writing of seditious libel clearly indicated dissatisfaction with the politician's activities: [211]

202 *Royal Female Magazine,* I(April, 1760), p. 150.
203 *Annual Register,* III, Pt. I (1760), p. 42.
204 *Annual Register,* III, Pt. I (1760), p. 39.
205 *Annual Register,* III, Pt. II (1760), p. 1.
206 *Annual Register,* VI Pt. I (1763), pp. 147 ff.
207 *Annual Register,* IV (Pt. I (1761), p. 82.
208 *Annual Register,* IV, Pt. II (1761), p. 301.
209 *Annual Register,* VI (1763), Preface.
210 *Annual Register,* VI, Pt. I (1763), pp. 143, 147.
211 *Annual Register,* VI, Pt. I (1763), p. 144.

So solemn a decision concerning privilege will, it is hoped, be attended with this good effect, that the ordinary employers of the press will be more cautious in their publications, when they perceive that even the great senators of the realm are not permitted to patronize seditious writings.

While more direct than those in most of the magazines, Burke's comments on the Wilkes controversy were more oblique than those in the reviews, at least the *Critical* and *Monthly*. However, in 1763, the two literary reviews were joined by the *Theatrical Review,* whose political views were only tangential to its main purpose.[212] In their political commentary, its writers were uncommitted to either side. Shocked by the depravity of the age as displayed by actors and audience alike,[213] the writers regarded neither the defenders nor detractors of Bute's ministry from a truly political point of view but rather from the standpoint of taste and decency, both of which were found lacking. Personalities rather than politics dictated the decisions of authors in the *Theatrical Review*. Their attack on the ministry centered upon the unfitness of the king's ability to speak English,[214] and their criticism of David Mallet's *Elvira* was concerned with the play's attempt to popularize the king's minister.[215] In the same way, they condemned a republication of the *Fall of Mortimer* (whose political purpose was to ridicule Bute) not because they disagreed with the politics of the play, but rather because the work was scandalous.[216] Of course, the reviewers assailed Charles Churchill, but their reaction to the co-author of the *North Briton* was caused by his abuse of actors in his *Rosciad* rather than the sentiments in his political journal.[217]

[212] *The Theatrical Review: or Annals of the Drama* first appeared in January, 1763, and continued until the end of the theatrical season in June. For the most part the review presented original material concerned with the history of the theater, lives of the dramatic poets and accounts of their work, biographies of actors, criticism of old and new plays, some gossip and occasional poetry.

[213] *Theatrical Review,* January, 1763, pp. 41-43; February, 1763, p. 48.

[214] *Theatrical Review,* February, 1763, pp. 50 ff.

[215] *Theatrical Review,* February, 1763, pp. 69 ff.

[216] *Theatrical Review,* April, 1763, pp. 149 ff.

[217] *Theatrical Review,* May, 1763, pp. 182 ff.; June, 1763, pp. 217 ff.

Although the writers in the *Critical* and *Monthly*, like those in the *Theatrical Review*, were concerned with more than politics, the nature of their reviewing necessitated political opinions. While neither was committed in the same way that the essay-journals were, both reviews made their political choices according to fundamental attitudes toward the nature of government. Although, for example, politics undoubtedly motivated the *Critical* reviewers' defense of the excise,[218] they were equally impelled by their conservative opposition to clamor.

Basic in their attitude toward government was their distrust of the people and their fear of rapid change. Describing a system in which human virtues were entrusted to restrain the forces of corruption and avarice, one reviewer rejected the possibility of success and forecast disaster.[219] For another writer in the *Critical*, the particular form of government was less important than the stability of order that restrained man's natural impulses, and even the British Constitution was not considered a sufficient guarantee against the vice and corruption that constantly threatened the civil peace.[220] Even in his praise for Pitt's administration prior to the minister's opposition to Bute, the reviewer emphasized especially Pitt's ability to quiet the voices of faction,[221] and in his concern for the monarchy, the writer in the *Critical* was motivated by a desire for the stability provided by the orderliness of inherited succession.[222]

But their principles were nowhere more apparent than in the review's treatment of the *North Briton* controversy. Despite the reviewer's expressed contempt for the *North Briton*,[223] he did not fully approve of the government's action in prosecuting the publishers of the *North Briton* for seditious libel. Although Smollett, the editor of the *Critical,* had formerly been a friend of John

---

[218] *Critical*, XVI (August, 1763), pp. 153-154; XVI (November, 1763), pp. 387-388; XVI (December, 1763), pp. 467-468.
[219] *Critical*, IX (June, 1760), pp. 465-467.
[220] *Critical*, XIII (January, 1762), pp. 1-3.
[221] *Critical*, XII (August, 1761), pp. 108-109.
[222] *Critical*, XV (June, 1763), pp. 453-454.
[223] *Critical*, XVI (November, 1763), p. 397.

Wilkes,[224] the reviewer's objections were not the result of sympathy for Wilkes' political argument, nor were they the outgrowth of a feeling that Number Forty-Five was anything other than indecent.[225] Instead, he disapproved of the government's action because it would encourage the public to look upon the culprits as messiahs. In an extensive article on the *North Briton*,[226] the *Critical* traced the disastrous effect of government censorship in the history of early eighteenth-century politics. As the reviewer pointed out, those journals that received the forebearance of the government died without notice, while those that evoked official action gained popular encouragement. Nevertheless, he examined the numbers of the *North Briton* to demonstrate what he regarded as an unfair, unfounded, and indecent attack upon Lord Bute and his administration.

For the writers in the *Critical,* the political controversy posed a particular problem. The review was committed, of course, to giving an appraisal of contemporary literary productions, among which were the poems of Charles Churchill, who, together with John Wilkes, was responsible for most of the papers in the *North Briton.*

The *Critical* had reason enough besides politics to be antagonistic to Churchill's work, for the poet, even before the political warfare, had engaged in literary controversy with the *Critical.*[227] Yet now, when the political antagonism was at its height, the writers attempted to separate Churchill's political ideas from his poetic talents. In an appraisal of the *Prophecy of Famine,* a work that must have been irksome to the Scottish reviewers of the *Critical,* the reviewer attacked its factious spirit, but fully

---

[224] Smollett sought Wilkes' help at the time of the trial for the Knowles libel, and Wilkes had been a friend, as well, to John Armstrong (Knapp, pp. 217-218). As late as January, 1761, the *Critical* was apparently still friendly toward Wilkes (XI, pp. 73-74).

[225] *Critical,* XV (May, 1763), p. 404.

[226] *Critical,* XVI (October, 1763), pp. 277-285. Nobbe, p. 181, is correct when he writes of the political bias of the *Critical,* but the details of the political controversy do more justice to the periodical.

[227] A. D. McKillop, "Notes on Smollett", *PQ*, VII (1928), pp. 371-374, gives an outline of the controversy between Churchill and the review.

acknowledged the poet's genius.[228] Indeed, the treatment of Churchill's poetry was more than fair; it was accurate. Recognizing the fine, spirited quality of his work, the reviewers were equally aware of his greatest weakness. His genius was given its due, but not without proper limitation: [229]

His genius is notwithstanding so extensive, his expressions so forcible, and his numbers, for the most part, so easy and harmonious, that when, from age and experience, he has learned what Pope calls,

The last and greatest art, the art to blot: he will, probably, be one day ranked amongst the first poets of this nation.

Coming as they did when the political furor was at its peak, the reviewers' judgments were an example of their ability to separate literary criticism from political sympathies.[230]

[228] *Critical*, XV (January, 1763), p. 60. *Cf., Monthly Review*, XXVIII (January, 1763), pp. 56-57.
[229] *Critical*, XVI (July, 1763), p. 67. See, also, XIV (October, 1762), pp. 301-302 and XVI (December, 1763), pp. 446, 446-448. The justice of the *Critical's* comments on Churchill's writing habits is supported by the statement of D. Grant in his introduction to *The Poetical Works of Charles Churchill* (London, 1956), p. xxi: "[Churchill] wrote so much in so short a time that he had little opportunity to revise."
[230] For lines in Churchill's work that refer to the *Critical*, see the following (page references are to Grant's edition):

Apology: p. 38, ll. 43 ff.
pp. 39-41, ll. 69-70, 108-123, 150-169.
p. 45, ll. 298-313.
Night: p. 53, ll. 105-108.
Ghost: p. 75, ll. 389-390.
Author: pp. 249-250, ll. 107-126, 256.

These lines are typical, and the following quotations – the first from the *Apology* and the other from the *Author* – will illustrate the nature of Churchill's attack:

Conscious of guilt, and fearful of the light,
They [the *Critical* reviewers] lurk enshrouded
in the veil of night:
Safe from detection, seize the unwary prey,
And stab, like bravoes, all who come that way.
(*Apology*, p. 38)

How do I laugh, when Publius [Smollett], hoary grown
In zeal for Scotland's welfare, and his own,
By slow degrees, and course of office, drawn
In mood and figure at the helm to yawn,
Too mean (the worst of curses Heaven can send)

Confronted by the same problems as the writers in the *Critical,* the *Monthly* reviewers had a political view far more given to an acceptance of change. Although, as their reaction to Rousseau indicated, they rejected the radical upheaval of the state, they were no advocates of conservative ideals. In their general comments on government and politics, the political writers clearly expressed their opposition to an absolute monarch. Ruffhead, for example, insisted that the king reigned through the grace of human, not divine, law, and he warned against the threat to public liberty that was being bred by political oppression.[231] While he opposed what he considered to be visionary political theories,[232] Ruffhead was not afraid of change. Indeed, Griffiths' chief political writer protested strongly against a system of government that did not take sufficient cognizance of the vast economic and social developments that characterized the new age: [233]

As social and commercial intercourse expand, a variety of cases daily revolve, which must either be provided for by a particular and express law, or referred to discretionary decision. A people however, jealous of liberty, will be cautious to entrust as little as possible to arbitrary discretion. In a free kingdom, the Judges are but the mouths of the law, and the King, no more than the supreme minister to execute its duress.

Convinced that civil rights devolved from natural rights,[234] the *Monthly* reviewers, at least in their general arguments, objected to the absolute prerogative of the king and opposed the extension of his powers.[235] Although the reviewers looked upon hereditary

---

To have a foe; too proud to have a friend;
Erring by form, which blockheads sacred hold,
Ne'er making new faults, and ne'er mending old,
Rebukes my spirit. . . .

Such comments as those by Whitridge, p. 23, and C. E. Jones, "Poetry and the *Critical Review*, 1756-1785", *MLQ,* IX (1948), p. 17, exaggerate the "log-rolling" techniques of the *Critical.*

[231] *Monthly*, XXIX (Appendix, 1763), pp. 551 ff.
[232] *Monthly*, XXVII (September, 1762), pp. 161 ff.
[233] *Monthly*, XXVI (January, 1762), pp. 1-2.
[234] *Monthly*, XXVIII (Appendix, 1763), p. 498 (Kenrick).
[235] *Monthly*, XXVI (January, 1762), p. 2 (Ruffhead).

kingship as being superior to elective,[236] they regarded the monarch as being responsible to the people, whose right it was to dispute and resist his actions if necessary.[237]

Much of the *Monthly* reviewers' general theory was repeated in their commentary on the specific political crisis. Griffiths' writers were convinced that personal liberty was being endangered,[238] and, arguing that no proper administration should object to an inspection of its measures, Kenrick warned: [239]

Certain it is, that as all government hath a natural tendency to despotism, it behoves every nation that hath freedom to lose, to keep a jealous eye on the conduct of its Ministers: and, perhaps, the very virtues of a Prince or his Minister, ought to be additional motives to the vigilance of the Subject.

According to Griffiths himself, this right of the people to interfere personally, "by offering their opinion, in any matter relating to the government", was not to be yielded beyond recall to their representatives.[240] The need for a people to act through representation for the sake of convenience was not to be misconstrued as yielding the individual's natural rights.[241]

But it is perfectly clear from their comments that what the reviewers meant by *people* was the London merchant class. In fact, Griffiths' own criticism of the argument that the citizens yielded their natural rights to representatives was, in part, owing to his belief that the City trade groups were inadequately represented in parliament.[242] Not surprisingly, therefore, Kenrick could praise the London trade interests at the same time that he rejected Wilkes' appeal to the multitude.[243] Despite their wholehearted oppo-

---

[236] *Monthly*, XXVI (March, 1762), p. 165 (John Langhorne).

[237] *Monthly*, XXIX (Appendix, 1763), p. 552 (Ruffhead).

[238] *Monthly*, XXVIII (June, 1763), p. 490 (Kirkpatrick); XXVIII (February, 1763), pp. 115-116, 119 (Kenrick); XXVIII (March, 1763), pp. 236-237.

[239] *Monthly*, XXVIII (March, 1763), p. 210. See, also, XXVII (December, 1762), pp. 469-470.

[240] *Monthly*, XXVIII (February, 1763), p. 140.

[241] *Monthly*, XXVII (December, 1762), pp. 469-470; XXVIII (February, 1763), pp. 141-142 (Griffiths).

[242] *Monthly*, XXVIII (February, 1763), pp. 143-144.

[243] *Monthly*, XXVII (September, 1762), p. 222.

sition to the excise,[244] the reviewers were generally unenthusiastic about the struggle of Wilkes against the Crown,[245] and as Kenrick described it: [246]

... tho' we have the greatest opinion of the cities and corporations of Great Britain, as the nursing fathers or mothers of our constitution, we should be very sorry to see the greatest monarch in the world so far degraded, as to be led about every where in the leading-strings of the multitude.

Their lack of commitment to Wilkes probably made easier the reviewers' task of literary criticism, for, like the writers in the *Critical*, they were expected to review the poetry of Charles Churchill as literature rather than polemics. If anything, their criticism of Churchill's poetry was more severe than the judgment offered by the *Critical*.[247] Despite some favorable comments by Langhorne and Griffiths,[248] interspersed among the derogation, the *Monthly* reviewers indicated a strong dislike for the cruelty of his satire and the lack of discipline and regularity of Churchill's verse.[249] Actually, Langhorne himself confessed his inability to

[244] *Monthly*, XXVIII (May, 1763), p. 396; XXVIII (June, 1763), p. 490; XXIX (September, 1763), pp. 232-233; XXIX (November, 1763), p. 393; XXIX (December, 1763), p. 474.

[245] *Monthly*, XXVIII (March, 1763), pp. 241-242; XXVIII (June, 1763), pp. 487 ff.; XXIX (July, 1763), pp. 78-80; XXIX (August, 1763), p. 157; XXIX (November, 1763), pp. 391-392, 409-411.

[246] *Monthly*, XXVII (September, 1762), p. 222.

[247] Nobbe, pp. 59-60, describes the *Monthly*'s timidity in its reviews. However, the examples cited here indicate that the *Monthly* was not afraid to criticize Churchill. In its review of the *Rosciad*, despite its praise for Churchill's talent, the *Monthly* termed his satire "cruel", and the periodical compared his justification with Pope's: "... the author's severity is more blameable than Mr. Pope's; for he [Pope] had received great provocation from the persons on whom, in just resentment, he let fall the weight of his satire; but the Reverend Author of the *Rosciad* could have no personal inducement to hurt these people in the estimation of the public, on whose favour they entirely depend for subsistence." (XXIV, April, 1761, p. 278.) If the *Monthly* did not come to the aid of the *Critical*, would the other, had the circumstances been reversed, have come to the aid of the *Monthly*?

[248] *Monthly*, XXIX (August, 1763), p. 138 (Langhorne); XXIX (November, 1763), pp. 385 ff., 397 (Griffiths).

[249] *Monthly*, XXIV (April, 1761), p. 278; XXVII (October, 1762), p. 316.

separate his criticism of Churchill's art from his judgment of the poet's morality: [250]

> We enter not into the disputes of parties; all that we have to do is to give our opinion of the literary merit of every new publication that comes before us; yet as citizens, we are sometimes called upon to oppose the torrent of obscenity, which we apprehend to be dangerous to moral virtue; and to obviate the calumny of ingenious satire, which we know to be inconsistent with truth and candour.

In the lack of sympathy displayed by the nominally Whig reviewers on the *Monthly* for the poetry of a man engaged in supposedly Whig partisan politics, there is a further reminder that party labels during the Seven Years' War require careful scrutiny rather than facile acceptance.

[250] *Monthly*, XXIX (Appendix, 1763), p. 532.

V

RELIGION AND THE STATE

In 1762 a visitor to England was struck by the overwhelming interest in politics. Earlier in the century religion had been the chief topic of controversy, but now, he reported, "when strangers struck up a conversation a political discussion was sure to follow".[1] Yet what the observer failed to note was the role that religion played in the political and military drama, which quite naturally had given rise to religious issues. The non-conformity of the Quakers threatened the training of the militia on Sundays and weakened the propagandistic effect of fast days in the early disaster years. Anti-papist feeling was used to encourage both support for Frederick the Great and opposition to the Catholic alliance of France and Austria, while the leveling effect of Methodist preachers was regarded as particularly dangerous in a nation at war.[2] Even the struggle between Wilkes and the Crown had its religious side, for the clerical opposition to Wilkes, including the Whig prelates, weakened his parliamentary support.[3]

What *had* happened was that religious arguments ostensibly

---

[1] R. N. Stromberg, *Religious Liberalism in Eighteenth-Century England* (Oxford, 1954), p. 170. The visitor was Count Frederick Kielmansegge, *Diary of a Journey to England in the Years 1761-1762* (London, 1902), p. 255. See Robbins, p. 324.

[2] Although Wesley was no social or political radical, the appeal of Methodism to the working classes was generally regarded as dangerous. *Cf.*, Stromberg, pp. 163-164; A. C. Underwood, *A History of the English Baptists* (London, 1947), p. 150; and J. Beresford, editor, *The Diary of a Country Parson, the Reverend James Woodeforde, 1756-1781* (London, 1924), p. 30.

[3] N. Sykes, *Church and State in the Eighteenth Century* (Cambridge, 1934), pp. 54-57, 59-60.

had largely ceased to be theological. In the words of Leslie Stephen, "Religion was regarded far less as providing expression for our deepest emotions, or as a body of old tradition invested with the most touching poetical associations, than as a practical rule of life." [4] The Established Church was a temperate institution, whose main business was to preserve religion from the excesses of superstition and the state from the degeneracy of anarchy.[5] Its clerics were involved in politics,[6] and the Church itself generally was regarded as an important means of strengthening the civil authority.[7] Where political alignment earlier had been determined by High and Low Church views, now political conviction as frequently led to Church attitudes.[8] Even belief in the importance of the Establishment was sometimes as much a matter of political concern as a sign of faith.[9]

To some, like Hoxie Fairchild, the Church of England in this period seems a failure: its inspirational power subservient to its social function; its fervor moderated by calm acceptance.[10] But such an argument neglects the reasons for the apparent lack of religious inspiration. No longer did the Anglican Church have to defend its theological position. It had come to accept naturally what the Archbishop of York had maintained earlier in the century: [11]

The Church of England is undoubtedly both as to doctrine and worship the purest church that is at this day in the world: the most orthodox in faith, the freest on the one hand from idolatry and superstition, and on the other hand from freakishness and enthusiasm, of any now extant.

[4] Stephen, II, p. 2.
[5] Sykes, *Church and State*, p. 284.
[6] Sykes, *Church and State*, pp. 39-41, 51, 81, 90, 147 ff. N. Sykes, "The Church", in *Johnson's England*, I, p. 17.
[7] Schilling, pp. 83-85, 87-88, 91-92, 186-188; Laski, pp. 80-81.
[8] Stromberg, p. 137.
[9] Stephen, I, p. 375.
[10] H. N. Fairchild, *The Noble Savage* (New York, 1928), p. 413. See, also, the same author's *Religious Trends in English Poetry* (New York, 1939-1957), II, pp. 13, 50-51.
[11] The quotation from Archbishop Sharp of York is given in Sykes, "The Church", in *Johnson's England*, I, p. 15. Sykes makes the point that the statement represents the orthodox view in the middle of the century.

Whatever challenge to doctrine existed, the Church responded confidently. In meeting the enthusiasm of the Methodists and the skepticism of the deists, most of its leaders were unafraid of putting the tenets of their faith to the test of reason. The widespread interest in scientific methods and discoveries became the tool, and the Church willingly used the arguments of natural religion to demonstrate the validity of revealed. Never stopping to consider that their religion might not be supported by scientific evidence, many of the orthodox readily employed the material of natural history to verify the Scriptures. After all, the science of Newton had demonstrated the orderliness, magnitude, and even the beneficence of God, and prior to the development of modern geology about 1760, no conflict between science and religion seemed apparent.[12]

In two areas, then, religious comment was abundant, those of the relationships between Church and state and those between science and religion. On the first, the orthodox point of view insisted that the proper working order of society was dependent upon the moral basis of religion, and a challenge to one represented a threat to the other. On the relationship of science and religion, the orthodox position was less clear. While even the most conservative believed in the reasonableness of Christianity and in the importance of individual acceptance of Protestant doctrine, the more liberal view was inclined to insist upon the primacy of reason and to argue that natural revelation was in itself sufficient.[13]

These are the lines, then, on which the religious orthodoxy of the comments by the various periodical writers must be examined.

[12]   Stromberg, pp. 26-27. Much of the background of this relationship between science, particularly geology, and religion has been discussed in Francis C. Haber, *The Age of the World* (Baltimore, 1959). Haber's evidence – without comment on the periodical literature – leads to the same conclusions as this study.

[13]   Stromberg, p. 62, notes, "[The] deists were prepared to subject the credentials of Christianity to as searching an examination as was then possible." More to the point, however, is C. L. Becker, *The Heavenly City of the Eighteenth-century Philosophers* (New Haven, Conn., 1932), p. 53: "Christian, deist, atheist – all acknowledge the authority of the book of nature; if they differ it is only as to the scope of its authority, as to whether it merely confirms or entirely supplants the authority of the old revelation."

Both religion and science were certainly important topics, particularly in the magazines. Although Carlson has described the essays on religion in the *Gentleman's Magazine* as indicating no specific point of view so much as they do a reflection of public opinion,[14] the comments on nonconformity and the relationships of Church and state and those of religion and science *do* reveal not only the climate of opinion but the particular editorial attitude of the magazine just as they do of all the other periodicals.[15]

Perhaps the best introduction to their religious position and view of Church-state relationships is in the comments of those periodical writers who took note of Voltaire. The evidence does not support Bernard Schilling's contention that although some opposition was expressed in the early 1750's, English opinion was not shocked by Voltaire's irreligion prior to the publication of *Candide*, but by 1763, his religious views were in grave general disrepute.[16] Instead, the comments in the periodicals indicate a greater variety at all times in their treatment of Voltaire than Schilling suggests.

On this subject the essay-journals are the least informative periodicals. Serious religious comment was not to be expected from those that adhered to the tradition established by Addison and Steele, and only the *Connoisseur* and *Bee* took even cursory notice of Voltaire.[17]

In the magazines, however, treatment of Voltaire was abundant and complex. His work aroused controversy, which editors used to advantage. Although a writer in the *Gentleman's* had praised the *History of the War of 1741*,[18] when an attack on Voltaire as an historian appeared, the editors printed it in full.[19] But even when their own comments berated him, they used excerpts from his writing to appeal to reader interest. After the publication of *Can-*

[14] Carlson, p. 124.
[15] Despite his remarks cited in the above note, Carlson, p. 18, seems to recognize the way in which the magazines expressed their religious views.
[16] Schilling, pp. 210, 212, 213, 216.
[17] *Connoisseur*, #126 (June 24, 1756), p. 170; *Bee*, #1 (October 6, 1759), pp. 28-30.
[18] *Gentleman's Magazine*, XXVI (April, 1756), p. 200.
[19] *Gentleman's Magazine*, XXVIII (November, 1758), pp. 521-522; XXVIII (December, 1758), pp. 577-578; XXVIII (Supplement, 1758), pp. 619-620.

dide, while they scorned his vanity, they reprinted his latitudinarian arguments,[20] laments about religious persecution,[21] and defense against malicious "libels".[22] Only when it came to face the
religious question directly in a review of *Candide* was the criticism
in the *Gentleman's* unrestrained.[23] Ridiculing Voltaire's reasoning, the writer insisted that the "malapert" metaphysician had
imperfectly understood the meaning of "whatever is, is right".[24]

Somewhat more conservative than the comments in the *Gentleman's,* those in the *London,* as early as 1757, objected to the conduct of Voltaire,[25] and the editors printed a letter criticizing his
scholarship, morality, and candor.[26] Nevertheless, until *Candide*
appeared, the magazine continued to contribute to his popularity
by plundering from his work.[27] With the publication of *Candide,*
however, the reviewer in the *London* condemned not only Voltaire's "invective . . . against mankind in general, . . . [and] against
Divine Providence itself", but also his aesthetic failure.[28]

The comments in the *London* show that some of the opposition
to Voltaire before *Candide* was stronger than Schilling had suggested; those in the *Gentleman's* indicate that the total rejection
after that book was incomplete; but the evidence in both magazines supports Schilling's assertion about the condemnation of the
novel. However, the remarks in at least one minor magazine re-
fute Schilling's contentions about the absolute opposition to Voltaire after the appearance of *Candide,* and to the work itself.[29] In

20   *Gentleman's Magazine,* XXXI (February, 1761), pp. 54-55.
21   *Gentleman's Magazine,* XXXII (June, 1762), pp. 255-258; XXXII (July,
1762), pp. 312-313.
22   *Gentleman's Magazine,* XXXII (August, 1762), pp. 347-349.
23   The *Gentleman's,* XXXI (June, 1761), p. 286, listed the publication of
the spurious continuation of *Candide,* giving Voltaire as author.
24   *Gentleman's,* XXIX (May, 1759), pp. 233-235.
25   *London,* XXVI (February, 1757), pp. 93-94.
26   *London,* XXVI (May, 1757), pp. 225-226. In July, 1758 (XXVII, pp.
364-365), the *London* printed an attack on Voltaire in its poetry.
27   *London,* XXVI (February, 1757), pp. 78-79, 82-85; XXVI (March,
1757), pp. 129-132; XXVI (December, 1757), pp. 598-599.
28   *London,* XXVIII (May, 1759), p. 264.
29   *Universal Magazine,* XXI (November, 1757), pp. 220-221; XXIV (May,
1759), pp. 268-269 (excerpt from *Candide,* no comment); XXV (July, 1759),
pp. 15-19 (from *Occasional Letters* – "To prevent the mistaken notions

its very first notice of Voltaire, the *Grand Magazine* gave a long
and favorable account of *Candide*, stressing its literary merits.[30]
After that, the editors of the *Grand* – published by Griffiths,
whose *Monthly Review* has commonly been depicted as less orthodox than the rival *Critical* – continued to publish Voltaire's
work, generally with high praise for his artistic talents and a defense of his philosophy.[31] Particularly in praise for the *Henriade,*
which the magazine printed in parts, the writer in the *Grand* expressed his approval· [32]

... the poet treats of the constitution of the universe, of the laws of
nature, and morality, like a modern philosopher; with the sentiments
of a man of humanity, and a person of superior genius. He seems to
render all his knowledge conducive to the great end of inspiring a
love of mankind, and a general horror for cruelty, and fanaticism.

But even more to the point, after its own laudatory notice, the
magazine offered a letter defending the book, absolving Voltaire
of all impiety, and charging that the critics, even the more moderate *Monthly* reviewers, had been unfair in their censure.[33]

Censure might take a less obvious form, as it did in the *Annual
Register*. Burke's failure to review the book was itself adverse

---

some may entertain from the reading of M. de Voltaire's *Candid, or All
for the Best*"); XXV (November, 1759), pp. 227-229; XXVII (November,
1760), pp. 246 ff.; XXVII (December, 1760), pp. 287 ff., XXVII (Supplement, 1760), pp. 346 ff; XXVIII (January, 1761), pp. 9 ff., 43; XXVIII
(February, 1761), pp. 67 ff. – All references to Voltaire in the *Universal
Visiter* were favorable, #1 (January, 1756), pp. 28 ff.; #2 (February, 1756),
pp. 74 ff. The comment in the *Weekly Magazine*, #10 (June 17, 1758), pp.
315 ff., is not that of the magazine, but it is an unfavorable excerpt. Both
the *Literary Magazine*, II (September, 1757), pp. 434 ff. and II (November,
1757), pp. 523 ff., and the *Universal Museum*, II (August, 1763), pp. 407 f.,
published without comment extracts from Voltaire's work. The one comment in the *British Magazine*, II (January, 1761), p. 45, called his *Critical
Essays on Dramatick Poetry*, "Sensible and sprightly". *Christian's Magazine*, II (April, 1761), p. 166, assailed his attempt to discredit Christianity.
[30] The *Grand Magazine of Magazines*, II (May, 1759), pp. 288-292; II
(June, 1759), pp. 329-334; III (July, 1759), pp. 17-25, reprinted the epitome
given in the *Grand Magazine*.
[31] *Grand Magazine*, II (July 1759), p. 375; II (August, 1759), p. 416; II
(October, 1759), p. 529; III (December, 1760), pp. 606-607.
[32] *Grand Magazine*, II (August, 1759), p. 425.
[33] *Grand Magazine*, II (October, 1759), pp. 533-535.

criticism since he reserved comment for works that he felt merited public attention.[34] Indeed, references to Voltaire were limited to some unfavorable remarks in the "Chronicle" and a satire, approved by the editor, in the section of "Characters".[35] Moreover, by refusing to print extracts from Voltaire's work, as magazine editors were doing, Burke protested silently against contributing to his reputation.

Similar silent treatment was not to be expected from the major literary reviews, which had committed themselves to giving an account of all publications.[36] The *Critical* and *Monthly* because of their policy had to assess Voltaire's literary merits as well as his philosophy.

Even in the treatment of Voltaire by the orthodox *Critical Review*, Schilling's account can be seen as not altogether accurate. The attack upon Voltaire's religious views was pronounced prior to the publication of *Candide,* and even after the appearance of that work, the reviewers were concerned with proper assessment of his literary talent. Although in 1756 Samuel Derrick, Smollett's assistant, discussed Voltaire's poetry in glowing terms,[37] and early the next year Voltaire's *History of the Voyages of Scarmantado* was described as having "marks of genius",[38] by the end of 1757, articles in the *Critical* were attacking him.[39] By October of the following year, his blasphemy had irked the reviewers, and his *Maid of Orleans* was said to "revolt the imagination".[40] When *Candide* appeared, there could be no question of the *Critical* reviewer's verdict, and the book was met with a solid rebuff, but one which hardly showed an understanding of the work: [41]

[34]   The purpose of the Book Review section was described in the *Annual Register* itself. See I (1758), pp. vi-vii.
[35]   In *Annual Register*, I (1758), pp. 237-239, Burke published among his "Characters" what he called a satirical but just attack on Voltaire. Then in IV, Pt. I (1761), p. 96, he commented unfavorably on Voltaire in the "Chronicle".
[36]   *Theatrical Review*, February, 1763, pp. 49-50, criticized Voltaire's tastelessness in *Candide*.
[37]   *Critical*, I (June, 1756), p. 456.
[38]   *Critical*, III (February, 1757), p. 176.
[39]   *Critical*, IV (November, 1757), pp. 385-386.
[40]   *Critical*, VI (October, 1758), p. 346.
[41]   *Critical*, VII (June, 1759), p. 550.

The writings of Mr. Voltaire are as much in fashion among the English as Chinese furniture, and some of them as fantastic. [He] has now published a satire upon the Creator of the Universe; for, such we take to be the design of his *Optimisme,* if he had any design at all, in writing this performance.

But derision of Voltaire as a free-thinker and resentment of his treatment of Milton and Shakespeare,[42] did not prevent one writer in the *Critical* from attempting to distinguish between the anti-Christ and the writer whose work Smollett, editor of the review, had engaged to translate for the entertainment of the English public.[43] To balance the condemnation of his skepticism, blasphemy, and irreligion, even after the appearance of *Candide,* there were statements in praise of his genius, style, and manner.[44]

For the *Monthly* reviewers, Voltaire's genius, certainly before *Candide,* was almost always enough to forgive his faults.[45] Before the publication of *Candide,* the novelist John Cleland, in the *Monthly,* defended his religious views,[46] and later, when Voltaire's reputation in England was supposedly at its lowest, not only did Robert Lloyd continue to praise his lively imagination,[47] but William Kenrick refused to accept the general condemnation of his principles and morals.[48]

Only in Kenrick's account of *Candide* was there any real condemnation of his character and talent,[49] and even Kenrick's treatment was certainly milder than the denunciation in the *Critical.* Instead of criticizing the novel as an attempt to undermine religious faith or "a satire upon the Creator of the Universe", he regarded it as an expression of Voltaire's "detestation of mankind

[42] *Critical,* IX (March, 1760), pp. 221, 227.
[43] *Critical,* XI (February, 1761), p. 158.
[44] The *Critical* reviewer accepted as genuine the spurious continuation of *Candide* (XII, August, 1761, pp. 131-138). None of the periodical writers detected the forgery.
[45] *Monthly,* XIV (February, 1756), p. 104 (Berkenhout); XIV (April, 1756), pp. 292-295; XIV (January, 1756), pp. 64-66 (Kirkpatrick).
[46] *Monthly,* XIV (Appendix, 1756), pp. 579-580.
[47] *Monthly,* XXV (September, 1761), p. 224.
[48] *Monthly,* XXIV (March, 1761), p. 139 [199]; XXIX (October, 1763), pp. 273-274.
[49] The spurious second volume of *Candide,* ascribed to Voltaire, was also attacked, XXV (August, 1761), p. 155.

in general" and saw his object, quite correctly, as an endeavor "to invalidate the opinion of some philosophers, respecting the moral and providential economy of the universe, viz. that *all is for the best*". Again, quite accurately, Kenrick distinguished between this philosophical doctrine and Pope's "whatever is, is right", claiming that the latter was not Voltaire's target.[50]

The variety of responses to Voltaire's work does more than invalidate Schilling's generalization; it suggests the differences to be found in the periodicals' pronouncements on religion in general and on the relationship of religion and the state in particular. To some extent the characteristics of a periodical type determined its treatment of religious material, but within each type, there were individual differences. Even magazine editors could indicate their attitudes, if not directly, then by their selection of material.

On the relationship of state and Church and in serious consideration of religion, it has been pointed out that the essay-journals were the least meaningful periodicals. Most of their comments on religion were expressions of fashionable commitment to the Establishment, popular opposition to Popery, conventional disdain for enthusiasm, or satirical denunciation of decadence.

Of all the non-political essay-journalists,[51] those in the *Connoisseur,* which achieved some reputation for its social and moral comment,[52] considered religion most seriously. Yet even they regarded the issues as social or aesthetic rather than theological. They related the decline in taste to the decline in religion,[53] and their derision of the Methodists was less doctrinal than a commentary on manners.[54] Indeed, in their discussion of religious

[50] *Monthly,* XXI (July, 1759), p. 84.
[51] *Centinel,* #2 (January 6, 1757), p. 5, offers a conventional religious statement.
[52] See, for example, *Critical Review,* III (April, 1757), pp. 314-315. However, Drake, II, p. 319, is correct in describing the *Connoisseur* as "critic on the manners and minor morals of mankind . . .".
[53] *Connoisseur,* #113 (March 25, 1756), pp. 100-102, 104 (John, Earl of Cork and Orrery); #118 (April 29, 1756), p. 129. Much of this unidentified comment was undoubtedly the work of the editors, Colman and Thornton, but as E. R. Page, *George Colman the Elder* (New York, 1935), pp. 27 ff. has pointed out, it is impossible to distinguish between their authorship.
[54] *Connoisseur,* #118 (April 29, 1756), p. 132; #123 (June 3, 1756), p. 155; #126 (June 24, 1756), p. 173.

practices, the writers turned the essay-journal into a conduct book rather than a religious tract.[55] However, in two comments they suggested their religious position. One, the conclusion to an ironic account of the "vulgar errors" that constituted true faith, reminded those freethinkers who believed in the chance creation of the universe that since everything in the world had been created by chance, perhaps chance had also made a hell.[56] The other comment seriously considered the relationship of conduct and religious practices. Despite this insistence that forms and ceremonies served to remind men of their sense of duty, the writer's warning against superstitious belief and acknowledgment of virtue without religious devotion suggest how much liberalism had entered into what was declared orthodox faith in the period: [57]

It must be allowed indeed, that if a man could constantly employ his mind in holy meditation, exercise the virtues, and believe the mysteries of our religion, he would be a true Christian, though he never complied with any outward forms, or so much as repeated a single prayer.

While the contributor both doubted the likelihood of such conduct and maintained the need to accept "the mysteries" of Christianity, his comment presented little defense against the deists' attack on the formalities of religion.

Neither the writers in the *Old Maid* nor the *World* had as much to say on religion as those in the *Connoisseur*. Apart from an argument in the *Old Maid* that true religion consisted in virtuous conduct,[58] discussion in both periodicals was limited to ironic remarks relating religious excesses to aesthetic and social faults.[59]

[55] *Connoisseur*, #106 (February 5, 1756), pp. 67-68; #109 (February 26, 1756), pp. 78-83.

[56] *Connoisseur*, #109 (February 26, 1758) pp. 83-84.

[57] *Connoisseur*, #106 (February 5, 1756), p. 66. See, also, *Connoisseur*, #106 (February 5, 1756), pp. 65-66.

[58] *Old Maid*, #22 (April 10, 1756) p. 184.

[59] *Old Maid*, #32 (June 19, 1756), pp. 262 ff. Straus, p. 185, notes that the *World* deliberately imitated the *Spectator* and was more concerned with the fashions and follies of mankind than with serious religious or political comment. See *World*, #163 (February 12, 1756), pp. 150 ff.; #168 (March 18, 1756), pp. 179 ff. (Soame Jenyns). The description of the Lisbon earthquake as a sign of "Divine displeasure" (#162, February 5, 1756, p. 146) is apparently ironic.

The same lack of serious discussion characterized Goldsmith's comments in 1759. Those in the *Busy Body* followed the conventional social criticism of the other essay-journals,[60] while his remarks in the *Bee* went only slightly further. In his famous essay on the "Time Machine", which appeared in the *Bee,* Goldsmith first excluded David Hume from the company of the great not because his position on religion was wrong, but because "he who disturbs religion is a blockhead".[61] Even in his criticism of Toland's atheism, Goldsmith lamented the moral consequences less than the literary effect.[62]

If the literary essay-journals, in general, were casual in their treatment of religion, the political essay-journals, concerned with the specific issues that had called them into being, were all but silent on the subject.[63] Only the writers for the *Monitor,* perhaps because its existence was not tied to any immediate need, expressed concern for religion. Religion for them served as useful propaganda to excite an idealistic fervor in a war that was being fought mainly for commercial interest. Throughout the disastrous early years of the fighting, Beckford's writers insisted upon strict compliance with the Established faith, but argued for it in terms that were military or political rather than theological. Both letters and articles described the alliance against the British as a combined effort of the Popish states to abolish the Protestant religion; [64] but as defenders of the faith the writers urged not a reliance upon the Divine Will but rather an effort to take Providence and turn it in the right direction.[65]

---

[60] *Busy Body*, #3 (October 13, 1759), pp. 17-18; #4 (October 16, 1759), p. 20. *Bee,* #4 (October 27, 1759), p. 85; #7 (November 17, 1759), pp. 181, 184.
[61] *Bee,* #5 (November 3, 1759), p. 135.
[62] *Bee,* #8 (November 24, 1759), p. 224.
[63] *Test,* #18 (March 1, 1757), pp. 99-100, offers casual support of the superiority of orthodox doctrine. Religion in the later quarrel between the *North Briton* and its adversaries has greater importance for the arguments about language than those about faith.
[64] *Monitor,* #124 (December 3, 1757), p. 754; #138 (March 11, 1758), pp. 834-835; #144 (April 22, 1758), p. 870; #175 (November 25, 1758), p. 1060.
[65] *Monitor,* #227 (November 24, 1759), pp. 1370-1372.

Despite such political liberalism,[66] whatever religious attitude seemed to challenge the speedy prosecution of the war was assailed on religious grounds. Blasphemy and atheism in young officers [67] and irreligion in the state [68] were condemned on a practical rather than a political basis. Quakers and Moravians, in their opposition to training the militia on Sundays and to observing fast days to gain God's support in battle, were cowardly traitors whose conduct threatened not the morality but the security of the state: [69]

Is not there reason to suspect the loyalty, as well as religion of a people, who would not, in a devout and solemn manner, humble themselves, and send up their prayers and supplications by the command and example of their king, to the Divine Majesty, for the safety and prosperity of his kingdoms and dominions? and does not any evasion or equivocation to excuse their contempt, or neglect of so religious and necessary a duty, as at this time to implore the Almighty's protection and blessing upon our fleets and armies, call aloud upon the government to examine into those principles, upon which they pretend to maintain such absurd and dangerous doctrines, and what, in other subjects, would be justly suspected of disaffection, and a ripeness to join in the first act of rebellion?

Not only the Quakers, but Jews and Dissenters were objects of suspicion,[70] and naturally when the religious practices of a quasi-neutral people like the Dutch could provide him with arguments that condemned a commercial rival, the writer in the *Monitor* was quick to take advantage. He deplored the laxity of a church gov-

---

[66] The *Monitor* is a good example of the danger that Stromberg, p. 124, has described in equating a liberal political tradition with a liberal tradition in religion. Indeed, a lack of strong religious feeling could easily permit the use of the Church in practical affairs.

[67] *Monitor*, #129 (January 7, 1758), pp. 783-784.

[68] *Monitor*, #137 (March 4, 1758), p. 831.

[69] *Monitor*, I (February 14, 1756), p. 254. See, also, *Monitor*, I (March 20, 1756), pp. 300-312; #138 (March 11, 1758), p. 833.

[70] *Monitor*, II (February 26, 1757), pp. 311, 316; #151 (June 10, 1758), pp. 914-915; #175 (November 18, 1758), p. 1050. A letter (#119, October 29, 1757, p. 720) defended the Dissenters. The use of a letter opposed to the views of the periodical was unusual for the *Monitor*, which commonly employed the epistolary device so that it is generally impossible to distinguish between genuine and fictional letters.

ernment that depended on the whims of the state and its ministers, while the nation itself became: [71]

... an asylum for blasphemers and for the most wicked livers, who have been exiled, or have fled from the justice of other nations. The Deist and the Atheist reject the Scriptures, and defy God publicly with impunity in the United Provinces. . . .

In contrast with the essay-journals, the magazines provide an abundance of comment on religion and its relation to the state. The multitude of letter-writers and the heavy borrowing from current works make difficult a determination of the particular editorial views of a magazine, but the very willingness to present a variety of opinion suggests a rather latitudinarian religious attitude, particularly in the *Gentleman's Magazine.*

Its editors made no effort to insist on the orthodox practices of the Established Church, whose ritual was variously described as necessary and unnecessary in the selection of essays.[72] One writer, at least, in a description of the customs of mankind, denied that salvation depended on an acceptance of Christianity,[73] while letters and articles stressed the importance of good works with or without the benefits of religious ritual.[74]

Not even the pressures of the war, which was being described by others in religious terms, produced any strong sentiments in support of the orthodox faith or a crusade against minority religious groups.[75]

---

[71]   *Monitor,* #169 (October 14, 1758), p. 1020.

[72]   *Gentleman's Magazine,* XXX (April, 1760), pp. 171-172; XXX (May, 1760), pp. 226-227.

[73]   *Gentleman's Magazine,* XXVI (May, 1756), pp. 229-230.

[74]   *Gentleman's Magazine,* XXVI (September, 1756), p. 431; XXVII (November, 1757), pp. 493-495; XXX (October, 1760), pp. 468-469; XXXIII (January, 1763), p. 28; XXXIII (February, 1763), pp. 60-61.

[75]   For letters deploring the bigotry and zeal of the Roman Catholics, see *Gentleman's Magazine,* XXVI (February, 1756), pp. 68-70; XXVI (March, 1756), pp. 111-113; XXVII (April, 1757), pp. 148-149; XXVII (June, 1757), pp. 254-256; XXIX (February, 1759), pp. 55-56; XXIX (March, 1759), pp. 129-130; XXIX (June, 1759), pp. 269-270; XXX (January, 1760), pp. 6-7. However, the *Gentleman's,* XXIX (March, 1759), pp. 126-127, printed a strong reply. For the balanced presentation of comment on Dissenters, see *Gentleman's Magazine,* XXVI (June, 1756), pp. 286-287; XXVIII (March, 1758), pp. 101-102; XXVIII (December, 1758), p. 599;

Comments on the Quakers were particularly sympathetic,[76] and when the magazine did offer criticism of the sect, it was reasonably stated and raised questions that were not religious but civil: [77]

Every civil society has a right to appoint certain laws and regulations, as the conditions upon which any individual shall be permitted to participate in common with other members, of the benefits and inconveniences which result from the mutual compact, by which such society was formed provided such laws and regulations enjoin nothing that is contrary to the law of nature, the express will of God, or the laws of a larger community, ot which such society is part.

While the comment clearly suggests the writer's dissatisfaction with the Quakers' objections to the civil demands, like the two letters advocating separation of Church and state which the magazine published,[78] his tone is urbane and reasonable.

Though not severely orthodox, the comments in the *London Magazine* were more conservative than those in the *Gentleman's*. Despite the abundance of religious controversy that the editors printed, particularly about the relationship of Church and state, their own editorial attitude is not more easily discovered than that of its rival. Much of the comment came in the many letters that were published in what seems an obvious attempt to create reader interest by encouraging argument; but only in an occasional book review or note did the editors reveal their own point of view. Perhaps the best contrast with the *Gentleman's* is expressed in the *London*'s attack on dissenters who sought to prevent the exercise

---

XXXI (May, 1761), p. 204; XXXI (June, 1761), pp. 251, 262-264; XXXI (July, 1761), pp. 299-300; XXXI (August, 1761), p. 345; XXXI (September, 1761), p. 395; XXXI (October, 1761), pp. 445-447; XXXI (November, 1761), p. 500; XXXI (December, 1761), pp. 570-572; XXXII (March, 1762), pp. 112-113.

[76] For defenses of the Quakers, see *Gentleman's Magazine*, XXVI (April, 1756), pp. 168-169; XXVII (February, 1757), p. 56; XXIX (June, 1759), p. 283. Quaker objections to Sunday training of the militia were printed without disparagement in the *Gentleman's*, XXVI (November, 1756), pp. 509-510; XXVII (January, 1757), pp. 29-30.

[77] *Gentleman's Magazine*, XXVII (April, 1757), p. 156.

[78] *Gentleman's Magazine*, XXVII (May, 1757), pp. 221-222; XXVII (June, 1757), pp. 270-272.

of the militia on Sundays. In its "History of the Last Session of Parliament", the writer defended the practice: [79]

It is not to be wondered, that the fanatical pharisaical spirit of some of the dissenters, especially the most ignorant sort, should prevail with them to oppose exercising the militia after divine service on Sunday; but it is to be hoped, that the members of the Church of England are generally of opinion, that the serving of mankind, or our country, is a serving of God; and that a man, who spent one half of his time on Sunday, in qualifying himself to defend his country in time of danger, would be a better Christian, than he who spent the whole of it, in attending prayers, singing psalms, or hearing even the best sermons, and thereby neglecting that other duty which he owes to mankind and his country, as well as to his Creator.

Of course, to call the principles of the *London* more conservative than those of the *Gentleman's* is not altogether accurate. While the objections to dissent were in support of the Establishment, the writers in the magazine, like those in the *Monitor*, were concerned with the practical purposes of religion. The attitude was consistent with their concern for a religion that would protect liberty and property, for such a religion would be in accord with "common sense and common reason"! [80] For the editors of the *London* the true principles of the Established Church were those which prepared a monarch to act in the best interests of his country when engaging in negotiations to conclude a peace.[81] Yet, in conducting religious debate without clearly indicating their own opinion, the editors, like those in the *Gentleman's,* gave full expression to the variety of views in the state.[82]

[79] *London*, XXVI (December, 1757), p. 577.
[80] *London Magazine*, XXIX (June, 1760), pp. 290-291.
[81] *London Magazine*, XXIX (1760), Preface. Similar views were expressed in letters published in the *London*, XXVIII (July, 1759), pp. 386-387; XXIX (October, 1760), pp. 449-450; XXIX (Appendix, 1760), pp. 689-690; XXX (March, 1761), p. 131.
[82] Compare the two book reviews in the *London*, XXIX (October, 1760), p. 559 and XXIX (November, 1760), p. 616, attacking the ignorance and subversiveness of the Methodists, with the editors' willingness to present debate on the subject: *London*, XXVI (October, 1757), pp. 482-484; XXVI (November, 1757), p. 527; XXVI (December, 1757), pp. 588-589; XXVI (Appendix, 1757), pp. 636-637; XXVII (January, 1758), pp. 38-39; XXVII (February, 1758), p. 81; XXIX (July, 1760), pp. 354-355, 364-366; XXIX (November, 1760), pp. 588-590; XXIX (Appendix, 1760), pp. 688-689;

Like the *Gentleman's,* the *London* was catering to the varied
views of its large reading audience, and the editorial attitude toward religion must be sifted from the mass of comments. With
some of the minor magazines, especially the *Christian's,* such a
job is unnecessary. The *Christian's,* first of the religious periodicals that were to develop rapidly after 1760,[83] was Anglican and
conservative,[84] and its editor, Dr. William Dodd, presented the
Church's own views on religion.

Dodd's main design was to popularize theology for the layman,
and both letters and articles made clear the editorial attitude on
the relationship between Church and state. Making evident its
agreement with a correspondent, the magazine printed his argument that "[religion], in a well-regulated state, ought to be adapted to the constitution of the government, without regard to the
dreams of bigots, or the talk of enthusiasts".[85] Despite its own
admittedly Anglican theological concern, the magazine ascribed
to Christianity, in general, a practical as well as spiritual importance, since of all systems it had proved "infinitely of [most] efficacy in perpetuating and establishing good government . . .".[86] To

---

XXX (January, 1761), pp. 19-21, 33-36; XXX (February, 1761), pp. 88-91;
XXX (March, 1761), pp. 145-146; XXX (July, 1761), pp. 356-358; XXXI
(April, 1762), pp. 190-191. Their only comment on the controversy explained the reasons for editing the correspondence, XXIX (August, 1760),
p. 440. – Roman Catholics were attacked in letters to the *London,* XXIX
(August, 1760), p. 410; XXIX (September, 1760), pp. 443-445; XXXI
(August, 1762), p. 429; XXXII (December, 1763), pp. 623-625, but a
defense was also printed, XXIX (September, 1760), pp. 445-446, and drew
a letter in response, XXIX (November, 1760), pp. 584-585. – For other
examples of the editors' presentation of correspondence that either ran
counter to their own opinions or merely reflected disagreement of correspondents among themselves, see *London,* XXV (April, 1756), pp. 168-171;
XXV (June, 1756), pp. 261-262; XXV (August, 1756), p. 384; XXIX (October, 1760), p. 543; XXIX (November, 1760), p. 614; XXIX (Appendix,
1760), pp. 692-693; XXX (March, 1761), pp. 132-133, 140-141; XXX
(April, 1761), pp. 197-198; XXX (July, 1761), pp. 354-356; XXX (August,
1761), p. 432.
[83]   F. E. Mineka, *The Dissidence of Dissent* (Chapel Hill, 1944), p. 36.
[84]   Mineka, p. 37. The editor of the *Christian's Magazine,* the Rev. Dr.
William Dodd, was later executed for forgery.
[85]   *Christian's,* I (July, 1760), p. 121.
[86]   *Christian's,* IV (January, 1763), p. 24.

support this point, the *Christian's Magazine* offered the evident superiority of Christian laws over those drawn by the wisest and best heathen philosophers.[87]

Specific comments on the effect of religious and philosophical systems gave particular consideration to political matters. They applauded the Scottish clergy for its support of the Hanoverian succession,[88] and criticized the Roman Catholics not only for their superstitious practices, but for their subversive tactics.[89] Criticism of the Methodists was not restricted to the madness of their enthusiasm, but extended particularly to the chaos they had created within the Establishment.[90] But any religion seemed better than none to writers who considered the most grievous fault of atheism to be its threat to the peace of the world; for Christianity properly practiced would bring complete peace, and even in its present shoddy condition was responsible for "the quiet, the security, the order, which a great part of the world enjoys at present".[91]

To a lesser extent, perhaps, than Dodd, the editors of the *Grand, Royal, Court,* and *Universal,* all clearly indicated their religious attitude. It is noteworthy that although they all had taken liberal positions on the necessity of extending the empire, only the *Grand* maintained what could be called a liberal attitude toward religion. The distinction between the *Grand* and the others serves as a further reminder of the difference between feelings of political and religious freedom.

The most meaningful comments on religion in the *Grand* were extremely liberal. While acknowledging that the Anglican Church granted as much freedom of conscience as any religion permitted, the writers refused to identify civil liberty with the Church and warned against religious wars which were the excuses that princes found to satisfy their political and military purposes.[92] Articles in the *Grand* objected to the pressures that organized religious

---

[87] *Christian's*, III (October, 1762), p. 433.
[88] *Christan's*, I (August, 1760), p. 170.
[89] *Christian's*, I (August, 1760), p. 167; I (November, 1760), p. 311; II (April, 1761), pp. 172-173.
[90] *Christian's*, I (August, 1760), p. 189; III (January, 1762), pp. 32-33.
[91] *Christian's*, III (August, 1762), p. 339.
[92] *Grand*, I (February, 1758), p. 55.

groups applied to individual morality,[93] and argued that unnatural restraints were repugnant to man's existence.[94] In comments on the English colonies in America, one writer especially reflected the religious liberalism in the magazine: [95]

... in short, the diversity of people, religions, nations and languages here is prodigious, and the harmony in which they live together equally pleasing. For though every man who wishes well to religion, is sorry to see the diversity which prevails, and would by all humane and honest methods endeavour to prevent it; yet when once the evil has happened, when there is no longer an union of sentiments, it is delightful to see men take and give an equal liberty; to see them live, if not as belonging to the same church, yet to the same Christian religion; and if not to the same religion, yet to the same fraternity of mankind.

Sharing the religious sentiments of the *Monthly* reviewers,[96] the magazine, because of the eclecticism of its type, printed letters that reflected opinions contrary to its own editorial views. With the exception of a letter opposing Methodism because it perverted liberty,[97] the correspondence in the *Grand* was less concerned with religious liberty than with emphasizing the purpose of the Anglican Church.[98] Comments in the letters urged the principles of the Establishment and argued the need to reform practices that corrupted the religious behavior of the people,[99] both with a force and interest that were not characteristic of either the magazine's articles or editorial statements. Where the writers in the *Grand* were concerned with conduct,[100] the editors, nevertheless, printed a letter that stressed the importance of orthodoxy as leading to virtue.[101]

In contrast to the articles in the *Grand*, those in the *Royal*

[93]   *Grand*, III (September, 1760), pp. 438-439.
[94]   *Grand*, I (January, 1758), p. 18.
[95]   *Grand*, II (February, 1759), p. 73.
[96]   *Grand*, I (May, 1758), pp. 220-222.
[97]   *Grand*, II (November, 1759), pp. 594-597.
[98]   *Grand*, I (February, 1758), pp. 63-67.
[99]   *Grand*, I (February, 1758), pp. 69-73; II (August, 1759), p. 432; III (February, 1760), pp. 76-77.
[100]   *Grand*, I (August, 1758), p. 388.
[101]   *Grand*, I (June, 1758), pp. 269-271.

Magazine insisted that religion was the moral basis of the structure of the state. In an argument explaining the need for reliance
on the Scriptures, one writer in the *Royal* concluded: "It is a
maxim founded on truth, that religion is the firmest foundation
of honour and true happiness in every state and nation, and the
most permanent pillar and strongest support in every form of
government." [102] Other writers contended, too, that the propriety
of order in the nation had been determined by divine intention and
that it was the duty of all Christians to accept the condition that
God had decreed.[103] According to writers in the *Royal*, the very
superiority of modern times to classical antiquity depended upon
an adherence to Christian principles in the conduct of life.[104]
Without religion there could be no true morality, and "as religion is the foundation of all duties, it is morally impossible for a
man to have any real merit, if he has not sound principles of religion".[105] To insure proper morality, the contributors to the magazine urged the inclusion of religious instruction in all education.[106]

While it offered no editorial statement on the assorted heresies
of Roman Catholicism, Methodism, Judaism, and deism, the
Royal printed letters condemning each variety of dissent. Romish
superstitions were to be eschewed,[107] and Jesuit activities were
described as machinations.[108] The Jews were berated for having
intentionally altered Scriptural chronology to confuse Christians
on the coming of the Messiah,[109] and deists, Methodists, Papists,
and infidels were grouped as a single target for assault.[110]

Like those in the *Royal*, the few significant comments on the
subject in the *Court* stressed the importance of using the Church
to foster morality in the state. The editors' own introduction to the
"Universal Oracle" section emphasized the relationship of reli-

[102] *Royal*, III (October, 1760), p. 183.
[103] *Royal*, II (May, 1760), pp. 242-243; III (September, 1760), p. 119; III
(November, 1760), p. 235.
[104] *Royal*, V (July, 1761), pp. 9-10; VI (January, 1762), pp. 1-2.
[105] *Royal*, V (September, 1761), p. 125.
[106] *Royal*, I (August, 1759), pp. 84-85; IX (September, 1763), pp. 137-138.
[107] *Royal*, VII (July, 1762), p. 4.
[108] *Royal*, VI (February, 1762), p. 96.
[109] *Royal*, II (February, 1760), pp. 59-60.
[110] *Royal*, VII (July, 1762), pp. 6-7.

gion, science, and conduct, all of which were to be used to instruct the readers.[111] In the same way, the *Court*'s comment on Rousseau's *Social Contract* left no doubt as to the role that religion played in the life of the state: [112]

After all, the meanest Christian must make a better patriot, and a much better social being, than the model of perfection, which John James exhibits in his Natural Man, who runs wild and naked in the woods upon his hands and legs, eats acorns, shuns his species, only when the spirit of copulation moves him, and lives and dies among his brother brutes.

For the writers in the *Court*, moral duties were efficaciously instituted only through the revelation of the true religion,[113] and both letters and articles opposed the leveling influences of Methodism and the political hypocrisy of the Jesuits because the two threatened the security of the English Church upon which the moral order was founded.[114]

While the religious opinions in the *Court* seem inconsistent with its political liberalism,[115] those in the *Universal Magazine* are even more perplexing. Although its writers were firm supporters of Wilkes, they were also extremely skeptical of man's virtue.[116] Their conservative religious views follow naturally enough from their skepticism, but hardly suggest their defense of Wilkes. Because of their skepticism, the writers in the *Universal* demanded good religious teaching to produce a better political state.[117] They

[111]   *Court*, I (June, 1763), p. 265.
[112]   *Court*, July, 1762, pp. 526-527.
[113]   *Court*, I (March, 1763), pp. 105-107.
[114]   *Court*, April, 1762, pp. 363-364; November, 1762, p. 719; I (March, 1763), pp. 97-100.
[115]   Some explanation for the discrepancy between the *Court*'s political and religious views stems from the fact that the political views were expressed chiefly in "The Politician", a single feature of the magazine, while the religious comments are taken from the entire magazine. – Robbins, pp. 295-296, says that although there was not an inevitable tie between religious dissent and questioning and civil and religious liberty, it was characteristic.
[116]   *Universal Magazine*, XIX (Supplement, 1756), p. 327; XX (April, 1757), pp. 153-158; XX (May, 1757), pp. 202 ff.; XXV (September, 1759), p. 118; XXVII (October, 1760), pp. 209-210; XXIX (August, 1761), p. 64; XXX (June, 1762), pp. 310 ff.; XXXI (July, 1762), pp. 1 ff.
[117]   *Universal Magazine*, XXII (May, 1758), p. 235.

contrasted the social and political effect of orthodox practices with the results of the unnatural Papist practices and the excesses of the dissenters.[118] Even in literary comment, one writer in the magazine admonished Christians to dismiss from their poetry "the fables and fictions of the pagan theology".[119]

In some of the other minor magazines, comment was sparse. Frequently the items were letters,[120] while articles like those in the *Philological Miscellany* were not greatly revealing.[121] Remarks on

[118] *Universal Magazine*, XVIII (April, 1756), p. 185; XXVI (June, 1760), p. 320.

[119] *Universal Magazine*, XXXI (October, 1762), p. 177.

[120] *Universal Museum*, II (August, 1763), pp. 415-417 is a letter attacking the Jesuits. *Lady's Museum*, II, #10, pp. 778-779, advocates Scriptural instruction for women, while a letter in I, #8, pp. 563-564, condemns Methodist teaching. Wesley's followers are attacked in a poem in the *Universal Visiter*, #3 (March, 1756), p. 142, and a letter in #12 (December, 1756), p. 560, chides the irreligious conduct of Britain's military men. *British Magazine*, II (March, 1761), pp. 131-133 and I (May, 1760), p. 110, offer letters on the importance of religion to the state, but another in III (July, 1762), pp. 351-352, opposed persecution of Irish and Scots for religious views. The magazine, III (August, 1762), pp. 413-414, printed a letter attacking French anti-scriptural writings. In one direct comment the editors of the *British* in II (January, 1761), p. 27, stressed the superiority of Christianity to the religion of Socrates and Cato.

[121] The title page of the *Philological Miscellany* announced that its contents consisted in select essays translated from the Memoirs of the Academy of Belles Lettres at Paris and other foreign countries, together with original pieces by eminent English writers. As the advertisement to the first volume (pp. iii-iv) indicated, the emphasis was on the French. The advertisement also made clear that further numbers, to appear every year at six-month intervals, depended on the success of the first volume. No further volume appeared, although the work received the approval and blessing of the *Monthly Review* (XXIV, June, 1761, pp. 373 ff.) and the *Critical* (XI, May, 1761, p. 341). – Comment in I (1761), pp. 174-175, 287-288, insisted on the superiority of Christianity, but generally the comparative-religion approach of the magazine's articles, I (1761), pp. 292-294, 395 ff., was latitudinarian. – Remarks in the *Grand Magazine of Magazines*, II (March, 1759), pp. 124, 155-156, stressed the Church and state relationship, but dismissed the importance of religious practices in themselves. The remarks were reprints from other magazines, but the indebtedness brought little gratitude. – In the Preface to its first volume (1758), the *Grand Magazine of Magazines* berated both the *Critical* and *Monthly* for their bias: "The managers of the *Reviews* are not, perhaps, incompetent judges, but they are too slovenly or too remiss: too partial or too much interested in the characters they give; too much bigotted, or too free thinkers; too zealous Tories or too rigid Whigs, to judge with candour of the labours of

the subject in the *Weekly* and *Literary,* although limited in number, at least suggest the editorial attitude of those magazines. Although insisting on the superiority of the orthodox faith, the writers in the *Weekly* maintained a liberal distrust of Church involvements in politics. A long article on bigotry argued for the Anglican religion as a proper mean between the excesses of superstitious and authoritarian Popery and the zealous fanaticism of the dissenters. For the writer, "An extraordinary religious zeal is always with good reason to be suspected"; and England itself was displaying a tendency to run to extremes.[122] Other writers, including Goldsmith, insisted that absolute sovereigns in Europe promoted Catholicism because they thought "it to be a religion far more favorable to civil despotism than Protestantism can possibly be"; but, although the writers equated Popery with slavery and Protestantism with liberty, they again sounded the warning that England was not safe from the dangers of excess.[123] Even in its demands for a reformation of the Established Church, an article in the *Weekly* urged a religion that would play a proper role in influencing the morality of the English people without endangering their liberty.[124]

In their relatively few comments on religion and the state, the writers in the *Literary,* too, displayed distrust for religious zealots. A description of an attempted assassination of Louis XV, when that monarch was England's arch-rival, deplored "the dreadful effects of enthusiasm [that] have been severely felt in every age and country, in which they have existed".[125] For one writer in the magazine, "inflamed religious zeal" was particularly characteristic of the Catholics,[126] and Johnson himself declared that the Es-

---

their contemporaries; hence it is, that the characters they give, often stand in contrast to each other." Nevertheless, the magazine continued to pillage the reviews (see, for example, II, January, 1759, pp. 11-16).

[122]   *Weekly,* #4 (May 6, 1758), p. 97.
[123]   *Weekly,* #5 (May 13, 1758), p. 129. See, also, *Weekly Magazine,* #1 (April 15, 1758), p. 20 (Goldsmith); #10 (June 17, 1758), p. 289. For the attribution to Goldsmith, see *CBEL,* II, p. 639.
[124]   *Weekly,* #6 (May 20, 1758), pp. 161-163.
[125]   *Literary,* II (January-February, 1757), p. 1.
[126]   *Literary,* II (January-February, 1757), p. 4.

tablished Church made the English natural enemies of the Popish powers.[127] Any attempt to disrupt that Establishment was regarded as an invitation to confusion and anarchy.[128]

Although articles in the *Annual Register*, like those in the minor magazines, commented sparsely on the relationship of Church and state, they left no doubt of Burke's editorial opinion. Burke himself depicted human wisdom as helpless before the interposition of Providence,[129] and an anonymous writer in the annual clearly regarded proper conduct to be dependent upon religion.[130] Such comment led naturally to a defense of the clergy, and comment in the *Annual Register* deplored their shabby treatment which kept them from their sacred studies and ministrations.[131] When a defender of the orthodox faith, like Warburton, attacked infidels, fanatics, and hypocrites, the writers in the annual ignored his vituperation and loudly applauded his cause: [132]

It is impossible for a man of real, that is, rational religion, to employ his time and abilities better than in discrediting jointly, as well those who openly attack that sacred bulwark [The State Church], as those whose conduct and opinions expose it to such attacks.

This directness and partisanship in dealing with the subject was less possible for reviewers in the *Critical* and *Monthly*.[133] Let their judgment suggest their religious partiality, and their critics would accuse them of incompetence.[134] In their many articles on religion, the reviewers were expected to deal objectively with the literary merits of works that presented ideas antithetical to their own. Moreover, not only were they expected to comment on the massive production of religious literature, but they also were in the

---

[127] *Literary*, I (April-May, 1756), p. 1. See, also, *Literary*, III (March, 1758), p. 103.
[128] *Literary*, II (January-February, 1757), p. 32.
[129] *Annual Register*, II (1759), p. 38.
[130] *Annual Register*, I (1758), p. 278.
[131] *Annual Register*, III, Pt. II (1760), p. 19.
[132] *Annual Register*, V, Pt. II (1762), p. 237.
[133] The *Theatrical Review*, February, 1763, p. 47, attacked priesthood's zeal for having annihilated the Bardic tradition, while another article, January, 1763, pp. 10-12, berated the bigotry of Medieval Catholicism.
[134] See, for example, footnote 121 on p. 190.

position of having to evaluate religious ideas in some works that were essentially literary or historical.

Yet in no periodical was the relationship of Church and state more emphatically argued than in the *Critical*. For its reviewers, religion and morality were interdependent, and the social order itself depended upon the perpetuation of traditional religious belief. Without religious morality to enforce civil duty, preservation of justice and mercy would rest upon "the written laws of men; and ... the unwritten laws of reason and conscience – both which [are] totally insufficient." [135] Skeptical of schemes and systems based on "human nature either better or worse than it is found by experience",[136] the reviewers expressed a conservative distrust of zealousness even in the name of religion: [137]

We need not enumerate the mischiefs intailed upon mankind by this religious zeal, because Mr. Weston [author of the book being reviewed] will say it was a false zeal; but we must observe, that zeal is like a fire kindled among straw; we know not how fierce the flames will burn.

In dealing with the Roman Catholics in England, one writer in the *Critical* recognized that they presented little direct threat to the Established Church and advised temperance in their treatment, suggesting that vehemence and abuse gave Popery a chance to evoke sympathy.[138] Another reviewer, recalling the period of Titus Oates and the Popish Plot, warned that zeal and bigotry might spark a dangerous conflagration, ending in the destruction of the existing social framework.[139] Nevertheless, the reviewers were unwilling to ignore the malevolence of Popish spirit and the persecution that was a part of the Jesuit policy.[140] For the writers in the *Critical*, hypocrisy and zeal were two heads of a single monster.

Their statements about Catholicism were part of their defense of the State Church, but the reviewers also recognized the need for the healthy condition of the established faith. Religion, and

[135]   *Critical*, II (November, 1756), p. 349 (Franklin).
[136]   *Critical*, X (October, 1760), p. 290.
[137]   *Critical*, VII (May, 1759), p. 428.
[138]   *Critical*, XI (January, 1761), pp. 44-45.
[139]   *Critical*, XV (April, 1763), p. 278.
[140]   *Critical*, V (February, 1758), p. 123; IX (June, 1760), p. 433.

respect for it, were serious matters in the *Critical,* whose writers looked with almost puritanical intolerance upon those who used the subject for poetry, even such poetry as *Paradise Lost.*[141] Furthermore, the reviewers were aroused by the lack of concern shown for hard-working, meritorious clerics, whose devotion and talents went unregarded by political leaders intent upon gaining the service and allegiance of clergymen in the interests of party. Public apathy, too, which led to the neglect of worthy churchmen, was scored: [142]

Had the author ... lived in an age, when people concerned themselves in things of this nature, when it was fashionable to patronize solid learning, and the study of divinity was more in vogue than it is at present; he might have stood the chance of being taken notice of, or perhaps even advanced to some dignity or preferment in that church, whose doctrines he had so well illustrated, and in whose defence he had so eminently distinguished himself; as it is, he will only be read and admired by the judicious few. ...

Even in such pronouncements, however, the writer was careful to distinguish between his attack on Church administration and his feeling toward religious doctrine and the Church constitution. In the review there was never any questioning of Church dogma, and while the reviewers deplored maladministration, they also lauded the self-sacrificing efforts of men like Chillingworth, Hooker, Leland, and Fothergill, who had entered upon clerical life without regard for temporal reward.[143]

But no matter how concerned they were with religious ideals, the writers in the *Critical,* which was sub-titled the "Annals of Literature", did not ignore form in their appraisal of devotional works. To be sure, the reviewers granted the primary value of utility in religious writing, but they also deplored the weaknesses of an author who had something to say but lacked the equipment to say it well.[144] When a work combined important subject matter with the ability to "excite the curiosity and command the atten-

---

[141]   *Critical,* XVI (December, 1763), p. 417. *Cf., Monthly Review,* XX (February, 1759), p. 142 (Kirkpatrick).
[142]   *Critical,* XI (April, 1761), pp. 282-283.
[143]   *Critical Review,* XIII (May, 1762), pp. 416-417.
[144]   *Critical Review,* V (February, 1758), p. 90.

tion of the public", Thomas Franklin, responsible for many religious articles in the *Critical*, was delighted.[145] For Franklin, clarity, simplicity, and effectiveness were at least as important as purpose where literary judgment was concerned,[146] but he found the ideal in a sermon by Ralph Heathcote: [147]

This sermon is, in our opinion, one of the best we have met with since the commencement of our *Review*: It is written in a plain, easy, and perspicuous stile, without pedantry or affectation: Every sentiment arises naturally from the subject, and is closely connected with the words of the text: Method is observed without tedious division and sub-division, and the whole is conducted as at once to convince, and to persuade.

Yet subject matter, as the *Critical*'s articles on Rousseau attest, could not be permitted to pass when it was detrimental to religion.[148] Regardless of their approval of Rousseau the artist, the reviewers could not tolerate his antipathetic remarks about revealed religion, remarks that they condemned as being dangerous to society, "as it is now impossible to unravel the complicated web of religion and government, or diminish the reverence for any established mode of the former, without oversetting the latter".[149] His arguments permitted one reviewer to declare with finality his own position: [150]

It is not for us to judge of the decrees of the Almighty, or cavil at the means he has taken to reveal himself, and promote our eternal felicity. Our understanding is too limited and imperfect to penetrate into the designs of Providence, or see clearly into final causes. We must take things as they are. . . .
    For our own parts, when we reflect on the danger not only to society, but to salvation in not believing, opposed to the inconveniences of resigning our judgment and giving implicit faith to what we sometimes do not understand, we think the latter ought to give way.

[145]   *Critical Review*, I (May, 1756), p. 347.
[146]   *Critical Review*, II (September, 1756), pp. 120-121.
[147]   *Critical*, II (November, 1756), p. 348.
[148]   Another fine example is Franklin's treatment of D'Argens' *Philosophical Visions* (II, November, 1756, pp. 339-340).
[149]   *Critical*, XIV (December, 1762), pp. 426-427.
[150]   *Critical*, XIV (December, 1762), pp. 430-431.

David Hume, too, presented a problem for the writers in the *Critical*. Although they admitted his greatness as an historian, they could not countenance his "illiberal and ungenerous" assault on the clergy, nor condone his infidelity.[151] Whatever Hume's merits as author, the reviewer adamantly refused to accept his remarks on the founders of English Protestantism,[152] and not even Smollett's desire for Hume's help – at a time when the novelist-editor was seeking a political appointment abroad – weakened the defense of the faith by writers in the *Critical*.[153]

But reviewing during the period did not often require judging between great artistic merit and questionable religious and social views. When an author like Archibald Bower appeared, the *Critical* reviewers, including Smollett, combined their attacks on his literary and religious frauds. He was notoriously dishonest in both his writing and conduct, and when he gained national attention as the perpetrator of a minor Popish Plot, the reviewers, despite their stated opposition to religious controversy,[154] took up the cudgel in defense of Church and state.[155]

As Bower moved, with the agility of an opportunist, from the Roman Catholic Church to the Church of England, and back and forth between the two, according to the advantages of the occasion, the *Critical* reviewers – particularly Franklin – followed him with scorn, astonishment, and shock.[156] Even before writers in the review had recorded Bower's forgeries, plagiarism, and general duplicity,[157] Franklin applauded his complete detection by

---

[151] *Critical*, XI (March, 1761), pp. 201-202.
[152] *Critical*, VII (April, 1759), p. 292.
[153] *Critical*, XIV (July, 1762), pp. 81-82. In each attack on Hume's religious views, however, the *Critical* reviewer noted his genius. He was described as an eminent writer and philosopher who somehow had been seduced into relgous error.
[154] *Critical*, II (September, 1756), p. 144 (Franklin); V (January, 1758), p. 61; XVI (September, 1763), p. 201.
[155] Smollett himself was responsible for one of these reviews, *Bower's History of the Popes*, V (XI, March, 1761, p. 219), according to a letter in E. S. Noyes, editor, *The Letters of Tobias Smollett, M.D.* (Cambridge, Mass., 1926), p. 70.
[156] *Critical*, I (July, 1756), pp. 536-537; III (February, 1757), p. 191.
[157] *Critical*, III (January, 1757), pp. 41-49, 52, 57; IV (August, 1757), p. 109; V (January, 1758), pp. 23-24.

John Douglas, whose identity was not yet publicly known.[158]
When Douglas, in turn, was attacked, the reviewers again celebrated his work and all but ignored his detractor [159] and, at the
same time, Franklin heaped contempt upon the defense and stall-
ing tactics of Bower in answering the charges.[160] Among Bower's
answers were two to the *Critical*, responses which served only as
an opportunity for the reviewer to remind his readers that he and
the periodical had only the interests of Church and state in view
when entering the controversy.[161]

In every way, the religious opinions in the *Monthly* appear
more liberal than those in the *Critical*. When Dr. Johnson described the *Monthly* reviewers as Christians with a minimum of
Christianity,[162] he was repeating, with moderation, charges that
others had made against the review. Among these was the accusation in the *Christian's Magazine* which described the *Monthly*
and its staff as the "very canker-worm ... in the republic of
letters, [and] enemies professed to the faith of Christ." [163] Despite
his reviewers' unwillingness to enter into religious controversy,[164]

---

158 *Critical*, I (July, 1756), p. 558.
159 *Critical*, V (February, 1758), pp. 122, 173-175.
160 *Critical*, II (August, 1756), p. 73; V (March, 1758), p. 228.
161 *Critical*, III (February, 1757), p. 150. Smollett's *British Magazine*, in a
brief comment on the fifth volume of Bower's *History of the Popes*, was
equally unfavorable: "The author has clapped a cracker to its tail, to
frighten away the criticks: but we look upon it as the last glimmer of a
farthing candle, that goes off in a stink" (II, February, 1761, p. 98). – The
magazines, however, did not generally comment on Bower, although they
gave excerpts from works that concerned him. After printing summaries
and parts of the controversy (XXVI, June, 1756, pp. 281-284; XXVI, July,
1756, pp. 336-344; XXVII, February, 1757, pp. 65-69), the *Gentleman's*
rejected his defense (XXVII, March, 1757, pp. 117-121). Other magazines
gave excerpts without comment: *London Magazine*, XXV (July, 1756), p.
344; *Universal Magazine*, XIX (Supplement, 1756), p. 316; *Literary Magazine*, I (June, 1756), pp. 126-133; I (December, 1757), pp. 442-453; *General
Magazine of Arts and Sciences*, Pt. V (April, 1757), pp. 530 f.; (May,
1757), pp. 541 ff.
162 Graham, p. 211.
163 *Christian's Magazine*, IV (August, 1763), p. 363. The immediate cause
of the magazine's attack was the *Monthly's* article in XXIX (July, 1763),
pp. 66 ff. However, the *Monthly's* unfavorable article on Dr. Dodd's work
(XXVIII, April, 1763, pp. 311-312, Kenrick), undoubtedly aroused the
magazine of which Dodd was editor.
164 See *Monthly Review*, XIV (March, 1756), p. 256 (Rose); XX (March,

Griffiths found the religious opinions in his periodical susceptible to attack.[165]

Perhaps the very lack of religious fervor in its comments explains, in part, the charges that the *Monthly* was no friend to Christianity. Unlike the reviewers in the *Critical*, those in the *Monthly* refused to defend such orthodox theologians as the illiberal Warburton,[166] nor would they condemn out of hand the unpopular Methodists when they were performing what the reviewer considered a useful social function.[167] Moreover, writers like Kenrick in the *Monthly* opposed persecution of the sect,[168] as well as censure of the Quakers.[169] When the latter had been attacked by the *Monitor,* an anonymous reviewer in the *Monthly* called such treatment scandalous and un-Christian,[170] an opposition of attitudes in two politically liberal periodicals which again points out the possible disparity between religious and political opinions.

Although some reviewers expressed conventional opinions supporting the "true religion",[171] it is in their refusal to identify Church and state that the charges of anti-Christianity against the *Monthly* probably had a justifiable basis. While their opposition to the Roman Catholic union of spiritual and temporal power would not disturb the orthodox Anglican,[172] their lack of enthusiasm for English Church power could hardly please the conserva-

---

1759), pp. 219-224 (Kenrick). Even in its treatment of Bower (XVI, January, 1757, pp. 67-74 [Rose]; XVI, April, 1757, pp. 340-341, 343 [Rose]; XVII, August, 1757, pp. 182-183; XVIII, March, 1758, pp. 241-244; XVIII, May, 1758, pp. 498-499 [Rose]; XX, April, 1759, pp. 332-339 [Rose]; XXIV, April, 1761, p. 237 [Rose]), the *Monthly* was not so aroused by religious fervor that it involved itself in controversy with him.

[165] *Monthly Review*, XVII (August, 1757), p. 186; XVIII (March, 1758), p. 215 (Benjamin Dawson).

[166] *Monthly Review*, XIX (November, 1758), pp. 417-418, 422 (Rose).

[167] *Monthly Review*, XIV (March, 1756), pp. 256-257.

[168] *Monthly Review*, XXIX (July, 1763), pp. 69-70 (Kenrick).

[169] *Monthly Review*, XIV (Appendix, 1756), pp. 588-589; XXV (September, 1761), p. 234.

[170] *Monthly*, XIV (March, 1756), pp. 253-254.

[171] *Monthly*, XVI (February, 1757), p. 113 (Sharpe); XXII (May, 1760), p. 422 (Ruffhead).

[172] *Monthly*, XVI (January, 1757), p. 5 (Ward); XIX (Appendix, 1758), p. 625 (Leman).

tive. Reviewers like John Seddon, who conducted a dissenting academy, clearly distinguished between religion and the state; one was not to intrude on the other, and no man was to be deprived of civil privileges because of his religious opinions.[173] Whatever the abuse of religious liberty, it was superior to religious tyranny, and according to Griffiths and his staff, the true freedom of England lay in its religious liberty.[174]

Opposed to the supremacy of a universal church,[175] reviewers like Ruffhead also distrusted "many, who pretend vast concern for the Established Church, and the mysteries of our holy religion".[176] The real concern of the *Monthly*'s writers was for a religion that was practical in its benefits; indeed, if a system led to morality, whatever its doctrines, the reviewers were impressed.[177] For the mysteries of religion, particularly when they led to controversy, denied man hope, or concerned themselves with supernaturalism, Griffiths' religious writers, led by William Rose, had little use.[178]

Unlike the writers in the *Critical,* those in the *Monthly* did not look upon the body of the Anglican Church as sacred beyond revision. Whereas the *Critical* reviewers acknowledged abuses in clerical practice but refused to attack the doctrines and constitution of the Church, Rose, a Scottish dissenter, urged the necessity for alterations that would modernize the religion to keep pace with the advances in government, arts, manufactures, and commerce.[179] To be sure, *Monthly* reviewers contrasted the Anglican religion with that of the Roman Catholics and praised the superiority

[173] *Monthly*, XXIX (August, 1763), pp. 127-130.
[174] *Monthly*, XXI (July, 1759), p. 88; XXVI (January, 1762), p. 22 (Langhorne); XXVI (May, 1762), p. 344 (Griffiths and Seddon); XXVIII (Appendix, 1763), p. 539 (Kenrick).
[175] *Monthly*, XXVIII (May, 1763), p. 408.
[176] *Monthly*, XX (January, 1759), p. 5.
[177] *Monthly*, XX (January, 1759), p. 2 (Ruffhead); XXII (April, 1760), p. 351.
[178] *Monthly*, XIV (January, 1756), p. 9 (Rose); XIV (March, 1756), p. 190 (Flexman); XVII (September, 1757), pp. 284-285 (Rose); XX (January, 1759), p. 32 (Rose); XXII (January, 1760), pp. 14, 79 (Rose); XXVIII (January, 1763), p. 73; XXIX (November, 1763), p. 363 (Rose).
[179] *Monthly*, XXII (June, 1760), pp. 470-471 (Rose).

of the English,[180] but that was no reason to rest secure with a religion that had become much outmoded. Indeed, Rose desired to see: [181]

our ecclesiastical constitution reformed in regard to doctrine, discipline, worship, and practice; the public forms of our Church purged from many things which at present disgrace them, and some of which, we will be bold to say, would have disgraced the most absurd system of Pagan superstition.

It is melancholy to consider, that in an age of so much knowledge, in a country blessed with higher and nobler privileges, both of a civil and religious nature, than any other under heaven, no attempt is made, by the Governors of our Church, to rectify what is amiss in her constitution, remove obstacles, supply defects, and, in a word, to make those alterations and improvements, which the wisest, most learned, pious, and judicious of her members acknowledge to be necessary.

Like the writers in the *Critical*, those in the *Monthly* had at the same time the task of reviewing these works for their literary as well as religious value. Recognizing the difficulties of devotional composition, which required gravity and dignity while it also needed plainness and simplicity,[182] Griffiths and his staff were usually inclined to forgive literary weakness when the work improved the understanding,[183] although an easy and flowing style was designated as desirable.[184]

For the genius of a writer like David Hume, both Rose and Ruffhead in the *Monthly* were able to put aside their religious objections.[185] Rose particularly was less concerned with Hume's skepticism than with his attack on reason, for, like the Papists, the philosopher took an approach that was more likely than reasoned

---

[180]   *Monthly*, XXIII (July, 1760), pp. 55-57 (Kenrick); XXV (July, 1761), p. 79.
[181]   *Monthly*, XXII (June, 1760), p. 470.
[182]   *Monthly*, XXVI (May, 1762), p. 343 (Griffiths and Seddon).
[183]   *Monthly*, XIV (March, 1756), p. 205 (Rose); XVIII (January, 1758), p. 25 (Dawson).
[184]   *Monthly*, XXI (Appendix, 1759), p. 578.
[185]   *Monthly*, XIV (April, 1756), p. 309; XVI (January, 1757), p. 36; XVI (February, 1757), p. 122 (all by Rose); XX (April, 1759), pp. 344-364 (Ruffhead); XXIV (January, 1761), p. 23 (Rose).

analysis to lead to infidelity.[186] Indeed, what becomes apparent in this difference between the *Critical* and *Monthly*'s treatment of Hume is that Griffiths and his writers were more inclined than the *Critical* reviewers to rely on reason in their examination of faith.

[186] *Monthly*, XVI (January, 1757), p. 50.

VI

RELIGION AND SCIENCE

Considered in itself, the progress of science in the eighteenth century was remarkable. The advances made from 1756-1763 in physiology,[1] natural history,[2] chemistry,[3] and seismology [4] represent only a small part of the general change that was taking place. In the allied field of medicine, for example, there was a virtual revolution that threw off the shackles of a classical tradition.[5] But even more importantly, by the middle of the century, scientific methods had themselves achieved the respectability for which the Royal Society had striven since its establishment. More careful observation of nature and more accurate experimentation were prized as much for themselves as for the practical contributions that they had made to knowledge.[6]

Recurring frequently in religious discussions during the Seven Years' War, the word *reason* suggests the effect that this scientific attitude was having upon matters of faith. To be sure, the impact was no more sudden than it was restricted to these years. But the discoveries and publications during the war helped to inspire "the intellectual development of the scientific movement" in the hands of the mathematicians and mechanists who contributed to the pure-

---

[1] A. Wolf, *A History of Science, Technology, and Philosophy in the Eighteenth Century, Second edition* (London, 1952), p. 488; C. E. Raven, *Natural Religion and Christian Theology* (Cambridge, 1953), p. 159.
[2] Wolf, pp. 460-461; C. Singer, *A Short History of Science to the Nineteenth Century* (Oxford, 1943), p. 328.
[3] Singer, p. 286.
[4] Wolf, p. 398.
[5] Sir D'Arcy Power, "Medicine", in *Johnson's England*, II, p. 256.
[6] J. H. Randall, *The Making of the Modern Mind* (Boston, 1926), p. 264.

ly materialistic outlook which led to the Victorian conflict between religion and science.[7]

The periodical writers, whatever their intentions, contributed to this development by popularizing science which had not yet become so complex that it required a specialist's knowledge for understanding. For the inquiring amateur who wanted to delve into the mysteries of science, dexterous fingers and sufficient curiosity were the only essentials, and great advances were as likely to come from the prelate, lawyer, or teacher as they were from the professional man of science.[8] Undoubtedly, the periodicals found in their audience many who, like Samuel Johnson, possessed chemical apparatus and delighted in experiments; or who, like Thomas Gray, devoted considerable time to the study of natural history; or who, like Adam Smith and Edward Gibbon, attended Dr. William Hunter's lectures on anatomy.[9] The periodicals had to cater to the hundreds of English naturalists, who had been inspired by the new edition of Linnaeus's *Systema*. Although botany had long enjoyed a public interest in England, during the latter part of the eighteenth century, all of natural history gained a popular vogue. The index of the *Monthly*, from 1749-1784, lists 348 reviews on the subject,[10] while the writers in the *Critical* declared that natural history was "a kind of national establishment",[11] and the magazines vied with one another to meet this special interest.[12]

Added to this general scientific curiosity was the practical interest in what scientific progress could do for a commercial nation dependent upon increased industry and agriculture. The many articles on subjects like husbandry, bleaching, and manufactures,

[7] The quotation is from Raven, p. 157. See, also, Raven, p. 158; W. P. Jones, "The Vogue of Natural History in England, 1750-1770", *Annals of Science*, II (1937), p. 348.
[8] E. J. Holmyard, "Science, Mathematics, and Astronomy", in *Johnson's England*, II, p. 244.
[9] L. L. Martz, *The Later Career of Tobias Smollett* (New Haven, Conn., 1942), pp. 1-2.
[10] Jones, "The Vogue of Natural History in England", pp. 345-348.
[11] Jones, "The Vague of Natural History in England", p. 347.
[12] Wolf, p. 37; Jones, "The Vogue of Natural History in England", p. 346.

in the periodicals, particularly the magazines, reflect national as well as individual concern: [13]

What Parliament did occasionally on a large scale private bodies did frequently in a less lavish manner. These bodies were the expression of that widespread interest in "improvement" and the "useful arts" which becomes so evident about the middle of the century. Agriculture and industry alike attracted attention, and while aristocrats, enterprising farmers, politicians, and retired tradesmen liked best to make and study experiments on the land, manufactures and commerce were not neglected. Encyclopaedias and dictionaries of science, arts, and commerce appeared: the *Gentleman's Magazine* and the *Annual Register* opened their columns to lists of patents or accounts of "Useful Projects"; the *Wonderful Magazine* was founded in 1764 to record the new and strange. Even the poets were affected. . . .

This general propagation of scientific information by the periodicals, however, was not restricted to the *Gentleman's Magazine* and *Annual Register*. Yet, it is odd, considering the attempt by the *Spectator* to popularize learning, that the essay-journals during the Seven Years' War had virtually nothing of importance on the subject. Concerned with either politics or light satire, they were all but devoid of comment on science. Only a straggling suggestion for good health,[14] and casual comment on the wisdom of the planning of the universe,[15] or an occasional Swiftian remark about scientific pretenders [16] is to be noted.

No such reticence characterized the magazines. With the amplitude of publications appearing on scientific subjects, the magazine editors had no difficulty providing extracts and abstracts as well as original articles for their readers. Although Carlson has designated the *Gentleman's* as "a magazine of 'popular science' in its day",[17] the same might be said of most of its competitors.

---

[13]   See Wolf, pp. 122-123; Singer, pp. 272-273; J. A. Williamson, "Exploration and Discovery", in *Johnson's England*, I, p. 124. The following quotation is from H. Heaton, "Industry and Trade", in *Johnson's England*, I, p. 246.
[14]   *Bee*, #6 (November 10, 1759), p. 153.
[15]   *Centinel*, #20 (May 18, 1757), p. 119.
[16]   *Connoisseur*, #106 (February 5, 1756), pp. 62-68; *Test*, #4 (December 4, 1756), p. 13.
[17]   Carlson, p. 151.

With few exceptions the editors made their magazines eager repositories for scientific and pseudo-scientific information. Both the *Gentleman's* and *London* offered excerpts from the *Philosophical Transactions, Medical Observations and Enquiries*, and the publications of academies of arts and science at home and abroad. Both magazines printed mathematical questions and solutions, remedies for everything from snake bite to consumption, and meteorological accounts. Charts and drawings of flora and fauna, lists of prizes to be granted by the Society for the Encouragement of Arts, Manufactures, and Commerce, and case histories submitted by physicians filled the pages of both major magazines. While the lack of genuine comment and the naive acceptance of unauthentic material in the *London* may be contrasted with the more critical observations in the *Gentleman's*,[18] both magazines were alike in their attempt to provide practical and useful information to their readers and to encourage a national science based on experimentation and observation.

But the major magazines were not alone in these endeavors. The minor magazines, with one exception, contributed to the awakening of reader interest in science and appealed to the public's curiosity about the subject. Only the *Philological Miscellany*, out of its editorial concern for the survival of *belles lettres*, opposed the development of what its writers called an exclusive taste in mathematics and natural philosophy.[19] Even Rolt in the *Universal Visiter*, the most literary of the magazines, urged the proper study of husbandry,[20] while the *British Magazine*, which also em-

[18] Cf., *London Magazine*, XXVII (April, 1758), pp. 164-165; XXVIII (August, 1759), pp. 425-428, and *Gentleman's Magazine*, XXVI (1756), Preface; XXVI (August, 1756), pp. 378-380; XXVI (September, 1756), pp. 418-420; XXVII (May, 1757), pp. 197-198; XXVII (September, 1757), p. 395; XXVIII (July, 1758), pp. 309 ff.; XXIX (October, 1759), pp. 454-455; XXX (September, 1760), p. 414; XXXI (August, 1761), pp. 340-341; XXXI (September, 1761), pp. 403-404; XXXII (December, 1762), p. 586; XXXIII (October, 1763), pp. 471-475. The only truly naive comment on the subject in the *Gentleman's* was XXXII (June, 1762), pp. 253-254.
[19] *Philological Miscellany*, I (1761), pp. 1-3, 7-11.
[20] *Universal Visiter*, February, 1756, p. 59. The *New Royal and Universal Magazine* also covered the subject. The file of the magazine, however, is incomplete. The identification of Rolt's authorship is from Jones, "Smart, Rolt, and the *Universal Visiter*", p. 214.

phasized literature, included mathematical problems, practical experiments, and medicinal remedies; and the *Court*, devoted to news, politics, and literature, in addition to presenting questions on mathematics and prescriptions, began a section on natural history in August, 1763, and one on astronomy in the next number. In the *Weekly Magazine*, whose purpose was described by Goldsmith, the editor, as political, commercial, and literary,[21] a regular selection from the *Gardener's Calendar* was introduced because of its usefulness [22], and even the *Christian's Magazine*, in addition to its regular section on physico-theology, included articles on the importance of a temperate diet, the success of cochineal as a medicine, and a chart on the lunar eclipse.

Other editors regarded science as a natural part of their magazine's content. When the *Universal Museum* introduced a compendious account of natural history in its second volume,[23] the addition was advertised as an improvement, but material on the subject had already appeared in the first volume, and the natural history itself was supplemented by a "Gardener's Calendar", practical experiments, and excerpts from the publications of the Royal Society and Royal Academy of Sciences at Paris. The *Imperial Magazine* also presented a section on natural history and a regular section on mathematical problems, while the *Grand Magazine of Magazines* took particular pride in its natural history plates.[24]

In four minor magazines of major importance – the *Universal, Royal, Grand,* and *Literary* – science received considerable attention. The *Universal*, whose long run rivaled the longevity of the *London* and *Gentleman's*, devoted as much space as its competitors did to the topic. Like the *London*, the *Universal* published extracts that were sometimes from unauthentic scientific works.[25] But its inclusion of mechanical plates, an important contribution to applied science, was more extensive than that of any other

21 *Weekly Magazine,* #1 (April 15, 1758), pp. 2-4.
22 *Weekly Magazine,* #2 (April 22, 1758), p. 36.
23 *Universal Museum,* II (1763), Preface.
24 *Grand Magazine of Magazines,* II (1759), Preface.
25 *Universal,* XXVI (May, 1760), pp. 232-237; XXXI (September, 1762), pp. 135 ff.

magazine. For the *Royal*, however, the greatest emphasis was upon natural history. Although the magazine printed mathematical problems and extracts from scientific society publications, its foremost interest was in that branch of science which demonstrated God's careful planning of the universe. On the other hand, the editors of the *Grand*, which also published a large quantity of natural history material and made the relationship of God and nature an important topic, was concerned with science as well when its implications were unrelated to religion. Tracing the history of science, evaluating systems of classification, and supporting the nationalistic aims of the Society for the Encouragement of Arts, Manufactures, and Commerce, were as important to the editors as presenting color plates for natural history. At the same time, the editors ignored neither excerpts from Royal Society publications nor simple remedies for complicated ailments. Finally, the *Literary Magazine*, whose editorial concern for the subject, Johnson himself declared, was only as it was entertaining to a general public,[26] showed no less range in its selection. Apparently the *Literary*'s general reader was as interested in the intricacies of the construction of a beehive as he was in a method for finding eclipses without the use of tables. Articles on the care of convulsions, the use of sarsaparilla root for treatment of venereal diseases, and Alexander Monro's *Treatise on the Lymphatics*, were all a part of the scientific material the *Literary* included for the entertainment of its readers.

But of all the magazines, the *General Magazine of Arts and Sciences* was naturally the most devoted to the subject of science. The magazine, published in parts,[27] presented on a popular level what is probably the most complete view of science in the middle of the eighteenth century. Here was no mere culling of the *Philo-*

[26] *Literary Magazine*, I (1756), p. iv.
[27] *The General Magazine of Arts and Sciences, Philosophical, Philological, Mathematical, and Mechanical* was published and sold in parts. The parts were indicated by five heads: 1. Young Gentleman and Lady's Philosophy; 2. Natural History of the World; 3. Compleat System of all the Philological Sciences; 4. Body of Mathematical Institutes, or Principles of Science; 5. Miscellaneous Correspondence, Essays, Poetry. Part five was also published as the *Miscellaneous Correspondence* by Benjamin Martin, who was editor of the magazine.

sophical Transactions, but detailed accounts of the telescope and microscope, solar system and animal world, mathematics and geography, chemistry and botany, anatomy and physics, actually a complete course of study in virtually every branch of science. Nor did the magazine neglect the mechanical arts and sciences with their emphasis on national pride and utilitarian principles. If any magazine can be singled out as an example of a "popular science" magazine, surely the *General* has a better claim to the title than the *Gentleman's.*

However, such material was not limited to the magazines. The *Annual Register* offered, in addition to a section on natural history, a division on useful or curious projects, discoveries, and inventions. Largely, these were of a practical nature, such as the medicinal values of hemlock, treatment of schirrous tumors, sprains, and lameness. But for all its practicality, Burke's attitude was far removed from the kind of opposition to seemingly fruitless experimentation that is reflected in Swift's *Tale of a Tub* and the third book of *Gulliver's Travels.* As the note to the *Annual Register*'s section on projects indicates, the view that experimental science often throws light on unexpected discoveries had become a commonplace,[28] and it could now be argued that inquiries into natural history, although they had no immediate usefulness, might one day prove of extreme importance.[29] At the same time, there can be no doubt that the *Annual Register*'s encouragement of scientific investigation was also motivated by Burke's desire to enable England to meet international competition in commerce [30] and to bring honor to the nation.[31]

Attempting to give notice to all publications, the two major reviews probably devoted more space to scientific and medical matters than did any other periodical with the exception of the *General Magazine of Arts and Sciences.* These subjects accounted for more than thirty percent of the content of the *Critical Review.*[32]

[28] *Annual Register,* V, Pt. II (1762), p. 86.
[29] *Annual Register,* II (1759), p. 472.
[30] *Annual Register,* V, Pt. I (1762), p. 6.
[31] *Annual Register,* II (1759), p. 285.
[32] Whitridge, p. 49, describes the *Critical* as built around literature, history, and medicine, but actually religion should be included. Science was

But despite its attention to the subject, the *Critical* was probably the most conservative periodical in the scientific attitude it presented. To be sure, in passing judgment upon the works of quacks and charlatans, Smollett and his staff did well to insist on common sense and practicality,[33] but their rigid insistence upon the immediate application and demonstrated accomplishment of experimentation,[34] often offered in mock-heroic irony,[35] displayed some of the same lack of foresight as the early Augustan satirists. Although sometimes leading to appropriate cautiousness against the use of popular remedies and a legitimate concern over improper hygienic practices,[36] the attitude also encouraged the rejection of diagnoses and treatment that were later to prove scientifically sound.[37]

Nevertheless, the writers in the *Critical*, like their contemporaries, were intent on encouraging the progress of English science, particularly applied science for which one writer was especially grateful: [38]

---

the most important subject. In Whitridge's comparison between the *Critical* and *Monthly* (p. 26), he uses the first numbers of the two reviews, and concludes, "[The] *Critical* was directed by a man of wider intellectual range than the *Monthly*." The judgment is not borne out by either perceptiveness or range in the articles of the two reviews.

[33] See, for example, *Critical Review*, I (May, 1756), p. 304 (Armstrong), pp. 321-322 (Smollett); I (June, 1756), pp. 461-462 (Smollett); III (January, 1757), pp. 24, 26; IV (December, 1757), p. 488; V (April, 1758), pp. 229-230.

[34] *Critical*, I (June, 1756), p. 414 (Smollett); II (August, 1756), pp. 32-33 (Smollett); V (May, 1758), p. 368; VI (July, 1758), p. 62; VI (October, 1758), pp. 285-287; VIII (July, 1759), pp. 31-32; IX (January, 1760), pp. 38-39; IX (June, 1760), p. 471; X (July, 1760), p. 20; XI (June, 1761), p. 446; XII (July, 1761), p. 15; XIV (November, 1762), pp. 321-322; XVI (August, 1763), pp. 117-118; XVI (September, 1763), pp. 210-219.

[35] *Critical*, I (January-February, 1756), p. 42 (Smollett); I (May, 1756), p. 304 (Armstrong), pp. 321 ff. (Smollett).

[36] *Critical*, III (June, 1757), pp. 512-513; IV (October, 1757), p. 296; V (January, 1758), p. 74; V (April, 1758), pp. 229-230; IX (May, 1760), p. 382.

[37] *Critical*, I (March, 1756), p. 141; I (June, 1756), p. 414 (Smollett); II (August, 1756), pp. 32-33 (Smollett); IX (January, 1760), p. 38; XI (April, 1761), pp. 270-271.

[38] *Critical*, V (April, 1758), p. 281.

The practical parts of navigation, geography, and astronomy, in common with the other arts and sciences, have lately made large advances towards perfection; a great variety of curious and useful instruments have been constructed; the mariner's compass considerably improved; the false methods of sailing used by the ancients exploded; and others far more accurate substituted in their place; the refraction of the heavenly bodies ascertained; the errors attending observations from the aberration of light corrected; and, lastly, the true figure of the earth determined as near the truth as it is possible to arrive by actual mensuration.

But unlike the other periodicals the *Critical*, even in its treatment of this subject, was deeply committed to controversy. To be sure, the function of a review lent to the possibilities of argument, but not even the *Monthly* engaged in scientific debate with the same intensity that Smollett and his bellicose staff engendered.[39] In a dispute between Alexander Monro, Jr., and William Hunter, involving claims for the "priority for the discovery of lacrimal ducts and the seminiferous tubules in man and for an explanation of the absorptive functions of the lymphatic system",[40] the *Critical*

[39]   A comparison of the *Critical* and *Monthly* in their treatment of Dr. John Hill shows the greater severity of the *Critical*. Although both were harsh in their criticism, the *Critical's* acerbity was such that it led to a direct conflict between Hill and the review. Hill was a multifarious writer whose energy was enormous. He had written a column of gossip called "The Inspector", and was a foe of Smollett. Cf., *Critical*, IV (November, 1757), pp. 412-426; VI (September, 1758), p. 226; VII (February, 1759), pp. 118, 122-123; VII (May, 1759), pp. 468-469; and *Monthly*, XIX (July, 1758), p. 93; XIX (September, 1758), p. 270; XX (April, 1759), p. 369.

[40]   J. M. Oppenheimer, "A Note on William Hunter and Tobias Smollett", *Journal of the History of Medicine and Allied Science*, II (1947), p. 482. The *Critical* immediately came to the defense of Hunter, who was a friend of Smollett (Knapp, p. 136; D'Arcy Power, "Medicine", in *Johnson's England*, II, pp. 269-270). According to Oppenheimer, p. 483, and Whitridge, p. 49, Smollett directed the defense in the *Critical*. However, Whitridge's statement erroneously restricts the controversy to Volume IV of the review. The involvement of the *Critical* can best be compared with the treatment given to the Hunter-Monro controversy in the *Monthly*, although the latter also concluded the justice of Hunter's claim. Cf., *Critical*, IV (September, 1757), pp. 225-227; IV (November, 1757), pp. 431-439; IV (December, 1757), pp. 523-532; VI (July, 1758), p. 39; VI (October, 1758), pp. 312-317; XIII (May, 1762), pp. 418-427; and *Monthly*, XVII (September, 1757), pp. 249-251; XIX (October, 1758), pp. 411-413; XXVII (November, 1762), pp. 319-327); XXVIII (June, 1763), pp. 442-444.

became a participant. Smollett was a friend of Hunter, but more important than the reasons for its participation in the argument is the fact that even here the review did not escape from controversy. This fact distinguishes the *Critical*'s treatment not only from that of the uncommitted magazines, but also from that of the rival *Monthly Review*.

Despite the suggestion that has been made that the *Critical*'s intellectual quality was superior to that of the *Monthly*, the latter's treatment of scientific material was equally extensive, and far more generous toward inquiry that was not immediately productive. The reviewers recognized that experimentation, unless finally systematized, could never be of practical value,[41] and they urged methods in medicine, agriculture, physics, and chemistry,[42] that expressed a forward-looking belief in careful diagnostic and experimental techniques. Indeed, presenting his conception of proper pathology, one writer argued that the best physicians in all ages had been those who observed in nature the details attendant in the case on hand and prognosticated and cured according to the accuracy of observation rather than those who depended on vain hypotheses.[43] Similarly, William Bewley, a friend of Priestley and himself a surgeon and apothecary, explained the character of modern science: [44]

If subtile disputations, founded on arbitrary hypotheses, could have given satisfactory reasons for the phaenomena of Nature, the doctrine of the schoolmen, or the principles of Des Cartes, would have rendered all sedulous enquiries, and accurate experiments, needless. But as all hypotheses, however plausible, are banished from the present method of philosophizing, and nothing admitted as a principle that will not bear the test of experiment, every attempt to account for natural phaenomena, on other principles, is justly looked upon as

[41] *Monthly*, XXII (January, 1760), p. 1 (Kenrick); XXIX (October, 1763), p. 284 (Goldsmith).
[42] See, for example, *Monthly*, XIV (February, 1756), p. 115 (Leman); XVI (February, 1757), p. 97 (Grainger); XVI (April, 1757), p. 328 (Kirkpatrick); XVI (May, 1757), pp. 385-386 (Okey); XVI (June, 1757), p. 541 (Grainger); XVII (July, 1757), pp. 92-93 (Leman); XVII (November, 1757), p. 388; XXI (August, 1759), p. 139; XXII (May, 1760), p. 399.
[43] *Monhtly*, XXI (November, 1759), p. 369.
[44] *Monthly*, XV (November, 1756), p. 466.

supposititious only, and denied a place among the discoveries of genuine philosophy.

But more important as an indication of their new scientific attitude was the *Monthly* reviewers' treatment, in contrast to that of writers in the *Critical*, of what would be called today pure science. Research, according to Sir Tanfield Leman, a physician, must go on despite the belief of many that ultimate knowledge may be unattainable by men. Whatever the final limitations, such research "may be repaid with some useful and curious occurrences by the way . . .".[45] Whether in physics or natural history, Kenrick and Sharpe also argued in the *Monthly,* minute researches were not only delightful but remarkable for the unlooked for information that they produced.[46]

Despite this modern scientific view, Griffiths and his reviewers did not scant the national importance of science. Like those in the *Critical*, they boasted of English accomplishments in agriculture, medicine, and natural history, and urged measures that would further enhance the progress.[47] Moreover, the writers in the *Monthly*, conscious of commercial and trade interests, sought to encourage experiments that would facilitate both trade and commerce.[48]

Whatever the significance of all this scientific curiosity expressed in the periodicals for the development of modern science,

[45] *Monthly*, XXIV (February, 1761), p. 137.

[46] *Monthly*, XIV (May, 1756), p. 418 (Sharpe); XX (April, 1759), p. 321 (Kenrick); XXII (January, 1760), p. 2 (Kenrick).

[47] See, for example, *Monthly Review*, XIV (May, 1756), p. 417 (Sharpe); XVI (June, 1757), p. 558 (Grainger); XVII (September, 1757), p. 197 (Leman); XVIII (January, 1758), pp. 1, 28 (Bewley); XIX (August, 1758), p. 142 (Kirkpatrick); XIX (October, 1758), p. 408; XXVIII (February, 1763), p. 119 (Griffiths); XXIX (October, 1763), p. 284 (Goldsmith). It should also be noted that the reviewers, particularly Kirkpatrick, were concerned with style in medical and scientific works, but did not expect elegance and were willing to forgive poor writing when the work was particularly useful, XVI (June, 1757), p. 558 (Grainger); XIX (August, 1758), pp. 142, 145 (Kirkpatrick); XIX (October, 1758), p. 371; XXI (July, 1759), p. 75 (Kirkpatrick); XXI (November, 1759), p. 373; XXII (June, 1760), pp. 441 ff. (Kirkpatrick); XXIII (August, 1760), p. 166.

[48] *Monthly*, XIV (January, 1756), p. 37 (Bewley); XIV (May, 1756), p. 428 (Leman); XXI (July, 1759), p. 81.

it was no less important for its effect on religious beliefs. From the earliest rise of the new science, its revelations were regarded as a means for improving and expanding the religious conception of the universe and of man.[49] Scientists like Boyle and Newton experienced no difficulty in reconciling a mechanistic view and a theistic philosophy.[50] For such men, as well as Galileo and Descartes, ". . . mechanism and teleology were by no means antagonistic, . . . indeed a machine was the product and instrument of purpose and itself always subordinate to and expressive of its controller." [51] Physico-theology and astro-theology were considered explanations of God's power and will,[52] and even the deists regarded a universe without plan and purpose to be incredible.[53]

But the persistent scrutiny of Christianity's credentials in the light of the new science, characteristic of the deists' attitude,[54] could lead through a mechanistic view of life and thought to what was virtually an atheistic outlook.[55] There was nothing sudden or spectacular about the change,[56] but by mid-century, it was difficult to distinguish between the Christian, deist, and atheist in their basic attitude toward the authority of nature. The difference was one of degree, measured by the extent to which they regarded natural revelation as having supplanted the necessity of supernatural intervention.[57] In focusing scientific attention on nature and its processes, the scientifically curious did not, after a while, always distinguish very clearly between "Nature's God" and His works.[58]

To be sure, a scientist like Linnaeus might be "deeply im-

---

[49] E. L. Tuveson, *Millennium and Utopia* (Berkeley and Los Angeles, 1949), p. 113.
[50] Raven, p. 132.
[51] Raven, p. 128.
[52] Wolf, pp. 283-284.
[53] Stromberg, p. 59.
[54] Stromberg, p. 62.
[55] Raven, pp. 143-144.
[56] Fairchild, *Religious Trends in English Poetry*, II, p. 10; Stephen, I, p. 177.
[57] Becker, p. 53; Fairchild, *Religious Trends in English Poetry*, II, p. 141.
[58] Fairchild, *Religious Trends in English Poetry*, II, p. 282; Tuveson, p. 146; Becker, pp. 21-22, 51-52, 55-57.

pressed by the problems presented by the ruthlessness of the natural order, [while] he nevertheless assigned that order to God without question or argument".[59] But already by Linnaeus's time, the advent of modern geology posed problems for religion which were suggestive of the serious conflict between religion and science that was to follow shortly: [60]

No major conflict between science and religion will occur in the first half of the eighteenth century. Geology offered almost as little opposition to theology as physics did. Later in the century, the poet Cowper will be heard murmuring about the impudence of those who "drill and bore the solid earth" in order to prove God a liar. But this was not until 1760, at about which time modern geology was born. Not until mid-century was the diluvian theory of the fossils seriously challenged, a theory which so comfortably adjusted Scripture to paleontology that Voltaire chose to regard fossils as an argument *for* Christianity. Theories as to the origin of the earth were numerous and fanciful, but, until . . . later in the century, they struggled to vindicate Genesis, and few suspected that this could not be accomplished.

In every way, the evidence from the periodicals presents a picture of the popular attempt not only to bring scientific theory into line with religious doctrine, but to explain religion in terms of the growing science. It may perhaps be a measure of the orthodoxy of a periodical that it relates the wonders of the universe directly to the beneficence and omnipotence of God, but a clearer indication of the orthodox point of view is the insistence upon the inability of human reason to perceive God without first having been granted the benefit of supernatural revelation. On the other hand, the extent to which a periodical stresses the importance of reason, the undeniable revelation in the works of nature, and the relative likenesses among all religions suggests the degree to which that periodical differs with the strictly orthodox point of view. Nevertheless, the demands for the use of reason in religious matters

---

[59]   Raven, p. 157.
[60]   The quotation is from Stromberg, pp. 26-27. See, also, Stephen, I, pp. 379-380, 389-392; Becker, pp. 62-63; Randall, p. 267; Bredvold, pp. 50 ff.; Holmyard, "Science, Mathematics, and Astronomy", in *Johnson's England*, II, pp. 243-244.

should not in itself be considered a departure from orthodoxy.[61] As early as the Renaissance, Richard Hooker was employing reason against the Roman Catholics on one side and the Dissenters on the other.[62] This had developed into a natural and necessary rationalistic theology by 1660 when, according to Bredvold, "The Anglicans were coming frankly to recognize that their final appeal must be to the power of the individual reason to interpret Scripture . . .".[63] Accordingly, the Anglicans like other Protestants had come to depend in varying degrees on the ability of the individual to establish religious truth.[64]

Against such a background, the importance of the periodicals may readily be seen. Their emphasis upon the obviousness of revelation in nature could easily be oversimplified by an audience unused to theological subtleties. Moreover, Scriptural analysis, which had been conducted by scholars ever since the sixteenth century,[65] could readily be construed as a challenge to the authenticity of the Scriptures themselves. Never before had the reasonableness of Christianity been put to the test by such a large group as the periodical readers of the mid-eighteenth century, and it came at a time when the enormous interest in science was easily transferred to other subjects.

The great bulk of significant material on the relationship of science and religion appeared in the magazines. While comments on reason in the essay-journals had a specific social or political application, science itself was a favorite topic in magazines as different as the *General* and the *Christian's*. Frequently, some of the best comment was in the minor periodicals, but even the *Gentleman's* and *London*, which emphasized the more practical aspects of science, were not without significant remarks on its relationship with religion.

[61]   Randall, pp. 273-274.
[62]   B. Willey, *The Seventeenth Century Background* (New York, 1953), p. 73.
[63]   L. Bredvold, *The Intellectual Milieu of John Dryden* (Ann Arbor, 1953), pp. 80-82. The quotation is from p. 82. Stromberg, p. 48, notes that a visitor to England in 1754 "observed that many Anglicans did not believe in the Trinity".
[64]   Bredvold, pp. 76 ff. Robbins, p. 12.
[65]   Willey, p. 73.

Comments in the *Gentleman's* urging the necessity of faith sought to persuade through reason. When they published arguments that attributed natural catastrophes to God's wrath, the editors balanced them with explanatory articles that either offered scientific causes or challenged the Scriptural authority.[66] Not only were Genesis and the Resurrection put to the test of scientific investigation,[67] but even the question of the immortality of the souls of animals became the object of analysis, perhaps beyond the reach of man's understanding, or at least demonstration, but not beyond legitimate inquiry.[68]

On the subject of Revelation, writers in the *Gentleman's* emphasized man's ability to perceive God in His creations. Whether in the magazine's history of botany,[69] or in the letters and abstracts published on astronomy and natural history,[70] the writers insisted that the wonders of creation – open to examination and experimentation – proved the omnipotence and beneficence of God. In poetry and correspondence, the *Gentleman's* offered the view that the articles of faith could only be effective when supported by the evidence of science and reason,[71] and, while rejecting the arguments of the deists, the magazine's own writers or correspondents were no less deistical in their insistence upon rational judgment and their belief that free reason was religion's best friend since Christianity stood upon positive proof.[72] Whatever its limitations, human reason remained a necessity in matters of faith for the re-

---

[66] *Gentleman's*, XXVI (January, 1756), p. 46; XXVI (February, 1756), pp. 70-71, 82-83; XXVI (March, 1756), pp. 138-139; XXVI (May, 1756), pp. 213-214; XXVII (October, 1757), p. 479; XXXIII (April, 1763), p. 195.

[67] *Gentleman's*, XXVI (January, 1756), pp. 16-17; XXVI (September, 1756), pp. 428 ff.; XXVII (September, 1757), p. 404; XXVII (November, 1757), pp. 495-496. See, also, XXVII (December, 1757), pp. 541-542; XXIX (Supplement, 1759), p. 622.

[68] *Gentleman's*, XXVI (February, 1756), pp. 57-59; XXVI (April, 1756), pp. 169-170.

[69] *Gentleman's*, XXVI (June, 1756), pp. 277-279.

[70] *Gentleman's*, XXVII (March, 1757), pp. 123-124; XXVIII (February, 1758), pp. 66-68; XXX (October, 1760), p. 466; XXXI (June, 1761), pp. 259-260.

[71] *Gentleman's*, XXIX (March, 1759), pp. 130-131; XXXIII (March, 1763), pp. 110-112.

[72] *Gentleman's*, XXX (March, 1760), p. 130; XXX (June, 1760), p. 279; XXX (July, 1760), p. 334.

viewer who rejected as nonsense Anthony Moore's deprecatory remarks on the faculty of reason: [73]

The author has taken occasion in several places to decry Reason as a faculty employed in the investigation of truth; but he is not aware that the ultimate appeal must be to Reason, even for his own hypothesis; for by what faculty are we to determine, whether Reason is or is not to be trusted in matters of Faith? By what faculty are we to determine, when Faith is to be substituted for Reason? And, why are we to believe one mystery and reject another?

For the other major magazine, the *London*, most of the pertinent comment on the role of science in religion appears in controversial correspondence. To be sure, there were the customary articles mildly relating the wonders of science to the glory of the Creator,[74] but the real interest lies in two quarrels that developed among the magazine's letter-writers.

One of these controversies, involving the self-educated scientist James Ferguson, indicates clearly the way in which science was being used to verify the Scriptures and the difficulty that arose from the method. Ferguson's *Astronomy Explained* was offered by a letter-writer to the *London* as evidence of the accuracy with which the Nativity and Crucifixion had been dated by the Scriptures: [75]

[This information] put[s] an end to the controversy among chronologers on that head [i.e., the dates of the Nativity and Crucifixion]. From hence likewise may be inferred the truth of the prophetick parts of Scriptures, since they can stand so strict a test as that of being examined on the principles of astronomy.

When another correspondent, challenging the support given to Christian dating of these events by Ferguson's work, concluded, ". . . it appears plain, that there is a great mistake in the Christian accounts; and that there is more credit to be given to this one astronomical criterion, than to the longest tradition",[76] Ferguson himself responded to defend both the accuracy of his work and the

---

[73] *Gentleman's*, XXVIII (October, 1758), p. 492.
[74] *London*, XXV (July, 1756), p. 321; XXVII (May, 1758), pp. 247-248.
[75] *London*, XXV (October, 1756), pp. 472-473.
[76] *London*, XXVI (April, 1757), pp. 190-191.

Scriptural evidence.[77] Perhaps what is most revealing in the controversy, however, is the assumption, by both Ferguson and his supporter, that the Scriptures required scientific proof, an assumption that Faith must be supported by Reason.

In the other controversy, too, Faith without Reason was challenged.[78] After the magazine had printed a letter, purportedly by an American Indian, that argued against the need for supernatural revelation,[79] a response appeared which raised a series of questions about the efficacy of natural religion, but failed to answer them.[80] This, in turn, was answered by the original querist with a challenge to supernatural revelation whose effectiveness had as its support a multiplicity of sects, all claiming to be the true faith.[81] Two later items in the magazine related to the same controversy. Edward Watkinson's "Power of Reason", while it insisted upon the superiority of the Anglican faith to human reason, declared that there could be no contradiction between the two,[82] and another letter-writer argued that careful historical study demonstrated the futility of trusting revelation to man's reason.[83] As answers to the original question, neither comment suggested that the articles of faith could not be proved by the evidence of science.

For the minor magazines, the subject of the meaning of science to religion was of great importance. Nowhere is the impact of the scientific development upon theological thought more apparent than in the *Christian's Magazine*, with its combination of science and Anglican orthodoxy. The editor, Dodd, candidly described his purpose as an attempt "to diffuse Sacred Science, to cultivate the

[77] *London*, XXVI (September, 1757), pp. 441-443.
[78] The response to the Methodists in the *London* was specifically concerned with their abuse of reason. For example, see XXIX (September, 1760), p. 469; "In my opinion, all religious points should be tried at the bar of reason, by the standards of revelation; but when men abandon the plain principles of sound reason for the wild flights of giddy enthusiasm, what are they not capable of doing?"
[79] *London*, XXIX (Appendix, 1760), pp. 694-696. See B. H. Bissell, *The American Indian in English Literature of the Eighteenth Century* (New Haven, 1925), pp. 76-77.
[80] *London*, XXX (February, 1761), pp. 92-93.
[81] *London*, XXX (June, 1761), p. 313.
[82] *London*, XXXI (July, 1762), p. 362.
[83] *London*, XXXII (September, 1763), pp. 465-468.

knowledge, and investigate the wisdom and wonders of God's world and His works . . .".[84] Without restricting their appeal to readers of the Established Church,[85] Dodd and his writers sought to demonstrate the superiority of theological sciences to all the lesser sciences which merely attested to the reasonableness and accuracy of Christian Revelation.

Although asserting the necessity of accepting supernatural revelation to demonstrate the attributes of God,[86] the articles in the magazine described Scriptural truth as capable of scientific and historical proof. Particularly those comments on systematical divinity urged a careful investigation of Christian doctrine before accepting its principles on faith. Indeed, one writer demanded scientific investigaton before he would acknowledge the authenticity of divine revelation.[87] While warning of the dangers of man's misinterpretation of particular prophecies or Biblical statements,[88] and cognizant of the limitations on man's reason,[89] other writers in the magazine appealed to the reasonable man,[90] for they were certain that the material of faith, properly explored, could convince: [91]

All faith is founded upon evidence; consequently the more and stronger evidence you have of any facts the stronger your faith must be. In divine things the more fully you are satisfied of the divine interposition, the more will your mind acquiesce; and the greater confidence will you place in the things revealed for your instruction and comfort.

Even when a writer was most insistent on the need for accepting Christian Revelation, he refused to reject the instrument of reason

84 *Christian's Magazine*, I (1760), p. i.
85 *Christian's Magazine*, I (1760), p. iv; III (April, 1762), p. 147.
86 *Christian's Magazine*, I (July, 1760), p. 100; II (March, 1761), p. 97; II (April, 1761), p. 145; II (May, 1761), pp. 193, 214-215; II (October, 1761), p. 497.
87 *Christian's Magazine*, III (May, 1762), pp. 193-194.
88 *Christian's Magazine*, III (December, 1762), p. 529; III (July, 1762), p. 290; III (September, 1762), pp. 407-408.
89 *Christian's Magazine*, I (May, 1760), p. 20; I (August, 1760), pp. 172-173; III (January, 1762), p. 2.
90 *Christian's Magazine*, III (July, 1762), p. 289.
91 *Christian's Magazine*, III (April, 1762), p. 145. The quotation is from III (June, 1762), p. 241.

as a means for examining the claims of supernatural evidence.[92]

In order to satisfy the skeptics' demands for a scientifically demonstrated religion, the *Christian's Magazine* devoted particular attention to Biblical exegesis, which was intended to remove all question of doubt about Scriptural inconsistencies.[93] Both the Old and New Testaments were examined on principles of reason,[94] for, as the editor explained, "[We are] not willing, therefore, to admit the pretensions of any mode of faith, or system of opinions, unexamined . . ." [95] Opening his pages to astronomical support for the text of Genesis,[96] Dodd displayed his willingness to demonstrate revelation by science.

Naturally, such demonstration involved the controversy with the deists, but the writers in the *Christian's* were unafraid of controversies, since they considered free debate by rational creatures to be the real glory of the Protestant religions.[97] Although regarding deism as the antithesis of Christianity,[98] they argued, like Bishop Joseph Butler, in the rational terms of their antagonists. Rather than agree that the deists had taken a scientific approach to religion, the magazine writers insisted that reason was on the side of Christianity.[99] The absorption of natural religion itself into the orthodox Anglican faith is most apparent in an article that used Bolingbroke's arguments to prove that by his own evidence not merely the existence but also the nature of God could be deduced.[100]

The argument with Bolingbroke's philosophy appeared in the magazine's section on physico-theology, and while this approach

---

[92] *Christian's Magazine*, II (September, 1761), p. 450.
[93] *Christian's Magazine*, II (October, 1761), p. 519.
[94] *Christian's Magazine*, I (May, 1760), p. 7; I (June, 1760), pp. 49-50; I (September, 1760), pp. 193-194; I (November, 1760), pp. 289 ff.; I (October, 1760), pp. 241 ff.; II (January, 1761), pp. 1 ff.
[95] *Christian's Magazine*, I (July, 1760), p. 97.
[96] *Christian's Magazine*, IV (September, 1763), pp. 416-417; IV (Supplement, 1763), pp. 577 ff.
[97] *Christian's Magazine*, I (May, 1760), p. 31.
[98] *Christian's Magazine*, I (May, 1760), p. 8.
[99] *Christian's Magazine*, I (May, 1760), pp. 7-8; III (March, 1762), pp. 97-98; III (August, 1762), pp. 338, 363-364; IV (July, 1763), pp. 318-320.
[100] *Christian's Magazine*, IV (June, 1763), pp. 254-255.

to religion was not original with the *Christian's Magazine*, the use of science to demonstrate the accuracy of Scriptures and to give evidence of God's nature was to prove a major difficulty for Christian theologians in the nineteenth century. In the abundance of natural history as a sign of God's providence, wisdom, and teaching published by orthodox periodicals like the *Christian's Magazine*, religion displayed its willingness to use science as a bulwark to religion; when later scientific development created a challenge to the Established Church, it was embarrassing for orthodoxy to argue that faith was independent of the need for scientific support.

But even at this point in the eighteenth century, physico-theology, with its emphasis on the evidence of God in nature, created the question of the need for supernatural revelation. The magazine writers insisted that even the ancients with all their wisdom had failed to recognize God's true nature when they were unaided by miraculous intervention; [101] but the argument could hardly have aroused the enlightened man of the eighteenth century with a fervor for revealed religion or zeal for the Church. In fact, the comments in the *Christian's Magazine*, insisting on the obviousness of the Creator in His creation, implied only that the ignorance of ancient scientists suggested less glory and grandeur than had usually been attributed to the civilizations of Greece and Rome.

In its praise for the evidence of order, regularity, and perfection in the universe,[102] the magazine's physico-theology could naturally conclude: [103]

---

[101] *Christian's Magazine*, I (May, 1760), pp. 20-21; I (July, 1760), p. 100; I (August, 1760), pp. 172-173; II (March, 1761), p. 97; II (May, 1761), p. 193; III (August, 1762), p. 338.
[102] *Christian's Magazine*, I (1760), p. ii; I (June, 1760), pp. 67-68; I (July, 1760), pp. 114-115; I (September, 1760), p. 207; I (December, 1760), pp. 354 ff.; II (January, 1761), p. 28; II (February, 1761), p. 76; II (March, 1761), p. 108; II (November, 1761), p. 557; III (January, 1762), p. 14; III (March, 1762), p. 110; III (May, 1762), p. 213; III (July, 1762), pp. 295 ff., 312 ff.; III (August, 1762), pp. 345 ff.; III (September, 1762), p. 399; III (October, 1762), p. 449; IV (February, 1763), p. 64; IV (July, 1763), p. 203; IV (August, 1763), pp. 346-347.
[103] *Christian's Magazine*, III (November, 1762), p. 495.

No man who contemplates an animal like this [the zebra], can doubt the existence of an original and all-wise Designer. –The view of *it alone* is sufficient to discredit all atheism. While the thinking mind must be filled with admiration on the reflection of His manifold wisdom, who has formed such a wonderful variety, and settled such a regular oeconomy through nature, that this variety uniformly continues, and will continue to the end of time.

In his use of the words *it alone*, the writer expressed an attitude that suggested supernatural revelation to be excessive in the presence of scientific information. The repetition of this opinion that an examination of science must lead to acceptance, adoration, and understanding of God by any rational, contemplative man indicates how fully the deistical principles had infiltrated the Anglican religion.[104]

At the same time, the magazine's use of natural history as a means for instruction in morality suggests what Lovejoy has described as the parallel between deism and neo-classicism. The *raison d'être* of the physico-theology section was to provide entertainment and instruction, and each article was an essay with a moral, a scientific-religious parable, which demonstrated God's purpose by offering examples of good or bad conduct in the animal and vegetable kingdoms.[105] Lessons in industry, important for a commercial society, were illustrated by the behavior of the silkworm and beaver,[106] and the bread plant of the West Indies demonstrated how men could use even the poisonous creations to produce required sustenance.[107] In the same way, God had provided the opossum, stork, and pelican as monitors for the instruction of human parents.[108]

Nothing better illustrates the extent to which the Anglican Church had accepted natural revelation as a part of the evidence

---

[104] *Christian's Magazine*, I (August, 1760), p. 165; II (April, 1761), p. 165; II (May, 1761), p. 216; II (August, 1761), p. 433; II (October, 1761), p. 508; IV (March, 1763), p. 108; IV (June, 1763), p. 257; IV (September, 1763), p. 399; IV (November, 1763), p. 500.

[105] *Christian's Magazine*, I (October, 1760), p. 256; II (July, 1761), p. 372.

[106] *Christian's Magazine*, I (August, 1760), p. 165; IV (April, 1763), p. 157.

[107] *Christian's Magazine*, II (January, 1761), pp. 28-29.

[108] *Christian's Magazine*, II (March, 1761), pp. 108-109; II (August, 1761), p. 433; III (February, 1762), p. 65.

for God's existence than a comparison between the *Christian's Magazine* and the *Spiritual Magazine*.[109] None of the former's physico-theology reached the pages of the latter. Not only did the *Spiritual's* letter-articles and poetry insist on miraculous revelation,[110] but, in "An Essay on Divine Teaching", the writer in the magazine, which was strongly Calvinistic,[111] specifically denounced attempts to relate science to religion.[112] Attacking the thesis that natural truths are of help in spiritual discernment and ascribing religious decadence to the confusion of the natural state,[113] he deplored the modern tendency of admitting everyone, and particularly persons of scientific pretensions, to argue the questions of divinity: [114]

Every one who finds himself able to solve a problem in metaphysics, calculate the time of an eclipse, discover the crisis in a disease, accurately pen a history, or write a romance; he imagines himself every way sufficient to examine divine things, and sit as umpire in the decision of inspired writings.

The comment was clearly a rebuke not only to skeptics like David Hume, but also to scientists who, like James Ferguson, were using the material of science to establish the chronology of Scriptures.

But apart from the comments in the *Spiritual Magazine*, those in the minor magazines overwhelmingly used science as an approach to religion. The differences among them were dependent upon the extent to which each was willing to admit evidences of faith without careful scrutiny according to reasonable principles, or the degree to which each argued the self-sufficiency of natural revelation.

---

[109]   The edition of the *Spiritual Magazine* used in this study was the reprint, *Divine, Moral, and Historical Miscellanies in Prose and Verse* (London, n.d.). The collection offers two volumes, bound in one, and part of the first volume bears the running head of dates, January-November, 1761. The divisions of the *Spiritual* for 1761-1762 included miscellanies, poetry, foreign affairs, domestic occurences, maritime affairs, promotions, preferments, pious thoughts, and biographies.

[110]   *Spiritual Magazine*, I, pp. 49 ff., 65 ff.; II, p. 16.

[111]   Mineka, p. 37.

[112]   *Spritual Magazine*, I, pp. 84 ff.

[113]   *Spiritual Magazine*, I, pp. 85-86.

[114]   *Spiritual Magazine*, I, p. 84.

Of all the magazine writers, indeed of all those in the periodicals, Benjamin Martin, editor of the *General Magazine of Arts and Sciences,* was most dedicated in his support of scientific progress and the scientific method. To be sure, he echoed the conventional opinion that the works of nature attested to the infinite power of God,[115] but unlike those periodical writers who merely accepted natural religion as an adjunct of revelation, he insisted that the design of the universe was in itself sufficient evidence "of the existence and providence of a Deity . . .".[116] Even the lowly louse, intricate in its physical structure, was "one of the strongest proofs of the existence and attributes of that superior Being, we call a God".[117] For the skeptic or infidel, the comments in the magazine did not offer the evidences of the Bible, but rather the "wisdom and contrivance in the formation of the mole-cricket": [118]

This creature alone is an undeniable proof of design and contrivance in the works of Nature; and such like themes as these, if they were more generally observed, and insisted upon, and made the subjects of public lectures, might prove a most effectual method to eradicate from the minds of men, the absurd principles of infidelity, causality, and necessity.

Indeed, in their treatment of the Scriptures, the articles were less than reverent.[119] At a time when orthodoxy regarded the Scriptures as an historical document, the *General Magazine* had its chief *persona,* Cleonicus, explain to his sister, Euphrosyne, whom he was educating, that literal Scriptural arguments were not intended to set forth a system of philosophy or astronomy, of which the writers were probably ignorant, but rather to offer the vulgar simplified explanations. Pointing to contradictory assertions in the Bible about the earth's position in the universe, he cautioned his sister that literal interpretation "is not only injurious to the

---

[115] *General Magazine of Arts and Sciences,* Pt. I, I, pp. iii ff., 27, 38, 170, 185, 247; Pt. I, II, p. 185; Pt. V, pp. 267-268.
[116] *General Magazine of Arts and Sciences,* Pt. I, II, p. 331.
[117] *General Magazine of Arts and Sciences,* Pt. V, p. 893.
[118] *General Magazine of Arts and Sciences,* Pt. V, p. 229; Pt. V, p. 793.
[119] *General Magazine,* Pt. I, I, pp. 105-106, 132-133, 284.

sciences, but even to religion itself".[120] According to Cleonicus,
the evidence of science was not to be refuted by the testimony of
the Scriptures: ". . . the figure of the earth is not the subject of
revelation . . .; and some of the Fathers of our Church have as
gravely defended the heathenish figure of the earth, as if they had
been the descendants of Ptolomy himself".[121] When Euphrosyne
replied that she could not imagine the earth's figure to have been
the subject for an article of faith, and that she recalled nothing of
it in the Thirty-Nine Articles, Cleonicus concluded: [122]

They [the notions of the earth's form and motion] are not; and our
principles and notions of religion are much more correct and rational
than they were formerly; and to what is this owing, my Euphrosyne?
To our having a more correct and rational philosophy; you will find
it a never-failing maxim, that the better you understand philosophy,
the better you will understand religion.

Taking a latitudinarian point of view toward religion,[123] and recognizing the impact of science on orthodox faith,[124] the articles in
the *General Magazine* regarded science with a truly religious fervor.[125] While acknowledging the limitation of man's knowledge,[126]
they scoffed at the superstitions that stood in the way of facts, and
they belittled the objections to scientific investigations.[127] Enlightenment resided in science and nature was revelation enough: [128]

It is always one good effect that philosophy has, to deliver the mind
from the infamy of ignorance, and those base sentiments and slavish
fears that continually subject it to unnecessary pain and anxiety. In
short, it gives the ingenious and liberal mind a pleasure in viewing
those phaenomena of wonder-working Nature, which vulgar and
superstitious souls construe into direful omens and prodigies of
Fate; and scare themselves, and their unthinking neighbours, with

[120] *General Magazine*, Pt. I, I, p. 14.
[121] *General Magazine*, Pt. I, I, p. 62.
[122] *General Magazine*, Pt. I, I, pp. 62-63.
[123] *General Magazine*, Pt. I, I, pp. 76-77.
[124] *General Magazine*, Pt. I, I, pp. 72-73, 79-80, 120, 138-139.
[125] *General Magazine*, Pt. I, I, pp. 5-6; Pt. I, II, p. 243; Pt. V, p. 641.
[126] *General Magazine*, Pt. I, II, p. 332.
[127] *General Magazine*, Pt. I, I, pp. 123, 311-312, 398-399; Pt. I, II, pp.
3-4.
[128] *General Magazine*, Pt. I, I, p. 111.

notions of divine wrath and judgment much oftner than there is occasion for.

None of the other magazines matched the *General*'s interest in science or reliance on natural religion, but the *Grand Magazine* was at least as demanding in applying the test of reason. In its pages, rational Christianity emerged as the ideal religion. Both in its letters and articles, the magazine presented arguments for the "rational Christian" against the attacks of the "formal pretences of the Pharisees of the age".[129] While supernatural revelation was not ignored, it was joined necessarily with the evidence of reason,[130] and science was regarded as a support to a Bible that was only a more finished version of the allegorical literature of pagan antiquity.[131]

Through the evidence of science, in original essays and letters, the *Grand* presented man and the creation as the work of a divine architect or a wonderful mechanic,[132] whose masterpiece, examined as a whole or in its parts, declared his wisdom: [133]

When we survey the whole creation like a map, we admire beyond measure the stupendous piece as a finished system: so when we contemplate the several parts of it, the same order and propriety are still observable, which corresponding, and united together, complete harmony and perfection of the whole.

In such Newtonian revelation, the need for God's supernatural revelation appears most untenable, especially since the writers in the *Grand*, in summarizing the purposes of agricultural study, concluded explicitly that such examination led naturally to a First Cause.[134]

While such magazines as the *Royal* and *Universal* displayed abundant interest in science, neither was as rationalistic as the *Grand* or *General*. Yet, once again, it is obvious from the comment in the *Royal* and *Universal* that natural revelation had be-

[129] *Grand*, II (January, 1759), pp. 19-20.
[130] *Grand*, I (September, 1758), pp. 433, 435; III (May, 1760), p. 235.
[131] *Grand*, II (September, 1759), pp. 481-483.
[132] *Grand*, I (September, 1758), p. 435; II (May, 1759), p. 226.
[133] *Grand*, I (October, 1758), p. 486.
[134] *Grand*, I (September, 1758), p. 456; II (August, 1759), pp. 427-429.

come an important part of the faith of even those who insisted on
the necessity of supernatural revelation. Like the *General Magazine*, the *Royal* devoted considerable space to the relationship between science – particularly natural history – and religion. In
letters, articles, and poetry, the writers in the *Royal* argued that
the teleological character of all creation demonstrated God's beneficence, practicality, and wisdom,[135] but – unlike Martin in the
General – were unwilling to concede that natural revelation was
more than additional evidence for the existence of a Supreme
Being.[136] Convinced of man's limitations in appreciating the handi-
work of God,[137] the *Royal*'s writers pointed to the inadequate concept of deity expressed by Greeks, Egyptians, Persians, Indians,
Chinese, and Jews, who lacked the benefit of Christian revelation.[138] While acknowledging the wonders of natural history, the
authors in the magazine did not regard them as more than an adjunct to supernatural revelation and did not consider them as obvious entries to God: [139]

If inquiries into natural history had nothing more for their object
than to display the innumerable variety of creatures observable in the
universe, they would claim our utmost attention; as they greatly
assist us in forming more enlarged ideas of the author of so many
astonishing works: for who can contemplate the amazing multitude
of different objects continually presented to his view, and not be
convinced that the Being who formed them is infinite in wisdom, in
power, and in goodness? . . . The body of the smallest and most dis-
regarded insect is a self-moving machine, a perpetual motion, the
*discovery of which has so long baffled, and will for ever defy, all the
attempts of human perspicacity.*

[135] *Royal*, III (July, 1760), p. 1; IV (February, 1761), p. 68; IV (March,
1761), p. 114; V (October, 1761), pp. 190-191; VI (May, 1762), pp. 233,
261-263; VI (June, 1762), p. 284; VII (September, 1762), p. 121; VIII
(May, 1763), p. 246; IX (July, 1763), p. 3; IX (October, 1763), pp. 179-
180; IX (December, 1763), pp. 291-293.
[136] *Royal*, II (January, 1760), pp. 1-4; VII (August, 1762), pp. 74-78; VIII
(March, 1763), pp. 119-120.
[137] *Royal*, I (August, 1759), pp. 55-57; II (January, 1760), pp. 1-2; II
(February, 1760), p. 95; IV (May, 1761), p. 235; V (August, 1761), pp. 75-
77; V (October, 1761), p. 177; VI (May, 1762), pp. 225-226.
[138] *Royal*, IV (May, 1761), p. 235.
[139] *Royal*, I (July, 1759), p. 7. Italics are added.

Indeed, in no uncertain terms, the articles in the *Royal Magazine* rejected the sufficiency of natural religion. Its "Historical Account of the Rise and Progress of the Arts and Sciences", in particular, described the necessity of supernatural revelation. Even the wisdom of Plato and Socrates had not been enough for them to perceive God behind the wonderful network of the universe.[140] Heathen philosophy, the writers in the *Royal* insisted, could have no effect on the improvement of men's manners because it failed to deal with the fundamentals of existence: "It was revelation alone that could display the real state of man, and explain the reason why, since his fall, he abounds with amazing contrarieties." [141] Moreover, a specific comparison between natural and revealed religion concluded that there was no difference in what they presented, but a Messiah was needed "to free mankind from their delusive errors, and draw the veil that concealed these mysteries".[142] Human reason was simply insufficient to see beyond the evidence to either the nature of the soul or the schemes of providence.[143]

Many letters supporting these views appeared in the *Royal*. In answer to a query about the discrepancy between Bishop Burnet's remarks on the smoothness of the earth before the flood and the account in Noah's story of the mountains and hills,[144] the editors published two letters in defense of Genesis. In each instance, the correspondent placed the evidence of Scriptures above that of nature, either attributing the contradiction to inadequate investigation or insufficient reason.[145] Other letters attempted to deprecate the arguments of deists by interpretation and examination of the Scriptures; [146] repeated the magazine's comments on the limitations of the human imagination in achieving true knowledge of

140 *Royal*, I (October, 1759), p. 184.
141 *Royal*, II (February, 1760), pp. 75-76.
142 *Royal*, V (July, 1761), p. 2.
143 *Royal*, I (August, 1759), p. 88.
144 *Royal*, VI (March, 1762), p. 162.
145 *Royal*, VI (April, 1762), pp. 193-194, 207. See additional comments in *Royal*, VII (July, 1762), pp. 14-15; VII (August, 1762), p. 26. For an earlier comment, see V (July, 1761), pp. 29-30.
146 *Royal*, IV (March, 1761), pp. 115-117; IV (May, 1761), pp. 237-238.

God without the aid of supernatural revelation; [147] or went so far as to explain science itself through Revelation.[148]

The peculiar combination of natural and revealed religion is more apparent in the articles of the *Universal Magazine* than in the *Royal*, although the latter devoted considerably more space to the subject. In a series of thoughts on several subjects, one writer in the *Universal* declared: [149]

There is more wisdom, goodness, and power of the Creator in the common course of nature, than in any miracle whereby He suspends or changes the course of nature. The restoring of a dead man to life doth not seem so wonderful, as giving constantly life by a continual course of nature in generation and sustenation. If we saw a grape grow on a pear-tree, we should greatly wonder at it; and yet this would not be comparable in any degree to the seed itself hidden in a pear, which contains in it the whole nature of the tree, the root, fruit, branches, and leaves; all which it is capable of producing in time; so that, on all such occasions, we may justly conclude, that the universe is the greatest of all miracles.

So great was this miracle of nature,[150] according to another article, that it was sufficient evidence of the existence of God, evidence adapted to the meanest capacities: [151]

Of all the proofs of the existence of God, none are so evident as those which are grounded upon the knowledge of the world, and of man in particular. This demonstration convinced the ancient philosophers, and ought to convince every attentive man.

Even to convince an atheist of God's being, in the language of a poem printed in the magazine, all that was necessary was to produce the facts of nature, since "Nature in every mystic scene / Declares a plastic author's reign." [152]

Yet it is also apparent in the *Universal*'s articles that the cele-

---

[147]   *Royal*, I (October, 1759), pp. 168-170; I (November, 1759), p. 227; IV (March, 1761), p. 108; VIII (January, 1763), pp. 25-26; IX (October, 1763), pp. 185-188.
[148]   *Royal*, VIII (January, 1763), pp. 4-8.
[149]   *Universal*, XXXI (July, 1762), pp. 24-25.
[150]   *Universal*, XXIV (April, 1759), pp. 184-185; XXIV (May, 1759), p. 232; XXV (August, 1759), p. 60; XXXI (July, 1762), pp. 32 ff.
[151]   *Universal*, XXIV (March, 1759), pp. 115-118.
[152]   *Universal*, XXVIII (April, 1761), p. 207.

bration of nature's miracles was not intended to demean the wonders of supernatural revelation. Indeed, an "Essay on the Judgment of the Holy Scripture, concerning the System of Nature" contended that the divine oracles not only were unopposed to the study of nature but encouraged it because God's works will teach His perfection.[153] Rather, the articles in the *Universal* permitted a choice of methods by which the glory of God might be discovered. For the well-disposed mind, for the man of sense, in general, the magazine's articles suggested, the evidence of divine planning was sufficient,[154] but it was possible to know God "either by revelation or the works of the creation",[155] and revelation certainly simplified the explanations of morality and immortality.[156]

For the writers in the *Universal*, as indeed for most of the magazine writers who regarded science and natural history as divine inspiration, the teleological character of all creation was the strongest evidence of a purposeful God.[157] Perhaps the greatest appeal in a practical Creator was His fitness to a growing commercial and industrial society. Certainly, the articles in the *Universal* stressed the practical nature of God and insisted that providence had given man the means for conducting a successful life dependent upon industry.[158] Particularly for the London middle class descendants of Robinson Crusoe, there was comfort in having a God whose revelation through nature sanctioned utilitarian values in man.

While the comments in other minor magazines are less exten-

---

[153] *Universal*, XXXI (August, 1762), p. 70.
[154] *Universal*, XXV (July, 1759), p. 30; XXVI (Supplement, 1760), p. 352. However, the *Universal*, XXVII (November, 1760), p. 231, warned that there was a mystery in the works of nature that man could not fully comprehend from their magnificence. Man remained ignorant of means, causes, and ends, but even here the magazine stressed the importance of biology and creation as symbols of providence.
[155] *Universal*, XXV (July, 1759), p. 28. See, also, *Universal*, XXIII (October, 1758), p. 166; XXV (July, 1759), p. 33.
[156] *Universal*, XXVI (January, 1760), pp. 2, 6.
[157] *Universal*, XIX (August, 1756), p. 69; XX (March, 1757), pp. 106-107; XXIII (October, 1758), pp. 165-166; XXV (July, 1759), pp. 2, 29, 33; XXVI (January, 1760), pp. 1-4.
[158] *Universal*, XVIII (January, 1756), p. 4; XXVI (February, 1760), p. 65; XXVIII (May, 1761), p. 247.

sive, they are equally revealing of the way in which Anglican orthodoxy had come to rely on the evidence of science. Although
for the socially and politically conservative authors in the *Lady's
Museum*, the question of conflict between natural religion and
supernatural revelation never arose,[159] their acceptance of natural
proof of God's existence is apparent. In presenting a teleological
explanation of the universe, the writer in the *Lady's Museum* felt
safe in instructing the young ladies by way of Providence in nature: [160]

[The protection, within limits, of creatures may be attributed to] the
infinite wisdom of the great First Cause in his works of creation,
who has thus contrived it so, that although it is necessary the different species of animals should mutually prey on one another, and
that each should find himself surrounded with a host of professed as
well as insidious enemies, yet that every kind should be supplied,
and that with a variety of invention which nothing less than infinite
wisdom could form, with the methods for preventing its race from
utter extirpation, and preserving the just and proper balance which
the use and the conveniency of man, and often some hidden cause
beyond the comprehension of his understanding, require to be maintained amongst the greater and the smaller wheels of this great
machine the universe.

While "some hidden cause beyond the comprehension of his
understanding" implied that human reason was not in itself sufficient to eliminate the need for supernatural revelation, the arguments in the *Lady's Museum* made it difficult to quarrel with the
deists' contention that nature's wonders made supernatural revelation redundant. In their tremendous respect for the probing of
science,[161] and in their insistence that this great machine, the

---

[159] The one comment on the subject in the other ladies' magazine, the
Royal Female, I (February, 1760), pp. 77-79, argued the need for a reasoned approach to sacred history and demanded strong evidence for God's
miracles.
[160] *Lady's Museum*, I, #5, p. 397. See, also, *Lady's Museum*, I, #3, pp.
184-185; I, #4, pp. 308-309.
[161] *Lady's Museum*, II, #8, p. 633: "There is nothing more trite and common than the ridicule which persons unused to the study of nature endeavour to throw on those whom a more speculative turn of mind induces
to follow her into her inmost recesses, and examine even into the extremest
minutiae of her works. The titles of gimcrack, cockle-shell merchant, fly-

earth, demonstrates in every way "that the whole must be the work of infinite power, of infinite wisdom, of infinite goodness",[162] the writers in the magazine might well have given the impression that Christian dogma was unnecessary for the young women who were advised: [163]

... look on the vast universe as one immense machine, whose complicated mechanism bespeaks an artist of almighty power and wisdom – a machine formed for our use, and consequently a most amazing proof of his benevolence and goodness – a machine whose several parts have all a wonderful connection, and all their several uses; which it is therefore a duty enjoined on us to endeavour at the discovery, and discovery itself a reward granted for the performance of that duty.

In the absence of specific comment in the magazine to remind them that science was not always so obvious an expression of God or so clear to the ignorant, little wonder if the readers confused telescopic and microscopic evidence with Christian revelation.

Comment in the remaining magazines was less extensive than that in the *Lady's Museum*. Despite the interest of Smollett and Goldsmith in science, the *British Magazine*, which the editors themselves regarded as a literary miscellany,[164] published far less material on subjects like natural history than most of the other important magazines offered. But in its comparatively few comments on the relationship of science and religion, the *British* again indicates how commonly the defenders of religion used the arguments of scientific evidence. Apart from those articles tracing God's hand in the teleological formation of the universe,[165] and insisting that mathematics presented "the only key whereby the

---

hunter, &c. are lavishly bestowed on them by such as either ignorance, indolence, or a natural want of curiosity, have excluded from the great garden of nature: they find no amusement or instruction [in such things] and therefore conclude that neither is capable of being drawn from them. . . ." See, also, pp. 634-635.

[162]   *Lady's Museum*, II, #11, p. 858. See, also, I, #2, pp. 140-141.
[163]   *Lady's Museum*, I, #2, pp. 136-137.
[164]   Graham, pp. 177-178.
[165]   *British Magazine*, II (February, 1761), p. 97; II (March, 1761), p. 130; III (May, 1762), p. 233.

springs of Nature can be unlocked . . .",[166] an article on free-thinking, stressed the importance of reason in religion.[167] According to the writer, religion had nothing to fear from independent judgment, open-mindedness, and a willingness to accept information. If God had meant man to be ignorant, He would not have created the instruments of reason for probing and finding religious truth.[168]

In the few comments in the *Imperial Magazine*, which described natural history as an instructive and entertaining study,[169] science appeared as an evidence of God's providence, but without challenge to Christian revelation.[170] But the *Weekly Magazine,* although offering little more than the *Imperial*, suggests the dangers to orthodoxy that were inherent in the emphasis upon the wonders present throughout the natural universe. For one writer in the *Weekly*, a magazine which printed scientific information that contradicted the Bible,[171] the presence of God in His own creations seemed obvious to all, and although supernatural revelation was not discussed, it hardly seemed necessary: [172]

Here [in the amazing objects of nature] we learn to adore our Almighty Creator, whose power, wisdom and goodness are conspicuous in all His works, which proclaim in a language understood by the whole human race, that they are the productions of an omnipotent hand.

A God so apparent to the entirety of mankind could surely need no recourse to supernatural intervention.

But reason was not enough for writers in three other minor magazines. Three comments from French sources in the *Philological Miscellany* emphasized the importance of supernatural revelation. An attack upon atheism offered scientific evidence of God's existence, but warned that, without miraculous intervention, man's

---

[166] *British*, II (March, 1761), p. 120.
[167] *British*, II (December, 1761), p. 640.
[168] *British*, II (December, 1761), pp. 640-641.
[169] *Imperial Magazine*, I (1760), p. 20.
[170] *Imperial Magazine*, I (January, 1760), pp. 5-6; III (March, 1762), pp. 116-119, 141.
[171] *Weekly Magazine*, #6 (May 20, 1758), pp. 174-175.
[172] *Weekly*, #1 (April 15, 1758), pp. 6-7.

reasoning powers were insufficient to permit him to perceive the divine plan.[173] Insisting that all man's knowledge does not depend for its truth upon his having experienced it, another article responded to those who questioned Christ's miracles: [174]

But God, who gave to men the law of nature, why may not He, upon seeing it disfigured by atheism in some, and by superstition in others, publish it anew, if I may be allowed the expression, and seal it by prodigies.

In much the same way, the articles in the *Universal Museum*, which insisted upon the reasonableness of Christianity,[175] explained that reason alone was not enough. Even a scientist like Robert Boyle, according to one writer, inquired into nature not to demonstrate the existence of God, but to add to the glory of His great creation.[176] Although another writer in the *Universal Museum* conceded that some excellent minds, through God's endowing them with superior wisdom, could discover in the "prospect of the universe, and in the contemplation of it" the Supreme Being, he concluded: [177]

But the unhappy prevalence which the greater part of mankind have permitted their irregular passions to gain over their reason, having vitiated and depraved it, it became absolutely necessary for God to declare His will, in a manner independent of their corrupt understandings.

Finally, the few comments in the *Literary Magazine* permit no real analysis, but suggest a position similar to those of the *Universal Museum* and the *Philological Miscellany*. To be sure, one article in the *Literary* rejected supernatural explanations for occurrences that could be attributed to natural causes,[178] but Johnson's famous review of Soame Jenyns's Enquiry into the *Nature and Origin of Evil* expressed skepticism of man's reason,[179] and, in describing the proper function of science, reminded the readers

173 *Philological Miscellany*, I (1761), pp. 184, 187-188, 278.
174 *Philological Miscellany*, I (1761), p. 161.
175 *Universal Museum*, I (January, 1762), pp. 26, 155.
176 *Universal Museum*, II (June, 1763), pp. 285-286.
177 *Universal Museum*, II (August, 1763), p. 430.
178 *Literary*, II (May-June, 1757), p. 220.
179 *Literary*, II (April-May, 1757), p. 171; II (May-June, 1757), p. 252; II (June-July, 1757), pp. 301-306. See, also, III (February, 1758), pp. 74 ff.

that science was not intended to challenge the "sacrosanctity of religion . . .".[180]

Clearly, the evidence of the magazines indicates the extent to which science had permeated religious thought. Differences of opinion concerned only the degree to which natural religion was regarded as a means of revelation, and few of the magazines were inclined to devalue the discoveries of biology, astronomy, and particularly natural history. The more conservative magazines placed limitations on man's reasoning power and argued that the evidence of nature was meaningful only after supernatural revelation, but even these orthodox publications used science as an illustration of divine attributes.

Like the writers in the conservative magazines, Burke in the *Annual Register* found no conflict between science and religion but placed the evidence of reason beneath that of revealed religion. Perhaps the *Annual Register* was even more orthodox than most of the conservative magazines. Although, beginning with its second volume, the annual had a long section on natural history and presented material to satisfy the scientific curiosity of its readers, its articles made no attempt to demonstrate the existence of God from the evidence of science or nature. Both a fictional piece called "Linnaeus's Dream" and passages from Johnson's life of Boerhaave [181] clearly expressed the view that science and reason for the most philosophical and intelligent beings were inferior to Christian revelation.

Of the writers in the two major reviews, those in the *Critical* shared Burke's opinion. Although Smollett himself believed that the universe and nature demonstrated the "power and wisdom of the Almighty Architect",[182] and an unidentified reviewer argued that scientific discovery heightened "our admiration of the wise Author of Providence, who has created nothing useless",[183] articles in the *Critical* did not equate scientific and metaphysical reason-

[180] *Literary*, I (July-August, 1756), p. 193.
[181] *Annual Register*, IV, Pt. II (1761), p. 182; I (1758), pp. 245-246. For Johnson's authorship of the second item (the life of Boerhaave), see Bloom, p. 275.
[182] *Critical*, I (July, 1756), pp. 520-521 (Smollett).
[183] *Critical*, X (August, 1760), pp. 122-123.

ing, and did not confuse the evidence of science with that of faith.[184] For Franklin in the *Critical*, human reason was "serviceable . . . in this life", although unimportant in the next,[185] but the word of God, Smollett himself noted, had to be defended against misrepresentation and it was wrong to pay "deference to *human* wisdom which is only due to the *divine*".[186]

While distinguishing between the inspiration of Newton, Homer, and the apostles,[187] the reviewers approved investigation of the Scriptures in order to convince the infidel of "the divine origin of those writings termed sacred".[188] Even when the investigation was Calvinistic and "tortured orthodoxy into heresy", the conservative reviewer was willing to praise the honesty of an effort that did not relinquish common sense,[189] but when the writer sought to demonstrate the credibility of gospel history, Franklin and others granted whole-hearted approval to the effort.[190]

Reason and common sense were handmaidens to religion for writers in the *Critical*, whose overwhelming opposition to the Methodists and enthusiasts was aroused by their distortion of reason. According to the reviewers – particularly Franklin – mere sense and argument were abhorrent to the followers of Hutchinson, Romaine, Wesley, and Whitefield, who threatened "to corrupt the pure stream of Christianity",[191] with their "striking examples of the abjectness of superstition . . .".[192] Franklin accused the enthusiast, like the deist, through the corruption of sense and reason, of building a sacrilegious temple "on the ruins of Scripture and common sense . . .".[193]

---

[184]   *Critical*, II (October, 1756), p. 193 (Franklin); XIV (August, 1762), pp. 81-82.
[185]   *Critical*, II (September, 1756), p. 155.
[186]   *Critical*, II (September, 1756), pp. 109-110.
[187]   *Critical*, XVI (December, 1763), p. 452.
[188]   *Critical*, XIII (January, 1762), p. 32.
[189]   *Critical*, VII (February, 1759), p. 118.
[190]   *Critical*, I (May, 1756), p. 347 (Franklin); IV (December, 1757), pp. 516-517; V (January, 1758), p. 59.
[191]   *Critical*, XIII (March, 1762), p. 227.
[192]   *Critical*, X (September, 1760), p. 207. See, also, II (November, 1756), p. 350 (Franklin); VI (July, 1758), p. 76; XVI (October, 1763), pp. 293-294.
[193]   *Critical*, II (October, 1756), p. 258. See, also, II (August, 1756), pp. 51, 61-62. Both by Franklin.

For the scientific pretensions of the enthusiasts, the writers in the *Critical* had only contempt. The reviewers, who acknowledged the proper use of science in supporting faith, ridiculed the growth of natural philosophy brought on by the earthquake at Lisbon. Particularly, they deplored the efforts of the enthusiasts to undermine Newtonian science, which suited so well the Anglican faith. Samuel Derrick, Smollett's "little Irishman", scornfully suggested that the fanatics who claimed the superiority of their system of discovering from Hebrew cryptography the character of natural phenomena could "contribute to the emolument of mankind".[194] And when Julius Bates, a follower of Hutchinson, used the Scriptures for natural philosophy, Franklin in the *Critical* replied: [195]

There lived heretofore a gentleman whom some of our readers may possibly have heard of, one Sir Isaac Newton, who was reckon'd, in his time, a man of no contemptible abilities, and who had a tolerable knack at a system; but the sagacious Mr. H . . . . . n and his followers have since discovered him to be a mere empirick in philosophy, and his system a very idle and improbable fiction. They have therefore taken the pains to substitute something else in its stead, infinitely more ingenious; for a perfect account of which we must refer our readers to Mr. Hutchinson's *Moses' Principia.* . . .

Unwilling to use science to distort religion, the *Critical* refused to permit religion to corrupt science.

While the *Monthly* reviewers' attitude toward religion has frequently been contrasted with that expressed in the *Critical*,[196] the specific difference has never been described adequately. In the scientific approach of the *Monthly* rests the challenge that the *Critical* reviewers detested most. For Rose and others in the *Monthly,* the very essence of Protestant faith was a reliance on the individual's right to take a reasonable approach to Christianity.[197] Reminding his readers that "Protestants, of all men, should be extremely cautious of offending against human reason: with-

---

[194] *Critical*, I (April, 1756), p. 257.
[195] *Critical*, II (October, 1756), pp. 259-260.
[196] See p. 197 of this study.
[197] *Monthly*, XV (September, 1756), p. 315 (Rose); XVIII (May, 1758), p. 494; XIX (August, 1758), p. 164 (Rose); XXVI (March, 1762), p. 240; XXIX (August, 1763), pp. 123-124 (Seddon).

out which we cannot reasonably expect converts to the Christian
faith, as professed by Protestants",[198] Gregory Sharpe, one of the
few *Monthly* reviewers prominent in the Established Church,
argued: [199]

Reason is to convince us of the truth of revelation; is it not also to
assist us in understanding it? Yes, surely, for should you tell the infidel, that tho' you appeal to his reason for the truth of the Christian
religion, yet when he has once admitted revelation, you would not
permit him to reason at all; he would certainly say, that he had
rather hear you talk of Christianity than become a Christian, for
whilst you only talked of religion, he was allowed to be a rational
being, but on his conversion, must become like the horse or the mule
who have no understanding. Nothing can discredit religion more
than the running down human reason, natural religion, and moral
virtues. . . .

Believing little in miracles,[200] Rose, one of the founders of the
Monthly, insisted that revelation itself be examined in the light of
reason and science: [201] "Natural religion, and the dictates of
reason, must never be given up, must never be contradicted. These
are first principles, the test and rule by which any doctrine that
comes recommended as revealed, should be tried." While not directly undervaluing revelation, Griffiths himself argued that they
must, at least, go hand in hand.[202] Asserting that all except the
most fanatic recognized Scriptural corruption,[203] Benjamin Dawson, who in 1759 renounced dissent and took orders in the
Church, objected to the argument [204]

that reason ought, in all mysterious points, to yield to revelation. For
certainly, where any doctrines are delivered, which are plainly contrary to reason, no man can so far give up his reason to revelation,

---

[198] *Monthly*, XIV (June, 1756), p. 503.
[199] *Monthly*, XIV (June, 1756), p. 499.
[200] *Monthly*, XIV (January, 1756), p. 68; XV (August, 1756), p. 199; XVI
(March, 1757), p. 201; XXVI (March, 1762), p. 239. All except the last
are by Rose.
[201] *Monthly*, XIV (May, 1756), p. 398. See, also, XV (September, 1756),
pp. 247-248 (Sharpe), p. 314; XV (November, 1756), p. 471.
[202] *Monthly*, XVIII (February, 1758), p. 151.
[203] *Monthly*, XIX (July, 1758), p. 96; XX (January, 1759), pp. 27, 37;
XXIX (October, 1763), pp. 293-294.
[204] *Monthly*, XIX (December, 1758), p. 550.

as to believe them true, at the same time that he sees them to be contrary to reason, or false; and as for those doctrines which may be reckoned though not contrary to reason, yet above reason, and surpassing the human comprehension, in this case there can be no yielding up of reason, because they are confessedly not the objects of reason, nor can any judgment be formed of them, as to their truth or falsehood, while the terms of the proposition are not understood.

While the quotation suggests that Dawson regarded some doctrines as not open to the scientific tests of reason, there were no examples of the reviewers' ready acquiescence to articles of faith. Rose and others insisted that religion must be based on truth, and even the credibility of the Gospels, divine interpositions in human affairs, and the very divinity of Christ's mission must be demonstrated.[205] While Rose urged the need to review the tenets and articles of the Church,[206] Griffiths joined him and others in repeatedly asserting that truth had nothing to fear from any test: [207]

But we have often said, and here repeat it, that *Truth*, like gold, has nothing to fear from any *test*; and that the more it is *tried*, the purer it will come forth at last: and, we do not scruple to add, that, in our opinion, every rational wellwisher to our holy religion ought to concur in a fair invitation to all intelligent unbelievers, openly to propose their doubts, and advance their utmost arguments; in order, that we may have the better opportunity of satisfying every candid enquirer, and of fully answering all objections.

The statement came in response to one of the attacks on the "deistic" principles of the *Monthly*. By their support of Shaftesbury and his ideas, the reviewers did little to discourage such charges.[208] Indeed, Ruffhead particularly admired Shaftesbury's ability to

[205] *Monthly*, XIV (January, 1756), p. 38 (Rose); XIV (May, 1756), p. 428 (Rose); XV (August, 1756), pp. 146-147 (Rose); XVI (March, 1757), p. 201 (Rose); XX (January, 1759), p. 5 (Ruffhead).
[206] *Monthly*, XIV (May, 1756), pp. 462-463.
[207] *Monthly*, XXIV (May, 1761), p. 359. See, also, *Monthly*, XIV (April, 1756), p. 356 (Rose); XVII (September, 1757), p. 287; XVIII (April, 1758), p. 309 (Rose); XVIII (Appendix, 1758), p. 652 (Dawson); XIX (October, 1758), p. 360 (Rose); XX (January, 1759), p. 8 (Ruffhead); XX (May, 1759), p. 419 (Rose); XXIV (April, 1761), p. 239 (Griffiths).
[208] See, for example, *Monthly*, XIV (June, 1756), p. 467 (Ruffhead); XVIII (February, 1758), p. 101 (Ruffhead); XXVII (July, 1762), pp. 32 ff. (Seddon).

demonstrate "divine truths conspicuously by the light of reason",[209] and Seddon went so far as to declare that true deism, that is, Shaftesbury's, was in no way opposed to Christianity.[210] While Rose was unwilling to denounce the honesty of the deists,[211] Sharpe declared, ". . . the superstructure of *revealed*, is properly raised on the foundation of *natural*, religion".[212]

For the *Monthly* reviewers, then, the new science was important for the ways in which it supported natural religion. Science was in no way a contradiction to religion.[213] Astronomy, according to Rose, further revealed the necessary "reverence towards the Original Parent Mind . . .",[214] and the light of revelation was hardly necessary alongside the light of nature.[215] God's beneficence, as well as omnipotence, was all the clearer before the instruments of science.[216] Only the ignorance of the enthusiasts could pervert such knowledge, and while tolerant of their religious heresy, the reviewers nevertheless regarded this strange enthusiastic "orthodoxy" as a disgrace to true Christianity.[217]

Once again, the difference between the *Monthly* and *Critical* is the difference between liberal and conservative opinion. Although other periodicals varied frequently from topic to topic, the two reviews only occasionally departed from their antithetical views.

---

[209] *Monthly*, XVIII (February, 1758), p. 101.

[210] *Monthly*, XXVII (July, 1762), p. 32.

[211] *Monthly*, XXIV (January, 1761), pp. 53-54.

[212] *Monthly*, XV (July, 1756), p. 78. See, also, XV (August, 1756), pp. 199-200 (Rose); XVI (June, 1757), pp. 481 ff. (Rose).

[213] *Monthly*, XIV (February, 1756), p. 155 (Sharpe); XX (March, 1759), p. 263 (Campbell).

[214] *Monthly*, XV (September, 1756), p. 236.

[215] *Monthly*, XVI (February, 1757), p. 187.

[216] *Monthly*, XVI (April, 1757), p. 303 (Rose); XVIII (March, 1758), p. 236 (Bewley); XXI (July, 1759), p. 2 (Rose); XXIV (March, 1761), pp. 169 ff. (Bewley); XXV (July, 1761), p. 26 (Griffiths); XXVI (June, 1762), p. 443 (Rose); XXVIII (June, 1763), pp. 441-442 (Kenrick).

[217] See, for example, *Monthly*, XIV (May, 1756), p. 392 (Sharpe); XVII (November, 1757), pp. 445-446 (Dawson); XVIII (Appendix, 1758), p. 635 (Dawson); XIX (August, 1758), p. 117 (Dawson), XX (May, 1759), p. 477; XXI (August, 1759), pp. 108-109 (Flexman); XXII (February, 1760), p. 172; XXIII (October, 1760), pp. 272, 309 (Rose); XXV (August, 1761), p. 121 (Rose); XXV (December, 1761), p. 114 (Rose); XXVI (January, 1762), pp. 78-79; XXIX (July, 1763), p. 70 (Kenrick).

VII

LANGUAGE, LITERATURE, AND THE ARTS

I. THE ESSAY-JOURNALS AND THE MAGAZINES

Less apparent than the political and social changes during the Seven Years' War was the continuing transformation of critical theories.[1] To be sure, the alterations were scarcely recognizable to orthodox critics who persisted in trimming the new ideas according to the old pattern, but the European standards which had remained substantially the same for two hundred years were undergoing a revision that would be complete by the beginning of the next century.[2]

To call that old pattern *neoclassicism* without elaboration would invite justifiable criticism, for the tag has unquestionably been used indiscriminately. But, as Rene Wellek has insisted, to deny the existence of a unified body of aesthetic values would be to ignore the historical truth: [3]

Whatever the arguments for caution in speaking of pre-romanticism and however justified may be the dissatisfaction of some scholars with the multiple meanings of the term "romanticism", it seems impossible to deny that we are confronted [in the second half of the eighteenth century] with the problem of the destruction of neoclassicism and its replacement by new and different theories. The problem should not be ignored and obscured by exclusive insistence on the undeniable survivals, the compromises, and the open contradiction of individual authors.

Varieties of modern interpretations as diverse as those by Lovejoy, Fairchild, Wimsatt, and Frye do not deny the conclusion of

---

[1] Rene Wellek, *A History of Modern Criticism, 1750-1950* (New Haven, 1955), I, p. 5.
[2] N. Frye, *Anatomy of Criticism* (Princeton, 1957), p. 83.
[3] Wellek, I, p. 106.

R. S. Crane that neoclassical criticism "constituted, from [1650-1800] a distinct and fairly consistent school . . .".[4] Whether discussing the entire period or limiting themselves to a particular author, scholars have emphasized the neo-classical insistence on general principles and laws relating to "kinds".[5] They have described the "central concept . . . of decorum" in Voltaire's criticism,[6] the conventions and generalization that led to Pope's abhorrence of singularity,[7] and the principles of clarity and regularity that characterized Blair's moral persuasiveness.[8] Whatever their differences in emphasis, critics like Frye and Abrams are in accord about neoclassical adherence to a theory that was governed by rules and order.[9]

To be sure, as Wellek and others have pointed out,[10] neoclassicism in the Age of Johnson must be distinguished in its methods and attitudes from those that existed earlier. What had constituted a change of degree ever since Dryden's period was ultimately to become a change in kind, and Johnson's own attitude toward Shakespeare and the unities indicated a shift in emphasis which Wellek has described as a liberal reinterpretation of "the main tenets of the tradition of neoclassical criticism".[11] Moreover, the very turn in the audience away from the "expert connoisseurship of a limited circle of readers" in the "London audience of Dryden and Pope" effected a practical alteration of critical principles.[12]

Nevertheless, to appreciate properly the distinctions of late

[4]   R. S. Crane, "On Writing the History of English Criticism, 1650-1800", *University of Toronto Quarterly*, XXII (1953), p. 375.
[5]   J. W. H. Atkins, *English Literary Criticism: 17th and 18th Centuries* (London, 1951), pp. 11-12.
[6]   Wellek, I, p. 45.
[7]   George Saintsbury, *A History of Criticism and Literary Taste in Europe* New York, (1950), II, p. 461.
[8]   Gordon McKenzie, *Critical Responsiveness: a Study of the Psychological Current in Later Eighteenth-Century Criticism* (Berkeley and Los Angeles, 1949), p. 113.
[9]   Frye, pp. 83-84; M. H. Abrams, *The Mirror and the Lamp* (New York, 1958), p. 17.
[10]   Wellek, I, p. 104; J. H. Hagstrum, *Samuel Johnson's Literary Criticism* (Minneapolis, 1952). For some suggestion of a likeness between the initial and final stages of neoclassicism, see Atkins, pp. 70, 145.
[11]   Wellek, I, p. 104.
[12]   Abrams, p. 17.

neoclassicism, they must be measured according to their divergence from those standards that modern critics have ascribed to the Augustan period. Even supposing the tradition of Boileau and Le Bossu dead and the late neoclassical critics giving only lip service to their doctrines,[13] it would still be necessary to describe what it was that the critics thought they believed. Perhaps the chief point of agreement on what constitutes neoclassicism centers around the notion that: [14]

... it assumed a stable psychology of human nature, a fundamental set of norms in the works themselves, a uniform working of human sensibility and intelligence allowing us to reach conclusions which would be valid for all art and all literature.

When combined with the critical attitude that emphasizes the effect of art on its audience,[15] the statement contains the basic concepts of universality (and hence an appeal to the ancients as models), a reason for imitation, rules and unities, correctness, a theory of the genres, a natural respect for reason, and a demand for morality in art.[16]

[13] Atkins, p. 185.
[14] Wellek, I, p. 12.
[15] Perhaps the best discussion of this point is in Abrams. See, especially, pp. 17 ff.
[16] In addition to those examples already cited, the following passages, despite their variety of views, lead to this general description of neoclassicism: William W. Appleton, *A Cycle of Cathay* (New York, 1951), p. 105; Fairchild, *The Noble Savage*, pp. 29 ff., and *Religious Trends in English Poetry*, II, p. 366; Heidler, p. 113; M. T. Herrick, *The Poetics of Aristotle in England* (New Haven, Conn., 1930), pp. 80, 81, 112-113, 119-121, 127; R. F. Jones, "Science and Criticism in the Neo-classical Age of English Literature", *JHI*, I (1940), p. 353; Samuel Kliger, "Whig Aesthetics: a Phase of Eighteenth-Century Taste", *ELH*, XVI (1949), pp. 136, 144; A. O. Lovejoy, *Essays in the History of Ideas* (Baltimore, 1948), pp. 70 ff., 79-89, 99-101, 147-148; J. J. Lynch, *Box, Pit, and Gallery* (Berkeley and Los Angeles, 1953), pp. 2-4, 31, 45, 180 ff., 264-266; Samuel Monk, *The Sublime: a Study of Critical Theories in XVIII-Century England* (New York, 1935), p. 101; A. W. Read, "Suggestions for an Academy in England in the Latter Half of the Eighteenth Century", *MP*, XXXVI (1938), pp. 145, 156; Saintsbury, II, pp. 391, 415-416; W. K. Wimsatt and C. Brooks, *Literary Criticism: a Short History* (New York, 1957), pp. 237-238, 258, 275, 288 ff., 296, 315, 318, 320-333. Most important of all, however, is Wellek, *passim*.

In the degree of both their insistence on these critical principles and their determination to apply them to aesthetic changes during the Seven Years' War, conservative periodical writers may be distinguished from liberal. All of what has since become known as "pre-romanticism" was present during these years. Aesthetic fashions like *chinoiserie*, Gothicism, primitivism, and the sublime, all required some trimming to fit the accepted critical theories, while writers like Young, Hurd, and Macpherson, in various ways, challenged orthodox rules and standards. In the extent of their attempts to assimilate these changes into the tradition, the periodical writers' allegiance may be seen to the old aesthetic establishment.[17]

Unlike studies which have extended the examination to 1770 or 1785 and emphasized examples from the later dates,[18] an investigation of these war years shows the periodicals generally to be far more reluctant to accept aesthetic than to accept social and political changes. At the same time, easy generalizations like Kliger's association of Gothic taste with political opinion require some modification when the evidence of the periodicals is presented.[19] The effect of the war itself upon attitudes toward

[17]   Although the term *pre-romantic* is used throughout this discussion, it should not be taken to mean a reaction against the Augustan Age. As both R. S. Crane and Northrop Frye have pointed out (J. L. Clifford, editor, *Eighteenth-Century English Literature: Modern Essays in Criticism*, New York, 1959, p. 311), such treatment of the period as one of reaction results in chaos. These ideas, like *chinoiserie*, Gothicism, and the sublime, are to be viewed, instead, according to the attempt to assimilate them in the aesthetic tradition. Particularly important for this discussion are, Appleton, *A Cycle of Cathay*; Kliger, *The Goths in England*; and Monk, *The Sublime*.

[18]   See, for example, E. N. Hooker, "The Discussion of Taste, from 1750 to 1770", *PMLA*, XLIX (1934), pp. 577-592, "The Reviewers and the New Criticism, 1754-1770", *PQ*, XIII (1934), pp. 189-202, and "The Reviewers and the New Trends in Poetry, 1754-1770", *MLN*, LI (1936), pp. 207-214; C. E. Jones, "Poetry and the *Critical Review*, 1756-1785", pp. 17-36, "The English Novel: a *Critical* View, 1756-1785", *MLR*, XIX (1958), pp. 147-159 and 213-224, "Dramatic Criticism in the *Critical Review*, 1756-1785", *MLQ*, XX (1959), pp. 18-26.

[19]   *Cf.*, Samuel Kliger, *The Goths in England: a Study in Seventeenth and Eighteenth Century Thought* (Cambridge, Mass., 1952). Kliger's thesis relates Gothic taste to Whig politics.

chinoiserie and romantic primitivism, the increasingly chauvinistic evaluation of Shakespeare, national literature, and language, and particularly the differences in periodical types add to the complexity of the picture.

For the non-political essay-journals, protection of public taste and morality virtually demanded a conservative adherence to aesthetic tradition. Satire, which was the chief stock-in-trade of these literary journalists, begins with the assumption of standards and proceeds on the belief that they are being perverted. In all four 1756 essay-journals, the view was satirical and the aesthetic attitude conservative.

Although the name *Connoisseur* suggests a critic of the arts, its writers were concerned primarily with correcting the manners and morals of its readers.[20] Their object was "to prevent the growth of vice and immorality",[21] and their comments, including some by William Cowper, on language were directed against fashionable swearing and the abuses of good taste.[22] Even in his objections to popular novelists and comic playwrights, the writer in the *Connoisseur* was aroused not by their impoverished talents but by their immoral portrayal of amiable villains.[23]

Taste, as an index of conduct and manners, received serious attention in this essay-journal. Borrowing a definition of the term, one of its writers declared: [24]

"Taste consists in a nice harmony between the fancy and the judgment." The most chastised judgment without genius, can never constitute a man of taste; and the most luxuriant imagination, unregulated by judgment, will only carry us into wild and extravagant deviations from it.

He ridiculed the fashions that passed for taste,[25] and, like Cowper,

---

[20]   Drake, II, pp. 318-319; *Critical Review*, III (April, 1757), pp. 314-315.
[21]   The quotation is from *Connoisseur*, #139 (September 23, 1756), p. 237. See, also, #136 (September 2, 1756), pp. 218-219.
[22]   *Connoisseur*, #104 (January 22, 1756), pp. 53-58; #108 (February 19, 1756), pp. 75 ff.; #138 (September 16, 1756), p. 230. The final comment has been attributed to Cowper.
[23]   *Connoisseur*, #136 (September 2, 1756), p. 220.
[24]   *Connoisseur*, #120 (May 13, 1756), p. 140.
[25]   *Connoisseur*, #120 (May 13, 1756), p. 138.

following the conservative line,[26] deplored Gothicism and *chinoiserie,* linking them with the corruption of the *nouveau riche.*[27]

Yet the moderns were criticized not only for their ludicrous innovations but for their lack of common sense and their inability to follow the classical rules. To be sure, servile imitation was never condoned by intelligent neoclassical critics,[28] but this emphasis upon common sense practice was especially characteristic after the middle of the century, and Colman, who was a classical scholar,[29] together with Thornton, scorned: [30]

> those who, despising the modern whims to which fashion has given the name of taste, pretend to follow, with the most scrupulous exactness, the chaste models of the ancients. These are the poets, who favour us with correct, epithetical, and tasteful compositions; whose works are without blemish, and conformable to the precise rules of Quintilian, Horace, and Aristotle: and as they are intended merely for the perusal of persons of the most refined tastes, it is no wonder that they are above the level of common understandings. These too are the critics, who, in their comments upon authors, embarrass us with repeated allusions to the study of *virtu:* and these too are the Connoisseurs in architecture, who build ruins after Vitruvius, and necessaries according to Palladio.

Even stronger denunciation of mechanical imitation of the classics appeared in a letter by Robert Lloyd, who chastized modern poets whose concern was with how and not what they should write: [31]

> . . . there is this material difference between the former and present age of poetry; that the writers in the first thought poetically; in the last, they only express themselves so. Modern poets seem to me

---

[26]   Here the distinction between conservative and liberal follows the decription of Kliger, *The Goths in England.* However, in the position of the *Connoisseur* and the *Monitor,* it may be seen that Kliger's linking of Gothic and Whig requires modification.

[27]   *Connoisseur,* #120 (May 13, 1756), p. 141; #134 (August 19, 1756), p. 209; #138 (September 16, 1756), p. 230; #139 (September 23, 1756), p. 236.

[28]   For a description of the variety of meanings given to the term *imitation,* see Abrams, pp. 8 ff.

[29]   Drake, II, pp. 321-322.

[30]   *Connoisseur,* #120 (May 13, 1756), p. 141.

[31]   *Connoisseur,* #125 (June 17, 1756), pp. 163-164.

more to study the manner how they shall write, than what is to be written. The minute accuracy of their productions; the bells of their rhimes, so well matched, making most melodious tinkle; and all the mechanism of poetry, so exactly finished; (together with a total deficiency of spirit, which should be the leaven of the whole) put me in mind of a piece of furniture, generally found in the studies of the learned, "in an odd angle of the room", a mahogany case, elegantly carved and fashioned on the outside, the specious covering of a – chamber-pot.

Implicit in the *Connoisseur*'s ironic comments on sterile imitation was the judgment of ancient superiority in the arts.

Like the writers in the *Connoisseur*, those in the *Prater* followed the Augustan tradition of light satire but offered little literary or aesthetic comment not bearing directly on social criticism.[32] Concern for purity of diction and objections to borrowing foreign words were related to moral censure.[33] In their ridicule of gaudy costumes and fashionable artistic taste, the journalists stressed moral rather than aesthetic values,[34] and their limited literary comments, as well as their choice of subject matter, emphasized morality and education.[35]

The same moral considerations characterized the writers' reactions to modern taste,[36] particularly for oriental fashions. By linking aesthetic excesses to reckless spending, the comments in the *Prater* clearly identified *chinoiserie* with the senseless indulgences of the *nouveau riche*.[37] Even when the writer himself used the

[32] The first number of the *Prater* (March 13, 1756), p. 5, set the tone by dedicating the periodical to the tradition of Isaac Bickerstaff and Nestor Ironside.
[33] *Prater*, #3 (March 27, 1756), p. 14 and #30 (October 2, 1756), p. 176. However, the *Prater*, #1 (March 13, 1756), p. 4, warned critics not to practice their malicious art by carping about trite sentiments and mean diction.
[34] *Prater*, #2 (March 20, 1756), p. 10 and #11 (May 22, 1756), pp. 61 ff.
[35] *Prater*, #1 (March 13, 1756), p. 2; #8 (May 1, 1756), pp. 45-46 and #24 (August 21, 1756), pp. 139 ff.
[36] Despite its statements deploring modern taste, the *Prater*, #1 (March 13, 1756), p. 4, aimed at no high level audience as suggested by the essay-journal's translations of commonplace Latin phrases.
[37] *Prater*, #18 (July 10, 1756), p. 105; #20 (July 24, 1756), p. 116; #21 (July 31, 1756), pp. 121-123; #25 (August 28, 1756), pp. 149-150; #29 (September 25, 1756), pp. 169-174.

oriental fashion to instruct his readers, his purpose was clearly a lesson in morality illustrating the precept by example: [38]

That my readers may the better discern, with what more than magic enchantment this Daemon [drinking] gains an ascendant over us, by artful approaches and unperceived gradations, I shall beg leave to illustrate precept by example.

Although essays in the *Old Maid*, too, were concerned enough with morality in literature to condemn Restoration poetry out of hand,[39] they were less restricted to social criticism than those in the *Prater* and *Connoisseur*. Mrs. Frances Brooke, the editor, was later to become an extremely popular novelist, and the aesthetic comments in the *Old Maid* reflected her interests.[40] Writers in the *Old Maid* prescribed the values of "truth, nature, and simplicity, the most animated fire, and the most studied correctness" for greatness in literature.[41] While arguing against the stock diction of neoclassical writing,[42] the journalists praised a song by Beaumont and Fletcher because its: [43]

images are not only fancied with the greatest beauty, strength, and propriety, but are heightened with all the colouring and ornament of the most exquisite poetry; and the versification, allowing for the distance of time, surprizingly smooth and harmonious, even to modern ears; though accustomed to the studied correctness of these latter days.

According to at least one writer, even the rustic charms of romantic primitivism required the restorative treatment of classical propriety, and for him the highest values in the arts were those that had the sanction of antiquity.[44]

The superiority of the ancients was described as plainly evident.[45] Satirically, the writers in the *Old Maid* extolled the "vir-

[38]   The quotation is from the *Prater*, #28 (September 18, 1756), p. 165. See, also, #13 (June 5, 1756), pp. 75-78; #15 (June 19, 1756), pp. 85-90; #16 (June 26, 1756), pp. 91 ff.
[39]   *Old Maid*, #28 (May 22, 1756), p. 237.
[40]   Foster, *History of the Pre-Romantic Novel in England*, pp. 145 ff.
[41]   *Old Maid*, #12 (January 31, 1756), p. 97.
[42]   *Old Maid*, #26 (May 8, 1756), p. 218.
[43]   *Old Maid*, #12 (January 31, 1756), p. 92.
[44]   *Old Maid*, #12 (January 31, 1756), p. 91.
[45]   *Old Maid*, #8 (January 3, 1756), pp. 54 ff.

tues" of the modern ode [46] and compared modern accomplishments in such trivialities as cook books and cockfighting with classical achievements in literature and the fine arts.[47] Close textual criticism of the *Aeneid* was used to teach, in Pope's words, "the world with reason to admire",[48] and to defend Virgil from charges of impropriety by demonstrating his satirical purpose.[49]

But alone, of the essay-journalists, those in the *Old Maid* were proud of national accomplishments in literature where they existed. Predecessors in periodical writing, especially Addison, were warmly praised,[50] along with poets and authors who have since been described as pre-romantic.[51] Although writers in the *Old Maid* stressed Milton's fancy and imagination as his greatest virtues,[52] their particular tribute was granted to Shakespeare, inimitable and immortal.[53]

No such charitable or favorable comments on the moderns appeared in the last of these four essay-journals, the *World*. Its literary comment was frequently related to taste, for although it has been criticized for lack of seriousness,[54] the *World*, like the other essay-journals, followed the tradition of the *Spectator* which sought to instruct as well as entertain.[55] Particularly in comments on language and *chinoiserie*, the writers for the *World* equated taste and morality. Critical of the fashionable use of such meaningless words as *vastly, horridly, abominably, immensely*, and *excessively*, one declared: [56]

[46] *Old Maid*, #16 (February 28, 1756), p. 130.
[47] *Old Maid*, #36 (July 17, 1756), pp. 290-293.
[48] *Old Maid*, #8 (January 3, 1756), pp. 54 ff. The quotation is from p. 54.
[49] *Old Maid*, #14 (February 14, 1756), pp. 115-116.
[50] *Old Maid*, #8 (January 3, 1756), p. 54; #12 (January 31, 1756), p. 91; #18 (March 13, 1756), p. 149.
[51] *Old Maid*, #28 (May 22, 1756), p. 237. Among these poets were Lady Winchelsea, Akenside, Young, Gray, and Warton.
[52] *Old Maid*, #12 (January 31, 1756), pp. 93 ff.
[53] *Old Maid*, #18 (March 13, 1756), p. 149.
[54] Drake, II, pp. 258-259 and Caskey, p. 144.
[55] *World*, #162 (February 5, 1756), p. 145 and #174 (April 29, 1756), p. 211. Straus, p. 185, notes that the *World* was written deliberately in the tradition of the *Spectator* and stresses its lightness.
[56] . *World*, #175 (May 6, 1756), pp. 216 ff. The quotation is from pp. 221-222.

It is certain, there is a distinction and subordination of *style*, as well as of *rank*, and a gradation to be preserved in point of *phraseology*, as well as *precedency*. Any encroachment in the one case being altogether as unseemly as in the other. An affectation of talking above our level, is as bad as dressing above it, and that which is current within the precinct of St. James's, will hardly pass any where else.

In the same way, others in the *World*, including Soame Jenyns, attacked the lack of decorum exhibited by those who displayed a ridiculous liking for Chinese fashions.[57] Particularly, the essayists deplored a public demonstration of such ignorance. If a man desired to place a head or figure of a mandarin between busts of Tully and Demosthenes or to raise Pekin's contributions to the levels of classical antiquity within his own gallery, that was unfortunate, "but if the same innovating taste should intrude upon the Muses shrine in our public seats of learning, I should wish for some authority to stop so sacrilegious an attempt".[58]

Clearly, the aesthetic opinions in the *World* were conservative. Its writers preferred the arts of the ancients to those of the moderns and scoffed at the new learning.[59] Romantic primitivism, whether in pastoral poetry, romances, or statecraft, held no lure for Jenyns and others,[60] and even in their refusal to judge modern work by ancient standards, these writers in the *World*, nevertheless, required genre criticism consistent with the rules.[61] For language, too, when a writer like Orrery did not relate the subject to taste, he still urged principles of authority based on gradual development: [62]

Custom is the tyrant of the language; it can alter, adjust, and new model, but it cannot annihilate. It can settle new phrases, introduce a whole colony of fashionable nonsense from foreign parts, and

[57]   *World*, #178 (May 27, 1756), pp. 240-241 (Jenyns) and #205 (December 2, 1756), pp. 381-385. In the latter, particularly, the relationship between Chinese fashions and the French is stressed.
[58]   *World*, #171 (April 8, 1756), pp. 195 ff. The quotation is from p. 195.
[59]   *World*, #189 (August 12, 1756), pp. 296 ff. and #191 (August 26, 1756), pp. 307 ff.
[60]   *World*, #178 (May 27, 1756), p. 242 (Jenyns) and #181 (June 17, 1756), pp. 252-254.
[61]   *World*, #171 (April 8, 1756), p. 198.
[62]   *World*, #166 (March 4, 1756), pp. 167-168.

render old words obsolete; but it cannot erase idea from language. It can do more than an absolute prince; because it can create new words; a privilege which was not allowed to the Roman Emperor Tiberius, who having coined a word in the senate, his flatterers desired it might be adopted into their language, as a compliment to the emperor; but an old senator, not quite degenerated from the honest sincerity of his ancestors, made this memorable reply – "You may give, Sir, the freedom of the city to *men*, but not to *words*."

Of the two essay-journals that appeared at the beginning of 1757, the *Centinel* offered opinions consistent with the orthodoxy of its predecessors, while the two comments in the *Crab-Tree* which expressed admiration for Pope provide little basis for judging their aesthetic principles.[63] Marr, who has described the *Centinel* as Thomas Franklin's imitation of the *Rambler*, properly emphasized its didacticism,[64] for Franklin himself declared that his purpose was to give "such intelligence as will amuse the fancy, meliorate the heart, and improve the understanding", but also noted that dullness would be intentional where otherwise the message might be obscured.[65] But didacticism was only one point on which the essay-journal reflected the orthodox aesthetic principles. The *Centinel*, which regularly employed Latin and Greek mottoes, contrasted ancient and modern talents in literature, and concluded with a condemnation of contemporary taste and creativity.[66] And, finally, in appointing a sub-centinel to guard the theaters, Franklin warned him to follow the precepts of decorum and insist that actors not "deviate from nature, either by soaring to bombast, or sinking to grimace and buffoonery".[67]

But for all these essay-journals, aesthetic comment was scarcely ever distinguished from social criticism; however, unlike any of these earlier essay-journals, the *Bee*, in 1759, was concerned with aesthetics as aesthetics. Together with the *Busy Body*, it had the services of Oliver Goldsmith, and its comments, like his work,

[63]   *Crab-Tree*, #12 (July 12, 1757), p. 68 and #13 (July 19, 1757), p. 74.
[64]   G. S. Marr, *The Periodical Essayists of the Eighteenth Century* (London, 1923), pp. 165, 168. See *Centinel*, #3 (January 20, 1757), pp. 17-18.
[65]   *Centinel*, #1 (January 6, 1757), p. 4.
[66]   *Centinel*, #21 (May 25, 1757), pp. 123-125. See, too, #22 (June 2, 1757), pp. 127-128, 131.
[67]   *Centinel*, #1 (January 6, 1757), p. 5.

reveal the method of transition in literary and aesthetic standards through the replacement of authority by the dictates of common sense.

While nothing of importance can be determined on aesthetics in the *Busy Body*,[68] the comments in the *Bee* exceeded both in number and significance those of any of the other essay-journals.[69] Its commitment was to a common sense neoclassicism which provided the artist or writer with the necessary rules and models but did not restrict his talent by mechanical restraints. Recognizing the need for the best models, the essays in the *Bee* nevertheless warned of the dangers of having "to imitate nature from an imitation of nature".[70] Goldsmith respected the importance of classical antiquity,[71] but demanded justice for modern writers.[72] An article on "The Characteristics of Greatness" advised writers and artists to break the mold, try new forms and inventiveness, despite the opposition of the age.[73] Particularly in his remarks on eloquence, Goldsmith put the rules in their proper perspective. Reminding his readers that "eloquence has preceded the rules of rhetoric, as languages have been formed before grammar", he declared: [74]

Rules will never make either a work or a discourse eloquent; they only serve to prevent faults, but not to introduce beauties; to prevent those passages, which are truly eloquent and dictated by nature, from being blended with others, which might disgust, or at least abate our passion.

[68] For its anti-romanticism see *Busy Body*, #8 (October 25, 1759), p. 44; #9 (October 27, 1759), p. 50, and #10 (October 30, 1759), pp. 55-60. In one comment, #4 (October 16, 1759), p. 24, the *Busy Body* describes its purpose to be to "instruct and amuse the publick . . .".

[69] The criticism in the *Monthly Review*, XXII (January, 1760), pp. 38-45, should be discounted since Goldsmith had recently left Griffiths' employ. See Marr, p. 173, for praise of Goldsmith's essays in the *Bee*.

[70] *Bee*, #1 (October 6, 1759), p. 12. However, if models were to be used, the *Bee*, #8 (November 24, 1759), pp. 214-215, insisted that it was important to find the best.

[71] *Bee*, #7 (November 17, 1759), p. 188.

[72] *Bee*, #4 (October 27, 1759), pp. 103-105 and #5 (November 3, 1759), pp. 127 ff.

[73] *Bee*, #4 (October 27, 1759), pp. 102 ff.

[74] *Bee*, #7 (November 17, 1759), pp. 174-175.

Or, again, he warned: [75]

[Rules] cannot make us eloquent, but they will certainly prevent us from becoming ridiculous. They can seldom procure a single beauty, but they may banish a thousand faults. . . . [Not in sublime portions, but in others,] rules may teach [the artist] to avoid any thing low, trivial, or disgusting. Thus criticism, properly speaking, is intended not to assist those parts which are sublime, but those which are naturally mean and humble, which are composed with coolness and caution, and where the orator rather endeavours not to offend, than attempts to please.

The same balanced view of freedom and restraint occurs throughout the comments in the *Bee*. "Follow nature", they advised,[76] but Goldsmith's admission of Smollett to fame for his romances was based on the precedent of Segrais and Cervantes.[77] Beware of "a conformity to critic rules, which, perhaps, on the whole have done more harm than good" by thwarting the vivacity of nature,[78] but remember that our imaginations are too easily misled by perpetual novelty and we are too often pleased by what is new rather than what is correct.[79] Seeking moderation, Goldsmith warned against the poet who "either drily didactive gives us rules, which might appear abstruse even in a system of ethics, or triflingly volatile, writes upon the most unworthy subjects; content, if he can give music instead of sense; content, if he can paint to the imagination, without any desires or endeavours to affect . . .".[80]

To be sure, it was a well-defined kind of imagination that the essays in the *Bee* advocated. They insisted upon the "illusion of nature" in the theater.[81] Whether in staging, casting, or acting, they demanded that nature be followed to maintain the illusion of reality.[82] There were objections to the notion that style could be forced upon subject matter contrary to nature. Similarly, in his comments on the sublime, Goldsmith argued that "the sublimity

[75] *Bee*, #7 (November 17, 1759), p. 180.
[76] *Bee*, #5 (November 3, 1759), p. 133.
[77] *Bee*, #5 (November 3, 1759), p. 136.
[78] *Bee*, #5 (November 3, 1759), pp. 139, 142.
[79] *Bee*, #8 (November 24, 1759), pp. 205-206, 217.
[80] *Bee*, #8 (November 24, 1759), p. 226.
[81] *Bee*, #2 (October 13, 1759), p. 56.
[82] *Bee*, #1 (October 6, 1759), p. 15 and #2 (October 13, 1759), p. 56.

lies only in the things; and when they are not so, the language may be turgid, affected, metaphorical, but not affecting".[83] Even comments on language in the *Bee*, although urging the necessity of an academy for reform, ridiculed attempts to force rules "to naturalize those absurdities [of our language], and bring them under a regular system", rather than restore the natural quality of the language itself.[84]

For the manifestations of romantic primitivism, the *Bee* had no welcome. The editor's own use and evaluation of orientalism was generally didactic, satirical, or critical of its anti-religious significance.[85] When the word *Gothic* appeared in the essay-journal, it was linked with ignorance and ridiculed for its mixing of orders.[86] And when confronted with the arguments for the noble savage, Goldsmith scrutinized them by the cold light of fact: [87]

... those savages and peasants are generally not so long-lived as they who have led a more indolent life; secondly, ... the more laborious the life is, the less populous is the country: had they [the advocates of primitivism] considered that what physicians call the *stamina vitae*, by fatigue and labour become rigid, and thus anticipate old age; that the number, who survive those rude trials, bears no proportion to those who die in the experiment, [what then must their opinion have been?]

Reluctant to accept literary conventions antithetical to common sense, Goldsmith was no more willing to approve attacks on tradition which were not themselves satisfactory examples of reason.

In effect, the literary essay-journals, whose social criticism was conservative, tended to reject aesthetic changes. Even the *Bee*, which was ready to yield to the transition when the aesthetic ideas were not related to the political and social, was more conservative in its response to romantic primitivism which challenged the social

---

[83]   *Bee*, #7 (November 17, 1759), p. 178.

[84]   *Bee*, #8 (November 24, 1759), pp. 223-224. In #6 (November 10, 1759), pp. 169-173, the comment in the *Bee* ridiculed academies where there was no culture.

[85]   *Bee*, #1 (October 6, 1759), pp. 17-24; #3 (October 20, 1759), pp. 67-70; and #5 (November 3, 1759), pp. 117-118.

[86]   *Bee*, #2 (October 13, 1759), p. 32.

[87]   *Bee*, #6 (November 10, 1759), pp. 152-153.

and political order. The problems were different for the political essay-journals, which, while literary themselves, were concerned with only the utility of aesthetic ideas.

For the *Test* and *Con-Test* in the intra-mural Whig battle early in the war, politics took precedence over all other subjects, and comments on aesthetics and language were used as tools in the art of polemics. The *Con-Test* had the advantage at a time when learning was still identified with a classical education. Despite his professed preference for ancient oratorical talents,[88] one of Murphy's writers in the *Test* blundered in classical allusions to history and literature and permitted Ruffhead's staff on the *Con-Test* to ridicule their rivals' lack of knowledge.[89] Murphy himself followed his Latin quotations in the journal by translations and criticized the *Con-Test* for failing to do the same,[90] which also proved a mistake in political judgment since it allowed Ruffhead's writers to scoff at their opponents' limited knowledge.[91] Pointing to a mistranslation of Latin in the *Test*, Ruffhead patronizingly promised to translate for the benefit of his rival, whose earlier objections to the Latin, he declared, now seemed demonstrated as illiteracy rather than satirical argument.[92] Moreover, he indicated in his comment on a translation of a Greek passage that the *Test* writer's lack of classical knowledge was tantamount to intellectual incapacity: [93]

For the benefit of the *Test* writer, we have translated the Greek; we ask his pardon, for having innocently affronted him by the un-translated Latin in our last; and we promise never to take advantage of him, in an *unknown* language for the future.

In the same way, the editors used comments on each other's diction and grammar as arguments in the political war. Again, the *Con-Test* had the intellectual advantage in describing the faulty

[88] *Test*, #3 (November 27, 1756), p. 8.
[89] *Con-Test*, #3 (December 7, 1756), pp. 13 ff. and #13 (February 12, 1757), p. 74.
[90] *Test*, #2 (November 20, 1756), pp. 2, 4; #3 (November 27, 1756), pp. 8-9; and #4 (December 4, 1756), p. 14.
[91] The passage in the *Con-Test* was #2 (November 30, 1756).
[92] *Con-Test*, #5 (December 18, 1756), p. 29.
[93] *Con-Test*, #3 (December 7, 1756), p. 14.

pronoun references and errors of diction in the *Test*.[94] The response in the *Test* weakly objected to the pedantry of verbal criticism,[95] once more affording the writer in the *Con-Test* an opportunity to regret having taken advantage of his opponent's ignorance but also to suggest that the mode of expression was related to the inferiority of ideas.[96] The comments in the *Con-Test* themselves objected to the use of *Jacobite* as a name-calling device,[97] and those in the *Test*, ignoring its own editorial rejection of verbal criticism, later ridiculed the romantic sentiment that characterized "high-flown phrases, strained metaphors, unnatural figures, [and] turgid diction".[98] While none of these comments was truly concerned with doctrines of aesthetics, literature, or language, the writers in the political essay-journals used the arguments of grammarians, rhetoricians, and literary critics to the ends of political controversy.

For the political essay-journals during the peace negotiations, too, interest in language and literature was restricted to propagandistic effects. Indeed, the writers in the *Monitor*, which had been publishing since 1755, had always regarded such things as the superiority of classical antiquity to the moderns and claims for American primitivism only in terms of their polemic utility.[99] When they sought to discredit the Newcastle administration, the journalists described the American Indians as undisciplined savages, a despicable band who, with no signs of nobility in their fighting capacity, had managed to defeat the British.[100] Yet one writer, in ascribing the cruelty of the Indians to the perversion by the French, foreshadowed the manner in which the American aborigines would later become the noble savages whose natural goodness was destroyed by corrupt society.[101] Similarly, during

[94]   *Con-Test*, #2 (November 30, 1756), pp. 7 ff.
[95]   *Test*, #4 (December 4, 1756), pp. 13-14 and #5 (December 11, 1756), p. 24.
[96]   *Con-Test*, #5 (December 18, 1756), pp. 25-26.
[97]   *Con-Test*, #12 (February 5, 1757), pp. 70-71.
[98]   *Test*, #31 (June 11, 1757), p. 180.
[99]   *Monitor*, II (October 16, 1756), pp. 118-120.
[100]   *Monitor*, I (February 28, 1756), p. 276; I (April 10, 1756), pp. 337 ff.; #117 (October 15, 1757), p. 709; and #129 (January 7, 1758), p. 780.
[101]   *Monitor*, #224 (November 3, 1759), p. 1351.

the controversy itself, Wilkes and Churchill in the *North Briton* made political use of anti-primitivism to ridicule their opponents. When Murphy in the *Auditor* employed the device of primitive spokesmen as political critics, Wilkes replied: [102]

... he has given us such a specimen of the Chinese in so simple a fellow, that we cannot but laugh in our turn at that *wise* nation. In a former paper he had referred the decision of some constitutional points to the stupid, drunken Cherokee king, who *would* not even articulate, and to his ideal majesty of Brobdingnag, who *could* not answer him. He has never once ventured to make the appeal to a candid Englishman.

Although Murphy made use of moral standards in literature to attack Churchill and Wilkes [103] and was himself denounced for his "Gothic stupidity",[104] in a way that suggests that Kliger's arguments relating the Goths to the Whigs are not altogether accurate,[105] the main concern that all these journalists had for literary matters was in a linguistic controversy aimed at making judgments of diction to suggest political allegiances.[106] Arnold Whitridge is certainly guilty of oversimplification when he ascribes these arguments about Scotticisms to puerility.[107] In the contest between the ministerial and anti-ministerial advocates from 1761 through 1763, language was used as an index of patriotism, and the defenders of Bute were assailed as Scots, Tories, and Jacobites, with the implication that to be a Scot and a Tory was to be no more than a traitor. Smollett, a Scotsman, called his essay-journal the *Briton*, and Wilkes was quick to respond with his ironically named *North Briton*. That Arthur Murphy, who wrote the *Auditor*, was an Irishman only made the supporters of Bute

---

[102] *Political Controversy*, II, p. 31.
[103] *Political Controversy*, I, p. 306.
[104] *Political Controversy*, I, p. 193.
[105] Although Kliger, *The Goths in England*, p. 4, himself limits the degree to which the connection existed between Whiggism in politics and admiration for the Gothic style, his main thesis stresses the relationship beyond factual support.
[106] See my own article, "Eighteenth-Century Political Controversy and Linguistics", *N&Q*, II (1955), pp. 378-379, in which much of this material is discussed.
[107] Whitridge, p. 71.

more vulnerable since the English gave the Irish as little claim to their nation, as the Scots.

While the writers in the short-lived *Patriot* merely suggested that the *Briton* learn English grammar and idioms or snidely offered to teach the Scottish dialect for those who sought Court positions,[108] the essays in the *North Briton* made all out attacks upon Scots, Tories, and Jacobites.[109] When Smollett in the *Briton* used mild language to describe the Jacobite uprising of 1745, Wilkes insisted that diction was dictated from a lack of patriotism: [110]

In his last number but one, speaking of the late rebellion, [the *Briton*] says, *the insurgents had defeated a body of regular forces.* How tenderly a true Scotsman speaks of rebellion! Is he afraid of wounding a father, uncle, or brother? An Englishman would have wrote, *the rebels had defeated a body of the king's forces*; but *rebels* are only *insurgents* in Scotland, and the *king's troops are* only *regular forces!* The other phrase had acknowledged a right in our sovereign, not quite so willingly own'd by all his subjects in the north of this island.

At a time when the *North Briton* and Wilkes were being accused of disloyalty to the Crown, the *Briton*'s terms were a convenient target for the anti-ministerial writer.

Another attempt to demean the patriotism of the *Briton* by suggesting that even the English language was alien to Bute's defenders was less successful.[111] To Churchill's criticism of the word *glorification* as a foreign word, Smollett responded: [112]

[*Glorification*] is an English word to be found in all the common dictionaries, and to be met with more than once in Scripture: his criticism therefore, is a little unfortunate, and the more extraordinary, as the author of it is said to be a clergyman, who ought to be better acquainted with his *Bible*, than to fall into such a palpable blunder.

[108]   *Patriot*, #3 (July 3, 1762), p. 16 and #4 (July 10, 1762), pp. 23-24. It is of some interest that in its choice of mottoes, the *Patriot* favored the moderns over the ancients by four to one: Mason, Churchill, Pope (2), and Horace.
[109]   *Political Controversy*, III, pp. 35 ff.
[110]   *Political Controversy*, I, p. 113. The footnote in the *Political Controversy*, probably by Wilkes, reinforced the argument of the *North Briton*.
[111]   *Political Controversy*, I, pp. 71-72.
[112]   *Political Controversy*, I, p. 138.

At the same time, Smollett answered the attack on his patriotism by questioning the *North Briton*'s use of the word *vouchsafement* as a substantive and declaring it "a word which I don't remember to have seen in any dictionary or writer of reputation".[113] If Churchill was going to denigrate the patriotism of Smollett in his failure to use proper English, then the latter surely had the right to insist on the same correctness in the home-bred patriot, not only in the purity of the language but in the adherence to the orthodox faith. The latter, of course, was a rebuke to both Charles Churchill, who was a clergyman, and John Wilkes, whose blasphemy was notorious.

In his rejoinder, Wilkes in the *North Briton* arraigned his rival's allegiance not only to the state but also to the Anglican religion. Wilkes, denying that he had said that *glorification* was not English, described it "as a *cant* word of the illiberal and illiterate Scottish Presbyterians", not to be found in the Scriptures.[114] As for *vouchsafement* used as a substantive, he suggested that his opponent read the quotation from Bayle in Johnson's English dictionary, and concluded, "I hope Johnson is *a writer of reputation*, because as a writer he has just got a pension of 300 £ *per ann.*"[115]

Further comment on Johnson and his pension used his own statements and definitions to label him, like the Tory *Briton* and *Auditor*, an enemy of the state.[116] But throughout their attacks, all these political journalists indicated a concern for more than haggling over genuine and supposed Scotticisms. Their general sensitivity to language reflected an awareness of its polemic significance, which is nowhere more apparent than in Murphy's consciousness and appreciation of linguistic changes, particularly as they are affected by political controversy. Despite the ironic intention of his statement, Murphy quite accurately depicted the character of language: [117]

[113] *Political Controversy*, I, p. 138.
[114] *Political Controversy*, I, pp. 189-190.
[115] *Political Controversy*, I, pp. 189-190.
[116] *Political Controversy*, I, pp. 222-224.
[117] *Political Controversy*, I, p. 229.

The advocates of despairing faction have at length advanced a true proposition, namely, That nothing conduces so much to the attainment of true knowledge as strict definitions of the terms in use. The fluctuation of living languages will for ever render exact precision a very difficult matter, and the causes of that fluctuation are so various, that it is impossible to enumerate them within the limits of this paper. One thing however that occasions much confusion in the use and application of words is party-rage, which is for ever introducing new modes of phraseology, even as fast as the views and interest of faction shift and alter.

Borrowing a device that Swift had used in the *Examiner*, the editor of the *Auditor* provided an ironic Political Dictionary for the admirers of the *North Briton* and *Monitor*. He adeptly chose terms most frequently used by his opponents and explained the connotations in order to ridicule the anti-ministerial writers. Words and phrases like *liberty of the press, pension, favourite*, and *faction* were included and analyzed to explain their use and implications.[118]

Whatever the partisan purposes of the *Auditor*, the dictionary indicates the role that linguistics played in the political controversy. Party-words and Scotticisms were objects of scrutiny because they implied political and national allegiance. But even more importantly, they show how the sensitivity to linguistic processes during the Seven Years' War was related to national pride and how, indeed, the aesthetic comments in these periodicals were as related to politics as those in the literary essay-journals were to social criticism.

By contrast writers in the magazines, which themselves were not heavily engaged in literary criticism, were far more willing to treat aesthetic problems as separate topics. To be sure, *chinoiserie*, American Indians, and language were not altogether isolated from national and international significance, but topics like the rules, genres, and imitation were considered primarily as aesthetic questions. The effect is frequently surprising, for comment in the magazines that were politically and socially conservative was not restricted to the same aesthetic views, and the extent of political liberalism was not the measure of the aesthetic. At the same time,

[118] *Political Controversy*, I, pp. 229 ff. See also *Political Controversy*, I, pp. 71-72.

while the overall picture in the magazines is one of the diminishing hold of the traditional criticism, the individual differences have never been noted before.[119]

Of the two major magazines, the *Gentleman's* is the more interesting. It represents the transition at the very outset of the major change: a dissatisfaction with the old standards; reluctance to accept the new; and an attempt to work aesthetic changes into the traditional pattern. To be sure, literary criticism, as such, was not extensive in the *Gentleman's*. Despite the impression given by Fred Boege, in his study of Smollett,[120] the magazine's imitation of the review feature of the *Monthly* was never considerable, and although the editors of the *Gentleman's* were severely critical of the reviewing method of the *Critical*,[121] their own writers did not effectively evaluate literary productions, particularly fiction.[122] Its review of *Rasselas* offered three paragraphs of unquoted material in two and one-half pages, with no more attempt at evaluation than the general assertion that the scenes describing Rasselas's birthplace "abound with the most elegant and striking pictures of life and nature, the most acute disquisitions, and the happiest illustrations of the most important truths".[123] *Tristram Shandy* received even less direct comment, and works like Young's *Conjectures on Original Composition* were presented almost entirely by quotations and excerpts rather than commentary.[124] For drama, the treatment was even less adequate, and the articles, such as those on *Douglas* and *Athelstan*,[125] were summaries rather than criticism.

[119] The important series of studies by Hooker (see note 18, p. 244) was concerned more with the aesthetic changes than with the individual periodicals, and Hooker restricted himself to the major magazines, the *Annual Register*, and the two reviews.

[120] Boege, p. 6.

[121] *Gentleman's Magazine*, XXVI (March, 1756), pp. 141-142.

[122] Heidler, p. 71.

[123] *Gentleman's Magazine*, XXIX (April, 1759), pp. 184-186. The quotation is from p. 186.

[124] *Gentleman's Magazine*, XXIX (May, 1759), pp. 230-232.

[125] *Gentleman's Magazine*, XXVII (March, 1757), pp. 124-127 and XXVI (April, 1756), pp. 155-159. See, also, XXVI (January, 1756), p. 47; XXVIII (March, 1758), pp. 117-121; XXVIII (April, 1758), pp. 178-179; XXX (July, 1760), pp. 325 ff.

Nevertheless, the *Gentleman's* did present information that is important for literary criticism.[126] Apart from its conventional expression of concern for Horace's dictum of *dulce et utile*,[127] and its characteristically neoclassical poetry,[128] the magazine displayed a balanced appraisal of those features designated as romantic and neoclassical. Its writers demanded no servile acceptance of the rules, no great reverence for the ancients, and no necessary imitation. At the same time, they showed no willing acceptance of romantic primitivism and attempted to assimilate new literary theory into the traditional aesthetics.

Even the comments on the English language in the *Gentleman's* were not excessive in making neoclassical demands for purity. Despite their attack on the *Critical* for the review's carelessness in grammar and diction,[129] the editors, particularly by comparison with the *Critical* reviewers, paid little attention to neologisms, foreign borrowings, syntax, and grammar.[130]

Their treatment of taste and the rules was also less authoritarian than was customary in neoclassical criticism. Despite their distinction between taste and judgment, the articles in the magazine insisted that taste was not to be achieved through the rules.[131] In agreement with one of its letter-writers who questioned the authority of criticism,[132] the editors of the *Gentleman's* flatly asserted, "It is extremely difficult to assign any rules by which questions of taste may be determined . . .".[133]

[126] Carlson, p. 58, overstates the case when he describes the development of the *Gentleman's* from a primarily political and historical to a scientific and literary magazine.

[127] See, for example, *Gentleman's Magazine*, XXX (May, 1760), p. 243; XXXI (April, 1761), p. 165; and XXXII (January, 1762), p. 17.

[128] Carlson, p. viii.

[129] *Gentleman's Magazine*, XXVI (March, 1756), pp. 141-142.

[130] However, see, *Gentleman's Magazine*, XXVI (January, 1756), pp. 11-12; XXVIII (March, 1758), pp. 117-121; XXVIII (September, 1758), pp. 437-438; XXIX (January, 1759), pp. 14-15, 26; XXIX (April, 1759), pp. 169-171; XXIX (November, 1759), pp. 543-544; XXXI (April, 1761), p. 148; XXXII (March, 1762), pp. 102-103.

[131] *Gentleman's Magazine*, XXX (March, 1760), p. 113.

[132] *Gentleman's Magazine*, XXX (Supplement, 1760), p. 611.

[133] *Gentleman's Magazine*, XXIX (February, 1759), p. 84.

Although its writers used Pope's work as a standard for criticizing poetry,[134] they were also chary about rules as a measure of artistic achievement. Not even in so simple a thing as the structure of verse, did the writers in the magazine believe in the infallibility of the rules as a guide,[135] and as for comedy, there no rules were to be followed, despite the critical approach that divided a drama into characters, diction, sentiments, and fable.[136] While one writer assented to the need for simplicity in contrast with confusion and perplexity, he warned: [137]

artful and judicious complication of incidents [is necessary for a satisfactory stage piece, and what is needed is a] rapid succession of events, where the plot is intricate without obscurity, and the incidents numerous without confusion. Such are all Shakespeare's, and the want of this variety is but ill attoned by a conformity to those rules, which can only restrain the powers of imagination, or sooth those who want them by the offer of an ineffectual *succedaneum*.

In letters to the periodical there was condemnation of the authority of the rules, together with that of the critic.[138] Instead, the attitude demanded by a critic of Goldsmith's *Enquiry into the Present State of Polite Learning* was one in which the rules could be used as a corrective. The position was made clear: [139]

[Goldsmith] observes indeed very justly, that works of genius should be judged by *feeling*, and not by *rule*; but it does not follow that what is *felt* to be a work of genius, must necessarily be such as would be condemned by rule; neither can the condemnation by mere rule prevent a work of genius from being felt. . . .

From various comments on the rules in the magazine, it might be imagined that homage to the ancients and demands for imitation would not be overwhelming. An insistence upon the rules logically presupposes a body of art from which aesthetic principles can be drawn and models that are worthy of study. In fact, however, the *Gentleman's* presented a preponderance of unfavorable com-

---

[134] *Gentleman's Magazine*, XXVIII (December, 1758), p. 600.
[135] *Gentleman's Magazine*, XXIX (February, 1759), p. 84.
[136] *Gentleman's Magazine*, XXXII (April, 1762), p. 161.
[137] *Gentleman's Magazine*, XXXII (April, 1762), p. 157.
[138] *Gentleman's Magazine*, XXX (Supplement, 1760), p. 611.
[139] *Gentleman's Magazine*, XXIX (April, 1759), p. 170.

ment on both the ancients and imitation. On modern English art, the writers in the magazine expressed sympathy for the neglect of the subject and certainly were not opposed to the idea of progress.[140] Remarks on Webb's *An Enquiry into the Beauties of Painting* particularly rejected a servile acceptance of antiquity and went on to argue for imitation of nature rather than art: [141]

of painting, nature is the standard; and though there are painted representations of beauty not existing in nature, yet this beauty either results from a combination in one object of those graces which provident nature has shared among many, or it is a mere creature of caprice, concerning which there can be no criterion. . . .

But such comment was not restricted to Webb's work. In its poetry, the magazine published William Whitehead's prologue to the *Orphan of China* which included the advice, "Enough of Greece and Rome. Th' exhausted store / Of either nation now can charm no more." [142] Again, in an extract from a poem entitled "Shakespear", which was addressed to Garrick, the mechanics of classical drama were scorned and exposure of "the folly of a servile imitation of the ancients in dramatic performance" was approved.[143] At the same time, the incongruity of the praise of antiquity by Boileau and Fontenelle at their own expense was cited by comments on the excellencies of these modern bards themselves.[144]

Even where the magazine printed laudatory comment on the ancients, it was balanced by warnings of the defects in classical art. A long heroic poem, while praising ancient achievements, opposed imitating the writers of antiquity. Recommended instead was original diction drawn from the inspiration of lavish nature, and denounced particularly was the use of classical tags.[145] In one instance, the balance required three and one-half years of waiting. On the publication of the first volume of *Engravings from Paintings Discovered in the Ruins of Herculaneum*, the magazine offer-

---

[140]   *Gentleman's Magazine*, XXIX (January, 1759), p. 15; XXIX (April, 1759), p. 169; XXIX (August, 1759), p. 367; XXXII (June, 1762), p. 248.
[141]   *Gentleman's Magazine*, XXX (March, 1760), p. 114.
[142]   *Gentleman's Magazine*, XXIX (May, 1759), p. 227.
[143]   *Gentleman's Magazine*, XXX (November, 1760), pp. 535-536.
[144]   *Gentleman's Magazine*, XXXI (June, 1761), p. 280.
[145]   *Gentleman's Magazine*, XXX (May, 1760), pp. 241-242.

ed two articles hailing the discovery. Genre criticism, rules of propriety, and arguments for imitation were used to celebrate the ancient artists, and only a small note of caution remarked that there were deficiencies.[146] Nevertheless, when the second volume was published, the reviewer declared that here was sufficient evidence to demonstrate that classical painters and architects were not superior to moderns, and the method of determining quality was to hold up imitation of nature as a standard.[147]

Aside from repeating Warton's categorization of poetry in his essay on Pope,[148] articles in the magazine paid fleeting attention to the genres, taking only occasional note of such lapses as the failure of the *Prussiad* to produce a convincing hero or at least one who was above the frailties of displaying human revenge or sinking to defeat.[149] Only remotely did writers in the *Gentleman's* suggest criticism of kinds in evaluating such plays as *The Sham Beggar*, which "wants a constituent part of comedy, dramatic action",[150] or in letters on music, considering Handel according to his type of composition,[151] or in commenting upon *Tristram Shandy* as a "masterpiece of its kind".[152]

Yet for all their reluctance to subscribe to a view of literature and criticism that was essentially neoclassical, the magazine's writers were unwilling to accept readily the growth of ideas that are conventionally labelled as *pre-romantic*. Most kinds of romantic primitivism were held only in contempt,[153] but the hard primi-

---

[146] *Gentleman's Magazine*, XXIX (September, 1759), pp. 414-415; XXIX (December, 1759), p. 584.

[147] *Gentleman's Magazine*, XXXIII (April, 1763), p. 158.

[148] *Gentleman's Magazine*, XXVI (May, 1756), pp. 249-251.

[149] *Gentleman's Magazine*, XXIX (November, 1759), p. 544. See, also, XXXIII (February, 1763), p. 57.

[150] *Gentleman's Magazine*, XXVI (April, 1756), p. 200.

[151] *Gentleman's Magazine*, XXXII (June, 1762), p. 248.

[152] *Gentleman's Magazine*, XXXII (January, 1762), p. 32. The particular comment comes after a condensed version of the story of Le Fever. Other references to Shandy are limited to an extract of the portrait of Yorick (XXX, January, 1760, pp. 35-37), a poem balancing the wit and wisdom with the bawdiness and immorality (XXX, May, 1760, p. 243), and a listing of volumes III and IV (XXXI, January, 1761), p. 45).

[153] An exception to this is the magazine's romantic biography of Shakespeare, *Gentleman's Magazine*, XXXI (June, 1761), p. 268.

tivism of the North especially had no appeal. A series of articles on Iceland portrayed severely both the climate and the people. Quoting Pope's "What happier natures shrink at with affright, / The hard inhabitant contends is right", the writer expressed his wonder not so much at those who never had known any better and tried to cope with the unhappy climate, but with those who inhabited "the more southern parts of the continent, [and] when they have wandered northward into the regions of cold and darkness, chuse rather to settle there, than to return. It is yet more difficult to account for the voluntary peopling and settling an island that lies in a climate so dreary and comfortless." [154] In the "wretched people",[155] their way of life, and their government,[156] he could find nothing attractive.

With the American Indians, writers in the *Gentleman's* found other things than climate objectionable. The magazine's reports of "the ravages and butcheries of the savages" were hardly conducive to sympathetic treatment.[157] Although they distinguished between the generally wretched savages and the nobler Iroquois [158] and presented a balanced view of the Indians in a description of the conclusion of a peace treaty,[159] the articles customarily characterized them as the most savage of all nations, ancient or modern, and contrasted their conduct with the principles of Christianity.[160] Those Indians allied with the French were particularly condemned, with such emphasis upon French responsibility for the corruption suggesting the manner in which the Indian was later to be idealized at the expense of civilized society.[161] In only one in-

[154] *Gentleman's Magazine*, XXVIII (January, 1758), p. 22.
[155] *Gentleman's Magazine*, XXVIII (March, 1758), p. 115.
[156] *Gentleman's Magazine*, XXVIII (April, 1758), p. 164.
[157] The quotation is from *Gentleman's Magazine*, XXXIII (September, 1763), p. 455. See, also, p. 456 and XXVII (October, 1757), pp. 475-476; XXVII (November, 1757), p. 510; and XXVIII (October, 1758), p. 499.
[158] *Gentleman's Magazine*, XXXI (August, 1761), p. 342.
[159] *Gentleman's Magazine*, XXIX (March, 1759), pp. 108 ff.
[160] *Gentleman's Magazine*, XXVI (March, 1756), pp. 131-132. For this opposition of Christianity to the noble savage view of the Indian, see Bissell, p. 52.
[161] *Gentleman's Magazine*, XXX (January, 1760), pp. 33-35. After 1759 it was easier for the British to regard the Indian more favorably. By then even the Canadian Indians were weakening in their loyalty to the French,

stance the *Gentleman's* presented material truly favorable to the Indian, and then it was neither in an editorial nor an article, but in a letter from a Dutch settlement in America: [162]

The Indians are in general more worthy of a national panegyric, than any people in the civilized part of the world. They clear the lands, and hunt and fish for such as have a friendly correspondence with them, and will every day supply their tables with a variety of game for such a trifle as a knife, or any little necessary, which they very justly value in proportion to its usefulness.

While the letter-writer's comments on the American Indian do not describe a noble savage, they are kinder than the general treatment of the American primitives in the magazine.

Orientalism fared somewhat better. Despite its declining popularity, *chinoiserie* still retained some mass appeal which was reflected in the magazine's selections. Accounts of performances or stories and abstracts of popular works suggest that general curiosity about the topic still remained. Without critical comment, the *Gentleman's* offered an account of Murphy's *Orphan of China*,[163] along with extracts from treatises that conjectured about the origin of the Chinese.[164] Letter-writers praised Chinese astronomy and even the introduction of oriental influences in gardening and music.[165] Some of the favorable comment was the result of such works as William Collins' *Persian Eclogues* and Chambers' book on Chinese gardens, both of which provided extracts for the magazine.[166] While Collins' book was perfectly consistent with neoclassical standards, the portions of Chambers' work which were

---

and others were willing to trade with the Britsh (Gipson, VII, pp. 448, 451). According to Gipson (VII, pp. 77-78, 85-86), neither the French nor their missionaries were able to control the Indians, and the English were equally guilty in arousing the Indians to scalp for mercenary reasons (Gipson, VII, pp. 41-42, 52).

[162] *Gentleman's Magazine*, XXVIII (June, 1758), p. 252.

[163] *Gentleman's Magazine*, XXIX (May, 1759), pp. 217-220.

[164] *Gentleman's Magazine*, XXX (January, 1760), pp. 12-15.

[165] *Gentleman's Magazine*, XXVII (January, 1757), p. 33; XXVIII (November, 1758), pp. 512-513; XXXI (December, 1761), p. 567.

[166] *Gentleman's Magazine*, XXVII (February, 1757), p. 81; and XXVII (May, 1757), pp. 216-219.

printed in the magazine were clearly less orthodox in their emphasis on nature "in all her beautiful irregularities".[167]

But most of the reprints and comments in the magazine were either less favorable to *chinoiserie* or attempted to use it for traditional purposes. Stories like John Langhorne's *Solyman and Almena* and John Hawkesworth's *Almoran and Hamet* were either judged by conventional critical standards or presented because they offered moral instruction similar to that of the pastoral.[168] In direct comparisons between oriental and British government, religion, and taste, articles in the *Gentleman's* insisted on the barbarism, tastelessness, and excesses of the East.[169] Even in their selection of letters, when the issues challenged orthodox religion or culture, the editors saw to it that oriental models were condemned. Despite their latitudinarian evaluations of religion at home, the writers in the *Gentleman's* identified Eastern religions with idolatry and superstition [170] and decried Voltaire's account of the Chinese as an attempt to sabotage the structure of the European states and the Christian churches.[171]

Unlike the material on orientalism, that on Gothicism was extremely limited and came from extracts and letters rather than editorial opinion. A reprint from the *Con-Test* for May 7, 1757, offered a Gothic tale that was intended to show the inferiority of those rude and unlettered days,[172] just as some extracts from *Letters on the Roman Antiquities and the Temples of Ancients* were used to describe the Gothic "perversion of taste and judg-

---

[167] *Gentleman's Magazine*, XXVII (May, 1757), p. 216. See, also, XXXI (Supplement, 1761), pp. 635-636, in which the work of a young lady poet, self-educated, is presented. Her inspiration was Johnson's *Rasselas*, and she describes his portrait as "romantic" in its contrast with cold English Decembers.

[168] *Gentleman's Magazine*, XXXI (June, 1761), pp. 273-277; XXXI (September, 1761), p. 399; XXXII (February, 1762), pp. 71-76.

[169] *Gentleman's Magazine*, XXVI (September, 1756), p. 445; XXIX (January, 1759), pp. 3-4; XXXII (July, 1762), pp. 300-305; XXXII (August, 1762), pp. 353-357; XXXII (September, 1762), pp. 397-400.

[170] *Gentleman's Magazine*, XXVI (May, 1756), pp. 217-221.

[171] *Gentleman's Magazine*, XXVIII (February, 1758), pp. 58-60 and XXVIII (September, 1758), p. 416.

[172] *Gentleman's Magazine*, XXVII (May, 1757), pp. 204-207.

ment . . .".[173] If the epitome of Bishop Hurd's account of the *Rise, Progress, and Genius of Gothic Poetry* presented a more favorable estimate of Gothicism, it also attempted to place Gothic poetry within a classical framework by relating the chivalric and Homeric periods and by applying rules of genre.[174] Aside from these extracts, an important letter in the magazine, although asserting the "barbarism of manners, and degeneracy of mind" in Gothicism, made a serious attempt to distinguish between its ancient and modern types and to explain the character of Gothic architecture: [175]

It is confessed on all sides, that there is an awful solemnity in these [Gothic] structures, that makes a more lasting impression on the mind, than all the studied exactness of the Grecian models; and yet this impression is far from being the result of *harmony* and *proportion;* while, at the same time, it must be allowed, it has not its rise from mere *savage* deformity. It is hard to account for this effect, unless it be, that the Goths rather studied strength than beauty; rather consulted how their buildings should appear bold and majestic, than rich and delicate; chose rather to animate the sentiments of posterity by a crude stateliness, than by a graceful symmetry.

Clearly, the letter-writer sought to explain the aesthetic appeal of the Gothic in terms of the sublime.[176]

Along with the Gothic, Macpherson's Ossianic poems must be considered, and, while cautious about accepting the work as genuine,[177] the writers in the magazine tried to explain *Fingal* in terms that were appropriate to the epic.[178] The comments, although offering little genuine criticism, indicate an attempt to adjust aesthetic innovations according to traditional devices.

The *London,* the other major magazine, offered even less direct

---

[173] *Gentleman's Magazine,* XXIX (August, 1759), p. 367.

[174] *Gentleman's Magazine,* XXXII (June, 1762), pp. 264-268.

[175] *Gentleman's Magazine,* XXVIII (November, 1758), p. 517.

[176] Burke's essay on the sublime was merely listed in the *Gentleman's,* XXVII (May, 1757), p. 243, but a poem on the sublime, XXXIII (April, 1763), p. 196, linked it with the best of Shakespeare's work.

[177] *Gentleman's Magazine,* XXX (June, 1760), pp. 287-288; XXX (July, 1760), pp. 335-336; and XXX (September, 1760), pp. 407, 421.

[178] *Gentleman's Magazine,* XXXII (January, 1762), pp. 9, 12; and XXXII (June, 1762), p. 248.

literary criticism than the *Gentleman's*, and its comments on aesthetics were more conservative. *Morality* and *utility* were key words in its literary pronouncements, and the editors' own boast of usefulness, entertainment, and instruction was acknowledged by many readers.[179] From the simplest sentimental novel to such works as *Rasselas* and *Tristram Shandy*, the judgments in the magazine depended upon morality.[180] In both editorial opinion and comment in letters, instructive writing was singled out for encouragement.[181] Biography and history were approved primarily for their didactic purpose, and the romance which idealized heroic personages and provided poetic justice was preferable to history because in addition to showing "us what men are; [it can also show us] what they ought to be".[182]

For the writers in the magazine and their readers, the didactic purpose necessitated an art that was generalized and universal, one that closely followed nature.[183] The importance of the ancients was that they had shown the way: "*Follow nature* was the advice and practice of the ancients"; the failure of the moderns lay in their opposition to nature.[184] Whatever indulgence might be granted to painters and poets, permission to break nature's rules was not one, and that came from the authority of Horace.[185] Whatever the need to attain variety, impropriety was not the means.[186]

Propriety applied as well to the genres. What belonged to the

[179] *London Magazine*, XXXII (1763), Preface. For examples of its readers' comments, see XXV (December, 1756), p. 585; XXVI (February, 1757), p. 74; XXVI (September, 1757), p. 443; XXXI (December, 1762), p. 636; and XXXII (May, 1763), p. 250.
[180] *London Magazine*, XXVIII (May, 1759), pp. 258 ff.; XXIX (February, 1760), pp. 111-112; XXIX (September, 1760), p. 496; XXX (January, 1761), p. 56; XXX (February, 1761), pp. 100-102; XXX (March, 1761), p. 168; XXXI (February, 1762), p. 112; and XXXII (April, 1763), pp. 200-201.
[181] *London Magazine*, XXVIII (April, 1759), pp. 191-193; and XXIX (December, 1760), p. 672.
[182] *London Magazine*, XXIX (March, 1760), pp. 139-140. See, also, XXXI (May, 1762), p. 224.
[183] *London Magazine*, XXIX (March, 1760), p. 140; and XXXI (May, 1762), p. 244.
[184] *London Magazine*, XXV (August, 1756), p. 380.
[185] *London Magazine*, XXVI (March, 1757), p. 122.
[186] *London Magazine*, XXXII (May, 1763), pp. 233-234.

farcical kind was not to be described as comedy.[187] In tragedy the adherence to the unities was required, and the sentiments and language were expected to be consistent with the type.[188] The emphasis in an excerpt from the introduction to *Fingal* was upon its claims to epic stature,[189] and where rules for a genre were nonexistent or unknown to an English audience, as in Italian comedy, the writers in the magazine provided them, but not without ironic comment on the kind of low drama that came from an ignorance of the unities and propriety.[190] Even where the writer was willing to accept a mixture of pathos in comedy, he did not approve of a violation of the unity of the fable.[191] Only Shakespeare was represented as above the critic's rules,[192] and even he, according to a letter-writer, had more classical learning and indebtedness than modern annotators recognized.[193]

The relationship between language and propriety was emphasized by another correspondent to the magazine,[194] and criticism of diction was made both in articles and correspondence.[195] Despite enlightened comment in the "History of the Last Session of Parliament", which chastized the lawmakers for their opposition to French words because the nations were at war,[196] writers in the magazine itself objected to Gallicisms and Scotticisms.[197] While there were no demands for an academy for the refinement of language, the *London* was less liberal than its statement in the parliamentary history indicated.

For romantic primitivism, there was no sympathy. At best, the

---

[187]   *London Magazine*, XXVI (March, 1757), p. 126.
[188]   *London Magazine*, XXX (December, 1761), pp. 664-665.
[189]   *London Magazine*, XXX (December, 1761), pp. 654-656.
[190]   *London Magazine*, XXX (August, 1761), p. 414.
[191]   *London Magazine*, XXXII (February, 1763), p. 94.
[192]   *London Magazine*, XXV (March, 1756), p. 144 and XXVIII (March, 1759), pp. 158-159.
[193]   *London Magazine*, XXVI (January, 1757), pp. 24-27.
[194]   *London Magazine*, XXXII (Appendix, 1763), p. 687.
[195]   *London Magazine*, XXVI (September, 1757), pp. 435-436 and XXVI (October, 1757), p. 503.
[196]   *London Magazine*, XXIX (March, 1760), p. 127; XXVII (September, 1758), pp. 456 f.
[197]   *London Magazine*, XXVII (September, 1758), p. 457; XXVIII (September, 1759), pp. 477-478; and XXIX (January, 1760), p. 56.

American Indians were simple beings who had been used by the French for barbaric purposes or perverted by the Jesuits,[198] and at worst, "Indians, like all other men in a state of nature, are prone to revenge . . ." [199] When the Governor of Philadelphia resorted to fixing a price upon even Indian women and children, he was excused because necessity demanded such cruel measures.[200] One letter-writer, deploring such treatment, nevertheless described the "barbarous ravages and massacres of the Indians".[201] The Cherokee warrior who was praised was an ally, a hope for better English relations with the savages in America.[202]

Extracts from Charlevoix on the Eskimo described the crude, rough, and gruff savages who inhabited Newfoundland and Labrador, the least inhabitable regions on earth, where only Eskimos belonged.[203] That orientalism fared better in the pages of the *London* is directly attributable to the didactic purpose served by the Eastern tale. The magazine's description of Langhorne's *Solyman and Almena* indicates the manner in which such works were viewed: "Told in the Eastern manner, or at least with some resemblance of it, in which a good intention is apparent, and many valuable truths are prettily enough expressed." [204] Among such truths, so long as the treatment was not designed to undermine orthodox faith, were Christian resignation, Christian virtue, the importance of a militia, the excesses of enthusiasm, and rules for the conduct of the fair sex.[205]

Between them the *London* and *Gentleman's* set the pattern for most of the minor magazines. To be sure, the *British Magazine* was more conservative than either of them and the *Royal Female*

---

[198]   *London Magazine*, XXVII (1758), Preface and XXXII (September, 1763), p. 459.
[199]   *London Magazine*, XXXII (January, 1763), p. 25.
[200]   *London Magazine*, XXV (June, 1756), pp. 298-299.
[201]   *London Magazine*, XXIX (June, 1760), pp. 279-280.
[202]   *London Magazine*, XXXI (August, 1762), p. 445.
[203]   *London Magazine*, XXX (January, 1761), pp. 25 ff.
[204]   *London Magazine*, XXXI (February, 1762), p. 112.
[205]   *London Magazine*, XXV (September, 1756), pp. 424-426; XXVII (March, 1758), pp. 128-131; XXVII (April, 1758), pp. 178-180; XXVII (May, 1758), pp. 239-244; XXVII (June, 1758), pp. 284 ff.; and XXXI (December, 1762), pp. 637-639.

was rather more liberal, but in all the magazines presented a balance that neither wholly rejected the traditions of the past fifty years nor desperately attempted to restrict aesthetic growth. On the necessity for artistic morality, the magazine writers were all agreed, but for the other standards, they varied in their desires, and the overall picture is consistent with the image of a general transition in aesthetics.

Not much is to be learned from the limited comments in the *Weekly, New Royal and Universal*, and *Imperial*. Didacticism is evident in the pointed moral of an oriental tale and in a reader's remark on the useful and entertaining in the *New Royal and Universal*,[206] whose articles also described "the gratification which results from imitation".[207] But such cursory items are insufficient for judgment.

If there is more evidence in the *Weekly Magazine*, it is not clearer in its pattern. Again, the didactic purpose is apparent in articles insisting that literature must be moral or in the magazine's presentation of a specific section on moral views,[208] and its authentic accounts of Indian cruelty could hardly lead to a favorable attitude toward romantic primitivism.[209] However, in their specific remarks on literature, the writers in the *Weekly* mixed a reverence for antiquity and genre criticism [210] with an attack on rules and authority and a wholly romantic view of poetry: [211]

An impulse, that reason cannot controul; nay, that reason cannot give: the true fire of poetry, it must be allowed, is enthusiastic, and consists alike, in harmony of thought and expression; so that a man can no more learn to imagine happily, without the gift of a poetic mind, than he can to compose harmoniously without the organic endowment of an excellent ear.

[206] *New Royal and Universal Magazine*, November, 1759, pp. 196 ff. and 219.
[207] *New Royal and Universal Magazine*, November, 1759, p. 201.
[208] *Weekly Magazine*, #6 (May 20, 1758), p. 181 and #13 (July 8, 1758), pp. 387-388.
[209] *Weekly Magazine*, #13 (July 8, 1758), pp. 397-400; #14 (July 15, 1758), pp. 408-411; and #15 (July 22, 1758), pp. 425-428.
[210] *Weekly Magazine*, #1 (April 15, 1758), p. 27; #10 (June 17, 1758), pp. 306 ff.; and #15 (July 22, 1758), pp. 436-437.
[211] *Weekly Magazine*, #11 (June 24, 1758), p. 328. See, also, #1 (April 15, 1758), pp. 2-3.

One's nature, not simply one's intelligence, must be suited to it, and nature was equated with genius, ". . . fire, fancy, invention, and enthusiasm being the necessary, and essential characteristics of exalted [poetic] genius . . .".[212]

The comments in the *Imperial Magazine* seem less contradictory. Although its book reviews disappointingly were epitomes of articles in the *Critical* and *Monthly*, the writers in the magazine from their conventional dictum of *utile et dulce* [213] to their arguments for language reform [214] and literary restraint [215] were conservative. For genre criticism and pure classicism, untainted by French influence, the remarks in the *Imperial* displayed a conservative taste.[216] Quite naturally, then, the magazine writers attacked the fashions of *chinoiserie*, not without a chauvinistic aside against the French,[217] and characterized the savage state of the American Indians not as a primitive ideal, but as an unhappy or unfortunate condition that could be corrected by "the intercourse occasioned by trade, which will introduce arts and sciences among them, [and] by degrees, tame the savage fierceness of those, hitherto, unhappy nations".[218]

Other minor magazines, like the *General Magazine of Arts and Science*, the *Christian's*, and the *Universal Visiter,* while offering limited aesthetic comment, suggested their editorial point of view, which for the *General* and *Christian's* might, at least in part, have been anticipated from their purpose. In its primary purpose, to celebrate the learning of the modern age,[219] the *General Magazine of Arts and Science* was committed to the neoclassical ideal of *utile et dulce* [220] and yet was automatically on the side of the

---

[212] *Weekly Magazine,* #11 (June 24, 1758), p. 329.
[213] *Imperial Magazine,* I (January, 1760), pp. 1-2, 7 ff.
[214] *Imperial Magazine,* III (June, 1762), pp. 309-310.
[215] *Imperial Magazine,* I (January, 1760), p. 27.
[216] *Imperial Magazine,* III (May, 1762), pp. 229-231, 249.
[217] *Imperial Magazine,* III (May, 1762), p. 231.
[218] *Imperial Magazine,* I (January, 1760), pp. 4-5.
[219] *General Magazine,* Pt. I, I, p. x.
[220] *General Magazine,* Pt. I, I, p. vii, and Pt. I, II, pp. 62, 128. With its general dialogues to inculcate scientific and philosophical learning and its biographies to instill the highest principles of virtue, the magazine was dedicated wholly to instruction. In Pt. V (December, 1760), p. 577, the

moderns in the controversy with the ancients. Although acknowledging the genius of Plato and Aristotle,[221] the articles in the magazine were at pains to describe the ridiculousness of ancient superstition, gullibility, stupidity, and ignorance,[222] and even their remarks on classical mythology were patronizing.[223]

The same reasoning that led Martin, the editor, to declare that all developments in science and technology were gradual [224] made him no more likely to approve of romantic than classical primitivism. Reporting the bestial scalpings by American Indians,[225] he could hardly look to the noble savage for instruction. With his great faith in education and a jibe at the enemy Frenchmen, Martin, indeed, argued not that the civilized man could learn from the savage, but that the ways of society might refine the manners of the American aborigines: [226]

Their cruelty of scalping their enemies is probably owing to long custom amongst them, and the base insinuations of those who may have an influence over them; but where they have had the advantage of different instruction, there are many instances of their discovering a different disposition.

While the subtle attack on the French, which tends to portray the Indian as a victim of corruption, again suggests the later development of the nobility of the American savage, Martin quite clearly had no such purpose in his arguments.

Like the *General*, the *Christian's Magazine* had a specific purpose that predetermined its few literary comments. Although it published poetry, occasional tales, and biographies (including many by Goldsmith),[227] the magazine offered little direct comment

---

magazine indicated the seriousness of its intention by refusing to print "Acrostics, rebusses, epigrams, &c, among the poetry of our magazine, as they are subjects too low for the generality of our readers . . .".

[221] *General Magazine*, Pt. IV, II, p. 52.
[222] *General Magazine*, Pt. I, I, p. 156 and Pt. I, II, pp. 3-4.
[223] *General Magazine*, Pt. I, II, p. 32.
[224] *General Magazine*, Pt. I, II, p. 302.
[225] *General Magazine*, Pt. V (July, 1758), p. 845.
[226] *General Magazine*, Pt. V (January, 1759), p. 1.
[227] See R. S. Crane, *New Essays by Oliver Goldsmith* (Chicago, 1927), pp. 140-141. These biographies were lives of the church fathers.

on literature. That it was didactic was obvious,[228] but even an editor committed primarily to instruction recognized the need to entertain,[229] and was not above using the oriental tale for moral and religious allegory. Yet it is in the attitude expressed in the *Christian's Magazine* toward primitivism that the incompatibility of such romanticism with religious orthodoxy is most clearly suggested. To sanction the primitive state necessitated condemnation of society's institutions – particularly the Church. Apart from the one oriental story, the magazine would have none of it. The barbarism of the religious practices of the American Indians was used to demonstrate the weakness of human reason without revelation; [230] the customs of Brahmans were depicted as savage because of their religious perversions; [231] and both African and Mexican aborigines were presented as horrible examples of man in the natural state, unenlightened by Christianity.[232]

If the position of the *Universal Visiter* could not be predetermined like that of the *General* and *Christian's Magazine,* its conservative aesthetic stance is at least clear enough from its comments, and only in one respect, its lack of didacticism, did the magazine take a weak stand. Although it borrowed its motto from Chaucer's description of the Clerk, whose speech was deep in morality and whose desire was not only to learn but to teach, the *Universal Visiter* was not a didactic magazine. To be sure, the editors made the conventional statement about the need to entertain and instruct,[233] and a life of Spenser was introduced by the

[228]   See, for example, the criticism in a poem on *Tristram Shandy,* attacking the novel as an example of vice and particularly deploring the fact that the author was a clergyman (*Christian's Magazine,* II, March, 1761, p. 133).
[229]   Even the *Spiritual Magazine* on its title page described its purpose as both instruction and entertainment, and in two comments on poetry (I, pp. 22, 110) insisted upon literary merit. *Christian's,* I (June, 1760), p. 90.
[230]   *Christian's Magazine,* II (July, 1761), pp. 378-379 and II (August, 1761), pp. 430-431.
[231]   *Christian's Magazine,* I (September, 1760), pp. 213-215 and II (February, 1761), p. 74.
[232]   *Christian's Magazine,* I (October, 1760), p. 268 and IV (December, 1763), pp. 539-542.
[233]   *Universal Visiter,* #1 (January, 1756), pp. 3-4.

notation of the importance of biography because of its instruction and pleasure,[234] but otherwise *dulce et utile* went unnoticed.

Yet in their reverence for the ancients, the writers in the *Universal Visiter* were more insistent than those in most of the magazines. Even the English language, which Christopher Smart described as superior to the French, Spanish, and Dutch, and regarded as rich because of its borrowings and useful for writers, was barren and barbarous alongside Greek.[235] In the arts, Grecian splendor had outlasted those of any other nation and Roman excellence was derived from it.[236] Italian rejection of ancient architectural styles for "the barbarous, foreign, confused, and irregular" Gothicism was shocking, and the writer, perhaps Johnson, distinguished between the favorable Gothic imitation of the ancient and the "massy, heavy, gross" style of the true Gothic.[237] Even a contrast between city and farm life, pre-romantic in its choice, was argued by Rolt, the co-editor, from classical authority.[238]

English authors were praised according to their relation to the writers of classical antiquity. Chaucer was seen (perhaps by Johnson) in his correspondence to Homer,[239] and when Shakespeare was discussed, Smart himself particularly attacked the notion that the Bard was without learning and without indebtedness to the ancients. He was weakest at those points where he neglected classical influences and was strongest when his borrowings could be traced to the ancients.[240]

Rules, imitation, and genres followed a classical tradition. De-

[234] *Universal Visiter*, #2 (February, 1756), p. 64.
[235] *Universal Visiter*, #1 (January, 1756), pp. 4-8. Identification is from Jones, "Christopher Smart, Richard Rolt, and the *Universal Visiter*", p. 214. For another example in the magazine, see #11 (November, 1756), p. 496.
[236] *Universal Visiter*, #6 (June, 1756), pp. 255-257.
[237] *Universal Visiter*, #6 (June, 1756), p. 258. In a comment on "novelty" (*Universal Visiter*, #1, November, 1756, p. 503), it was said to appeal only to the vulgar. For authorship, see Bloom, p. 270.
[238] *Universal Visiter*, #2 (February, 1756), p. 62. Jones, "Christopher Smart, Richard Rolt, and the *Universal Visiter*", p. 214.
[239] *Universal Visiter*, #1 (January, 1756), pp. 9 ff. Bloom, p. 270.
[240] *Universal Visiter*, #3 (March, 1756), pp. 126 ff. Jones, "Christopher Smart, Richard Rolt, and the *Universal Visiter*", p. 213.

scribing the proper rules for an epitaph, Johnson insisted, "Every art is best taught by example. Nothing contributes more to the cultivation of propriety than remarks on the works of those who have most excelled." [241] Nature could not properly be opposed to art because nature itself was merely the best effect of art.[242] Whether describing the work of the French poets or Geoffrey Chaucer, Rolt, Smart, and their writers used the rules of genre criticism, giving the hierarchy and characteristics of types.[243] A comment on drama, perhaps by Arthur Murphy, and a correspondent's remarks on the pastoral carefully followed the genre approach.[244] The one comment in praise of an opera adapted from Shakespeare's *The Tempest* is the exception to prove the rule; for once, the English success, the use of native superstitions and appeal to fancy were lauded despite the absence of the type in classical antiquity, but even here there was the concern for types.[245]

In two other minor magazines with special interests, the comment was more extensive and significant than that in either the *General* or *Christian's*. None of the surprises in the *Royal Female* are met with in the *Philological Miscellany*. Since the sources of the articles in the latter were mainly the essays from the Academy of Belles Lettres at Paris and other foreign academies, authority and rules were to be expected recommendations. The primary basis for both was the assumption of universality which the magazine presented in a discourse upon the historical certainties of Rome: [246]

He who will turn his attention to the history of the world in general, will upon that theatre often see the scenes changed; he will see new actions advance and others retire; but the same spectator will also observe, that so many different scenes always introduce the same interests; that from the same interests rise the same passions, and

---

[241]   *Universal Visiter*, #5 (May, 1756), p. 207. *CBEL*, II, p. 619.
[242]   *Universal Visiter*, #5 (May, 1756), p. 208.
[243]   *Universal Visiter*, #1 (January, 1756), pp. 8, 12 ff.
[244]   *Universal Visiter*, #3 (March, 1756), pp. 116 ff. and #7 (July, 1756), pp. 303-304. For the attribution to Murphy, see Arthur Sherbo's *New Essays by Arthur Murphy* (East Lansing, Mich., 1963), pp. 179 ff.
[245]   *Universal Visiter*, #2 (February, 1756), p. 86.
[246]   *Philological Miscellany*, I (1761), pp. 134-135.

that these passions often engage mankind in the same enterprizes, and produce the same effects.

There is but one principle of action in all men, and the springs are so similar that we might justly be astonished if the actions were always different, and never resembled each other. . . . 'Tis but natural then, that those who have the same views should employ the same means, and why may not what we call hazard bring about the same combinations of causes and effects?

History itself could be examined for a determination, then, of rules applicable to modern times; antiquity could be used as an example,[247] not only because modern learning was based on it,[248] but because the progress in one age resembled that in another.[249]

Without exaggerating the modern indebtedness to antiquity or servilely ignoring the faults of the ancients,[250] the articles in the *Philological Miscellany* re-examined the ancient-modern contro- versy. The manner in which general esteem for ancient achieve- ment had been inverted to gross contempt was deplored, for in science as well as in the arts, the modern advances had been made possible only by ancient discoveries, and even Christianity had been anticipated by the Greeks: [251]

If the moderns have some real advantage over the ancients, it is because they came after them, and trod in paths that were already beaten; it is because they had the benefit not only of their dis- coveries, but of their mistakes to guide them.

But the writers in the magazine were unwilling to concede that the moderns had the advantage. France would do well if posterity were as indebted to it as it was to Greece and Rome.[252] A particu- lar evaluation of ancient and modern merits pointed out the spe- cific faults in Plato, Herodotus, and Aristotle, and warned against excessive praise, but insisted upon the superiority of ancient writ- ing and advised using it as a model.[253] If there were failures in

247   *Philological Miscellany*, I (1761), pp. 33 ff.
248   *Philological Miscellany*, I (1761), pp. 24-25, 237.
249   *Philological Miscellany*, I (1761), p. 62.
250   *Philological Miscellany*, I (1761), p. 155.
251   *Philological Miscellany*, I (1761), pp. 296-303. The quotation is from p. 319.
252   *Philological Miscellany*, I (1761), pp. 21-22.
253   *Philological Miscellany*, I (1761), pp. 50-55.

Roman drama, science, and philosophy, there was strength in its law, eloquence, and grammar,[254] and unquestionably the ancients excelled in taste, elegance, and sentiment.[255] The importance of ancient learning was urged in the arguments for study of the ancient languages.[256]

Classical letters stimulated the demand for an academy in the modern age, an academy that by making such knowledge available would halt the "spreading contagion of bad taste".[257] But the need for an academy was not restricted to the importance of preserving classical learning. Writers in the magazine argued the need for rules, whether for science, history, the arts, or language, and they were to be understood and promulgated for the preservation of learning.[258]

Like the *Philological Miscellany*, the *Royal Female Magazine* had a special interest. Its function was the instruction of women; in this respect, its editorial attitude was predetermined, and indeed, the magazine was strongly didactic. Its review of the *Sermons of Mr. Yorick*, although commending the sentiments, disapproved of the licentious appeal.[259] An article on the romances rejected Fielding's work, particularly for female readers, and the power of Fielding's art caused only more concern, while Richardson's writing was wholeheartedly approved.[260] The editor recommended the study of history as "most pleasing to the human mind, as it interests our passions at the same time that it informs our reason . . .".[261] That the magazine impressed its readers as a watchdog of public morality is evident from a letter it published asking that the *Royal Female* take notice of indecent performances and entertainments at such places as Ranelagh and Vauxhall, and at the Saddler's Wells, where women bared their legs and postured with their bodies in vile lessons to the youth of either sex.[262]

[254] *Philological Miscellany*, I (1761), pp. 66-67.
[255] *Philological Miscellany*, I (1761), p. 86.
[256] *Philological Miscellany*, I (1761), p. 20.
[257] *Philological Miscellany*, I (1761), pp. 387-388.
[258] *Philological Miscellany*, I (1761), pp. 158 ff., 219 ff., 440 ff., 481.
[259] *Royal Female Magazine*, I (May, 1760), p. 238.
[260] *Royal Female Magazine*, I (January, 1760), pp. 9-10.
[261] *Royal Female Magazine*, I (January, 1760), p. 14.
[262] *Royal Female Magazine*, I (April, 1760), p. 147.

But more important than these didactic comments in the magazine were its remarks on literature as literature. Robert Lloyd, the
editor, may have felt that the *Royal Female* had to be conventional in its moral pronouncements, but was certainly not orthodox in
his aesthetic demands. No opposition to ancient authority in the
arts was more apparent than that in the *Royal Female*. Perhaps
the explanation is to be found in the comments of an article and
letter which proclaimed that taste and judgment were not truly to
be distinguished; whatever their degree, they were parts of the
same faculty – feeling.[263] No rules and no authority are necessary
to inform us of what we know intuitively.

Antiquity did not impress the writers in Lloyd's magazine. Ossianic poetry was judged not by its age but by its intrinsic merit,[264]
and no reverence was due to Grecian and Roman accomplishments, for those of Shakespeare and Milton were superior, and a
host of modern English poets had produced literature at least
equivalent to the classics.[265] But more particularly, the magazine
writers struck at adopting the ancients as standards. An article on
the entertainment of the theater attacked the unities of ancient
drama as being not only inappropriate to the modern stage, but as
being "too hastily founded on a necessity that might easily and
much better have been removed, and are therefore universally laid
aside now . . .".[266] According to one writer in the magazine, there
could be no "invariable standard for universal imitation", and an
attempt to insist upon classical authority was merely "pedantic
affectation". *Lear* and *Othello* were the best arguments for not
adhering to the unities; they were proof that the ancients simply
lacked sufficient experience.[267]

Practical criticism of drama in the magazine questioned the use
of the laws of unity in *The Siege of Aquileia*. To be sure, it would
gain the approval of the lovers of antiquity, "but whether [the
strict adherence] does not embarrass the action, may be a question

---

[263]   *Royal Female Magazine*, I (April, 1760), p. 146 and I (May, 1760), p.
195.
[264]   *Royal Female Magazine*, I (June, 1760), pp. 275-276.
[265]   *Royal Female Magazine*, I (January, 1760), pp. 3-5.
[266]   *Royal Female Magazine*, I (January, 1760), p. 17.
[267]   *Royal Female Magazine*, I (January, 1760), p. 18.

with those who prefer the feelings of nature to the most revered authority: as the emotions raised by the liveliest relation must be languid in comparison of what is felt from the immediate object . . .".[268] Again, on a practical level, one writer remarked on the *Desert Island,* a dramatic poem, "The veneration for antiquity, which prevails at present, is so extensive, as to afford a sanction to every thing, that even claims a resemblance to it." [269] Such reverence writers in the magazine obviously did not have, and, indeed, in an article on comedy, their attitude was clearly summarized: [270]

This general view of the ancient theatre proves how unnessary a critically exact knowledge of it is, to form a judgment of the modern; and delivers common sense, and the feelings of nature, from the tyranny of pedantic affectation, by shewing that those boasted models are much beneath the present productions of the same kind, in every instance of excellence.

The same article argued that if rules were to be formed, they must be pertinent to the modern theater. However, the magazine's comments on synesthesia indicated no particular delight in the rules. For *synesthesia* breaks the rules of art, and its noble irregularity, through disdain of the rules, rises to beauty.[271] In his criticism of *Tristram Shandy,* the reviewer combined this supreme rejection of the rules with a most conventional regard for morality: [272]

as it affects (and not unsuccessfully) to please, by a contempt of all the rules observed in other writings, and therefore cannot justly have its merit measured by them. It were to be wished though, that the wantonness of the author's wit had been tempered with a little more regard to delicacy, throughout the greatest part of his work.

Apart from concern for the extent of ancient authority and the rules, however, the writers in the magazine had little more to contribute on literature. Obviously, their appraisal of the oriental tale

---

[268] *Royal Female Magazine,* I (February, 1760), p. 91.
[269] *Royal Female Magazine,* I (February, 1760), p. 65.
[270] *Royal Female Magazine,* I (February, 1760), p. 44.
[271] *Royal Female Magazine,* I (March, 1760), p. 100.
[272] *Royal Female Magazine,* I (February, 1760), p. 56.

was related to their own didactic purposes,[273] and although their comments on the American Indians were sympathetic and opposed to the cruel treatment the savages had received from the French,[274] the evidence is too limited for judgment on primitivistic characteristics.

Surprisingly, the other woman's magazine, the *Lady's Museum*, in which Charlotte Lennox, its editor, published her own novel, *The History of Sophia*, as well as poetry, was virtually devoid of literary comment. Its didactic purpose was expressed not only in conventional statements about *utile et dulce*,[275] but in specific praise of the importance of dictionaries [276] and in particular condemnation of idle reading habits: [277]

There is scarcely a young girl who has not read with eagerness a great number of idle romances, and puerile titles, sufficient to corrupt her imagination and cloud her understanding. If she had devoted the same to the study of history, she would in those varied scenes which the world offers to view, have found facts more interesting, and instruction which only truth can give.

Even the classical fables and oriental tales were unacceptable according to the standards of the *Lady's Museum*. No advocates of primitive supremacy, classical or romantic,[278] the writers in the magazine warned, "As for the heathen stories, it will be happy for a girl to remain totally ignorant of them all her life-time; because they are impure, and abound with impious absurdities . . ." [279]

Comment in the remaining seven magazines was more extensive, and the magazines themselves generally had longer runs than those minor magazines already discussed. Four – the *British, Literary, Royal,* and *Universal Museum* – were clearly conservative, while the others – the *Universal, Grand,* and *Court* – repre-

---

[273] *Royal Female Magazine*, I (January, 1760), p. 20 and I (April, 1760), p. 154.
[274] *Royal Female Magazine*, I (January, 1760), p. 35 and I (April, 1760), p. 182.
[275] *Lady's Museum*, I, #2, pp. 130, 145.
[276] *Lady's Museum*, II, #8, p. 593.
[277] *Lady's Museum*, I, #1, p. 13.
[278] *Lady's Museum*, I, #3, p. 193.
[279] *Lady's Museum*, II, #10, p. 776.

sented varying degrees of the aesthetic transition. Perhaps the most conservative magazine of all was the *British*. Its expression of the importance of instruction and entertainment was more than conventional.[280] Letters, articles, and policy statements stressed the need for literature as a means to morality. Biography was offered to readers in order to provide examples of the good life or illustrations of the bad.[281] History was regarded, in Bolingbroke's words, as "the science that teaches morality by example . . .",[282] while comedy and tragedy were described as methods of improving mankind.[283] Even in their treatment of novels, the writers in the *British* gave primary attention to their didactic qualities, so that "chaste, entertaining, and moral" sufficed as literary judgment, and perverse moral teachings resulted in critical disfavor.[284] So closely related were the subjects of literature and morality that the magazine offered a letter comparing Horace, Boileau, and Pope, using their literary work as a guide to their characters.[285]

But such reliance upon Horace's dictum was only one example of the attitude toward the ancients. For writers in the *British*, classical antiquity was unassailable. Whether attempting to raise the level of Britons to Athenian glory,[286] or simply defending classical achievement from modern depreciations,[287] the articles in the magazine left no doubt of their allegiance. In matters of rhyme [288] as in matters of manners,[289] the ancients were superior, and not even the purity of Christianity had enabled the moderns to reach them.

---

[280] *British Magazine*, II (1761), p. i; III (1762), Preface; and III (June, 1762), pp. 306-310.

[281] *British Magazine*, I (October, 1760), p. 561; II (December, 1761), p. 624; and III (July, 1762), p. 358.

[282] *British Magazine*, I (August, 1760), p. 471.

[283] *British Magazine*, I (July, 1760), p. 410; and II (December, 1761), p. 646.

[284] *British Magazine*, I (July, 1760), p. 420 and IV (February, 1763), p. 98.

[285] *British Magazine*, I (August, 1760), pp. 467-468.

[286] *British Magazine*, III (January, 1762), p. 37.

[287] *British Magazine*, I (December, 1760), p. 714.

[288] *British Magazine*, IV (January, 1763), pp. 17-18.

[289] *British Magazine*, II (October, 1761), p. 525.

Naturally, it was to the classical rules that the magazine writers turned for aesthetic models. Upon ancient authority, they argued for idealization in art. Follow nature, but extend it with judgment and taste, even as Homer and Virgil had done. If the *Iliad* and *Aeneid* do not strictly follow nature, they imitate it and heighten it in order to be striking.[290] In the methods of the ancients was inherent the doctrine of imitation, a method prescribed in the magazine for all the arts.[291] Writing generally about emulation, one writer in the *British* declared, "It is indeed the most certain road to excellence in art, learning, politeness, virtue, and even religion." [292] For poetry and epistolary writing, imitation was the prescribed method.[293]

While recognizing that genius was above the methodology of rules,[294] the writers in the magazine, nevertheless, were strong advocates of both the rules and genre criticism. An article on Horace's *Art of Poetry* depicted the rules as the best means of frightening away the unskilled. Although generally praised, the rules were especially lauded for their importance to drama, which could not be successful without them.[295] They were needed in poetry to produce a poem that was excellent in its own kind,[296] and both letters and articles were at pains to distinguish between the poetic genres and to observe the mechanical aspects of verse.[297]

Consistent with their concern for the rules, the writers in the *British* admired regularity and symmetry [298] and insisted upon pro-

---

[290]   *British Magazine,* II (October, 1761), pp. 541-542.
[291]   *British Magazine,* II (October, 1761), p. 543.
[292]   *British Magazine,* IV (May, 1763), p. 222.
[293]   *British Magazine,* II (November, 1761), p. 584 and III (January, 1762), p. 38.
[294]   *British Magazine,* I (June, 1760), pp. 364-365.
[295]   *British Magazine,* II (January, 1761), p. 17.
[296]   *British Magazine,* II (January, 1761), p. 19. *Cf.,* the treatment of *Fingal,* I (August, 1760), p. 479; II (December, 1761), p. 662; III (January, 1762), p. 46; and IV (March, 1763), p. 158.
[297]   *British Magazine,* I (October, 1760), pp. 586-588; I (November, 1760), pp. 631-632; III (February, 1762), pp. 89-91; III (March, 1762), p. 150; III (April, 1762), p. 184; III (June, 1762), pp. 310-312; IV (June, 1763), p. 311; and IV (July, 1763), p. 334.
[298]   *British Magazine,* I (August, 1760), p. 477 and I (October, 1760), p. 594.

priety in art. Whether the author discussed was Shakespeare, who was described as the "father of dramatic poetry" in England,[299] or the immortal Virgil and Homer, the articles in the magazine did not approve of a "deviation from propriety", attributing it to the "erroneous judgment of the writer, who, endeavouring to captivate the admiration with novelty, very often shocks the understanding with extravagance".[300] No matter that Shakespeare, like Pope, not merely copied nature, but was nature itself,[301] he was not to be forgiven his lapses from decency and his descent to obscenity.[302] Whatever his genius, his irregularities could not be overlooked, and even the soliloquy in *Hamlet* was described as "a heap of absurdities, whether we consider the situation, the sentiment, the argumentation, or the poetry".[303] Although the mob might sanctify Shakespeare because of these very errors, the writer in the magazine insisted on the lack of propriety of expression as well as logic, and declared the words, "Ay, there's the rub" to be a "vulgarism beneath the dignity of Hamlet's character . . .".[304]

As these remarks on *Hamlet* suggest, the rules were applied not only to literature, but to language. Although the extent of comment is limited, it clearly indicates the conservative attitude. In bantering tone, a writer in the magazine struck at innovators, who fashionably dropped the *k* from *back, lack,* and *stick,* or who emasculated words in the manner of Italians "in hopes of gaining an elegant sweetness", or who freely omitted the *u* in *honour.* He warned that an absence of standards meant the certain decline of the language, and that the only salvation was in Johnson's dictionary, with its reliance upon the writings of Shakespeare, Milton, Dryden, and Pope.[305] Brief essays on fashionable words or

---

[299] *British Magazine,* I (June, 1760), p. 363. See, also, I (August, 1760), p. 462 and IV (June, 1763), p. 313.
[300] *British Magazine,* III (November, 1762), pp. 596-597.
[301] *British Magazine,* IV (July, 1763), p. 334.
[302] *British Magazine,* IV (July, 1763), p. 335.
[303] *British Magazine,* III (April, 1762), pp. 186-187.
[304] *British Magazine,* III (May, 1762), pp. 263-264.
[305] *British Magazine,* IV (March, 1763), p. 131.

extravagant usage attempted to perform their little part in holding the barbarians at bay.[306]

For writers with the generally conservative literary attitudes of those on the *British,* romantic primitivism could hardly prove attractive.[307] To be sure, the *British* published pastoral pieces to contrast life in a Golden Age with the contemporary degeneracy, but these were in the classical tradition.[308] The noble savage himself did not exist in its pages. While Negroes from the Gold Coast bore strong physical and animalistic traits, they had no desirable social qualities. Their laziness, craftiness, fraudulence, and villainy were not the result of society's institutions but of nature's freedom.[309] The squalid life in the Congo was contrasted with the glories of civilization, and its people were indolent, slothful, "mistrustful, jealous, envious, and treacherous", caught in the stupidity of idolatry and superstition.[310] If a writer in the magazine sought to condemn the behavior of the English, it was by way of comparison not contrast with that of the Hottentots.[311]

The American Indian fared no better than the African Negro. Although the editors presented an engraving of Austenaco, head of the Cherokee nation, in which he looked, except for his shaven head, every bit the European potentate,[312] the articles in the magazine did not romanticize their description of the Cherokees and detailed their account of the cruelty of the Indians.[313] A history of Canada described the Hurons, who were allies of the French, as beasts of prey, unchangeable, incapable of enlightenment or humanization.[314]

---

[306] *British Magazine,* IV (June, 1763), p. 322 and IV (October, 1763), p. 542.

[307] *British Magazine,* I (April, 1760), p. 193, gives the term *Gothic* the meanings of *monstrous* and *illiberal.*

[308] *British Magazine,* I (June, 1760), pp. 354 ff. and I (July, 1760), pp. 405-408.

[309] *British Magazine,* I (September, 1760), pp. 525 ff. and I (August, 1760), pp. 481 ff.

[310] *British Magazine,* II (November, 1761), p. 571.

[311] *British Magazine,* IV (July, 1763), pp. 336-338.

[312] *British Magazine,* III (July, 1762), facing p. 337.

[313] *British Magazine,* III (July, 1762), pp. 354, 377-378.

[314] *British Magazine,* II (March, 1761), p. 153.

Perhaps because of Oliver Goldsmith's connection with the magazine, orientalism was the one branch of primitivism that the writers on the *British* regarded favorably. Then, too, the close association between England and its African and American colonies which made the noble savage argument difficult to uphold in the face of experience did not exist to the same extent between Britain and the orient. Aside from both these considerations, the tradition of using oriental stories for moral purposes was consistent with the magazine's didacticism, and it was the moral tale, not Chinese architecture or decor that received approval. An introduction to the *Chinese Letters* [315] in the *British* indicated its value lay in instruction as well as entertainment, and terms like *instructive* and *moral* accompanied most offerings on the subject, while the tales themselves generally pointed their morality.[316]

Despite their admiration for the ancients, the writers in the *Literary Magazine* offered a more complex conservative pattern than those in the *British* in their aesthetic judgments. To be sure, a direct contrast of ancient and modern taste favored antiquity,[317] and despite their lack of later advantages, the classical painters "excelled the moderns in strength of genius and boldness of their fancy",[318] while Gray's *Odes* were praised on classical authority,[319] and the sublime was accepted by virtue of its Longinian ancestry.[320]

[315] *British Magazine*, I (July, 1760), p. 431. For the remainder of the extracts from the *Chinese Letters*, see I (August, 1760), pp. 487-488; I (September, 1760), pp. 523-524; I (December, 1760), pp. 707-709; II (March, 1761), pp. 137-139; and III (June, 1762), p. 324.

[316] *British Magazine*, I (June, 1760), pp. 373-375; I (August, 1760), pp. 457-460; I (November, 1760), pp. 625 ff.; II (January, 1761), pp. 19 ff.; II (February, 1761), p. 65; II (March, 1761), pp. 143-145; III (March, 1762), p. 158; IV (May, 1763), pp. 238 ff.; IV (August, 1763), pp. 402-404. In its treatment of Confucius, the *British Magazine* acknowledged his grasp of religious essentials, but warned that it was limited to what could be done without revelation and that his disciples had made too much of it (III, July, 1762, pp. 355-358).

[317] *Literary Magazine*, II (January-February, 1757), p. 27. For tentative ascription of this and other articles in the *Literary Magazine* to Arthur Murphy, see Sherbo, *New Essays of Arthur Murphy*, pp. 99 ff.

[318] *Literary Magazine*, II (August-September, 1757), p. 378.

[319] *Literary Magazine*, II (September-October, 1757), p. 425 and II (October-November, 1757), p. 467.

[320] *Literary Magazine*, II (October-November, 1757), p. 468.

At the same time, to pretend to imitate the ancients without following their precepts, as Home had done in *Agis* and *Douglas*, was to commit a double fault and to open the way to criticism on two accounts, the failure of imitation and perfection.[321] Nevertheless, one writer, perhaps Goldsmith, in the *Literary*, in his judgments of Shakespeare, refused to accept French classicism, with its ridiculous adoption of ancient blemishes and weaknesses,[322] and insisted, in his comments on both imitation and the rules, upon the model of nature rather than merely the ancients.

Whether for painting or poetry, nature was the best guide. In his review of Warton's *Essay on the Writings and Genius of Pope*, Johnson himself disagreed with the author that Pope should have written American pastorals: [323]

... for as he must have painted scenes which he never saw, and manners he never knew, his performance, though it might have been a pleasing amusement of fancy, would have exhibited no representation of nature or of life.

In their identification of the arts with instruction, the writers in the magazine emphasized truth, and in judgments of poetry, all of which is imitation of nature, "the question should be whether the imitation is true ...".[324] On such a criterion, in addition to the authority of antiquity which was based on following nature, Gray's *Odes* were approved,[325] and painters were advised that the way to art is a practical imitation of nature.[326] The demands for universality were answered not by the particular artistic models but as those models were drawn from nature,[327] and even the sublime was

[321] *Literary Magazine*, III (March, 1758), pp. 109 ff.
[322] *Literary Magazine*, III (January, 1758), p. 8. For the possible attribuiton to Goldsmith, see Crane, *New Essays*, p. 131.
[323] *Literary Magazine*, I (April-May, 1756), p. 36.
[324] *Literary Magazine*, II (January-February, 1757), p. 35. See, also, II (January-February, 1757), p. 30.
[325] *Literary Magazine*, II (September-October, 1757), p. 425.
[326] *Literary Magazine*, II (October-November, 1757), pp. 464-465.
[327] *Literary Magazine*, III (February, 1758), pp. 59-60. For the attribution to Goldsmith, see M. Golden's note in *Notes and Queries*, III (1956), pp. 434-435.

justified because natural variety and irregularity, despite their rudeness, provided an absolute standard.[328]

Such absolute standards required absolute rules, and criticism of Hume's essay on taste expressed disappointment in his failure to settle "some fixed and immutable standard", for "surely a criterion of beauty might be established . . .; [and] fixed principles of right and wrong . . . may be settled in literature as well as religion . . .".[329] To be sure, writers in the *Literary* had their own standards, which were best expressed, perhaps by Goldsmith, in a rating scale that was provided for evaluating poets. The divisions were *genius, judgment, learning*, and *versification*. While the greatest art depended upon genius, "those excellencies that no study or art can communicate: such as elevation, expression, description, wit, harmony, passion, &c.", the other three criteria were important matters of training.[330] On such a basis, Shakespeare's limited learning and judgment might prove no impossible handicap,[331] but for others it was necessary to peruse models and rules to achieve success.[332]

Ancient authority, drawn from nature, was an important crite-

---

[328]   *Literary Magazine*, II (March-April, 1757), pp. 115-116 and II (April-May, 1757), pp. 184-185.
[329]   *Literary Magazine*, II (January-February, 1757), p. 35.
[330]   *Literary Magazine*, III (January, 1758), pp. 6 ff. For attribution to Goldsmith, see Crane, *New Essays*, p. 131.
[331]   For other comments on Shakespeare, see *Literary Magazine*, I (April-May, 1756), p. 37 and II (March-April, 1757), p. 152. The first was by Johnson.
[332]   The following is a partial list from the poetical scale in the *Literary*, III (January, 1758), pp. 6 ff. Twenty was the maximum score for each category.

Author	Genius	Judgment	Learning	Versification
Chaucer	16	12	10	14
Spenser	18	12	14	18
Shakespeare	19	14	14	19
Jonson	16	18	17	8
Cowley	17	17	15	17
Waller	12	12	10	16
Otway	17	10	10	17
Milton	18	16	17	18
Dryden	18	16	17	18
Addison	16	18	17	17

rion.[333] The critics were reminded that "the first inventors of an art seldom attain perfection; it is from subsequent observation that improvements are made". Through taste and ingenuity the principles must be reduced to a regular system, such as that provided by the ancients,[334] and the result is quite naturally a theory of the genres. An article on Dyer's *Fleece* presented the rules for Georgic poetry, or what it called the "Georgic kind".[335] Whether describing farce, tragedy, or poetry, writers, including Johnson, in the *Literary*, were concerned with the propriety and rules of the type.[336]

Perhaps the insistence upon following nature and the regard for truth were related to the magazine's didactic demands on literature. The theater was described as an important source for morality whose function was to promote virtue and retard the progress of vice.[337] The argument for biography was its ability to provide "knowledge of the human heart"; by fixing "the most useful knowledge with pleasure and utility in the mind of the reader", it served the best purpose of literature.[338] In his attack on the popular novel and its readers, the critic applied standards of morality rather than aesthetics,[339] as did a letter-writer whose principles of *dulce et utile* were underscored by a demand for sentiments judged by their measure of truth and diction whose purity had an educational value.[340]

Prior	16	16	15	17
Swift	18	16	16	16
Pope	18	18	15	19
Thomson	16	16	14	17
Butler	17	16	14	16

For attribution to Goldsmith, see Crane, *New Essays*, p. 131.

[333] *Literary Magazine*, II (September-October, 1757), p. 425.
[334] *Literary Magazine*, II (January-February, 1757), p. 28.
[335] *Literary Magazine*, II (March-April, 1757), pp. 134 ff.
[336] *Literary Magazine*, I (April-May, 1756), pp. 35-38; II (February-March, 1757), pp. 77-78; and II (March-April, 1757), pp. 136 ff. The second was by Johnson.
[337] *Literary Magazine*, II (February-March, 1757), pp. 87-90.
[338] *Literary Magazine*, II (May-June, 1757), p. 228.
[339] *Literary Magazine*, II (April-May, 1757), pp. 180 ff.
[340] *Literary Magazine*, II (January-February, 1757), p. 30.

Not unnaturally, articles in the *Literary* advocated a refinement of the English language, and, indeed, urged the necessity for forming an English academy.[341] Viewing the forces at work to destroy the language,[342] Goldsmith and Johnson objected to Gallicisms, Scotticisms, abuses of grammar and diction in their articles on language and literature.[343] Arguing for standards of clarity and simplicity,[344] the comment in the *Literary* reproached even the *Philosophical Transactions* because its editor had too little "regard to the purity of our language, which is too frequently vitiated by their correspondents and translators . . .".[345]

This sense of refinement, this view that civilization was necessary for the cultivation of the arts precluded a taste for romantic primitivism. For the Gothic, there was only scorn,[346] and the magazine's excerpts from Chambers on Chinese gardens and abstracts of accounts of the Eskimo were offered as oddities without comment.[347] Without ennobling the American Indians, Johnson himself deplored their treatment by both the English and French, and noted that the English traders had defrauded the "simple hunter of his furs".[348]

Although the *Royal* was also conservative, it was not nearly so insistently so as the *Literary* and *British*. Didacticism was the one artistic principle on which its writers truly insisted. Not merely conventional pronouncements and letters from subscribers but

[341] *Literary Magazine*, III (May, 1758), p. 199.
[342] *Literary Magazine*, III (February, 1758), pp. 56 ff. For the attribution to Goldsmith, see Golden, *Notes and Queries*, III, pp. 434-435.
[343] *Literary Magazine*, I (May-June, 1756), p. 57; I (June-July, 1756), p. 136; I (August-September, 1756), pp. 239-240; II (January-February, 1757), p. 26; II (April-May, 1757), p. 161; and III (February, 1758), pp. 57-58. The first three were Johnson's work. For the attribution of the last to Goldsmith, see the preceding footnote.
[344] *Literary Magazine*, III (March, 1758), p. 105.
[345] *Literary Magazine*, I (July-August, 1756), p. 193. For possible attribution to Johnson, see Bloom.
[346] *Literary Magazine*, II (July-August, 1757), p. 362 and II (October-November, 1757), p. 474.
[347] *Literary Magazine*, II (February-March, 1757), pp. 63 ff., 68 ff., 73 ff. and II (April-May, 1757), pp. 199-201.
[348] *Literary Magazine*, I (April-May, 1756), pp. 8-9; I (June-July, 1756), pp. 153-154; I (July-August, 1756), pp. 161-162. All have been attributed to Johnson.

also specific criticism indicate the magazine's didactic purpose.[349] The importance of biography, from ancient and modern authority, was argued as a precept to be followed.[350] Accounts of the drama judged as much from moral virtue as artistic merit. *The Way to Keep Him* was approved for its instructive moral, instructive characterization, just ridicule, and useful satire.[351] Praise for a farce was granted on negative values, such as the absence of low jests, obscene hints, or particular scandal and wantonness,[352] while Whitehead's *School for Lovers* was rewarded as much for its morality and instruction for women as it was for its contribution to the new genre of sentiment.[353] But drama was not alone in its moral significance. Again citing ancient and modern examples, writers in the magazine demanded that poetry be constructive in the building of virtue,[354] and described the purpose of both sculpture and painting to be their moral effect.[355]

But for all this didacticism, articles in the *Royal* were not nearly so dogmatically conservative as those in the *British*. Their treatment of the remnants of the ancient-modern controversy certainly was balanced. Although the editors claimed rediscovery of the glories of antiquity as one of their objects,[356] and articles in the magazine particularly praised the Greeks for their sculpture,[357] much of the comment in letters and articles compared modern achievement favorably with that of the ancients. In a letter which described a fictitious Temple of Taste, Pope, Voltaire, Shakespeare, and three Restoration dramatists shared equal fame with Aristotle, Longinus, Plautus, and Aristophanes, while Boileau

[349] *Royal Magazine*, I (September, 1759), pp. 129-134; II (1760), p. ii; IV (June, 1761), p. 295; VI (April, 1762), p. 195; and IX (November, 1763), p. 249.
[350] *Royal Magazine*, I (August, 1759), p. 66.
[351] *Royal Magazine*, II (January, 1760), pp. 34-35.
[352] *Royal Magazine*, IX (November, 1763), p. 247.
[353] *Royal Magazine*, VI (February, 1762), p. 76.
[354] *Royal Magazine*, IV (January, 1761), p. 4.
[355] *Royal Magazine*, III (November, 1760), pp. 242-243.
[356] *Royal Magazine*, I (1759), pp. i-ii.
[357] *Royal Magazine*, II (May, 1760), pp. 245-246 and III (November, 1760), p. 242.

came close, and only Descartes was rejected.[358] Then, a long article on the literary merits of ancients and moderns sought to credit judiciously the arguments of Boileau, who rejected the modern Tasso, and Voltaire, who had placed Tasso above Homer.[359] Working through the genres, the writer compared favorably the epic achievement of Tasso and Milton with that of Homer and Virgil; declared that the minor epics of Lucan and Statius were not superior to those of Camoens and Voltaire; placed the dramatic poetry of Racine, Voltaire, Corneille, Shakespeare, Otway, and Rowe above that of Sophocles, Euripides, and Seneca, and insisted upon the ascendancy of modern comic writers. However, the ancients were acclaimed for history and oratory, and their lyric poetry was admittedly beyond the best work of the moderns. In satire, there was little to judge between Horace, Juvenal, and Persius, on the one hand, and Dryden, Pope, and the Italian satirists, on the other, just as in morals, despite the benefit of Christianity, there was little to choose between them, although Locke, in logic and metaphysics, was clearer than Aristotle.

Whatever the relative merits of particular arguments in the *Royal*, they were intended to balance the virtues of ancients and moderns. Yet the aesthetic values of writers in the magazine were chiefly those of classical regularity and universality, perhaps related to the moral quality of their criticism. The relationship is clearest in those arguments against Gothic irregularity as a means for achieving devotion through church architecture: [360]

The holy awe, thus mechanically incited [by the Gothic sublimity, the magazine warned,] would be as friendly to paganism as Christianity; and indeed, this awe is so far from being holy, that it is a thing entirely distinct from rational piety and devotion, and may be felt without any inclination to enter the choir.

Not only religion but conduct was associated with the demands for regularity in art. Singularity, marring instead of mending nature, and extravagant excesses were fashionable decadence,[361] but

---

[358]   *Royal Magazine*, III (December, 1760), pp. 282-283.
[359]   *Royal Magazine*, IX (September, 1763), pp. 125-128.
[360]   *Royal Magazine*, VIII (April, 1763), p. 172.
[361]   *Royal Magazine*, IX (July, 1763), p. 33.

more particularly, the mind was properly formed through examples of good order: [362]

Good taste is an habitual love of order, and influences the manners as well as the several productions of genius. A symmetry of parts between themselves, and with the whole, is as necessary to the conduct of a moral action, as to a piece of painting. This love of order is a virtue in the soul, which extends itself to every object that has any connection with, or relation to us; when this love of order is concerned in things of pleasure or amusement, it is called taste; when it relates to the manners, it is stiled virtue.

With one major exception, articles in the magazine found regularity and order a necessity for art, while the ornamental and irregular were absurdities.[363] To be sure, writers in the magazine did not approve of dull imitations of the classical,[364] and were willing to treat a new genre according to its own rules,[365] but these were rules of uniformity and regularity. Only Shakespeare was above these, and critical remarks on the English tragic poets defended him from the attacks of Bolingbroke and Voltaire.[366]

But this approval of Shakespeare did not extend to romantic primitivism. "Painting, like all other arts, was very gross and imperfect in its beginnings. The shadow of a man marked by the outlines, gave birth to it, as well as to sculpture." [367] For the primitive existence itself, a letter-writer reminded the *Royal*'s readers that civilized man had a far longer lease on life than his barbarian contemporaries.[368] Only in the didactic possibilities of romantic primitivism were writers in the *Royal* interested, and both orientalism and the American Indian provided material for instruction.

In their treatment of orientalism, Goldsmith and others in the

[362] *Royal Magazine*, III (November, 1760), p. 233.
[363] *Royal Magazine*, VI (January, 1762), p. 9; VI (March, 1762), p. 151; VIII (March, 1763), pp. 152-153; VIII (April, 1763), p. 177; VIII (May, 1763), p. 235; IX (August, 1763), p. 77; and IX (November, 1763), p. 233.
[364] *Royal Magazine*, V (December, 1761), pp. 293-294.
[365] *Royal Magazine*, V (August, 1761), pp. 66-67.
[366] *Royal Magazine*, IX (July, 1763), pp. 39-41. See, also, VIII (May, 1763), p. 236.
[367] *Royal Magazine*, III (July, 1760), p. 21. See, also, I (July, 1759), pp. 35-38.
[368] *Royal Magazine*, III (July, 1760), p. 3.

magazine did not hold up the East as an ideal,[369] but used the pseudo-oriental tale for lessons in morality. Subtitles and moral tags suggest the character of stories that were often exempla for Christian virtue: "the proceedings of Providence are just, regulated by infinite Wisdom, and tempered by mercy and loving kindness".[370] Moreover, it was not at all inconsistent for the editors to use a moral motto from Dryden to introduce an oriental tale.[371]

The American Indian served the same instructional purposes, although there was less information about him. His ignorance was deplored,[372] and, as a savage, he was not to be used as a model,[373] except to demonstrate that even "the Indians, if properly instructed, might be rendered useful members of society".[374] That they had not been was attributed to the white man, and here the contributor to the magazine was using the savage to attack the enemy French,[375] a form of didacticism that was political rather than intellectual or social.

If less conservative than the *British Magazine*, the *Universal Museum* was more orthodox than the *Royal*. Aesthetic comments in the *Universal Museum*, with few exceptions, were conservative. If those on language were restricted to the regularly printed essays, the *Author* and the *Witling,* and were limited in number, they were at least insistent upon principles of purity and refinement.[376] No such limitations existed in the concern for instruction and

---

[369]   *Royal Magazine*, III (September, 1760), pp. 138-139. See, also, letters, II (February, 1760), pp. 60-62 and IX (November, 1763), p. 232. For attribution of the September comment to Goldsmith, see Crane, *New Essays*, pp. 48 ff.

[370]   *Royal Magazine*, VIII (January, 1763), pp. 1-4. See, also, I (December, 1759), pp. 296-299; II (February, 1760), pp. 90-92; II (January, 1760), pp. 9-12; II (March, 1760), pp. 115-118; II (April, 1760), pp. 174-176; II (June, 1760), pp. 317-318; III (September, 1760), pp. 127-129; and IX (October, 1763), pp. 202-204. For attribution of the December, 1759, comment to Goldsmith, see Crane, *New Essays*, p. xxxiii.

[371]   *Royal Magazine*, V (July, 1761), pp. 6-8.

[372]   *Royal Magazine*, VII (July, 1762), p. 16.

[373]   *Royal Magazine*, VII (August, 1762), pp. 83-84.

[374]   *Royal Magazine*, III (October, 1760), pp. 175-176.

[375]   *Royal Magazine*, III (October, 1760), p. 176 and IX (August, 1763), p. 104.

[376]   *Universal Museum*, II (March, 1763), p. 121 and II (October, 1763), pp. 541-542.

entertainment with the emphasis upon instruction. Not only its general statements [377] and its biographical feature, but its very method of criticism indicate the magazine's didactic emphasis. To the moral climate of the age, articles in the *Universal Museum* attributed the development of writers.[378] Judgments of novels depended upon their instruction and morality,[379] and heathen mythology was objectionable in modern poetry.[380] Satire was defended because of its utility,[381] while the language of the theater was expected to be pristine, genteel, and free of double entendre.[382] Drama itself was regarded as much for its moral as aesthetic qualities, so that the purpose of comedy was to attack the vices and foibles of the times at the same time that its characters should be worthy of imitation. Moreover, as one writer explained, "The stage ought, on all occasions, to be made the school of virtue . . .".[383]

Plainly admiring the ancients,[384] writers in the *Universal Museum* sought regularity, propriety, and rules in the arts. Johnson's critical remarks on Pope's epitaphs were quoted with approval, "Every art is best taught by example. Nothing contributes more to the cultivation of propriety, than remarks on the works of those who have most excelled." [385] The magazine's long digest of a *View of the Fine Arts* stressed the functions of rules and imitation in creating harmony and universal principles.[386] At the same time, a life of Otway judged his drama by Aristotelian rules,[387] and one reader of the magazine questioned the application of Aristotelian principles to a three act play in order to determine how the prima-

---

[377]   *Universal Museum*, I (January, 1762), pp. 26-27, 52 and I (September, 1762), p. 481.
[378]   *Universal Museum*, I (October, 1762), p. 569.
[379]   *Universal Museum*, I (November, 1762), p. 616 and I (February, 1762), p. 97.
[380]   *Universal Museum*, I (February, 1762), p. 98.
[381]   *Universal Museum*, II (September, 1763), pp. 462-464.
[382]   *Universal Museum*, I (February, 1762), p. 109.
[383]   *Universal Museum*, I (February, 1762), p. 108.
[384]   *Universal Museum*, I (November, 1762), p. 598; II (September, 1763), pp. 462-464; and II (November, 1763), p. 563.
[385]   *Universal Museum*, II (September, 1763), p. 472.
[386]   *Universal Museum*, I (January, 1762), pp. 7-9 and I (February, 1762), pp. 78-80.
[387]   *Universal Museum*, II (November, 1763), p. 563.

ry parts of a drama were to be conducted and whether it constituted "a just and regular play". The authority of Aristotle was
placed alongside that of Horace, not to challenge, but to arrive at
a workable formula.[388] Even when a critic was willing to yield to
the modern mixture of the tragic and comic, he was still insistent
upon unity of the fable and judged its sacrifice as a loss to the
drama.[389]

Stressing the word *propriety*,[390] articles in the *Universal Museum*
linked rules, regularity, and the genres in their criticism. Versification was the mechanical part of poetry, but it was essential to
the character of the art.[391] The writers in the magazine desired to
distinguish between sentimental tragedy and comedy.[392] They
sought the appropriate models for a genre,[393] attempted to prescribe rules for success within a type,[394] and recognized, in painting and poetry, a hierarchy of classes.[395] The chief values of the
works themselves were those of symmetry, simplicity, regularity,
and order.[396]

Of the two exceptions to these general principles, one – the
magazine's review of *Fingal* – was not altogether a contradiction.
The reviewer denied the necessity of applying Aristotle's rules to
all epic poetry. While they were applicable to the *Iliad*, from
which they had been drawn, the reviewer insisted, they were not
important here. Nevertheless, his own analysis followed the divisions of fable, sentiments, characters, and language, and clearly
the objection was intended to elevate the importance of Macpherson's work, which the reviewer took to be genuine but confessed
was not to give the same pleasure as Homer or Milton.[397]

The other exception, of course, was Shakespeare. He was plain-

---

[388]   *Universal Museum*, II (July, 1763), p. 357.
[389]   *Universal Museum*, II (February, 1763), p. 90.
[390]   *Universal Museum*, I (April, 1762), p. 227 and II (May, 1763), pp.
250-251.
[391]   *Universal Museum*, II (July, 1763), p. 357.
[392]   *Universal Museum*, I (January, 1762), p. 44.
[393]   *Universal Museum*, I (January, 1762), p. 52.
[394]   *Universal Museum*, I (December, 1762), pp. 689-690.
[395]   *Universal Museum*, I (January, 1762), p. 5.
[396]   *Universal Museum*, I (March, 1762), p. 139 and I (April, 1762), p. 194.
[397]   *Universal Museum*, I (February, 1762), pp. 98-99.

ly above the rules, even beyond the need for observance of the unities.[398] Whatever his faults, he was the supreme dramatic writer.[399] Truly there were no rules for him to follow, for he was not an imitation of nature, but its instrument; he did not speak from nature, but nature spoke through him.[400] Of the scene after Macbeth's murder, a writer in the magazine declared, it "consists of nothing but the pure strokes of nature".[401] For such an artist, the rules, unities, and genres were unimportant.

But Shakespeare was the only acceptable child of nature. Demands for simplicity and regularity in art precluded a taste for the Gothic. While writers in the magazine accepted a climatic theory of character development,[402] which might well have led to a consideration of hard and soft primitivism, the noble savage did not arise in its pages. One Indian chief who was courageous and honorable did not constitute a tribe,[403] and at least one writer recognized the extent to which imagination affected the description of savage nations.[404]

If orientalism appears to have fared better in the magazine, it is only because of the didactic use to which oriental tales were put. Each of the stories specifically stated its moral,[405] and the editors of the magazine described the purpose of the genre itself to be entertaining and instructive,[406] just as Lady Mary Wortley Montague's description of Turkish manners and customs was to delight and educate.[407] For oriental taste or *chinoiserie*, writers in the *Universal Museum* had no more respect than for Italian fashion.

[398] *Universal Museum*, I (March, 1762), p. 172.
[399] *Universal Museum*, II (November, 1763), p. 561.
[400] *Universal Museum*, II (November, 1763), p. 563.
[401] *Universal Museum*, I (January, 1762), p. 45.
[402] *Universal Museum*, I (March, 1762), p. 146; I (May, 1762), pp. 279-281; and I (October, 1762), p. 569.
[403] *Universal Museum*, I (July, 1762), p. 357.
[404] *Universal Museum*, I (September, 1762), p. 508.
[405] *Universal Museum*, I (January, 1762), pp. 3-5; I (July, 1762), pp. 361-363; I (August, 1762), pp. 430-432; I (December, 1762), pp. 663-665; II (January, 1763), pp. 9-10, 18-20; II (February, 1763), pp. 67-69, 79-80; II (April, 1763), p. 185; II (June, 1763), p. 301; and II (July, 1763), pp. 348-349.
[406] *Universal Museum*, I (1762), Preface and I (February, 1762), p. 96.
[407] *Universal Museum*, II (May, 1763), p. 241.

This mad enthusiasm was contrasted with the taste of the cultivated English: ". . . it was a certain uniformity of sentiment and
action, a harmony of thought, with a discerning judgment; in
every science they endeavour'd to improve on the models left
them by the ancients . . ." [408] That which was best in English and
Chinese fashions was based on tradition and custom, not on the
naive intuition of romantic primitivism.[409]

The three important minor magazines whose comments on aesthetics were transitional differ not in kind but in degree, not only
from the three conservative magazines that have just been described, but from each other. From their emphasis on didacticism,
the comments in the *Universal Magazine* would seem far more
conservative in their literary opinions than their lack of enthusiasm for either the authority of the ancients or the necessity of the
rules demonstrates them to have been. The magazine's stated editorial purpose was to entertain and instruct the gentry, merchants,
farmers, and tradesmen, to provide a "Repository of the Utile
and Dulce",[410] and whether in biographical sketches,[411] scientific
articles,[412] or sensational news accounts,[413] Horace's dictum was
insisted upon.[414] More particularly, writers in the magazine, like
other periodical writers who related art to its effect on the public,
demanded moral standards in criticism of both literature and the
fine arts. From that point of view, even the origin of music was
described in terms of its didactic purpose, and its refinement was
successful only when it followed its original design.[415] Novels were
praised more for their good intentions than for their aesthetic

---

[408]   *Universal Museum*, I (December, 1762), pp. 656-657.
[409]   *Universal Museum*, I (August, 1762), p. 415.
[410]   *Universal Magazine*, XXXIII (1763), p. 2. See, also, XXI (November,
1757), p. 229.
[411]   *Universal Magazine*, XIX (1756), Preface; XXIII (Supplement, 1758),
p. 329; XXIV (January, 1759), pp. 22 ff.; XXVII (Supplement, 1760), p.
337; and XXXII (Supplement, 1763), p. 337.
[412]   *Universal Magazine*, XXIII (July, 1758), p. 4 and XXVIII (June,
1761), pp. 299 f.
[413]   *Universal Magazine*, XXXI (August, 1762), pp. 100 ff.
[414]   In *Universal Magazine*, XXIII (December, 1758), p. 274, even the
sublime was included in the attempt to instruct and please, as the magazine added "to move" and made it, at the same time, part of the latter.
[415]   *Universal Magazine*, XIX (July, 1756), pp. 1-3.

accomplishments,[416] and dramas were evaluated according to their capacity to teach proper conduct.[417] Indeed, there was a puritanical note to the magazine's comments on sculpture. Despite favorable remarks on the ancients' achievement in the art, writers in the *Universal* pointed to the immoral purposes suggested by naked figures: "What loose ideas do not these naked figures of young persons suggest to the imagination, which sculptors so commonly take the liberty of exhibiting? They may do honour to the art, but never to the artists." [418] From such a moral code, it was natural to advocate a censorship of art.

The same censorious attitude characterized comments on language which were as much moral as literary criticism. Despite his praise for *Tristram Shandy,* the reviewer scored the "indecent expressions" in the novel, labeling them "gross and obscene" and relating them to the questionable morality of Sterne's treatment of midwifery and baptism. Again, the critic was judging art from the point of view of its effect on the audience, and the author was criticized for using smut, as the playhouses did, to encourage mass interest.[419] But *Shandy* was not alone. Another reviewer in the *Universal* equated unnatural diction and stylistic corruption with moral indecency in his account of *Polly Honeycombe, a Dramatic Novel of One Act.*[420]

Apart from this use of diction as an argument for morality, there was surprisingly little comment on language in the *Universal* – no objections to borrowings, no demands for an academy, no lamentations about syntax and grammar,[421] all of which generally characterized periodical writers whose literary attitudes were conservative. Moreover, neither did statements about the authority of

---

[416]   *Universal Magazine,* XXIV (May, 1759), p. 238 and XXVII (December, 1760), p. 321. See the first of the extracts from *Rasselas* in XXIV (May, 1759), pp. 238-245.

[417]   *Universal Magazine,* XXII (March, 1758), pp. 119-120; XXV (November, 1759), pp. 245-248, 265; and XXIV (Supplement, 1759), pp. 341-342.

[418]   *Universal Magazine,* XVIII (January, 1756), p. 3.

[419]   *Universal Magazine,* XXVI (April, 1760), pp. 189-190.

[420]   *Universal Magazine,* XXVII (December, 1760), p. 321.

[421]   The only example of concern with language problems was a reprint of an ironic political dictionary, *Universal Magazine,* XXXII (Supplement, 1763), pp. 356-358.

the ancients, the necessity of rules, and the desirability of imitation, follow a line that was consistent with the didactic and moral arguments.

To be sure, writers in the magazine praised Grecian contributions to musical development,[422] used Aristotelian authority to judge tragedy,[423] and admitted architectural and sculptural perfection in the ancients.[424] But even this praise was offered with reservations. The perfection was only relative, for the sculpture was not without its abuses, nor the music without its corruption. In morality, the Greeks were vain and filled with self-conceit,[425] and in scientific achievement, the moderns had surpassed them.[426] While they intended comparisons between Pitt and Pericles,[427] Milton, Shakespeare, and Homer [428] to be complimentary approval of the moderns, writers in the *Universal* did not hesitate to commend Shakespeare beyond praise for the ancients. His work gave no knowledge of the ancients, but "his own great genius [was] equal, if not superior to some of the best of theirs . . .". Had he known their writing, his own might have had fewer blemishes, but perhaps such regularity and deference would have cost him his fire: [429]

And there is reason to believe we are better pleased with those thoughts, altogether new and uncommon, which his own imagination supplied him so abundantly with, than if he had given us the most beautiful passages out of the Greek and Latin poets, and that in the most agreeable manner it was possible for a master of the English language to deliver them.

Indeed, with Shakespeare's capacity to express the passions, the same writer in the *Universal* declared, ". . . what a task would it

---

[422]   *Universal Magazine*, XIX (July, 1756), p. 3.
[423]   *Universal Magazine*, XXV (November, 1759), pp. 245-246.
[424]   *Universal Magazine*, XVIII (January, 1756), p. 3 and XX (January, 1757), p. 1.
[425]   *Universal Magazine*, XXIV (Supplement, 1759), p. 350.
[426]   *Universal Magazine*, XXXI (August, 1762), pp. 86 ff.
[427]   *Universal Magazine*, XXV (July, 1759), p. 3.
[428]   *Universal Magazine*, XXII (January, 1758), pp. 1 ff. and XXIX (August, 1761), pp. 70-71.
[429]   *Universal Magazine*, XXVIII (Supplement, 1761), p. 337.

have been for the greatest masters of Greece and Rome" to have matched him.[430]

As these comments on Shakespeare suggest, the writers in the *Universal* were no great proponents of the rules. While they indicated the importance of developing artistic talent,[431] noted that the "nicest and most scrupulous critics" had insisted upon the unities,[432] and outlined the rules for historical writing,[433] the magazine writers also argued that true merit depended upon more than the simple adherence to basic principles [434] and that reducing a work to dramatic rules might, in great measure, destroy its power of affecting the passions.[435] Certainly, to follow the excellent rules of the ancients was neither the sole way of achieving greatness nor a guarantee of anything more than mediocrity.[436] The supreme example of deviating successfully from the classical rules, of course, was Shakespeare, for whom "art had so little, and nature so large a share in what he did . . .".[437] Judged by Aristotelian rules, his plays were defective, but why apply such standards to them? Shakespeare "lived in a state of almost universal license and ignorance; there was no established judge, but every one took the liberty to write according to the dictates of his own fancy". What really mattered was his achievement.[438]

Without rejecting the use of classical models, writers in the magazine stressed imitation of nature. Admittedly, a good style, a certain eloquence, and practical standards could be achieved by working with ancient predecessors as guides,[439] but servile imitation was not enough, and the object of proper imitation was to im-

---

[430] *Universal Magazine*, XXVIII (Supplement, 1761), pp. 340-341.
[431] *Universal Magazine*, XIX (July, 1756), p. 2; XX (January, 1757), p. 2; XXI (July, 1757), p. 2 and XXXIII (July, 1763), p. 6.
[432] *Universal Magazine*, XXIV (Supplement, 1759), p. 340.
[433] *Universal Magazine*, XXV (October, 1759), pp. 174 ff.
[434] *Universal Magazine*, XXI (July, 1757), p. 2.
[435] *Universal Magazine*, XXVIII (January, 1761), p. 23.
[436] *Universal Magazine*, XX (January, 1757), pp. 2-3.
[437] *Universal Magazine*, XXVIII (Supplement, 1761), p. 338.
[438] *Universal Magazine*, XXVIII (Supplement, 1761), p. 341.
[439] *Universal Magazine*, XXV (July, 1759), p. 4 and XXV (November, 1759), pp. 245-248.

prove on the original.[440] Even so, the best imitation was not of the ancients but of the nature from which they had copied, whether it was nature in its regularity or irregularity.[441] Consequently, the true Gothic was as appealing as the true classical, for both represented nature, if in different ways. On the one hand, nature could be praised because it "always takes the easiest and shortest way in all her works: He therefore who would imitate her must do the same"; [442] and on the other hand, imitation of nature, did not have to mean simplicity and regularity: [443]

... the nearer these gardens approach to nature, the longer they will please; for what is a garden, but a natural spot of ground, dressed and properly ornamented? There are those who have erred in copying of what they call nature, as much as those who have drawn a whole garden into straight lines, great alleys, stars &c. by bringing the roughest and most deformed part of nature into their compositions of gardens. . . .

Comments on imitation, like those on classical rules, argued for the consistency of Gothic and sublime taste with proper aesthetic appreciation.[444]

Despite this generally liberal interpretation of neoclassical aesthetics, the articles in the magazine retained the standards of genre criticism. *Tristram Shandy* was described, for all of its deficiencies of taste and morality, as a "book . . . truly excellent in its kind".[445] A biographical article on Ben Jonson lamented the absurdity of the modern mixture of farce and comedy,[446] and an account of Dodsley's tragedy, *Cleone,* discussed the appropriateness of parts of the composition in relation to the genre. [447] The same genre criticism was applied to both opera and modern trage-

---

[440] *Universal Magazine,* XXIV (Supplement, 1759), pp. 341-342 and XXXI (July, 1762), p. 24.

[441] *Universal Magazine,* XXIV (Supplement, 1759), p. 348.

[442] *Universal Magazine,* XXVI (February, 1760), p. 66.

[443] *Universal Magazine,* XXX (February, 1762), p. 70.

[444] *Universal Magazine,* XX (January, 1757), pp. 2-3; XXII (January, 1758), p. 2; XXIV (January, 1759), pp. 12-13; and XXVII (December, 1760), p. 297.

[445] *Universal Magazine,* XXVI (April, 1760), p. 190.

[446] *Universal Magazine,* XXIV (Supplement, 1759), p. 341.

[447] *Universal Magazine,* XXIII (December, 1758), pp. 283-290.

dy,[448] and even Shakespeare, who was above classical rules of criticism when they concerned the unities, was found guilty of appealing to the ignorance of his age in the mixture of tragedy and comedy, and it mattered not that the result still appealed to English taste: [449]

[His histories and some of his comedies are actually tragedies] with a run or mixture of comedy amongst them. That way of tragi-comedy was the common mistake of that age, and is indeed become so agreeable to the English taste, that, though the severer critics among us cannot bear it, yet the generality of our audiences seem to be better pleased with it than with an exact tragedy.

For the signs of romantic primitivism, the reaction was less clear. While they attempted to explain the Gothic and sublime, the writers in the *Universal* had little sympathy for the noble savage. They lamented the lack of development in Africa and recognized that commerce rather than Christian principles would guide that continent's future.[450] Yet the rejection of Christianity of these savages indicated an opposition to civilization,[451] and the positive values of civilization were contrasted with the humble conditions in primitive life, without romantic sentiment clouding the picture.[452]

In dealing with the American Indians, comment in the *Universal* was not more favorable. Although they were given the usual animal attributes, and the French were described as doing nothing, even by way of example, to improve their status, the Indians were presented, without malice or nonsense, as rude, ignorant, and barbarous.[453] The obvious relationship between the portrait of the Indian and England's commercial rivalry with France was made not only in the attack upon the French treatment of the Indian, but in an article on colonial trade which described the uncivilized

[448] *Universal Magazine*, XXV (November, 1759), pp. 245-248 and XXVIII (March, 1761), pp. 122-123.
[449] *Universal Magazine*, XXVIII (Supplement, 1761), pp. 339-340.
[450] *Universal Magazine*, XXXIII (August, 1763), p. 59.
[451] *Universal Magazine*, XXX (June, 1762), pp. 294-295.
[452] *Universal Magazine*, XXII (May, 1758), pp. 228 ff.
[453] *Universal Magazine*, XVIII (February, 1756), p. 73; XX (May, 1757), pp. 193-195; XXVIII (February, 1761), pp. 59-60; XXVIII (March, 1761), pp. 113-114; and XXXII (Supplement, 1763), pp. 342 ff.

state as shameful in its nakedness, barren in its accomplishments, and a source worthy of the attention of business interests.[454]

Only the oriental primitivism came in for favorable treatment, despite an article attacking the bad effects of tea and warning that the English were in danger of degenerating "to the delicate effeminate stature of the diminutive people of China".[455] The editors found the oriental tale suitable to their own didactic purposes,[456] and the appeal of oriental design to their taste for the sublime.[457]

The same transitional pattern is to be found in the *Grand Magazine*. Because they offered no original book reviews but merely condensed those of the *Monthly*,[458] the editors of the *Grand* considerably limited original comments on literature, language, and the arts. What remains is a combination of neoclassical remarks on language and morality, a more liberal attitude toward the rules, and a mixed response to primitivism. Antiquity and the genres were scarcely discussed,[459] and sentiment was treated cursorily.[460]

While the comments on language are not extensive, they clearly indicate a conservative attitude. In both letters and extracts, the abuse of words, alterations in spelling, and borrowings from foreign languages were excoriated.[461] The dropping of *u* in *honour* and *neighbour*, the intrusion of *encroach, encroachment, vouchsafe, deign*, and *condescend* were specifically deplored. Comments on language were concerned with literary propriety, and even when the words were intended to distinguish the characters in a tragedy, the writer in the *Grand* objected to their impropriety and insisted that the audience would recognize the distinctions without them.[462]

---

[454]   *Universal Magazine*, XX (March, 1757), pp. 104-105.
[455]   *Universal Magazine*, XXXIII (July, 1763), p. 29.
[456]   *Universal Magazine*, XX (January, 1757), pp. 16-18; XX (June, 1757), pp. 254 ff; and XXVIII (Supplement, 1761), pp. 370 ff.
[457]   *Universal Magazine*, XXX (April, 1762), p. 172.
[458]   *Grand Magazine*, II (April, 1759), p. 206.
[459]   See, however, *Grand Magazine*, I (April, 1758), pp. 181-183 and III (March, 1760), p. 132.
[460]   *Grand Magazine*, I (July, 1758), p. 332 and III (December, 1760), p. 581.
[461]   *Grand Magazine*, I (June, 1758), pp. 266-267, 279-280.
[462]   *Grand Magazine*, III (March, 1760), p. 135.

But the fact that the number of examples is limited suggests that the editors were no fervent supporters of an academy for the refinement of the language. In the same way, the absence of repeated demands for instruction and entertainment, except for female readers,[463] indicates a lack of concern for *utile et dulce*.[464] Even the question of morality did not arouse interest in the *Grand* except in its treatment of *Tristram Shandy*. In addition to printing a poem and letter attacking Sterne's masterpiece for a lewdness unbecoming a clergyman and a sacrilegious mixture of a sermon with a smutty tale,[465] the editors presented an original article taking him to task for his obscenity.[466]

If these comments on morality and language are too few to argue for the magazine's conservatism, they are not offset by other statements and cannot be ignored. However, remarks on the rules were clearly antithetical to the conservative arguments. Extracts as well as articles espoused views that opposed a literature created by rule. Distinguishing between taste and genius, an extract from John Armstrong's *Sketches* limited the former to the proper disposition of parts,[467] and other comments on the subject concluded that knowledge of the rules was insufficient to produce good literature.[468] Genius, particularly for poetry, was necessary in the arts,[469] and one writer in the magazine deplored the "cold phlegmatic critics, who judge of poetic merit, with all the *sang froid* that a geometrician would examine a corollary of Euclid." The familiar, limited ideas of critical rules were no more than the blind judgments of those who pretended that their bias had universal approval.[470]

---

[463] *Grand Magazine*, III (January, 1760), p. 30; III (February, 1760), pp. 80 ff.; III (March, 1760), pp. 140 ff.; III (September, 1760), pp. 454 ff.; III (October, 1760), pp. 501 ff.; and III (November, 1760), pp. 542 ff.

[464] See, however, *Grand Magazine*, I (April, 1758), p. 157 and I (September, 1758), pp. 471-472.

[465] *Grand Magazine*, III (April, 1760), pp. 194-198 and III (June, 1760), pp. 317-319.

[466] *Grand Magazine*, III (June, 1760), pp. 308-311.

[467] *Grand Magazine*, I (June, 1758), pp. 264-265.

[468] *Grand Magazine*, III (May, 1760), pp. 250-251.

[469] *Grand Magazine*, II (April, 1759), p. 214.

[470] *Grand Magazine*, II (June, 1759), p. 310.

For romantic primitivism, the emotions were mixed, although the overall opinion was unfavorable. In order to celebrate the wonders of natural religion, a dissertation on wild animals contrasted the natural state of freedom with the forced condition of society,[471] and critical of European enemies one writer declared them more barbarous than the savages.[472] But the idea of a Golden Age, even Biblical, was described as allegorical,[473] and suggestions about evolution in the *Grand* were unlikely to make primitive man an example worthy of imitation.[474] Indeed, specific comments about the African, noting the importance of trade, suggested the need to introduce Christianity for the sake of lifting the Negro from his state of ignorance,[475] and the inhabitants of Turkey and Japan were regarded as "strangers to the refinements of society. ... Men in a rude unpolished state are but little alarmed at the instances of severity inflicted on others. The ferocity of their tempers exempts them from tender feelings . . ." [476]

The American Indian posed a different problem. Although comment in the *Grand* described him as a treacherous barbarian, whose mores were deplorable, and whose intellect was limited,[477] he was placed above the Negro in the chain of being.[478] But more importantly, the Indian was used as a means for propagandizing against the French, and as a consequence, it was sometimes necessary to present him as the victim of French corruption whose natural goodness had been subjected to the perversions of European cruelty.[479]

Finally, writers in the *Grand* considered primitivism in literary terms. Two letters offered contradictory views on the "peasant

---

[471] *Grand Magazine*, I (January, 1758), pp. 15-16.
[472] *Grand Magazine*, I (March, 1758), p. 113.
[473] *Grand Magazine*, II (September, 1759), p. 481.
[474] *Grand Magazine*, I (May, 1758), pp. 205-206.
[475] *Grand Magazine*, I (December, 1758), p. 616.
[476] *Grand Magazine*, II (February, 1759), p. 94.
[477] *Grand Magazine*, I (April, 1758), p. 199; I (June, 1758), pp. 271 ff.; I (December, 1758), p. 619; II (January, 1759), pp 5-6; II (February, 1759), p. 76; and III (April, 1760), p. 211.
[478] *Grand Magazine*, I (November, 1758), p. 576.
[479] *Grand Magazine*, II (June, 1759), pp. 296-298 and II (September, 1759), p. 466.

poet". In one, a young tradesman was advised that poetry required an education that he did not have,[480] while the other presented the work of an untrained American, correct in the art, a natural genius – although his poetry, published in the magazine, was clearly imitative.[481] The other literary manifestation of primitivism, orientalism, was ridiculed through parody and direct comment. A long oriental tale parodied the many absurdities of the type,[482] and a policy statement about rival magazines declared that Oliver Goldsmith's oriental language for oriental tales made him "nothing less than herald to the great Cham of Persia", an honor equalled only by his fellow editor, Tobias Smollett, a Tory and a Jacobite.[483]

In one sense, the final magazine is a disappointment. Although the *Court* promises much in the way of literary criticism because of its theatrical department, called the "Green Room", even the dramatic criticism was concerned more with actors, theater gossip, and productions than with the principles of the genre. In the same way, the magazine's book reviews, which were intended to give complete titles, summaries, principal parts, author's purpose, and specimens,[484] provide virtually no literary criticism.[485] There emerges, however, from the comments and editorial selection a pattern favorable to the new developments in literature while insistent upon criticism by the traditional rules.

To be sure, the editors of the *Court* were kindly disposed to the sentimental and oriental tale. Their "Secret History of the Court", for example, offered a tender romance complete with fainting spells and love conquers all.[486] But it was in their taste for

[480] *Grand Magazine*, II (March, 1759), p. 151.
[481] *Grand Magazine*, II (February, 1759), pp. 100-104.
[482] *Grand Magazine*, III (January, 1760), pp. 38-40; III (February, 1760), pp. 65-70; III (March, 1760), pp. 117-123; III (April, 1760), pp. 188-194; and III (June, 1760), pp. 284-290.
[483] *Grand Magazine*, III (February, 1760), pp. 90-91.
[484] See *Court Magazine* (September, 1761), p. 35.
[485] For example, the review of *Tristram Shandy*, volumes V and VI, in the *Court* (December, 1761), p. 184, was one paragraph, offering the simple comment that those who found something to like in earlier volumes would no doubt do so here, but "I cannot meet with any thing to recommend".
[486] *Court Magazine* (November, 1761), pp. 102-106.

the oriental tale that the editors displayed their willingness to accept the new. To be sure, they presented Percy's didactic comment on his translation of *Hau Kiou Choaan* and stressed moral purpose in two Eastern tales,[487] but they were also willing enough to publish oriental stories without the ostensible moral lesson.[488] While comments on the American Indian which ascribed scalping to the barbarian and savage nature of uncultivated humanity might suggest a less favorable attitude toward primitivism, the Cherokee chief, Outacite, was in the same article compared with the Marquis of Granby. His great courage and dignity were extolled and his height and stature described in terms of the noble savage.[489]

Some support for the argument that the writers in the *Court* were no strong advocates of tradition may be derived from their lack of enthusiasm for the ancients, their virtual lack of concern for the refinement of the language,[490] and their limited regard for the dictum of *utile et dulce*.[491] A direct comparison of the ancients and moderns stressed the modern supremacy in science,[492] while an article on the importance of Great Britain described a visit to the tombs of Shakespeare and Milton as worthy as a trip to that of Virgil, and considered the poetry of Horace of no greater worth than that of Pope.[493]

Yet, for all that, the articles in the *Court* were concerned with the rules and genres, and, while not insistent upon instruction and entertainment, held morality high as a standard. One of the few important comments in the "Green Room" praised the *Discovery* both for its adherence to the rules and its effective moral pur-

---

[487] *Court Magazine* (November, 1761), pp. 107-110, 137 and (November, 1762), pp. 700 ff.

[488] *Court Magazine*, I (May, 1763), pp. 226 ff. and II (July, 1763), pp. 323 ff.

[489] *Court Magazine* (July, 1762), pp. 515-517.

[490] See, however, *Court Magazine* (October, 1761), p. 77 and I (May, 1763), p. 235.

[491] *Court Magazine* (February, 1762), p. 256, is the one strong example of concern for the dictum of *utile et dulce*. More conventional statements are characterized by (September, 1761), p. 6.

[492] *Court Magazine*, II (August, 1763), pp. 374 ff.

[493] *Court Magazine* (September, 1762), p. 594.

pose.[494] Shakespeare's *Tempest* was cited for the fact that here he observed the unities more than in any other play that he wrote, and the moral effectively taught "a dependance upon providence".[495] If his *Cymbeline* was to be approved, it was despite the irregularity and because of the sweetness of the work.[496] Although Chaucer, Lydgate, and Gower were described as deriving "their chief value from their antiquity",[497] a biography of Chaucer made amends to the poet, romanticizing the facts of his education in order to explain the methods by which he "refined and improved" upon his sources, although his manner remained free.[498] Chaucer like Shakespeare was being brought within the pale of the rules.

The rules and genres were specifically argued for in a letter to the magazine in which lyric poetry was called the chief composition of the age.[499] The purpose of the writer was "to observe what kind of measure is best adapted to that species of writing, and perhaps an endeavour to fix a standard for it".[500] By way of example and rules, the letter-writer described to his own satisfaction the characteristics of the genre, and, in a sense, he was doing no more than what the majority of critics were attempting to do with the changes in aesthetic fashions.

---

[494] *Court Magazine*, I (February, 1763), pp. 65-66. See, also (November, 1761), pp. 118-120.
[495] *Court Magazine*, I (June, 1763), pp. 298-299.
[496] *Court Magazine* (December, 1761), p. 172.
[497] *Court Magazine* (September, 1761), p. 15.
[498] *Court Magazine* (November, 1761), pp. 99-102.
[499] *Court Magazine* (March, 1762), pp. 326 ff.
[500] *Court Magazine* (March, 1762), p. 326.

VIII

LANGUAGE, LITERATURE, AND THE ARTS
II. THE *ANNUAL REGISTER* AND THE REVIEWS

While in most subjects the gap which separated the direct criticism of the *Critical* and *Monthly* from the oblique comments of the magazines was bridged by the *Annual Register* and sometimes the *Theatrical Review*, neither periodical offered effective aesthetic judgments that differed greatly in method from those in the magazines. The failure of the *Annual Register* is particularly disappointing because of the hopes raised by Burke's connection. Nevertheless, Copeland's remarks describing Burke's reviews on aesthetics as being "neither extremely numerous nor extremely enthusiastic" [1] may be extended as well to the periodical's articles on the subject.

Yet its comments are not without interest, particularly those which attempted to place the sublime within the accepted aesthetic tradition. Both articles on this subject were reprints to which Burke gave his approval. An excerpt from Montesquieu's essay on taste contrasted Grecian and Gothic architecture, condemning the latter not for its attempts to provide variety but rather for its method or means of presenting ornaments. The pleasure of variety was no less than that of order, but Gothic architecture failed to achieve variety through "the very means that were chosen to make it agreeable".[2] The point was repeated in connection with oriental taste in the *Annual Register*'s excerpt from Chambers' essay on Chinese gardens, and Burke specifically made application of his theory on taste to Chambers' arguments. Through a

---

[1] Copeland, p. 141. Throughout Chapter IV Copeland demonstrates Burke's close connection with the reviews in the periodical.
[2] *Annual Register*, I (1758), pp. 313-314.

contrast of scenes of terror, "impending rocks, dark caverns", and the like, with pleasing scenes, the pattern of nature could be imitated in all its beautiful irregularities.[3] The possibilities themselves were without limitations, for there were "as many variations as there are different arrangements in the works of the creation".[4] Clearly, the sanction for the sublime was, throughout, the imitation of nature which, when associated with ancient authority, was at the heart of neoclassical theory.

Whatever their arguments to justify orientalism or to evaluate Gothicism, comments in the *Annual Register* firmly rejected romantic primitivism. There was no charm in the "gloom of ignorance and barbarism" of the Middle Ages,[5] and savages were ignoble, whether they were African slaves or American Indians.[6] Even opposition to satire on civilized society derived from dread of the natural state without its notions of right and wrong.[7]

Not unnaturally, the concern for morality was characterized by an insistence upon the didactic purpose of literature. In his expansion of the section called "Characters", Burke explained, ". . . we know no kind of reading that can be at once more useful and agreeable".[8] Fables were important in turning a "rude and fierce people" into a civilized group,[9] while the purposes of biography lay in the need for amusement and instruction.[10] Where a work like Johnson's *Rasselas* lacked sufficient incidents for diversion, Burke emphasized the purity and soundness of its morality, and for *Rasselas* to have inverted the values of the genre was, in this instance, an achievement rather than a failure.[11]

While he offered little comment on the rules, ancients, imitation, and language, Burke did not waver from an orthodox critical

---

[3] *Annual Register*, I (1758), pp. 319-320.
[4] *Annual Register*, I (1758), p. 323.
[5] *Annual Register*, I (1758), p. 464.
[6] *Annual Register*, II (1759), pp. 32-34, 77; III, Pt. I (1760), pp. 61-62; VI, Pt. I (1763), pp. 20, 22-23, 32.
[7] *Annual Register*, II (1759), pp. 479-484.
[8] *Annual Register*, II (1759), pp. v-vi.
[9] *Annual Register*, III, Pt. II (1760), p. 265.
[10] *Annual Register*, IV, Pt. II (1761), p. 1.
[11] *Annual Register*, II (1759), pp. 477-479.

viewpoint.[12] Clarity was the chief strength of style,[13] and judgment was to be imposed as a restraint on fancy.[14] The fancy of the moderns was a madness to be contrasted with the sanity of the ancients,[15] and the favorable review of Macpherson's work was largely on the basis of a comparison with the ancient epics and with a sublimity that had classical antecedents.[16] Even comments on language were prescriptive and opposed borrowings like *cordon, maneuver, reconnoiter, bagatelle, trifle,* and *nude.*[17]

The same orthodoxy characterizes the articles in the *Theatrical Review,* whose limited comments on aesthetics are, at least in one respect, even more disappointing than those in the annual. Articles on plays were rarely extensive in the other periodicals, but to find a dramatic review given to the same method of summarizing and epitomizing as the magazines is as unexpected as it is distressing. The remarks in the review rarely rise above commonplace journalism, and their only real virtue is to suggest the superficial conservative judgments that might be expected from the conventional playgoer of the period.

For the writers in the *Theatrical Review* dramatic criticism was founded upon moral evaluation. The object of drama was the "delight and improvement of society" in a theater which, "if properly conducted, [could] be one of the best supports to morality and virtue . . .".[18] Despite the need for development of taste in modern society, the editors commended the new attitude toward the theater which was becoming more respectable and more reputable: [19]

[12] It should be noted, however, that the review of *Tristram Shandy* in 1760, III, Pt. II, pp. 247-249, explained the success of the novel by remarking, ". . . it is not surprizing, that at a time, when a tame imitation makes almost the whole merit of so many books, so happy an attempt at novelty should have been so well received". Nevertheless, the periodical writer complained of the lack of plot and the "tiresome" digressions in the novel.

[13] *Annual Register,* I (1758), p. 257.
[14] *Annual Register,* II (1759), p. 310.
[15] *Annual Register,* IV, Pt. II (1761), pp. 204-205.
[16] *Annual Register,* IV, Pt. II (1761), pp. 276-286.
[17] *Annual Register,* I (1758), pp. 373-374; III, Pt. II (1760), p. 249.
[18] *Theatrical Review* (1763), p. i.
[19] *Theatrical Review* (1763), pp. iii-iv.

Indecency no longer usurps the place of wit, nor does any elevation of language gild over, in these days, an illiberal immorality of sentiment – nothing has now a chance of succeeding that has not an apparent tendency to improve; nor is any author confident enough to expect the approbation of the public at the expence of decency and virtue.

The relationship of literature to morality was such that criticism of one automatically affected the other.[20] In an immoral state, depravity doomed even the finest art,[21] but the purpose of drama always remained, "To purge the passions, and reform the mind, / To give to Nature all the force of Art, / And, while it charms the ear, to mend the heart." [22]

Criticism of particular plays reinforced these demands for morality. Describing the *Elopement*, the reviewer insisted, ". . . 'tis the business of every poet to make his amiable characters always worthy of imitation." [23] Unstinted praise for Mrs. Sheridan's *Discovery* stressed its moral import, "As this piece is extremely moral, it is replete with sentiment, and indeed, such as are justly calculated to instruct the world, and prove the goodness of heart for which the author is so highly distinguished." [24] In the same way, the terms of critical disapproval of *The Sketch of a Fine Lady's Return from a Rout* were moral epithets like "vile" and "execrable".[25]

Quite naturally, a drama that was expected to instruct had to conform to rules of propriety and was dependent upon imitation of nature. In considering propriety, the reviewers made clear the necessity for realistic literature, "The nearer any dramatic exhibition can be brought to the appearance of reality, in a proportionable degree will it strike the senses, and affect the breast of every auditor." [26] Nothing is more revealing of neoclassical criticism than the judgment of a work of art according to its effect on the audience. Whatever interfered with the reality that was neces-

[20] *Theatrical Review* (1763), p. v.
[21] *Theatrical Review* (February, 1763), p. 60.
[22] *Theatrical Review* (January, 1763), p. 7.
[23] *Theatrical Review* (May, 1763), p. 199.
[24] *Theatrical Review* (March, 1763), p. 122.
[25] *Theatrical Review* (April, 1763), p. 146.
[26] *Theatrical Review* (May, 1763), p. 212.

sary to enforce the moral was unsatisfactory; whatever conveyed properly that instruction was desirable.[27] In every sense the proper way was to follow nature.[28] Distortions of nature, like Italian opera, were scorned,[29] and that which portrayed human nature at its best reflected "the greatest merit of polite literature . . .".[30]

As the review's comments on antiquity, the rules, and unity made clear the nature that was to be followed had regularity and order. Contrasting ancient and modern drama, and relating them to their audiences, the *Theatrical* reviewers found the greatest merit in the simplicity of ancient drama, and deplored the "intrigue, shew, contradiction, noise, and incident" in the modern.[31] They bemoaned the absence of sufficient "classical educated persons in the theater",[32] and the inadequacy of modern tragedy.[33] Not only did they seek the three great unities of ancient drama, but, concerned with the regularity of tragedy,[34] the reviewers insisted as well upon the unity of character which had been introduced by the best of the moderns.[35]

But all this seems little more than superficial comment in comparison to the abundance of aesthetic opinion in the *Critical* and *Monthly*. To be sure, the limitations of earlier methods of reviewing persisted even in the two major reviews.[36] The abstract serials' form and extended summarizations had been altered by the *Monthly*,[37] but it, together with the *Critical*, too often substituted quotations for criticism. Nevertheless, direct aesthetic judgment,

[27] *Theatrical Review* (January, 1763), p. 10; (March, 1763), p. 122.
[28] *Theatrical Review* (January, 1763), p. 41; (February, 1763), pp. 74 ff.; (March, 1763), pp. 106-107.
[29] *Theatrical Review* (February, 1763), pp. 47-48.
[30] *Theatrical Review* (March, 1763), p. 88.
[31] *Theatrical Review* (January, 1763), pp. 9-10.
[32] *Theatrical Review* (January, 1763), p. 14.
[33] *Theatrical Review* (February, 1763), p. 74.
[34] *Theatrical Review* (March, 1763), p. 90.
[35] *Theatrical Review* (March, 1763), p. 123.
[36] For the development of early book reviewing, see Walter Graham, *The Beginnings of English Literary Periodicals* (Oxford, 1926), particularly the first chapter.
[37] Graham, *English Literary Periodicals*, pp. 207-209, suggests that the analysis which the *Monthly* added to quotations in its reviewing may have been borrowed as a form from the *Literary Journal* of Dublin, which ran from December, 1744-June, 1749.

even of fiction, a subject which had been treated previously in the *Gentleman's Magazine,* was nowhere given as serious attention as in the two reviews.[38]

While in politics and religion, the *Critical* and *Monthly* generally represented the conservative and liberal impulses of the age, their comments on aesthetics were at times remarkably alike. They insisted on morality and didacticism, and yielded, if at all, only reluctantly to changes in the canons of literary criticism. For the reviewers in the *Monthly,* this sometimes led to an unusual position, but those on the *Critical* were merely following their usual course which was dictated by a dedication to the stabilization of the existing order.

In an age when "improvement" was the key word in industry, trade, the arts and sciences,[39] the *Critical* was dedicated to the defense of public taste and morals.[40] From its outset the review performed a task that was consistent with the role of an academy of *belles lettres.*[41] Its sections on Foreign Articles and its notices on Sculpture, Painting, and Engraving were part of a plan to encourage genius and prevent dullness. In their comments on language, literature, and the arts, the reviewers judged with a concern for morality that was the chief characteristic of neoclassicism.

Although engaged in controversies that inevitably appealed to public interest, the gentlemen who conducted the *Critical* could ill afford to be thought gutter-fighters and back-alley ruffians. They were – as they frequently reminded their readers – defenders of the public taste, and even as they engaged in back-biting and quibbling, Smollett was at pains to point out: [42]

The task of professed critics, who undertake to reform the taste of mankind, is like that of cleansing the Auguean stable; they must not only wade through dunghills of dulness, but also be exposed to the stench and stings of all the vermin hatched amidst such heaps of noisome pollution. . . .

The *Critical* reviewers, secure from personal abuse, will persevere

[38]   Heidler, p. 71; Knapp, p. 97.
[39]   Heaton, "Industry and Trade", in *Johnson's England,* I, p. 246.
[40]   Jones, "Poetry and the *Critical Review*", p. 17.
[41]   Jones, p. 82.
[42]   *Critical Review,* I (April, 1756), p. 288.

in the execution of their plan, without paying the least regard to the undistinguishing clamour and impotent threats of bad writers, or their employers. . . . Every author who writes without talents is a grievance, if not an imposter, who defrauds the public. . . .

Whatever the particular merits or defects of their controversy with Griffiths, Hill, and Shebbeare, among others,[43] the *Critical* reviewers argued chiefly against the sins of poor taste, creative inability, and literary fraud. According to one writer in the review, any work that would help "prevent the arts and sciences from falling into utter contempt and oblivion" should be particularly praised at a time when there was every evidence of the growing degeneracy in society.[44] The editors declared their regret at having to condemn a book and their pleasure when a work of any merit fell their way, but if the imposture of author or bookseller demanded condemnation, the review, Samuel Derrick insisted for the editors, would not hesitate to point out the imposition.[45]

To be sure, much of this has the self-righteous acclaim common to popular journalism, but there was a strong moral fervor, consistent with the neoclassical concern for the relationship of art to its audience, in the tone of the *Critical*'s comments. Under constant attack were schemes used by booksellers to promote sales and hoodwink the public into buying a falsely represented commodity. One reviewer condemned the practice of taking a collection of poems which had previously been published, adding to them slightly, and offering the work as though it were composed entirely of new pieces.[46] Misleading title pages and outright plagiarism suffered the justifiable condemnation of Smollett and his colleagues.[47]

Pretense, generally, was as intolerable to the writers in the

[43] In the *Critical*, I (March, 1756), p. 98, Smollett naturally argued for his own objectivity. But for some idea of the extent of the controversy in which the review was constantly engaged, see the list of attacks by maligned authors and irate competitors in Jones, pp. 107 ff., and my own lists in the *Periodical Post Boy* (June, 1955), pp. 6-7; *Notes and Queries*, II (1955), p. 535; III (1956), p. 425; IV (1957), p. 121; V (1958), p. 308.

[44] *Critical Review*, IV (July, 1757), p. 46.

[45] *Critcial Review*, II (September, 1756), p. 140.

[46] *Critical Review*, XVI (November, 1763), p. 338.

[47] *Critical Review*, I (March, 1756), p. 98 (Smollett); I (May, 1756), p.

Critical as it had been to the satirists of Queen Anne's day, and pomp and pedantry nearly always brought down the axe of Smollett and his fellows. When a writer, or his publisher, said of one offering that it was designed for "supplying the place of all other books; as it will contain whatsoever there is in them worthy regard...", he invited the reviewer's sermon on modesty and merit.[48] But it was not in their attacks on pompous writers alone that the writers in the *Critical* proclaimed modesty to be "an inseparable companion on true merit, and presumption on ignorance",[49] thereby closely identifying morality with literature. While quick to make their point in castigation of such writers as *Estimate* Brown,[50] they were equally ready to praise the learned Mrs. Carter, who commented on "her own performance with that modesty and diffidence which always accompanies real merit".[51] Nor did the reviewers hesitate to approve an author whose modest title page, unlike many that abounded in liberal promises, led to "a work of true ... merit".[52] It was an unusual writer who could parade his own praises and receive the plaudits of the *Critical* reviewers.[53]

If they could not permit pompous authors to pretensions of superiority, neither could they allow the opinion of the town to influence their decisions. Griffiths and the *Monthly* had made

---

374 (Franklin); I (June, 1756), p. 391 (Smollett), p. 420 (Franklin); IV (November, 1757), p. 472; IX (March, 1760), pp. 229-231.

[48] *Critical Review*, IV (October, 1757), pp. 298-299. Oddly enough, the first important attack on the *Critical* itself was for the affectation that it deplored in others: "The public has been prepared to receive this elaborate work with proper respect, by a long ostentatious advertisement, that, like another Goliath, has come forth 'morning and evening, and presented itself more than forty days', with insult and defiance. The authors are said to be gentlemen, and not hirelings of booksellers...." (*Gentleman's Magazine*, XXVI, May, 1756, pp. 141-142).

[49] *Critical Review*, VIII (December, 1759), pp. 462-463.

[50] *Critical Review*, V (April, 1758), p. 319.

[51] *Critical Review*, VI (August, 1758), p. 153.

[52] *Critical Review*, VII (January, 1759), p. 15.

[53] Benjamin Donn, whose *Mathematical Essays* the *Critical* reviewer praised, was such an exception, although the reviewer expressed his displeasure with the author's being "too full of his own consequence, and vain of his reading...". (*Critical Review*, VI, September, 1758, p. 201.)

things easier for Smollett's periodical by proving criticism to be the province of the literary review,[54] and the *Critical*'s editors had no intention of returning it to its former claimants. Like Addison and Steele, Smollett described himself as taking philosophy out of closets and bringing it to the general public: [55]

This charitable task of improvement, the learned, who enjoy their ease, ought to undertake for the benefit of mankind. This is the professed aim of us, who publish our monthly lucubrations in the *Critical Review*. . . .

In order to hold such a relationship to the public, the reviewers had to assert their superiority over the taste of their audience or the town and to display independent and avowedly impartial judgment: [56]

While the public esteem is thus capricious, our province it is, as *Critical* reviewers, to discriminate between personal and literary reputation; to distinguish the forced productions of necessity, from the spontaneous growth of genius; to estimate every performance by its own intrinsic merit; and to render the particular cast of every writer of the utmost utility to our readers. . . .

Smollett and his staff felt compelled to render their decisions on a work, regardless of "the sentiments of those gentlemen who call themselves the Town...".[57]

This relationship to their audience, a relationship which also derived from the editor's concept of the review as an academy, predetermined their attitude toward taste and the Horatian dictum of the *utile et dulce*. Although, like their contemporaries,[58] the *Critical* reviewers were unable to solve the complicated problems of taste or even provide a simple definition,[59] they offered descrip-

54   Elizabeth E. Kent, *Goldsmith and His Booksellers* (Ithaca, 1933), p. 2.
55   *Critical Review*, I (April, 1756), p. 227.
56   *Critical Review*, VIII (October, 1759), p. 271.
57   *Critical Review*, IX (February, 1760), p. 133. See, also, XIV (October, 1762), p. 294.
58   See, for example, *Connoisseur*, #120 (May 13, 1756), p. 140 and *Monthly Review*, XX (June, 1759), p. 534.
59   Hooker, "The Discussion of Taste", p. 584, points out the hopeless situation in which Hogarth, Burke, and Reynolds were engaged. The arguments of each were toppled by the others, and not one principle endured against the opposition of their reasoning.

tions that maintained the audience's dependency upon the review. According to the writers in the *Critical*, "The regions of taste can be travelled only by a few"; and "[taste] is the gift of nature, and cannot be communicated by the rules".[60] In the *Critical*'s basically aristocratic standards, universality and common sense applied to taste rested upon an assuredness that the innate qualities of a gentleman permitted him to know what was worthwhile in literature.[61] The readers were to rely on the astuteness of the critic, who, depending on the discrimination of a gentleman in matters of judgment, used a method remarkably similar to Matthew Arnold's touchstone: ". . . a man may be struck with the performance of a second rate artist, and believe that human art could not possibly go farther; until he sees a perfect capital piece, and the other immediately sinks into contempt".[62]

In this capacity of arbiter, the *Critical* reviewers naturally followed Horace's principle that insisted upon instruction and gave emphasis to the moral values in literature.[63] Over and over again writers in the review commended works that could not "fail to afford both entertainment and instruction".[64] A piece that was "equally entertaining and instructive" might be "freely recommended" by Smollett.[65] His accolades went to a book "fraught

[60]   These are cited in Jones, "Poetry and the *Critical Review*", p. 22.
[61]   *Critical Review*, VI (November, 1758), p. 389: "Taste is a delicate, acute perception, in the powers of fancy, as well as in faculties of the understanding. One man has a keener sense of smelling than another; and why may he not also have a finer imagination?" VII (May, 1759), p. 394: "Some philosophers, whom we shall venture to call fantastical, have ascribed all sense of beauty, external as well as internal, to fashion and custom. Our author rejects this absurd opinion. . . ." IX (January, 1760), p. 11: "Common sense is perhaps one of the first requisites in a critic. . . ." XIII (May, 1762), p. 378: ". . . there actually exists a common nature or standard of taste. . . ."
[62]   *Critical Review*, IX (March, 1760), p. 198.
[63]   For the importance of the principle of *dulce et utile* in neoclassical literature, see Wellek, I, p. 23 and Saintsbury, II, pp. 436-437, 488. McKenzie, p. 12, declares that Horace was "as solidly on the side of neoclassicism as it is possible to be". For the importance of the Horatian principle to the *Critical*, see Jones, "Poetry and the *Critical Review*", pp. 24, 36.
[64]   *Critical Review*, II (November, 1756), p. 363.
[65]   *Critical Review*, I (January-February, 1756), p. 10.

with entertainment and instruction...",[66] and Derrick particularly praised Richardson's writings, being rendered into volumes for children, because rarely were books of entertainment "so well adapted to the instruction of youth".[67]

Judgment and taste were related to the principles of morality. Edward Watkinson's estimate of Chaucer, for example, stressed his contribution in moralizing the British muse and rendering virtue amiable.[68] Blank verse, Oriental tales, and philosophy were all praised in the good name of morality,[69] while Georgic poetry was cited for its nationalism, pleasure, and instruction.[70] Mixture of genres might be forgiven by the reviewer if the aim were virtuous and the outcome instructive.[71] Not only were sponsors of moral works applauded for contributions to piety and learning,[72] but sins of style might be overlooked for the sake of moral virtue,[73] and productions designed for young people could be granted approval despite a "rambling" and "incorrect" form if only they were educational.[74] Even a publication by the despised firm of Noble received the sanction of the *Critical* when the novelist wrote for the instruction of the public.[75]

Yet Dr. John Armstrong, Smollett's friend and author of *The Art of Preserving Health*, led the reviewers in reminding their readers that the ideal was the combined virtues of *utile et dulce*.[76] When a work by a man of genius was valuable as moral instruc-

[66] *Critical Review*, I (April, 1756), p. 226.
[67] *Critical Review*, I (May, 1756), p. 315.
[68] *Critical Review*, VII (January, 1764), pp. 2-3. The article, an important part of a series by Edward Watkinson, is, of course, after the period of this study. The point is included, however, because C. E. Jones, "The *Critical Review* and Some Major Poets", *Notes and Queries*, III (1956), p. 114, fails to notice its importance.
[69] *Critical Review*, III (February, 1757), p. 123; VII (May, 1759), pp. 398-399; XI (June, 1761), pp. 469-474.
[70] *Critical Review*, III (May, 1757), p. 402.
[71] *Critical Review*, XV (February, 1763), p. 112.
[72] *Critical Review*, VIII (December, 1759), p. 486.
[73] *Critical Review*, I (June, 1756), p. 455 (Franklin).
[74] *Critical Review*, I (March, 1756), pp. 133, 134 (Smollett and Derrick).
[75] *Critical Review*, X (October, 1760), pp. 280-290.
[76] *Critical Review*, I (March, 1756), p. 115. Probably the review's favorable treatment of Metastasio was encouraged by his didactic and moral qualities (see Wellek, I, p. 199). See, also, III (March, 1757), p. 193.

tion, the writers in the *Critical* were unstinting in their praise, and Laurence Sterne's *Sermons of Mr. Yorick* received their plaudits because the author, whose *Tristram Shandy* had offended the reviewer by its impurity, grossness, and lack of decorum,[77] taught while he entertained: [78]

> The excellent sermon, so humorously inserted in *Tristram Shandy*, raised our expectations of this publication; and we must frankly confess, that we are not disappointed in the perusal, whatever learned divines may think, who look for the formality of heads, explications, proofs, and controversial quibbles. The reverend Mr. Sterne aims at mending the heart, without paying any great regard to the instruction of the head; inculcating every moral virtue by precepts, deduced from reason and the sacred oracles. Would to God his example were more generally followed by our clergy, too many of whom delight in an ostentatious display of their own abilities, and vain unedifying group of theological learning.

Refusing to sanction what they considered an abuse of morality, regardless of the merits of an author,[79] the writers in the *Critical* prescribed rules for authors. According to one reviewer, "One great aim of novel-writers ought to be, to inculcate sentiments of virtue and honour, and to inspire an abhorrence of vice and immorality." [80] Able to praise a play that had less talent than decency,[81] the critics lamented the mores of the theater in which, "Wit, humour, character, and sentiment, have been entirely banished, and their places supplied by intrigue, ribaldry, and impertinence . . .".[82] Satirists were warned against falling prey to the vanity, affectation, conceit, and pride that they were striving to

---

[77] *Critical Review*, XI (April, 1761), p. 317 and XIII (January, 1762), pp. 66-69.

[78] *Critical Review*, IX (May, 1760), pp. 405-406.

[79] The *Critical*, XIV (October, 1762), pp. 270-271, for example, presents criticism of Goldsmith's waste of talent on the *Life of Richard Nash*, of Bath. Despite the review's favorable comments on Swift (March, 1758, pp. 249-260; VI, August, 1758, pp. 99-100; XIV, September, 1762, p. 178), it would not forgive the "impurity . . . of his . . . poetical pieces". (XIV, September, 1762, p. 184.) See, also, I (April, 1756), p. 261 (Derrick) and XV (May, 1763), pp. 378, 388.

[80] *Critical Review*, VII (May, 1759), p. 409.

[81] *Critical Review*, XII (December, 1761), p. 437.

[82] *Critical Review*, XV (February, 1763), pp. 96-97.

correct in others,[83] and the author who wrote for a general public was admonished by Smollett not to concern himself with the reformation of an incorrigible and meaningless minority.[84] When the writer offended the sensibility of his readers or presented a threat to the public morals, Smollett himself advocated the even more dangerous censorship by the civil authorities.[85]

Obviously, their concern for morality led to the reviewers' consideration of the effect of art on the public, which they felt the need to shelter.[86] For it was a public, according to Smollett and his colleagues, led by indolence, idleness, and fashion;[87] unappreciative of works of scholarship, it was devoted to the nonsense of the circulating libraries.[88] It was gullible, vain, and defenseless in the foolishness of its own pride.[89]

The situation permitted the editors of the *Critical* to present themselves as the public defenders of morals and taste. With no small degree of self-acclaim, Franklin and others reminded their readers of the labors performed in the public interest and accepted credit for any literary achievement of which the age could boast.[90] As a part of this responsibility, Smollett, Derrick, and Franklin damned the concoctions of travel writers whose inspiration was "the desire of their booksellers",[91] historians who offered little or imagined information,[92] and publishers who encouraged the growth of "literary mushrooms" of little value and less duration.[93]

It was all a part of the *Critical*'s role as an academy, and in its

[83]   *Critical Review*, XI (February, 1761), p. 109.
[84]   *Critical Review*, I (January-February, 1756), p. 79.
[85]   *Critical Review*, I (January-February, 1756), p. 90.
[86]   The tone of the following comments on the public should be compared with the equally conservative remarks of the *Annual Register*, I (1758), p. 476.
[87]   *Critical Review*, II (August, 1756), p. 48 and IX (April, 1760), p. 306.
[88]   *Critical Review*, VI (August, 1758), pp. 149-150; VI (October, 1758), p. 266; VII (February, 1759), p. 174.
[89]   *Critical Review*, II (September, 1756), p. 121 (Smollett); V (May, 1758), pp. 400-403; V (June, 1758), pp. 501-507.
[90]   *Critical Review*, I (July, 1756), p. 490 (Franklin) and XV (March, 1763), p. 161.
[91]   *Critical Review*, I (July, 1756), p. 523 (Derrick).
[92]   *Critical Review*, I (March, 1756), pp. 99-100; I (June, 1756), p. 391. Both are Smollett's.
[93]   *Critical Review*, II (October, 1756), pp. 275-276 (Franklin).

specific standards for language, literature, and the arts, the review was directed by the same principles. To be sure, when the *Critical,* under Smollett, attacked abuses of the language, there was more behind it than the pugnacious character and national origin of the Scottish editor.[94] The call for rules and regulations to be applied to language was consistent with the *Critical's* conservative attitude. Earlier in the century, Swift had even gone so far as to propose an academy for language reform and stabilization, and in the pages of the *Critical,* Thomas Sheridan's similar plan was quoted with approval.[95] In another article the reviewer voiced whole-hearted approbation of the French academy's having corrected, polished, and refined its language in a way that the English had not, and he bemoaned: [96]

the hard fate of the English language, when even our public orators, and authors, who ought to be her guardians, improvers, and re-finers, are, from their negligence (for we are ashamed to say ignorance) likely to prove her corrupters.

This note is echoed throughout the *Critical.* Grammar, spelling, and diction all came under the careful scrutiny of the reviewers. Examples of the first two are not so numerous as those of diction,[97] but there is no dearth of them. Misuse of demonstrative adjectives,[98] incorrect particles and participles, confusion of *will* for *shall* and *would* for *should,*[99] all bore the censure of the *Critical's* reviewers. Spelling errors – although as likely to have been the result of a printer's delinquency as an author's ignorance – stirred the wrath of the periodical writers.[100]

---

[94]   Much of what follows has been discussed in my article, "Language Control in the Eighteenth Century", *Word Study,* XXVII (1951), pp. 1-2. The period covered there is 1756-1760.

[95]   *Critical Review,* XIV (September, 1762), p. 170.

[96]   *Critical Review,* IX (January, 1760), pp. 9-10.

[97]   Jones, "Poetry and the *Critical Review*", pp. 27-28, cites the *Critical* reviewers' dissatisfaction with archaisms, low diction, foreign words, neologisms, obsolete words, Scottish and French idioms, and vulgarisms.

[98]   *Critical Review,* I (May, 1756), p. 361 (Armstrong).

[99]   *Critical Review,* I (January-February, 1756), p. 67 (Armstrong) and XV (January, 1763), p. 43.

[100]   *Critical Review,* V (April, 1758), pp. 349-350. The *Critical* reviewers also objected to David Hume's spellings of such words as *favor, labor,*

Chief object of the editors of the *Critical*, however, was to stabilize the vocabulary and to keep it pure. Among the greatest offenders against this purity of language were the writers from the North, not the least of them, David Hume. Perhaps because the Scottish origins of the *Critical*'s editors made them particularly vulnerable to attack by political opponents,[101] but certainly because refinement of the language was one of the standards of the review, the reviewers were severe in their judgments. Words that have become an accepted part of the English language were objected to in Hume's *History of Great Britain*. *Rescind* and *succumb* provoked the reviewer, and *insurgents* – the exact word that Smollett was to be taken to task for by the *North Briton* – evoked the comment: [102]

Such a word [of doubtful authority, and not very pleasing to the ear] may be convenient on many occasions . . . but if this reason were admitted for the coining of new words, we should hardly have any standard of language remaining.

But Hume was not the only Scot to offend against the *Critical*'s purist code. Smollett and his staff attacked others for using such words as *adroitly, abandonment, tramp,* and *lint,*[103] and, in many instances, the reviewers did not hesitate to label the culprits as being from north of the Tweed.[104]

---

honor, and *ardor,* arguing that the author's use of etymology to produce these was unreasonable, and that such borrowings should be made consistent with words already in the language (II, December, 1756, p. 393 [Smollett]). However, Armstrong in the *Critical* also objected to an author's changing proper nouns from Greek and Latin to English equivalents (I, January-February, 1756, p. 67 [Armstrong]).

[101] See my article "Eighteenth-Century Political Controversy and Linguistics", pp. 378-379.

[102] *Critical Review,* VII (April, 1759), p. 290. Smollett was chastized for using the word in place of *rebels* to describe the Jacobites. In another place (I, January-February, 1756, pp. 74-75), however, the writer in the *Critical* recognized the importance that sound played in the adoption of a word into the language.

[103] *Critical Review,* I (March, 1756), p. 114 (Smollett) and III (April, 1757), p. 289.

[104] *Critical Review,* I (January-February, 1756), p. 38 (Murdoch); I (March, 1756), pp. 139-140 (Derrick); I (April, 1756), p. 228 (Smollett); II (October, 1756), p. 278 (Smollett); VI (December, 1758), p. 463.

The Scots were not without company at the whipping post. Foreign authors writing in English were not forgiven their lapses or unfamiliarity with the English language. The reviewer suggested the writer had an obligation to submit the work to an inspector or native,[105] but under no circumstances was ill use of English to be tolerated.[106] Translators themselves came in for a full share of the chastisement. Many felt the lash, but none more severely than the writer who translated the *Philosophical Visions* from the French. Of such words as *foibles, tinted, propelled, condemnable, misanthropes, orient, occident, tranquilly, emanate, devastated,* and *bilious*, Franklin asked, ". . . to what language [do] these most properly belong", and concluded, ". . . most certainly not to our own".[107]

English writers in their own publications were as likely to employ unsatisfactory language as the others, and the *Critical* reviewers were not inclined to pass them by. John Grose, in a travel book, used: *population, insistence, supplemented, aggrandizement, intermediary, generalized, paternity,* and *simplification.* The reviewer responded: "In what part of his travels our author pick'd up these uncouth strangers, we know not; certain it is, they are not of English growth; nor shall we, perhaps, very readily admit of their naturalization." [108]

To be sure, these examples offer only those words that have subsequently become acceptable, and there were many others in which the judgment of the reviewers was supported by history. It is equally true that the opportunities that the *Critical* had to comment on the simple grammatical failings of authors indicate the slovenliness of Grub Street productions. Yet the circumstances do not alter the fact that in every instance the judgment was made

---

[105] *Critical Review*, IV (December, 1757), p. 480.
[106] *Critical Review*, XII (July, 1761), p. 54.
[107] *Critical Review*, II (November, 1756), p. 340.
[108] *Critical Review*, IV (October, 1757), p. 319. Obviously, this discussion has been concerned only with those words that have since become a part of the English language. There were, of course, numerous instances in which the reviewers' judgment proved accurate. At the same time, the examples of the reviewers' concern for purity of the language do not exhaust the material present in its pages.

from an authoritarian point of view. Moreover, in the admiration they expressed for lexicographers and their work, the reviewers indicated a distinct taste for principles and rules.[109] They were not willing to settle for usage even when that usage represented the work of Shakespeare, Milton, or Pope.[110] As arbiters of taste and opinion, the writers in the *Critical* found no authority more reliable than their own – an English Academy *de facto*.

The same principles characterized the *Critical*'s evaluation of literature and the arts. In these early years, the writers did not hesitate to judge according to the rules.[111] Derrick, for example, discouraged the efforts of a "clever" writer who imagined himself superior to the accepted standards: [112]

It appears to us, that the author of this piece sat down determined to write whatever came uppermost, without paying the smallest regard to order, connection, probability, manners, or stile; being perhaps of a genius not to be confined by vulgar rules; and he has this advantage that he finds himself either witty or comical, or both, in every page; and lest the reader should not discover it, he takes care to tell him of it.

Praising a work in which "the rules of the drama were well preserved",[113] the reviewers rejected another in which they were broken.[114] Painting, fiction, and travel books, all were expected to follow the designated pattern.[115] Those critics who waived the rules argued not from their unimportance, but rather from the

---

[109] See the article on *An English and Swedish Dictionary*, in the course of which Johnson comes in for the *Critical* reviewer's praise (V, May, 1758, p. 421).

[110] *Critical Review*, VII (January, 1759), p. 88; VII (February, 1759), pp. 149, 154-155. In answer to Johnson's being cited as an authority for a word the writer in the *Critical* had questioned, the reviewer noted the errors in Johnson's *Dictionary*. However, the writer in the *Critical* was careful to point out that he intended no disparagement of Johnson by his remarks.

[111] See Jones, "Poetry and the *Critical Review*", for a contrary view. However, in his examples there is no citation earlier than December, 1759, and most are considerably later than this earlier period.

[112] *Critical Review*, I (March, 1756), p. 126.

[113] *Critical Review*, V (March, 1758), p. 206.

[114] *Critical Review*, XI (April, 1761), pp. 332-333.

[115] *Critical Review*, I (April, 1756), p. 219 and I (July, 1756), p. 524 (Armstrong and Derrick). See, too, Heidler, p. 47.

audience's lack of appreciation. The standards of Aristotle and Horace were pointless to those who could not recognize a "perfect play".[116] At least one reviewer abjured the "new criticism", and with a display of Greek and Latin quotations, stressed a fondness for the devices and ornaments of classical literature.[117]

At the same time, the writers in the *Critical* were more attracted by ancient standards than modern French practices. While expressing approval of the clarity, order, and planning of many French productions,[118] the reviewers defended Shakespeare's departure from the rules by recommending that modern writers of tragedy beware of following those "who are grown so fond of imitating the dull regularity and declamation of the French drama".[119] Not the French imitation, but the "true classical taste" of Milton was necessary to raise the inferior taste of the age.[120]

The attitude was reverent toward the ancients and led naturally to an acceptance of imitation. While the common sense orthodoxy of late neoclassical criticism prevented them from falling prey to simple idolatry or neglecting the value of such modern contributions as those by Newton,[121] the reviewers repeatedly fought on the side of antiquity. They ridiculed claims for modern superiority,[122] deplored the "expiring taste for ancient literature",[123] argued for a standard of classical prosody in English,[124] and gave wholehearted approval to ancient writers on agriculture and moderns who had imitated them.[125] Indeed, in his attack on Brown's *Estimate*, the writer in the *Critical* fought his own battle of the books. Scoffing at the author's claim "that the ancients were but pigmies in history, poetry, oratory, ethics, war, and what not, to the moderns", the reviewer reduced Brown's arguments to absurdity.

[116] *Critical Review*, IV (November, 1757), p. 427.
[117] *Critical Review*, VI (December, 1758), pp. 464-466.
[118] See Joliat, pp. 160-161.
[119] *Critical Review*, XIII (May, 1762), p. 404.
[120] *Critical Review*, VI (July, 1758), p. 81.
[121] *Critical Review*, III (January, 1757), pp. 21-23; VI (November, 1758), p. 353; X (October, 1760), p. 262; XI (May, 1761), p. 342.
[122] *Critical Review*, XIV (August, 1762), pp. 39-46.
[123] *Critical Review*, XIII (June, 1762), p. 489.
[124] *Critical Review*, V (May, 1758), p. 383.
[125] *Critical Review*, III (January, 1757), p. 2.

Without question, his concluding and ironic comments placed the critic on the side of Swift and Pope, and shared the Augustan attitude toward antiquity: [126]

After so much judicious criticism, and refined taste, will the reader doubt, that our author deserves a place on the same shelf with the learned Wotton, a member of the same seminary, and the worthy hero of that waggish performance, called the *Battle of the Books*.

In their comments on imitation, the reviewers naturally recommended that great works be used as models for modern writers.[127] To be sure, the writers warned against choosing the idiosyncratic and personal performances for guides and opposed slavish copying,[128] but their views on the subject were dictated by the common sense principles expressed by Edward Young in his *Conjectures on Original Composition*, a work which was considered conventional in its own time.

Respect for the rules, the ancients, and imitation prefigures genre criticism, and the *Critical* reviewers were indeed more concerned with the genres than was customary even among conservative critics during the period.[129] In recommendations for painting, the writers in the review called upon artists to try their talents with historical subjects, recognized as the highest genre of the art.[130] Heroic poetry was described as "the master-piece of human wit, as the most fertile genius, the happiest tastes and the most extensive knowledge must necessarily unite in the formation of it".[131] Particular praise for Pope stressed his appropriate technique for working within a genre,[132] but whether the author himself classified a work, the writers in the *Critical* judged according to the requirements of a particular genre, indicating points of divergence

---

[126] *Critical Review*, IX (April, 1760), p. 296.

[127] See Joliat, p. 161.

[128] *Critical Review*, III (February, 1757), p. 187; VII (April, 1759), pp. 377-378; IX (April, 1760), p. 303; XI (March, 1761), p. 186.

[129] See Wellek, I, pp. 19-20, 115; Atkins, p. 275; Saintsbury, II, pp. 483-484, 572.

[130] This genre criticism characterized the entire section on painting and engraving.

[131] *Critical Review*, IV (July, 1757), pp. 27-28.

[132] *Critical Review*, XIII (May, 1762), pp. 401-402. See, also, III (April, 1757), pp. 300-306; IX (May, 1760), p. 417.

from the proprieties of the kind.[133] It did not matter whether a production was an epic, ode, or history; there were the rules by which each must be judged; and although the reviewers were willing to accept a modern genre, there were standards to be met and principles to be followed.[134]

Typical of the genre criticism and standards of the review were its comments on French poetry: [135]

The French poetry, all the world knows, is in general but very indifferent; their language, which is properly the language of conversation only, is by no means adapted to verse, especially on sublime and lofty subjects; their epic is utterly contemptible, and their best writers rough and inharmonious. Some of their most sensible authors have, within the last century, discovered this defect; and, conscious that they could not arrive at any degree of perfection in the higher paths of Pindus, have struck out a new road on the side of the mountain, where they might travel with more ease and safety. La Fontaine, in his fables, and Rousseau, in his odes, set the example of looser measures; where the rhime, not returning so often, met the ear with more pleasure. This has since been followed with great success by Chaulieu, la Farre, Mad. Deshoulieres, Gresset, and some others, who by an ease of diction, and familiarity of expression, joined to a natural simplicity, and sprightliness peculiar to themselves, have gained a seat on the poetical mountain, which was never occupied before.

Within their criticism of the genre, which they thought extremely important because of the success of contemporary English poets,[136]

---

[133] *Critical Review*, VII (April, 1759), p. 331. For an excellent example of the *Critical's* genre criticism of the ode, see I (April, 1756), pp. 209 ff. The article considers not only the ode, in connection with a work by Mason, but takes the occasion to comment on different species of poetry and the relative difficulties of executing the ode form. The article was by Franklin. In VIII (December, 1759), p. 480, the review objected to mixing comic and tragic scenes. See, also, II (December, 1756), p. 386 (Smollett).
[134] *Critical Review*, XV (January, 1763), pp. 13-14, is an excellent example of the application of the standards of genre criticism to the modern romantic novel.
[135] *Critical Review*, IV (December, 1757), p. 499. The article indicates why the *Critical* did not judge odes according to the old rules for the genre: new odes required a standard consistent with modern forms. *Cf.*, Jones, "Poetry and the *Critical Review*", pp. 27, 29-30, and Paston, p. 163.
[136] *Critical Review*, III (May, 1757), pp. 426-427. *Cf.*, Jones, "Poetry and the *Critical Review*", p. 21.

the reviewers were particularly concerned with the purity of diction. While condemning "quaint conceits, far-fetched metaphors, and indifferent versification", they approved "fine sentiments, native and genuine simplicity, great elegance of diction, and harmony of numbers...".[137] They lauded poetry in which "the stile is chaste and animated, the language pure, the sentiments grave and sublime, and extremely well adapted to the dignity of the subject".[138] Such terms were characteristic of neoclassical criticism, whether in the age of Dryden, Pope, or Johnson, and the writers in the *Critical* left no doubt of their position as they railed against inaccurate rhyme, inappropriate metaphors, and unguided attempts to elevate and surprise.[139]

Genre criticism also characterized the *Critical*'s comments on drama. Reviewing published plays rather than performances,[140] Smollett and his staff considered not only the literary merits of a piece, but also the benefits that acting, costumes, and scenery had brought to the production.[141] Their criticism combined genre requirements with neoclassical standards of propriety, diction, imitation, and the rules.[142] The reviewers expected a good tragedy to take advantage of blank verse to elevate the beauties of poetry and elocution, and argued against the use of prose.[143] They looked favorably upon the unities, particularly the unity of action;[144] and the method of criticism employed by the review divided a drama into the customary fable, characters and manners, sentiments, and diction.[145]

There is no better example of its dramatic criticism than its

---

[137] *Critical Review*, XI (April, 1761), p. 302. See, also, II (October, 1756), p. 270.
[138] *Critical Review*, IV (October, 1757), pp. 366-367.
[139] *Critical Review*, XVI (September, 1763), pp. 192-194.
[140] C. H. Gray, *Theatrical Criticism in London to 1795* (New York, 1931), p. 154.
[141] *Critical Review*, I (January-February, 1756), pp. 78-79 (Smollett); VI (July, 1758), p. 17; XV (February, 1763), pp. 96-97.
[142] *Critical Review*, III (March, 1757), p. 259; XIII (January, 1762), pp. 53-54.
[143] *Critical Review*, XIV (September, 1762), p. 163.
[144] *Critical Review*, V (March, 1758), pp. 237-238.
[145] *Critical Review*, I (March, 1756), p. 162 (Franklin); V (March, 1758), pp. 237-238; XV (February, 1763), pp. 96-97.

articles on John Home's *Douglas*, probably the most important play of the period.[146] Beginning with a commentary on the plot or fable, the *Critical* reviewer indicated his presumption of rules, by criticizing the familiarity of the narrative, lack of motivation for the main action, too early presentation of the discovery scene, and the failure to produce "poetical justice". Turning to the characterization, which was described as inadequate, the critic advanced nothing significant to theory. But his treatment of the sentiments of the play, lauding their propriety, and his unfavorable comments on the diction, which had been applauded by "superficial judges, [for whom] ranting will pass for passion, and bombast for sublimity, [and by whom] low and vulgar expression may also be mistaken for simplicity" – both demonstrate the orthodox standards of the reviewer. At the same time, judging according to type, he concluded that *Douglas* was infinitely superior to other plays in the same category that had appeared in recent years.[147]

For criticism of fiction, especially the novel, the writers in the *Critical* had fewer genre rules by which to judge. Yet they applied their divisions of fable, characters, diction, and thought, which, although seemingly making a cleavage between form and content, was an attempt to gain unity through Aristotelian analysis.[148] Whether the work was a French romance, a fictionalized travel book, or a satirical novel, the reviewer demanded propriety and scorned "wild imagination, little judgment, [and] no probability...".[149] Criticism of *Candide*, indicative of the reviewer's inability to divorce art from life and to judge literature without regard for morality, attributed Voltaire's failure to aesthetic as well as moral ineptitude. Arguing that there were no characters in na-

---

[146]   *Critical Review*, III (March, 1757), pp. 259 ff.
[147]   See Mossner, pp. 42 ff. for a description of the part played by Scottish patriotism in the success of *Douglas*. The *Critical Review*, III (March, 1757), pp. 287-288, gives a description of the Scottish attempt to defend Home's play from adverse criticism.
[148]   See Wellek, p. 19, and Heidler, p. 46. However, Heidler's view that criticism had ceased to see in the genre anything more than the possibility of instruction is not borne out in the *Critical* or *Monthly*.
[149]   The quotation is from *Critical Review*, XV (May, 1763), pp. 343-344. See, also, VIII (October, 1759), p. 302; IX (May, 1760), p. 419; XI (March, 1761), p. 198.

ture such as Voltaire had presented, the critic described the incidents as "the ravings of a delirious poet, strung together without order, or the least shadow of verisimilitude . . .".[150] The *Critical's* evaluation of *Tristram Shandy* was severely limited by the demands for unity in the unconnected rhapsody,[151] and even the favorable treatment of Johnson's *Rasselas* balked at the genre inadequacies of the work.[152] Moreover, the reviewers' insistence upon an art that mirrors nature suggests that the novel, to be worthy of regard, was expected to contribute to morality.[153]

In their attempt to apply genre criticism to the novel may be seen the *Critical* reviewers' characteristic method of dealing with the aesthetic changes that are now regarded as pre-romantic. Suggestions that editorial refusal to remain dogmatic in the face of changing taste implies an alteration in the basic attitude expressed in the *Critical* come no closer to the truth than assertions that the review's maintenance of orthodox standards signifies an inflexible, obstinate neoclassicism.[154] To be sure, Smollett and others in the *Critical* gave a warm reception to Gray, Young, Akenside, and Warton,[155] but in each instance the reviewer attempted to fit new ideas into an old pattern, to reject out of hand the radical departures from the accepted standards, and to apply a rule of common sense wherever that was possible. For all his approval of the "enthusiasm, exstasy, and prophetic fury, that alarms, amazes and transports the reader" in Gray's *Odes*, the reviewer judged them according to classical standards and the correctness of the Pindaric form.[156] Certainly for the expressedly

---

[150]   *Critical Review*, VII (June, 1759), p. 551.
[151]   *Critical Review*, XI (April, 1761), p. 317 and XIII (January, 1762), pp. 66-69.
[152]   *Critical Review*, VII (April, 1759), pp. 372-375.
[153]   *Critical Review*, IX (May, 1760), p. 419.
[154]   Hooker, "The Reviewers and the New Trends in Poetry", p. 207, emphasizes the rigid neoclassical approach, while C. E. Jones, "The *Critical Review's* First Thirty Years", *Notes and Queries*, III, pp. 78 ff., ignores the methods in which the review assimilated changes.
[155]   *Critical Review*, I (April, 1756), p. 276 (Smollett) and V (March, 1758), p. 197.
[156]   *Critical Review*, IV (August, 1757), pp. 167, 169. See W. P. Jones, "The Contemporary Reception of Gray's *Odes*", *MP*, XXVIII (1930), pp. 61-82.

romantic, at least Samuel Derrick in the review did not hesitate to pronounce his complete dislike.[157]

For works by Edward Young, Bishop Hurd, the Wartons, and Macpherson, a similar pattern was used. Young's *Conjectures on Original Composition* posed little problem for the orthodox critics.[158] Greeting the work as an accurate statement of the principles of imitation, the reviewer, probably Goldsmith, tailored Young's comments to fit the needs of standard criticism.[159] According to the critic, the chief point of the *Conjectures* was its insistence that moderns not be intimidated by ancient writings, and that the best way to write was to draw from nature, which, after all, had been the inspiration for antiquity. Use the spirit and taste but not the materials of classical authors was advice consistent with the common sense approach of critics in the Johnsonian age, who regarded ancient authority and universality as being based on the principles of following nature and criticized slavish imitation of any models. The degree to which a periodical was conservative depended on how much its writers were willing to acknowledge the ancients' achievement in following nature and thus proving acceptable models in their own work. The *Critical* insisted on their reliability. Where, as in his comment on *Night Thoughts*, he was unable to adapt Young's melancholy to the standards of an orthodox creed, the *Critical* reviewer withheld approval.[160]

Like Young, Bishop Hurd offered enough to appease the conservative demands of the *Critical*. Not only did he present a systematic and scholastic criticism in his *Letters on Chivalry and Romance* but he also demonstrated a great regard for the hierarchy of genres, dealt with kinds, and was not antipathetic toward standard views of imitation.[161] Indeed, criticism such as Hurd's

[157] *Critical Review*, I (May, 1756), pp. 312-313.
[158] Atkins, p. 193.
[159] *Critical Review*, VII (June, 1759), pp. 483-485. For the possible attribution to Goldsmith, see A. Friedman, "Goldsmith's Contributions to the *Critical Review*", *MP*, XLIV (1946), pp. 41-42.
[160] *Critical Review*, III (February, 1757), pp. 118-119; III (June, 1757), p. 532; XIII (June, 1762), p. 461. However, it is clear from these reviews that the *Critical* did admire Young as a poet.
[161] See Hooker, "The Reviewers and the New Criticism", pp. 194-195; Wellek, I, p. 130.

was exactly what the reviewer needed in his evaluation of a work like Thomas Warton's *Observations on the Fairy Queen of Spenser*.[162] Depending upon rules rather than intuition, the writer in the *Critical* sought principles for judging Gothic poetry. The reviewer was still concerned with finding rules for genres even when the kind did not exist in classical antiquity.

With Warton's brother Joseph, although approving his *Essay on the Writings and Genius of Pope* without understanding its affect on Pope's reputation, Smollett himself took sharp issue on the important points that involved orthodox taste.[163] Defending the artificial diction of Pope's pastorals, Smollett attacked Warton's praise of *Grongar Hill*, calling attention to its "indifferent painting and hobbling measure, [and noting that it] contains a number of strained applications and distorted reflections . . .". In addition, the editor disapproved of Warton's "excessive" regard for the talents of Thomson, Akenside, Young, Glover, and Gray, four of whom have come to be considered among the precursors of romanticism.[164]

But perhaps the most interesting and in some ways the most important articles on a work that departed from the main currents of neoclassical literature were those that the review devoted to Macpherson's grand Ossianic forgeries. Whatever role Scottish patriotism might have played in the reviewer's willingness to accept the authenticity and genius of the work, the genre criticism in his analysis remains significant.[165] After specifically noting the absurdity of applying the standards of the epic to Macpherson's poem, the *Critical* reviewer relied on the principles of the orthodox creed in evaluating the merits of Ossian, terming the achievement superior in many places even to the classics of Homer and Virgil,[166] regretting only its lack of polish. Furthermore, in enthusiastically approving of Macpherson's efforts, the critic based

---

162 *Critical Review*, XVI (September, 1763), p. 220.
163 William D. MacClintock, *Joseph Warton's Essay on Pope* (Chapel Hill, 1933), p. 25.
164 *Critical Review*, I (April, 1756), pp. 228-231.
165 *Cf.*, Mossner, pp. 86-87 and Bosker, p. 87.
166 *Critical Review*, X (July, 1760), pp. 28-29; XII (December, 1761), pp. 405 ff.; XV (February, 1763), pp. 120-126. *Cf.*, Bosker, pp. 168-169.

his opinion on the most fundamental value of neoclassical criticism – morality.[167] There is no question that in his judgment the writer in the *Critical* was attempting to fit *Fingal* into the framework of a neoclassical design.

With similar determination and varying success, the *Critical* reviewers tried to trim the new fashion in ideas according to the pattern of the past. Romantic primitivism, Gothicism, orientalism, and the sublime all posed problems, and even Shakespeare had to be explained as an exception to the *Critical*'s rules. To be sure, the reviewers, including Smollett, described Shakespeare as the "British Homer",[168] to be defended against detractors and idolators alike.[169] Regardless of the distortions of Shakespeare's plays on the eighteenth-century stage, Smollett himself recognized him as the father of English drama, whose virtues managed to shine through the abominations of modern adaptations.[170] Nevertheless, at a time when even conservative critics had given wholehearted approval to his work,[171] the reviewers did not permit their admiration to blind their judgment. Despite his genius, Smollett and others criticized Shakespeare for his lack of learning, "absurdities", and "confusion" of tragedy and comedy.[172] For Smollett the playwright's greatness was not enhanced by his failure to observe the rules, and his faults were not minimized: [173]

... though we revere the might of that creative genius, we are not so dazzled with his excellencies, but that we can perceive a number of imperfections scattered up and down his works. These his warmest admirers will not deny, and there are an hundred characters in his plays, that ... speak out of character.

In their criticism of Shakespeare's lack of learning and in their suggestions that *Fingal* wanted polish, the reviewers indicated

[167] *Critical Review*, XII (December, 1761), pp. 410-411; XIII (January, 1762), pp. 45-53.
[168] *Critical Review*, I (March, 1756), p. 145 (Smollett).
[169] *Critical Review*, X (August, 1760), pp. 154-155.
[170] *Critical Review*, I (March, 1756), pp. 144-146.
[171] The older view of Saintsbury, II, p. 485, is adequately disposed of by Krutch, p. 335.
[172] *Critical Review*, I (March, 1756), p. 145 (Smollett); VIII (July, 1759), p. 14; XI (February, 1761), p. 164.
[173] *Critical Review*, I (April, 1756), pp. 234-235.

what their reactions must be to romantic primitivism, to the concept of the noble savage and the Rousseauistic natural man. Antiquarianism itself was looked upon as a waste of time, learning, and talents,[174] but an acceptance of a natural society was considered a positive danger or, at best, ridiculous nonsense. How trust the natural man, Franklin asked in the *Critical*, if in the refined and civilized state he is unreliable: [175]

In regard to our author's arguments . . . we cannot but esteem them weak and inconclusive: for although it will very readily be granted, that every species of society, and every form of civil government is attended with many evils, and subject to inconveniences and abuse, it will yet, by no means follow, that total anarchy and confusion, which would be inevitable consequences of (what he terms) *natural* society, are therefore eligible. The grievances and imperfections of which he so heavily complains, must always continue whilst men are men, unless he could persuade his friends in the shades to send us one of his Utopia patriot kings to govern us, and a better rule than his first philosophy to regulate our moral conduct.

Questions of natural goodness and benevolence were set aside as unworthy of serious consideration.[176] Peasant poets, American Indians, and theories of climatic effect on character were just so much tomfoolery to the conservative reviewers, who rejected any suggestion of the superior morality of the aborigines.[177]

Perhaps the best measure of their deep distrust of romantic primitivism is to be found in their treatment of Rousseau's work. Despite his high regard for Rousseau's talents as a writer, one reviewer labeled the French author's observations "superficial" and his conclusions "false".[178] Were Rousseau's arguments for rejecting the drama and banishing the arts accepted, another reviewer declared, ". . . we should be no better than rude savages and fierce barbarians . . .".[179] Their rejection of Rousseau's social

[174] *Critical Review*, VI (September, 1758), p. 239; XIV (September, 1762), p. 222.
[175] *Critical Review*, I (June, 1756), p. 426.
[176] *Critical Review*, V (June, 1758), pp. 461-468.
[177] *Critical Review*, IV (September, 1757), p. 193; IX (January, 1760), pp. 51-53; XIII (February, 1762), p. 108.
[178] *Critical Review*, XVI (November, 1763), pp. 375-377.
[179] *Critical Review*, VII (January, 1759), p. 54.

ideas indicates the *Critical* reviewers' fundamental opposition to the primitivism of the romantics: [180]

> To confess the truth, society hath introduced some evils into life, but it hath also been the instrument of manifold blessings and comforts; it hath given birth to numberless crimes, but it has likewise been the kind parent of an equal number of virtues: benevolence could have no existence in the savage state of man, nor the chearing reflection of worthy actions, the heartfelt joy of communicating happiness; and though it might be exempted from dishonesty, falsehood, malice, ingratitude and the catalogue of the blackest vices, it must exclude the tender ties, and the tenderer offices of love and friendship, the endearing relations of husband, father, son, and brother, and all those soft emotions, and feeling sympathies, which kindle all their affections, rouse the finer passions, and polish and refine humanity.

While on a purely literary basis a writer in the review might find praise for some aspect of primitivism,[181] in general, the critics were too much concerned with refinement, culture, manners, and decorum, and too little convinced of the goodness of man to give ear to the arguments for noble savages.

When that noble savage was oriental, the writers in the *Critical* were no more disposed to lend their approval. Although the Chinese madness hit its peak during the 1750's, the association of *chinoiserie* with the French lessened its popularity during the Seven Years' War, and led to its decline.[182] But the antipathy of the *Critical* reviewers was more fundamental than nationalistic sentiment. To be sure, they approved of individual pieces, such as Walpole's *A Letter from Xo Ho* and Percy's *Hau Kiou Choaan*, a "Europeanized" translation,[183] but such favorable commentary was certainly the exception to the rule. More typical was Smollett's attack on the depraved judgment of those moderns who preferred Chinese to Grecian and Roman architecture,[184] or the reviewer's description of the Chinese fashion in furniture as "fantastic".[185]

---

[180] *Critical Review*, XIII (February, 1762), p. 101.
[181] *Critical Review*, XIV (July, 1762), pp. 21-22.
[182] Appleton, pp. 77, 112, 140.
[183] *Critical Review*, III (May, 1757), pp. 466-467 and XII (November, 1761), p. 381. See Appleton, pp. 85-86, 140-141.
[184] *Critical Review*, I (April, 1756), pp. 224-225.
[185] *Critical Review*, VII (June, 1759), p. 550.

With complete agreement, one critic quoted Cibber's remarks on the current theatrical fare, "These Arabian rickshaws, – or Chinese festivals, – call them what you please – as any silly name may suit them all alike – These mockeries of sense – These larger kind of puppet-shews – These idle amusements . . .".[186]

Yet taste was a minor matter in the *Critical*'s concern with *chinoiserie*. Recognizing that the oriental manifestation of primitivism was a further attack upon the institutions of society, particularly the religious, the orthodox reviewer objected: [187]

Of late years, some writers of the French nation, partly from an effectation of singularity, and partly with a view to deprecate the religion of Christ, have set up the Arabians and the doctrines of Mahomet, as it were in opposition to the people of Europe, and the worship they profess. They have represented the natives of Arabia as a civilized, polite people, who possessed the arts and sciences at a time when Europe was buried in ignorance and barbarity. They have praised their caliphs as the best of men, and their tenets as the dictates of reason and humanity. But, in fact, the Arabians were never otherwise than ignorant barbarians, and cruel fanatics.

If the main opposition to orientalism stemmed from the orthodox religious beliefs of the writers in the *Critical*, their primary reaction to Gothicism probably emerged from their political conservatism. Actually, the interrelationship of the two branches of primitivism may be easily traced,[188] but here, in the example of the *Critical*, Samuel Kliger's identification of the Gothic and Whig-Liberal positions seems more important than the religious implications of Gothicism. According to Kliger, attitudes toward Gothic taste were related to party principles. For the Whigs the freedom from neoclassical restraints, characteristic of Gothic architecture, was connected with popular government, while the Tories viewed the symmetry and balance of Grecian buildings as corresponding to monarchal and aristocratic interests in maintain-

---

[186] *Critical Review*, II (August, 1756), p. 49.
[187] *Critical Review*, V (February, 1758), pp. 136-137.
[188] Sitwell and Barton, "Taste", in *Johnson's England*, II, p. 35; Kliger, p. 212.

ing national stability.[189] In addition to this political significance of Gothic taste and its opposition to the classical tradition,[190] there was a correlation between art and morals, with the Gothic again representing fewer rules and restraints.[191]

Kliger's thesis, unsubstantiated by most of the comments in the magazines and essay-journals, does seem appropriate at least to the *Critical*. No better index to the sympathies expressed in the conservative review can be found than its writers' use of the term *Gothic*. To condemn the adversaries of Charles I for their lack of culture, taste, and respect for tradition, the reviewer labeled them *Goths*.[192] Contemptuously, Smollett himself linked democratic enthusiasm and republican virtues, both of which he despised, with Gothicism, and when he chose to depreciate the age and the productions of its artists, he merely noted: "This is one of the few productions of this Gothic age, which we can with pleasure recommend to the public notice. – It breathes the spirit of true criticism, unbiased by sordid prejudices or partiality." [193]

At the same time, comments on Gothic productions were unfavorable. Smollett paid little respect to the traditions of the Druids,[194] and even where the reviewer was being most generous, he attributed his own choice to his training and standards, but was still unable to admire the Gothic.[195] If he had to make a decision, he was forced to conclude, "... we are apt to believe that the beauties of Grecian architecture will at once recommend themselves to every unprejudiced beholder...".[196] Only, as in *Fingal*, where the work could be molded to the old standards, did the reviewers approve.

Despite the obvious significance of the sublime for the development of romantic doctrines,[197] the writers in the *Critical* found

[189]   Kliger, pp. 1, 4.
[190]   Kliger, pp. 25-26.
[191]   Kliger, "Whig Aesthetics", p. 144; also see Kliger, p. 20.
[192]   *Critical Review*, VI (August, 1758), p. 126.
[193]   *Critical Review*, I (April, 1756), p. 227.
[194]   *Critical Review*, I (January-February, 1756), pp. 56-57.
[195]   *Critical Review*, VII (May, 1759), pp. 440-447.
[196]   *Critical Review*, XIII (March, 1762), pp. 241-242.
[197]   Monk, p. 101.

little difficulty in working the concept into their traditional theory of aesthetics. Undoubtedly, the classical origins recommended it to the taste of the reviewers, but in addition they perceived the foundations of the sublime to rest in a groundwork of order, a progression of surprises,[198] a view which was hardly at odds with a neoclassical standard of criticism. Their identification of the *sublime* as "an impression made on the fancy, by an object that indicates power and greatness", and, "whatever is capable of raising a strong emotion in the soul" [199] would permit the reviewers to judge even epic poetry along those lines.

It does not matter much that a writer in the *Critical* could approve of a work rendering Newton's principles in accord with those of the sublime,[200] or that a reviewer could display little appreciation for the sublimity of mountains.[201] What does matter is that even in his treatment of a subject like the sublime, the *Critical* reviewer sought rules and standards.[202] He did not trust to emotions alone; his appeal to common sense, authority, and reason demanded explanations.

One such explanation, of course, was Edmund Burke's *Philosophical Enquiry into the Origins of Our Ideas of the Sublime and the Beautiful*. Although the writer in the *Critical*, like others in contemporary periodicals, had high praise for Burke's work, he also shared their view that Burke had limited the sublime too closely, excluding all emotions but terror from its compass.[203] Again, however, the *Critical* reviewer's approach to the sublime related it to ancient standards, indicating that this was no new literary theory, but one which had been taken into account by classical criticism.[204]

Between the overall aesthetic opinions in the *Critical* and *Monthly*, there was often agreement, indicating the danger of

---

[198] *Critical Review*, VII (May, 1759), p. 442.
[199] *Critical Review*, III (April, 1757), pp. 363, 369.
[200] *Critical Review*, XI (January, 1761), p. 53.
[201] *Critical Review*, I (March, 1756), pp. 185-186.
[202] *Critical Review*, III (March, 1757), pp. 212-213.
[203] Monk, pp. 98-99; Herbert A. Wichelns, "Burke's *Essay on the Sublime and Its Reviewers*", *JEGP*, XXI (1922), pp. 646-647.
[204] *Critical Review*, III (April, 1757), pp. 363-364.

oversimplifying the conservative tendencies of the one and the more liberal impulses of the other. Although not always for the same reasons, writers in the *Monthly* not infrequently shared the views of Smollett's writers on language, literature, and the arts, and particularly in matters of morality and didacticism the values of the reviewers were alike if not identical. Both groups were influenced by the general climate of opinion, but while writers in the *Critical* assumed their role of public defender chiefly from Smollett's aspirations to form an academy, Griffiths' reviewers, through their need to establish the supremacy of their taste over that in the town and coffee houses, were no less insistent in their demands for an art that was both moral and instructive.

Like the writers for the *Critical*, Griffiths and his staff objected to common indecency and lack of refinement.[205] They opposed the impositions of booksellers [206] and castigated plagiarism.[207] At the same time, the reviewers identified an author's character with the quality of his work, not merely by praising his modesty [208] or reviling his conceit,[209] but by ascribing the merit of his writing to his personality and by relating his public image to its effect on his audience.[210] Swift's weakness, therefore, James Ralph contended, was the result of "the bitterness of his own nature"; [211] Voltaire, according to Kenrick, had been betrayed by the giddiness of pub-

---

[205] *Monthly Review*, XVII (December, 1757), p. 568; XVIII (June, 1758), pp. 581-582 (Griffiths); XXIV (April, 1761), p. 278; XXIX (October, 1763), p. 320.

[206] *Monthly Review*, XVII (July, 1757), p. 89 (Ruffhead); XXII (May, 1760), p. 435 (Kenrick); XXIII (November, 1760), p. 408; XXVI (May, 1762), p. 360 (Langhorne); XXVIII (January, 1763), p. 69 (Griffiths); XXIX (October, 1763), pp. 273-274 (Kenrick).

[207] *Monthly Review*, XIX (December, 1758), pp. 580-581; XXVII (December, 1762), pp. 428-429 (Langhorne).

[208] *Monthly Review*, XVII (November, 1757), p. 401 (Kirkpatrick); XVIII (February, 1758), p. 124 (Ruffhead); XX (February, 1759), p. 178 (Kirkpatrick).

[209] *Monthly Review*, XIV (April, 1756), pp. 360-361 (Berkenhout); XIV (May, 1756), p. 445 (Bewley); XVII (October, 1757), p. 307 (Ruffhead); XXVII (August, 1762), p. 116 (Ruffhead), p. 122 (Kenrick),

[210] An exception appears in the *Monthly Review*, XIV (April, 1756), pp. 334-335 (Berkenhout).

[211] *Monthly Review*, XVIII (March, 1758), p. 258.

lic acclaim;[212] and Ruffhead found Sterne culpable as much for the fashion he set as a clergyman as for the indecency of his performance: [212a]

Had these Discourses been sent into the world, as the *Sermons of Mr. Yorick,* . . . every serious and sober reader must have been offended at the indecency of such an assumed character. For who is this *Yorick?* We have heard of one of that name who was a *Jester* – we have read of a *Yorick* likewise, in an obscene romance – But are the solemn dictates of religion fit to be conveyed from the mouths of buffoons and ludicrous romancers? Would any man believe that a preacher was in earnest, who should mount the pulpit in a Harlequin's coat?

However, had his first title-page *only* appeared, we might have had the satisfaction to have supposed, that some licentious layman had presumed to publish these Discourses, under this assumed character, as a ridicule on religion. But what shall we say to the second title-page, in which the *Reverend* and *dignified* author does not scruple to avow his real name. . . .

Is it possible that a man of such wit and understanding as our author possesses, should have so little decency and discretion? How can he suppose that the second title-page will ease people's minds? Will it not rather disturb them the more, to find a dignitary of the Church so lost to virtue, and so insensible of shame, as openly to acknowledge himself the author of so indelicate a novel; and what is still worse, to use it as a recommendation of works which he publishes in his sacred character.

Not surprisingly, some writers for the *Monthly* made the customary demands, as well, for utility and entertainment, citing Horace as an authority in making their judgments.[213] Many of these comments, to be sure, were perfunctory, conventional tags applied to such subjects as geography, history, biography, and even the *Odyssey*,[214] with an occasional admonition for more *dulce*,[215] but

[212] *Monthly Review*, XXI (July, 1759), p. 83.
[212a] *Monthly Review*, XXII (May, 1760), pp. 422-423. See, also, XXIII (July, 1760), p. 83; XXV (December, 1761), p. 451 (Griffiths); XXVI (January, 1762), pp. 31-32 (Langhorne).
[213] *Monthly Review*, XV (September, 1756), pp. 235-236 (Ward); XVI (March, 1757), p. 246 (Grainger); XVII (September, 1757), p. 262 (Clarke); XVII (November, 1757), p. 401 (Kirkpatrick); XIX (September, 1758), p. 318; XX (January, 1759), p. 20 (Bewley); XX (March, 1759), p. 257 (Campbell).
[214] *Monthly Review*, XIV (January, 1756), p. 29 (Bewley); XVII (August, 1757), p. 150 (Goldsmith); XVII (December, 1757), p. 493 (Ruffhead);

an equal appreciation of the simple *utile*.[216] Yet even here an important aesthetic note may enter, as with Benjamin Dawson's explanation of the qualities that make for a successful biography. For here, despite his conventional warning against biographical narratives that aimed "merely to please" or those that disgusted through an "affected importance, by moralizing on every circumstance", Dawson added a note that was considerably different from the customary standard. Where most advocates of the instructive importance of biography would have asked that those qualities of the subject that were most universal in their importance be brought forth, he demanded that the emphasis be on the "particular manner and disposition", or that which "particularly" characterized the man and showed the individuality of his conduct.[217] If biography were to have a moral purpose, Ruffhead, like Dawson, believed, then, it must be made to live, and it could only come alive by bringing forth the *personal* quality of its subject.[218]

Other comments on the moral importance of literature put the *Monthly* closer to the traditional views expressed in the *Critical*. Perhaps the sense of commercial rivalry with France, apparent in the *Monthly* reviewers' remarks on language, was related to Ruffhead's and others' demands for literature that brought improve-

---

XVII (Appendix, 1757), p. 577 (Leman and Griffiths); XVIII (February, 1758), p. 129 (Ruffhead); XVIII (May, 1758), p. 448 (Griffiths); XIX (July, 1758), p. 12 (Ruffhead); XX (January, 1759), p. 49 (Campbell); XX (March, 1759), p. 231 (Kenrick), p. 234 (Ruffhead); XXI (December, 1759), p. 461 (Ruffhead); XXII (February, 1760), pp. 81-82 (Kenrick); XXII (March, 1760), p. 234 (Berkenhout); XXII (April, 1760), p. 314 (Kenrick); XXIII (October, 1760), p. 257 (Leman); XXV (July, 1761), p. 27 (Griffiths); XXV (September, 1761), p. 161 (Ruffhead); XXV (October, 1761), p. 242 (Kenrick); XXV (November, 1761), p. 337 (Rose); XXVI (January, 1762), p. 13 (Rose); XXVIII (January, 1763), pp. 30-31 (Seddon), p. 46 (Griffiths); XXVIII (April, 1763), pp. 250-251 (Ruffhead); XXIX (July, 1763), p. 41 (Langhorne); XXIX (September, 1763), p. 179 (Kenrick).
[215] *Monthly Review*, XVII (July, 1757), p. 51 (Goldsmith); XVII (October, 1757), pp. 301, 317; XXVII (November, 1762), p. 395.
[216] *Monthly Review*, XVII (November, 1757), p. 462; XVII (December, 1757), p. 550 (Stuart); XVIII (January, 1758), p. 25 (Dawson); XX (February, 1759), p. 163 (Ruffhead); XXVIII (April, 1763), p. 327.
[217] *Monthly Review*, XIX (July, 1758), p. 64.
[218] *Monthly Review*, XIX (October, 1758), p. 385; XXII (March, 1760) p. 177.

ment.[219] But whatever the reason, the reviewers regarded instruction as the primary concern of literature. "It is the business of poetry to instruct as well as to entertain", Langhorne insisted in a review of two elegiac poems.[220] When it was necessary for a poet to include barbarous material for the sake of historical truth, his obligation, according to Ruffhead, was to indicate his condemnation.[221] Even when the age he lived in was unpolished, the poet was constrained not to "accommodate his language to the grossness of their ideas", but to refine their taste, for the business of genius was to "polish public manners, instead of endeavouring to give a grace to barbarity, by the colouring of art".[222] In his defense of Pope from the criticism of Warton, James Grainger, himself a poet, asked, "If a moral sentiment is couched in poetical language, and adapted to numbers, is it not poetry?" [223] The question was rhetorical, for Grainger at once answered: [224]

The inventive faculties are much more circumscribed than is commonly supposed. A few simple ideas are all its exhaustless stores. Our author [Warton] has not sufficiently attended to this when he accuses Pope of barrenness. He who inriches a work with a new moral sentiment, is as much an inventor as he who recites a tale of fancy.

While his concern for morality and instruction in art led to Grainger's strong arguments for the values of Georgic poetry,[225] the *Monthly* reviewers by no means limited such comments to verse. To be sure, Kenrick argued that dramatic poetry should instruct by example and not by precept,[226] but Ruffhead was equally insistent that the particular purpose of dramatic poetry was "to expose the vices and follies of the age, to inculcate principles of virtue, and exalt the dignity of human nature".[227] In tragedy the

219   *Monthly Review*, XVII (October, 1757), p. 340 (Ruffhead); XXVI (February, 1762), p. 157.
220   *Monthly Review*, XXVIII (March, 1763), p. 185.
221   *Monthly Review*, XXII (February, 1760), p. 126.
222   *Monthly Review*, XXII (February, 1760), pp. 124, 126. Ruffhead wrote both.
223   *Monthly Review*, XIV (June, 1756), p. 529.
224   *Monthly Review*, XV (July, 1756), p. 62.
225   *Monthly Review*, XVI (April, 1757), pp. 328-329.
226   *Monthly Review*, XX (June, 1759), p. 508.
227   *Monthly Review*, XXIII (December, 1760), p. 456.

groundwork of every fable, Goldsmith observed, must be its moral,[228] and the purpose of comedy, according to Grainger, was the punishment of vice and the rewarding of virtue, making sound sense and morals a greater concern than the "strokes of wit and humour which excite laughter...".[229] Neither Griffiths nor his staff would countenance anything that interfered with refinement of taste and improvement of morality.[230]

Even stronger than these remarks on drama were those on the novel. Although it has become customary to think of the attack on the genre as opposition to the type itself, the *Monthly*'s comments indicate both a high regard for what the novel might accomplish in morality and a dissatisfaction with the practice itself. In discussing Rousseau's *Eloisa*, Berkenhout, the former Prussian officer, declared: [231]

We confess our difference in opinion from those who consider all romances merely as books of amusement. It is certainly in the power of a moral, sensible, writer, to convey instruction in any form or guise he shall think fit to assume; and, considering the prevailing taste of the present age, we know not whether, as a novelist, his lessons are not most likely to command attention.

Particularly for the young, Berkenhout believed, the novel could serve its effective purpose, since for them morality must have its candied coating.[232]

But the novel was not serving such a purpose, and the *Monthly* reviewers decried the debasement of the genre. Citing the remarks of a French writer who looked upon romance as the one way to administer morality to the corrupt public, Berkenhout lamented the failure of English novelists,[233] and Ruffhead contrasted the modern and earlier examples of the genre: [234]

[228] *Monthly Review*, XVI (May, 1757), p. 428.
[229] *Monthly Review*, XVII (July, 1757), p. 48.
[230] *Monthly Review*, XVII (July, 1757), p. 48 (Grainger); XXII (February, 1760), p. 136 (Griffiths); XXIV (March, 1761), p. 183 (Ruffhead).
[231] *Monthly Review*, XXIV (April, 1761), p. 227.
[232] *Monthly Review*, XIV (April, 1756), p. 289; see, also, XXVI (March, 1762), p. 237 (Lloyd).
[233] *Monthly Review*, XXIV (April, 1761), p. 260.
[234] *Monthly Review*, XXIV (June, 1761), p. 415. See, also, XXVI (March, 1762), p. 236 (Lloyd).

The genius of romance seems to have been long since drooping among us; and has, of late been generally displayed only for the basest purposes; either to raise the grin of ideotism by its buffoonery, or stimulate the prurience of sensuality by its obscenity. Novels, therefore, have circulated chiefly among the giddy and licentious of both sexes, who read, not for the sake of thinking, but for the want of thought.

So shameful a prostitution has brought this species of writing into such disrepute, that if the more serious and solid reader is at any time tempted to cast an eye over the pages of romance, he almost blushes to confess his curiosity.

Compositions of this kind, nevertheless, when conducted by a writer of fine talents and elegant taste, may be rendered as beneficial as delectable. They have this peculiar advantage, that by making a forcible impression on the imagination, they answer the purposes of conviction and persuasion, with the generality of mankind, much better than a direct appeal to the judgment.

Such writers "of fine talents and elegant taste", however, were unusual, and the reviewers had to contend mainly with Noble's ignoble novel manufactory and the tasteless females whom the circulating libraries served.[235] The few novels that were praised were generally accredited only by virtue of their relative superiority, and fiction was commonly relegated to notices in the Monthly Catalogue.[236] Productions like *Tristram Shandy* and *Eloisa*, approved on other merits, were condemned for their moral failures [237] by reviewers like Goldsmith who also found impropriety in Richardson's *Pamela* because the heroine had designs on finally marrying the villain.[238] Few novelists could succeed as Sarah Fielding had done in accomplishing her purpose: [239]

[235] *Monthly Review*, XIV (March, 1756), pp. 268-269 (Rose); XVI (February, 1757), p. 178; XVII (November, 1757), p. 478; XVII (December, 1757), p. 563; XX (January, 1759), p. 81; XX (March, 1759), pp. 275-276 (Dawson).

[236] *Monthly Review*, XIV (April, 1756), p. 289 (Berkenhout); XVIII (March, 1758), p. 273; XX (April, 1759), pp. 380-381 (Kenrick); XXI (November, 1759), pp. 449-450 (Berkenhout); XXIV (April, 1761), pp. 260 ff. (Berkenhout) (full review); XXIV (June, 1761), pp. 416 ff. (Ruffhead) (full review); XXIX (August, 1763), p. 159.

[237] *Monthly Review*, XXIV (February, 1761), pp. 101-116 (Ruffhead); XXV (September, 1761), p. 194 (Kenrick).

[238] *Monthly Review*, XVII (July, 1757), p. 45.

[239] *Monthly Review*, XVII (July, 1757), p. 39 (Leman).

To excite an abhorrence of vice, by exposing its deformity and wretchedness, tho' attended with the dazzling circumstances of pomp and power; and to inspire a reverence for even afflicted virtue, by exhibiting its present amiableness, and lasting felicity. . . .

If this treatment of morality bore a genuine resemblance to that in the *Critical*, the two reviews shared only a superficial likeness in their comments on language. To be sure, despite their acknowledgment of the mechanical difficulties involved in commercial publishing,[240] the *Monthly* reviewers, as responsible critical authorities,[241] were compelled to take note of abuses of spelling, grammar, and diction, all of which were frequently no more than lapses in typography. While there was less stress on the general subject by writers in the *Monthly*, like those in the *Critical*, they took note of such simple grammatical errors as misplaced modifiers, improper agreement, and incorrect tense, whether these appeared in original productions or translations.[242]

Again like the *Critical* reviewers, Griffiths and his staff objected to alterations of standard diction,[243] ridiculed fashionable jargon,[244] and rebuked the use of peculiar coinages or compounds.[245] Owen Ruffhead scornfully repeated Johnson's use of *excogitation,*

---

[240] *Monthly Review*, XVI (February, 1757), p. 111 (Leman); XVII (August, 1757), p. 192.

[241] *Monthly Review*, XXI (September, 1759), p. 192 (Berkenhout); XXIII (July, 1760), p. 9 (Ruffhead).

[242] *Monthly Review*, XIV (January, 1756), p. 63 (Kirkpatrick); XIV (June, 1756), p. 557 (Grainger); XV (September, 1756), p. 235 (Ward); XVII (October, 1757), p. 302; XVIII (January, 1758), p. 38 (Ruffhead); XVIII (February, 1758), p. 183; XIX (October, 1758), pp. 378-379 (Kirkpatrick); XX (February, 1759), p. 178 (Ruffhead); XXI (September, 1759), p. 265 (Kenrick); XXI (October, 1759), p. 301 (Kenrick); XXI (November, 1759), pp. 416-417 (Kirkpatrick); XXIII (August, 1760), p. 116 (Kenrick); XXIV (January, 1761), p. 6 (Kenrick); XXV (September, 1761), p. 187 (Ruffhead), pp. 223-224 (Kirkpatrick); XXVIII (February, 1763), pp. 100-102 (Kirkpatrick).

[243] *Monthly Review*, XIV (April, 1756), p. 424 (Sharpe); XV (August, 1756), pp. 128 ff. (Griffiths).

[244] *Monthly Review*, XVII (December, 1757), p. 568; XX (February, 1759), pp. 189-190; XX (April, 1759), pp. 317-318. Last two are by Kenrick.

[245] *Monthly Review*, XV (Appendix, 1756), p. 679 (Berkenhout); XXV (November, 1761), p. 328 (Lloyd).

exaggeratory, multifarious, and *transcendental* in *Rasselas,*[246] and, although without the vehemence of those in the *Critical,* other reviewers in the *Monthly* rejected Scotticisms, Gallicisms, Irishisms, and Londonisms,[247] at the same time that they objected to low expressions.[248]

Yet for all that, there was a fundamental difference between the attitudes on language expressed in the two reviews. Where writers in the *Critical* sought stabilization of the language in keeping with conservative pressures for purity, the *Monthly* reviewers sought a language that would serve the commercial interests of the nation. The objections by Griffiths and his writers to Gibbon's writing his little study of literature in French,[249] to the neglect of English in the schools and universities,[250] and to the translation of Prior's *Alma* from English into Latin [251] may seem no more than narrow chauvinism, but their meaning becomes clear when the reviewers relate their strictures to the rivalry with the French for domination of national trade interests on the continent.[252]

An even greater distinction between the attitudes expressed in the two periodicals concerns the nature of language. To be sure, reviewers like Ruffhead and Goldsmith recognized the need for rules,[253] but unlike the writers in the *Critical,* they sought no academy to fix the language. Where the *Critical* reviewer had taken

---

[246]   *Monthly Review,* XX (May, 1759), p. 428.

[247]   *Monthly Review,* XV (October, 1756), p. 344 (Leman); XV (November, 1756), p. 451 (Grainger); XVI (January, 1757), p. 40 (Rose); XVII (September, 1757), pp. 233-234 (Griffiths); XIX (August, 1758), p. 202; XX (January, 1759), p. 26 (Rose); XXIII (December, 1760), p. 430 (Kenrick); XXIII (Appendix, 1760), p. 507; XXVI (January, 1762), p. 13 (Ruffhead). But see XIV (June, 1756), p. 489 (Rose) and XVI (February, 1757), p. 122 (Rose).

[248]   *Monthly Review,* XV (November, 1756), p. 451 (Grainger); XVIII (February, 1758), p. 12 (Grainger); XXIV (March, 1761), p. 183.

[249]   *Monthly Review,* XXV (September, 1761), pp. 224-225 (Lloyd).

[250]   *Monthly Review,* XIV (February, 1756), p. 92 (Rose); XXVI (January, 1762), pp. 27-28 (Griffiths).

[251]   *Monthly Review,* XXVIII (April, 1763), p. 320 (Langhorne).

[252]   *Monthly Review,* XIX (October, 1758), p. 335; XX (January, 1759), p. 20. Ruffhead did both.

[253]   *Monthly Review,* XIX (October, 1758), pp. 335, 342; XIX (December, 1758), p. 520.

the occasion of Sheridan's *British Education* to argue for an academy, Rose in the *Monthly* presented the author's proposals without making any special plea.[254] Recognizing the necessity of change in all living languages,[255] the *Monthly's* reviewers looked to the learned writers to preserve by their practice, "the elegance, the purity, and the perspicuity of [English]".[256] It was not the business of dictionary makers and their colleagues to prescribe; "they are the servants, not the masters of language; and ... their only business is to give us the language as they found it, – not to form a new one".[257] Whatever the benefits of uniformity, the writers in the *Monthly* did not believe it could be achieved.[258] Indeed, in one article Kirkpatrick admired the "very genius of our language ... both in deriving and compounding boldly ...",[259] and, in a comparison between English and foreign poetry, Kenrick noted the advantages that had accrued to the native tongue because it was "a compound of many others, [and] is possessed, in a great degree, of their several advantages ...".[260]

Even in their attitude toward dialects, the *Monthly* reviewers proved more liberal than those in the *Critical*. Kirkpatrick's review of Home's *Medical Facts and Experiments* considered the appropriateness of Scottish idioms and concluded with a statement suggestive of what has since been called "levels of usage": [261]

We are well aware, that as language itself is local, the very correctness and elegance of it are, in some sort, relative also; and certain words and idioms are as right in Edinburgh, as very different ones are in London. But when a book, whose subject is suppos'd to be interesting, is publish'd in the last place as well as the first, it seems expedient, that its language and idiom should be that of a great majority of those to whom it is address'd: and however persons may commonly discourse, all valuable and scientific books publish'd in Great Britain ought to be in *proper* English.

---

254 *Monthly Review*, XIV (February, 1756), pp. 81-104.
255 *Monthly Review*, XXVIII (May, 1763), p. 359 (Langhorne).
256 *Monthly Review*, XX (January, 1759), p. 19 (Kirkpatrick).
257 *Monthly Review*, XVII (July, 1757), p. 83.
258 *Monthly Review*, XXVII (July, 1762), p. 69 (Rose).
259 *Monthly Review*, XX (January, 1759), p. 19.
260 *Monthly Review*, XX (March, 1759), p. 225.
261 *Monthly Review*, XXI (July, 1759), p. 75.

From comments by Griffiths and his staff on "dead languages",[262] their attitude toward the ancients may be anticipated, and certainly the reviewers regarded the emphasis on classical learning as detrimental to the progress of a commercial nation. Although the study of classical languages was made the focal point of attack, an article by Rose made clear that this educational emphasis was only symbolic of a lack of concern for all subjects except the classical,[263] and whether the objection by Griffiths and his staff was merely to the method of instruction in which Greek and Latin were taught as though "they were desirable only for their own sakes",[264] or to the belief that English could be taught through their study,[265] the reason for the opposition was clear: [266]

The attention paid to Latin and Greek, in our public schools and universities, to the manifest neglect of what is of infinitely greater moment in the business of education, is attended with very pernicious consequences to the community.

To be sure, there were areas in which the *Monthly* reviewers praised the ancients. The government of Rome,[267] the art of oratory and argument,[268] and especially Grecian architecture [269] were admired.[270] The reviewers particularly approved of the ancient achievements when these were contrasted with Gothic and Chinese productions [271] or when some modern writer had the temerity to advance his personal work or discoveries ahead of the classical.[272]

[262]   *Monthly Review*, XXVI (January, 1762), pp. 27-28 (Griffiths); XXVII (November, 1762), p. 390; XXVIII (January, 1763), pp. 75-76 (Griffiths); XXVIII (April, 1763), p. 320 (Langhorne).
[263]   *Monthly Review*, XXVII (July, 1762), pp. 40-41.
[264]   *Monthly Review*, XIV (February, 1756), p. 92 (Rose).
[265]   *Monthly Review*, XXVIII (January, 1763), pp. 75-76 (Griffiths).
[266]   *Monthly Review*, XXV (November, 1761), p. 366 (Rose).
[267]   *Monthly Review*, XV (July, 1756), pp. 1 ff.
[268]   *Monthly Review*, XVIII (February, 1758), p. 97; XXI (November, 1759), p. 427. Ruffhead did both.
[269]   *Monthly Review*, XXV (December, 1761), pp. 454-455 (Bewley); XXVIII (April, 1763), p. 303 (Kenrick).
[270]   For a contrast, however, see *Monthly Review*, XIV (March, 1756), p. 178 (Bewley) and XXV (July, 1761), pp. 1-2.
[271]   *Monthly Review*, XVI (March, 1757), p. 266 (Kirkpatrick); XVIII (January, 1758), p. 59 (Sharpe); XXVIII (May, 1763), p. 384 (Kenrick).
[272]   *Monthly Review*, XVII (September, 1757), pp. 228-229 (Goldsmith);

However, using the ancients as standards was unusual.[273] While Ruffhead claimed he was unwilling to underestimate classical accomplishments even as he noted the many areas in which the moderns had surpassed them,[274] others like Kenrick and Grainger, without apology, were at pains to point out the foolish reverence for antiquity, a veneration that age rather than achievement had lent to it.[275] The reviewers noted the ancients' ignorance of harmony [276] and satirized the taste for classical odes and their stock devices.[277] While describing the popular failure of Mason and Gray to impose classical odes on a modern audience, Goldsmith in the *Monthly* regretted that "those talents so capable of giving pleasure to all [were] exerted in efforts that, at best, can amuse only the few", and added, "we cannot behold this rising poet [Gray] seeking fame among the learned, without hinting to him the same advice that Isocrates used to give his scholars, study the people".[278]

For the *Monthly* reviewers classical poetry, while representing an achievement for the age in which it was written, was no monument for worship. Pope, Grainger argued, had surpassed both Theocritus and Virgil in the pastoral art,[279] and whatever the virtues of Homer,[280] Ruffhead insisted he was not worth the labored analysis of modern criticism.[281] Indeed, Ruffhead criticized Homer's work both in itself and as a reflection of the age in which he lived. At best, "Homer, as a poet, will always command the

---

XXVII (August, 1762), pp. 135 ff. (Langhorne); XXVIII (April, 1763), p. 276 (Kenrick). But see XVI (April, 1757), pp. 377 ff. (Goldsmith).
[273] *Monthly Review*, XIV (June, 1756), p. 535 (Grainger); XVII (September, 1757), p. 259 (Ward); XXI (November, 1759), p. 417 (Clark).
[274] *Monthly Review*, XXII (May, 1760), pp. 397-398.
[275] *Monthly Review*, XVIII (February, 1758), p. 127 (Grainger); XIX (August, 1758), pp. 161-162 (Kirkpatrick); XXVIII (Appendix, 1763), p. 528 (Kenrick); XXIX (August, 1763), p. 95 (Kenrick); XXII (April, 1760), p. 314 (Kenrick).
[276] *Monthly Review*, XXIV (May, 1761), p. 294 (Berkenhout).
[277] *Monthly Review*, XV (November, 1756), p. 478 (Ward).
[278] *Monthly Review*, XVII (September, 1757), p. 239. See, also, XIV (May, 1756), p. 434 (Grainger).
[279] *Monthly Review*, XIV (June, 1756), p. 542.
[280] *Monthly Review*, XX (March, 1759), p. 234.
[281] *Monthly Review*, XXII (February, 1760), p. 118.

admiration of every reader of taste: but that the *Iliad* is a proper model for poetry at this day, is what perhaps, no man of judgment will allow." [282] But Homer himself was not to be excused for his vulgarity. Whether his defects were attributable, as Goldsmith and Ruffhead claimed, to the age in which he lived or to his own weaknesses,[283] his work was no index to modern taste and must not be used as a guide to modern achievement.

In the same way, and to a greater degree, classical drama – both tragic and comic – was severely treated in the review. With Shakespeare as their foremost example, the *Monthly* reviewers regarded modern drama as superior to the ancient,[284] and neither the correctness of classical expression nor the richness of its language was impressive.[285] Again Ruffhead regarded the frailties of ancient art as a reflection of the times, but added: [286]

but whether their pieces, founded mostly on fabulous absurdities, are, at this time, proper entertainments for rational and enlightened minds, or worth the attention which this writer [Thomas Franklin] and others have bestowed upon them, will still remain a question.

It was a question that Ruffhead and other reviewers answered negatively in their depreciatory attitude toward Sophocles, Seneca, and Euripides,[287] and in their utter rejection of Aristophanes. Of a translation of *The Clouds*, the *Monthly* reviewer, terming it "worthless comedy", declared: [288]

A blind reverence for antiquity may induce some to put a high value upon the author of *The Clouds*; but for our parts, we scruple not to

---

[282] *Monthly Review*, XXII (February, 1760), p. 128.

[283] *Monthly Review*, XVII (September, 1757), p. 230; XXII (February, 1760), pp. 120, 124.

[284] *Monthly Review*, XXI (October, 1759), pp. 318 ff. (Kenrick); XXIII (July, 1760), pp. 4-5 (Ruffhead); XXIII (November, 1760), pp. 371 ff. (Kirkpatrick); XXV (December, 1761), p. 461 (Langhorne).

[285] *Monthly Review*, XXIII (October, 1760), p. 287; XXIV (June, 1761), p. 395 (Lloyd).

[286] *Monthly Review*, XXIII (July, 1760), p. 7. See, also, XXIII (December, 1760), p. 462.

[287] *Monthly Review*, XXIII (July, 1760), pp. 1-2 (Ruffhead); XXV (December, 1761), p. 462 (Langhorne).

[288] *Monthly Review*, XX (May, 1759), p. 462.

own, that we deem him no better than a scurrilous buffoon, whose name ought long ago to have been buried in oblivion. . . .

But the reviewers went further and condemned classical drama in its entirety as having no value for the modern theater. Kenrick, describing the devices derived from the ancients as ridiculous, maintained that the lovers of the classical had made sacred and inviolable what had been wrought by the limitations of the Greek theater.[289] In particular, the *Monthly* reviewers abjured the use of a chorus,[290] but challenged as well the propriety of using ancient tragedy itself as a model, so that Kenrick declared of *Caractacus*, that he would prefer to see Mason "give the world a tragedy, adapted to the present taste, and the customs of the English stage".[291]

At least implicit in their opposition to ancient authority was the reviewers' rejection of imitation. To begin with, the classical age was inappropriate as a model for writers in a more refined society. Homer, for example, "wrote at a time when the ferocity of mankind took a horrid pleasure in [descriptions of blood and gore]. But it is undoubtedly a proof of false taste in a modern to copy him in such circumstances".[292] The *Iliad* itself was no proper model in modern times.[293] As for imitating classical writing in the drama, that, too, was to no purpose. Kirkpatrick argued that an intimacy with Greek tragic poets led to no perfection in original writing,[294] and Kenrick observed that had Shakespeare written after a Greek original, what was best in his work would have been lost.[295] In poetry, the pagan mechanism of the ancients was wholly unsuited to modern taste,[296] and, according to Goldsmith, Greek

---

[289] *Monthly Review*, XXII (June, 1760), p. 455.
[290] *Monthly Review*, XXI (July, 1759), p. 185 (Berkenhout); XXIII (July, 1760), pp. 4-5 (Ruffhead); XXIII (November, 1760), p. 373 (Kirkpatrick).
[291] *Monthly Review*, XX (June, 1759), pp. 507-509. The quotation is from p. 507.
[292] *Monthly Review*, XXIX (October, 1763), p. 258 (Langhorne).
[293] *Monthly Review*, XXII (February, 1760), p. 128 (Ruffhead); XXIX (September, 1763), p. 193 (Langhorne).
[294] *Monthly Review*, XXIII (November, 1760), pp. 371-372.
[295] *Monthly Review*, XX (June, 1759), pp. 507-508.
[296] *Monthly Review*, XXII (February, 1760), p. 120 (Ruffhead).

odes were repellent to the contemporary English taste,[297] while Kenrick argued that imitations of Lucan were better left undone.[298] Only in architecture was the reviewer, Bewley, willing to concede the values of classical models.[299]

But this opposition to imitation was not restricted to models of classical antiquity. In their narrower arguments, Griffiths and his staff objected as well to following French originals in all the arts,[300] while in their broader view all imitation and waste of original power were regarded as faults.[301] The *Monthly* reviewer, Kenrick, found particular merit in Young's arguments for original writers and his objections to imitation.[302]

For the writers in the *Monthly* rejection of ancient authority was not the sole reason for denying the propriety of imitation. More fundamental was their denial of the principle of universality, which became apparent when they offered their peculiar arguments about the imitation of nature. To be sure, Griffiths and his writers advocated the importance of nature as a model in all the arts [303] and recommended that authors follow the rules drawn from reason and knowledge rather than from ancient writers.[304] But nature itself, as Ruffhead pointed out in his rejection of an argument by Lord Kames, had not provided universal qualities for judgment.[305] From one society and from one age to another, au-

[297] *Monthly Review*, XVII (September, 1757), p. 240.
[298] *Monthly Review*, XXVII (July, 1762), p. 25.
[299] *Monthly Review*, XXV (December, 1761), pp. 454-455. There was also mild praise in XVII (September, 1757), p. 259 (Ward) and XXVI (January, 1762), pp. 41-42 (Kenrick).
[300] *Monthly Review*, XVII (September, 1757), p. 244 (Goldsmith); XVIII (January, 1758), p. 78 (Kirkpatrick); XIX (July, 1758), p. 78 (Ruffhead); XXVIII (January, 1763), p. 67 (Griffiths).
[301] *Monthly Review*, XVII (September, 1757), p. 244 (Goldsmith); XXIV (June, 1761), pp. 393-395 (Lloyd).
[302] *Monthly Review*, XX (June, 1759), pp. 502, 506.
[303] *Monthly Review*, XVII (July, 1757), p. 48 (Grainger); XXI (November, 1759), p. 387 (Kenrick); XXII (February, 1760), p. 120 (Ruffhead); XXV (July, 1761), p. 54 (Griffiths); XXV (October, 1761), p. 259 (Kenrick); XXVI (March, 1762), p. 263 (Ruffhead); XXVI (April, 1762), p. 282 (Langhorne); XXIX (September, 1763), pp. 184-185 (Langhorne).
[304] *Monthly Review*, XXII (June, 1760), p. 455 (Kenrick); XXVI (June, 1762), p. 417 (Ruffhead).
[305] *Monthly Review*, XXVII (August, 1762), p. 115.

thority, custom, and fashion altered interpretations of nature,[306] so that even had the ancients copied carefully from nature's original, which they had not,[307] their models, transfigured by their manners and customs, would have been inappropriate for imitation.

These objections to universal principles, quite naturally, affected the reviewers' opinions on taste and shaped their attitude toward the rules. Unlike the writers in the *Critical*, those in the *Monthly* denied the universality of standards of taste even among the aristocracy. As Ruffhead's comments on imitation indicated, although each period proclaimed true standards of taste, they later proved to be no more than local customs, governed by fashion and dictated by the authority of a limited number of individuals.[308] While the mechanical parts of art required knowledge and their principles might be determined by judgment, taste had its source in feeling and had no absolute standards.[309]

Nevertheless, the *Monthly* critics *had* to argue the superiority of their own taste to that of the town and that it was the function of the critic, as the prevalent authority, to point the way in the arts.[310] Ruffhead, the man of taste who set the fashion,[311] could at least explain to sensitive readers how their perceptions were produced,[312] or Grainger, the man of learning, indicate the striking and beautiful particulars of a work of art.[313] Although taste could not be acquired, it could be improved,[314] and criticism itself, according to Grainger, was "the result of judgment, and the per-

[306] *Monthly Review*, XVII (August, 1757), pp. 104-105 (Goldsmith); XIX (August, 1758), p. 185 (Ruffhead); XXVI (June, 1762), p. 414 (Ruffhead); XXVII (August, 1762), p. 115 (Ruffhead).
[307] *Monthly Review*, XXVI (June, 1762), p. 417 (Ruffhead).
[308] *Monthly Review*, XXVII (August, 1762), p. 115.
[309] *Monthly Review*, XIV (January, 1756), p. 74 (Leman); XX (June, 1759), p. 534 (Rose); XXII (April, 1760), p. 307 (Kenrick); XXVI (April, 1762), pp. 241-242 (Kenrick).
[310] *Monthly Review*, XX (March, 1759), p. 225 (Kenrick); XXVI (May, 1762), p. 375 (Griffiths).
[311] *Monthly Review*, XXII (February, 1760), p. 119.
[312] *Monthly Review*, XXVII (July, 1762), p. 13.
[313] *Monthly Review*, XV (July, 1756), pp. 77-78.
[314] *Monthly Review*, XXII (April, 1760), p. 314 (Kenrick); XXII (May, 1760), p. 398 (Ruffhead); XXV (August, 1761), p. 106 (Ruffhead).

fection of taste. It neither extenuates beauties, nor aggravates errors; but, placing both in a proper point of light, teaches when to applaud, and when to censure, with reason." [315]

In the same way that it influenced comments on taste, imitation, and the ancients, the *Monthly* reviewers' unwillingness to accept principles of universality led to a distinctive attitude toward the rules. On the surface, there was apparent agreement between the critics on the *Monthly* and *Critical*. Griffiths' writers, like their competitors, did seek polish, regularity, refinement, and propriety in the arts.[316] Like the reviewers on the *Critical*, too, the *Monthly* writers naturally opposed authors like Warton and Goldsmith when they attacked criticism and the rules for destroying creative work.[317] Nevertheless, there was a basic difference, for while the *Critical* reviewers founded their rules on universal practices as demonstrated by the ancients, such orthodox dependency upon antiquity was anathema to Griffiths' staff.

The keynote was struck in Goldsmith's article on *Douglas*: [318]

A mechanically exact adherence to all the rules of the drama, is more the business of industry than of genius. Theatrical lawgivers rather teach the ignorant where to censure, than the poet how to write. If sublimity, sentiment, and passion, give warmth, and life, and expression to the whole, we can the more easily dispense with the rules of the Stagyrite; but if languor, affectation, and the false sublime, are substituted for these, an observance of all the precepts of the antients, will prove but a poor compensation.

In their criticism of the drama, in general, the *Monthly* reviewers (Kenrick, Ruffhead and Kirkpatrick) noted the "mere preserva-

---

[315] *Monthly Review*, XIV (June, 1756), p. 528.

[316] *Monthly Review*, XVIII (April, 1758), p. 334 (Grainger); XIX (October, 1758), p. 335 (Ruffhead), p. 380 (Kirkpatrick); XIX (December, 1758), p. 520 (Goldsmith); XX (February, 1759), p. 183 (Kirkpatrick); XX (May, 1759), pp. 462-463 (Kenrick); XXI (August, 1759), pp. 171-172; XXI (November, 1759), p. 455 (Berkenhout); XXI (Appendix, 1759), p. 562 (Kenrick); XXII (February, 1760), p. 136 (Kenrick); XXVI (February, 1762), p. 151. But see XVI (March, 1757), p. 228 (Ward); XIX (October, 1758), p. 383 (Kirkpatrick).

[317] *Monthly Review*, XV (July, 1756), p. 62 (Grainger); XXI (November, 1759), pp. 383, 386-387 (Kenrick).

[318] *Monthly Review*, XVI (May, 1757), p. 427.

tion of the unities of time and place",[319] advocated the violation of the unity of action to give the poet "a larger field for the display of native genius",[320] and applauded comments that approved of Shakespeare's refutation of the unities.[321] Their rejection extended as well to the uses of the ancient choruses, and urged, finally, a reliance upon the rules only that were founded on nature.[322] If the reviewer discovered virtue in Horace's *Art of Poetry*, it was only because "all his rules ... are founded in nature, and, therefore, require only common sense to judge of their propriety".[323]

This opposition to the simple orthodoxy of antiquity led to the *Monthly* writers' approval of critical heresy,[324] so that even where the reviewer described the rules of the drama, it was not with the sense of the importance of adherence that was rather common in the *Critical's* remarks. In his article on Murphy's *Desert Island*, Kenrick depicted variety of action and characterization as consonant with the dramatic rules,[325] and Langhorne's review of a masque favored the genre precisely because it gave full breadth to genius by dispensing with the worries about unity, order, and probability.[326] Other comments by Grainger, dealing with rules for a type, also illustrated the reviewer's preference for natural rather than artificial rules, the latter being the product of a reliance upon ancient practices that had come to be regarded as universal.[327]

While they did not give complete license to a poet to ignore the rules, the reviewers, particularly Kenrick and Ruffhead, did acknowledge his right to create his own genre,[328] and emphasized

---

[319] *Monthly Review*, XXII (March, 1760), p. 220. See, too, XXII (June, 1760), p. 456. Both were written by Kenrick.
[320] *Monthly Review*, XXIII (December, 1760), p. 462 (Ruffhead).
[321] *Monthly Review*, XXIII (November, 1760), p. 372 (Kirkpatrick).
[322] *Monthly Review*, XXII (June, 1760), p. 456 (Kenrick); XXIII (November, 1760), pp. 371, 373 (Kirkpatrick).
[323] *Monthly Review*, XVI (June, 1757), p. 34.
[324] *Monthly Review*, XVII (September, 1757), p. 229 (Goldsmith); XXVII (August, 1762), p. 81 (Rose).
[325] *Monthly Review*, XXII (February, 1760), p. 136.
[326] *Monthly Review*, XXVIII (February, 1763), p. 109.
[327] *Monthly Review*, XVI (April, 1757), pp. 328-329; XVIII (March, 1758), p. 278.
[328] *Monthly Review*, XXVI (January, 1762), pp. 41-42 (Kenrick).

especially the fact that genius made its own rules.[329] The sensitive artist like the sensitive critic might be improved by a study of the arts, but that sensitivity, unlike mechanical ability, was not to be acquired from the rules.[330] Indeed, the rules themselves were sometimes too vague to be practicable,[331] and criticism could afford to ignore them when a work, like Smart's *A Song to David*, was both "greatly irregular" and "irregularly great".[332]

For all this lack of emphasis on the rules, imitation, and ancient models, the writers in the *Monthly*, nevertheless, were as insistent as those in the *Critical* on genre criticism. Some of the comments already quoted, particularly those on the novel,[333] suggest this genre approach. To be sure, works like Smart's translations from Horace and Warton's essay on Pope called naturally for such discussion,[334] but perhaps more importantly the *Monthly*'s reviewers, as Kenrick suggested, recognized that readers expected genre criticism.[335]

Whatever the reason, the reviewers concerned themselves with what was appropriate to a kind. Goldsmith's objections to memoirs arose from an inability to classify them either as history or romance,[336] while historical novels were condemned as a bastard type, impure in the mixture of truth and fiction.[337] Goldsmith in-

[329]   *Monthly Review*, XXIII (October, 1760), p. 311 (Ruffhead).
[330]   *Monthly Review*, XXIV (May, 1761), p. 294 (Berkenhout); XXV (August, 1761), p. 106 (Ruffhead); XXVI (June, 1762), pp. 413-414 (Ruffhead), pp. 417-418 (Ruffhead); XXVII (July, 1762), p. 13 (Ruffhead).
[331]   *Monthly Review*, XXVI (May, 1762), p. 331 (Kenrick).
[332]   *Monthly Review*, XXVIII (April, 1763), p. 320 (Langhorne). See, also, XXI (July, 1759), p. 85.
[333]   *Monthly Review*, XIV (March, 1756), pp. 268-269; XIV (April, 1756), p. 334 (Berkenhout); XVI (February, 1757), p. 178; XVII (July, 1757), p. 48 (Grainger); XVIII (April, 1758), pp. 289 ff. (Ruffhead); XVIII (May, 1758), p. 448 (Griffiths); XX (June, 1759), p. 508 (Kenrick); XXI (November, 1759), pp. 449-450 (Berkenhout); XXIV (February, 1761), p. 101 (Ruffhead); XXIV (April, 1761), p. 227 (Berkenhout), p. 260; XXIV (June, 1761), p. 415 (Ruffhead); XXVI (March, 1762), p. 236 (Lloyd); XXVIII (February, 1763), p. 109 (Langhorne).
[334]   *Monthly Review*, XIV (June, 1756), pp. 534 ff. (Grainger); XVI (January, 1757), p. 34.
[335]   *Monthly Review*, XXVIII (February, 1763), p. 104.
[336]   *Monthly Review*, XVII (July, 1757), p. 80.
[337]   *Monthly Review*, XX (February, 1759), p. 188.

sisted upon the appropriate designation when essays or medita-
tions were offered as letters,[338] and Griffiths himself assigned
proper requisites for epistolary writing.[339] Their concern for appropriate form led also to the critics' careful distinction between
biography and history, consigning human nature to one and human policy to the other and recommending methods of approach
for both.[340]

The same regard for characteristics of a genre marked the reviewers' criticism of the novel, a type for which they displayed
little taste, except when they considered the possible moral effects.[341] Here, where there were no rules prescribed by classical
tradition, the writers in the *Monthly*, like those in the *Critical*,
borrowed their divisions from the drama. Language, fable, characters, and sentiments were made the basis for judgment, with the
emphasis placed on a novel's being founded in truth and nature,[342]
although even a favorable review was generally assigned to the
Monthly Catalogue.[343] Indeed, Ruffhead, who was a leading reviewer, expected even the oriental romance to remain within the
bounds of probability and to follow nature in order to instruct.[344]

With the drama, too, the *Monthly* reviewers applied genre distinctions. Robert Lloyd's article on Richard Cumberland's *The
Banishment of Cicero: a Tragedy* objected that it should have
been called a *dramatic poem*, "since ... the language seems too
metaphorical and declamatory to rouze our passions, which are
more easily awakened by the genuine simplicity of nature, than by
all the colouring of the richest classical expression." [345] Farce was

---

[338]   *Monthly Review*, XVII (July, 1757), p. 51.
[339]   *Monthly Review*, XXIX (August, 1763), p. 148.
[340]   *Monthly Review*, XVI (June, 1757), pp. 530 ff. (Goldsmith); XIX (July,
1758), pp. 64-65 (Dawson); XX (June, 1759), p. 513 (Ruffhead); XXII
(March, 1760), pp. 177-178 (Ruffhead); XXVIII (April, 1763), pp. 250-251
(Ruffhead).
[341]   *Monthly Review*, XX (February, 1759), p. 190 (Kenrick).
[342]   *Monthly Review*, XIV (April, 1756), p. 289 (Berkenhout); XVIII
(March, 1758), p. 273; XXIX (August, 1763), p. 159.
[343]   *Monthly Review*, XVIII (March, 1758), p. 273; XXIX (August, 1763),
p. 159.
[344]   *Monthly Review*, XXIV (June, 1761), pp. 415-416.
[345]   *Monthly Review*, XXIV (June, 1761), p. 395.

to be distinguished from comedy, and the critics detailed the distinctions of the types,[346] just as they explained the genre characteristics of the opera.[347] For comedy the reviewers were insistent upon the propriety of language that did not pander to a low taste, and Ruffhead's article on The Jealous Wife objected to the use of coarse dialogue from common life as well as the impropriety of character and improbability of incident.[348] At the same time, the Monthly reviewers regarded drama on a hierarchal basis, with the five-act comedy and tragedy at the head of the genres,[349] and it was on this basis that Goldsmith condemned Douglas for its weaknesses by comparison with other members of the type.[350]

Propriety according to type and an awareness of the characteristics of each genre were also the pronounced points of the Monthly's criticism of poetry. Griffiths' of monody and Kirkpatrick's of burlesque included discussions of kinds,[351] while the editor and his staff, in comments on the epistle, distinguished between the heroic, love, and elegiac, and demanded appropriate treatment of each type.[352] Quick to criticize a religious poem because the author's attempt at plainness had led to a lack of dignity for that species of poetry,[353] Langhorne insisted that heroic poetry be written in refined diction.[354] Even rhyme was discussed according to its fitness for a genre, and Grainger concluded that it was essential for sonnets, pastorals, eclogues, elegies, satires, and "even odes".[355]

Elegies and odes called for particular discussion because modern poets used the names indiscriminately. The Monthly reviewers scoffed at the tendency to label irregular rhymes as Pindaric

---

346   Monthly Review, XVI (April, 1757), p. 362; XXIX (December, 1763), p. 464.
347   Monthly Review, XIV (March, 1756), p. 238 (Berkenhout).
348   Monthly Review, XXIV (March, 1761), p. 183.
349   Monthly Review, XXIII (July, 1760), p. 83.
350   Monthly Review, XVI (May, 1757), p. 426.
351   Monthly Review, XIV (April, 1756), p. 352; XVIII (June, 1758), p. 528.
352   Monthly Review, XVI (April, 1757), p. 289 (Grainger); XX (January, 1759), p. 58 (Griffiths); XXVI (March, 1762), p. 224 (Langhorne).
353   Monthly Review, XXVII (December, 1762), pp. 426-427.
354   Monthly Review, XXIX (September, 1763), p. 186.
355   Monthly Review, XVIII (March, 1758), p. 277.

Odes [356] and ridiculed, in general, the lack of appreciation for the form.[357] In a comment on the Pindaric Ode, Goldsmith designated the characteristics of the species,[358] and in another on the elegy, Robert Lloyd depicted its language as the utmost in simplicity without debasement to meanness.[359] The qualities and distinctions of both genres were brought together by Lloyd in a single article on *Woodstock: an Elegy:* [360]

The terms *Elegy* and *Ode*, among the moderns, are frequently bestowed on compositions that have neither simplicity of sentiment, which is the particular ornament of the first species of poetry, nor that variety and fire which are absolute requisites in the last. It seems as if measure were all in all, and that alternate verse were sufficient of itself to constitute an elegy: as irregular metre, falsely called Pindaric, has often been the only apparent reason for affixing the title of *odes* to the most dull and phlegmatic performances.

Comments on the epic were even more insistent upon the protection of the genre from modern debasement. *Fingal*, which had been presented as an epic, had to be judged according to the genre, and Macpherson's poem was found wanting alongside the *Iliad* and *Odyssey*, both of which themselves had been severely criticized in the review.[361] Although Kenrick, the reviewer, regretted that the poem's admirers had compelled it to be judged on epic terms, he proceeded with a full delineation of the epic characteristics.[362] More importantly, he insisted that where a work was to be judged according to the genre, the standards must be rigidly applied so that the form itself be protected from corruption.[363]

While Kenrick not only maintained genre criticism, but placed the epic properly at the head of all types, other reviewers in the

[356] *Monthly Review*, XVI (March, 1757), p. 233; XXIII (Appendix, 1760), p. 525. Kirkpatrick did both.
[357] *Monthly Review*, XV (November, 1756), pp. 477 ff. (Grainger).
[358] *Monthly Review*, XVII (September, 1757), p. 239.
[359] *Monthly Review*, XXV (November, 1761), p. 328.
[360] *Monthly Review*, XXV (July, 1761), p. 62.
[361] *Monthly Review*, XXVI (February, 1762), pp. 139-140.
[362] *Monthly Review*, XXVI (January, 1762), pp. 41-57.
[363] *Monthly Review*, XXVI (January, 1762), pp. 41-42.

Monthly particularly admired Georgic poetry, with its didactic qualities. Here, again, the criticism was according to the species, as Langhorne, for example, gave the characteristics of the kind as simplicity in communicating pleasure and instruction.[364] John Dyer's *The Fleece* called forth a review of the type and a comparison with the epic. The Georgic fared well, for, according to Grainger, who practised the art himself, not even the epic "demands such glowing and picturesque epithets, such daring and forcible metaphors, such pomp of numbers, and dignity of expression . . .".[365] Grainger went on to note the need for a subject of great national interest, which suggests why the genre could be particularly appealing to a reviewer who sought the commercial expansion of the country, and concluded:

such precepts ought only to be delivered, and such objects painted, as can be represented to the imagination in agreeable colours; that pathetic strokes ought frequently to be introduced; and lastly, that the attention ought often to be awakened by pleasing and naural episodes and digressions.

In another comparison between the epic and Georgic, giving the characteristics of descriptive poetry, Grainger again clearly stated a genre theory, even while praising a lesser genre beyond a degree that would have been acceptable to most neoclassical critics:[366]

Tho' descriptive poetry is doubtless inferior both in dignity and utility, to ethic compositions, yet it ought to be remembered, that as in a sister art, landscape claims the next rank to history – painting, so a poet, as Virgil, for instance, in the Georgics, never stands more in need of the Muse's inspiration, than when he draws either natural or artificial objects. But, to describe with propriety, minuteness is not so necessary as enumeration of the more striking, picturesque, and peculiar circumstances: the former is the province of the naturalist and philosopher; the latter is the characteristic of a poet. Nor is a selection of appearances the only thing required in descriptive poems; they should be diversified with moral reflections, naturally brought in; and above all, with short, enlivening strokes, which may arouse and exercise the affections.

---

[364]   *Monthly Review*, XXVI (January, 1762), pp. 65.
[365]   *Monthly Review*, XVI (April, 1757), pp. 328-329.
[366]   *Monthly Review*, XVIII (March, 1758), p. 278.

Like this genre criticism the *Monthly* reviewers' treatment of pre-romantic subjects was not far removed from the conservative point of view in the *Critical*. Despite their arguments in favor of Shakespeare's drama compared with that of the ancients,[367] the writers in the *Monthly* did not regard his work as inviolable. To be sure, they placed him above the rules, but only so far as he copied from nature,[368] and although foolish emendations of the plays were scored,[369] his weaknesses were not condoned, especially when they were counter to the neoclassical principles of correctness and propriety.[370]

Correctness, propriety, and morality influenced the critics' judgments not only of Shakespeare, but of romantic primitivism in general. While Kenrick's criticism of both Shakespeare and *chinoiserie* flouted the orthodox principles of universality,[371] Kenrick himself, along with Griffiths and his staff, generally measured the new developments according to the old standards. The Chinese, for example, were depicted by Griffiths as a race apart, not merely in their inferior taste, but physically and physiologically removed from Western society.[372] Yet the reviewers, who themselves noted that it was absurd to use the conventional rules to judge such productions, applied the normal standards of rhetoric, correctness, and propriety.[373] The reasons are not difficult to discover, for they are clearly related to criticism that judged according to the relation of art to the audience. Where orientalism was praised, it conformed with the demands of correctness and didacticism, even though the reviewers had their reser-

---

[367] *Monthly Review*, XX (June, 1759), pp. 507-508 (Kenrick); XXI (July, 1759), p. 85; XXIII (July, 1760), pp. 4-5 (Ruffhead); XXIII (November, 1760), pp. 371-372 (Kirkpatrick).

[368] *Monthly Review*, XXI (November, 1759), p. 386 (Kenrick).

[369] *Monthly Review*, XIV (March, 1756), p. 270 (Berkenhout); XV (August, 1756), p. 153 (Griffiths).

[370] *Monthly Review*, XX (May, 1759), pp. 462-463 (Kenrick); XXII (February, 1760), p. 121 (Ruffhead); XXVI (February, 1762), p. 151; XXVIII (January, 1763), p. 75 (Griffiths).

[371] *Monthly Review*, XXIV (March, 1760), p. 138 *bis*.

[372] *Monthly Review*, XXV (December, 1761), pp. 427-428, 431-432, 436; XXVIII (March, 1763), p. 176.

[373] *Monthly Review*, XXV (December, 1761), p. 431 (Griffiths).

vations about public taste which demanded fanciful stories before it would accept instruction.[374]

Chinoiserie was also linked with the Gothic, and once again the relationship of Whig politics and Gothic taste, noted by Kliger, fails to materialize. While orientalism was linked with the French enemies, Gothicism was connected with papist superstition and idolatry.[375] Rather than the freedom that the Whigs were supposed to have found in the Gothic, Griffiths himself discovered "critical barbarism" [376] and Kenrick damned together "the Gothic barbarism, and monkish jingle, of rhime . . .".[377]

But pre-romanticism, apart from the sublime, had *no* aesthetic appeal for the *Monthly* reviewers (particularly Kenrick), and the primitive man had no allure. Kenrick considered the American Indian too exotic to have meaning for a European audience.[378] Praise for the Icelander was derided by Bewley in the review,[379] and, according to the *Monthly* reviewers, the unschooled artist, like the untutored man, was restricted by his ignorance.[380] Whatever the advantages for poetry in a primitive society, Kenrick believed that they were unequal to the disadvantages of lack of refinement and polish.[381] He found the achievement of Macpherson due precisely to the measure in which the Ossianic poems had become his own and consequently gained as poetry from the benefits of a cultivated society.[382] As for the absurdities of pre-

---

[374] *Monthly Review*, XVI (June, 1757), p. 487 (Grainger); XX (January, 1759), pp. 79-80; XX (April, 1759), p. 380 (Kenrick); XX (May, 1759), pp. 428-437 (Ruffhead); XXIV (June, 1761), p. 415 (Ruffhead); XXVI (April, 1762), p. 254 (Ruffhead); XXVIII (May, 1763), p. 384 (Kenrick).
[375] *Monthly Review*, XVI (March, 1757), p. 266 (Stuart); XVIII (January, 1758), p. 59 (Sharpe).
[376] *Monthly Review*, XV (December, 1756), p. 654.
[377] *Monthly Review*, XXI (October, 1759), p. 352.
[378] *Monthly Review*, XXII (February, 1760), pp. 85-86; XXIII (December, 1760), p. 424.
[379] *Monthly Review*, XVIII (March, 1758), p. 205.
[380] *Monthly Review*, XIV (January, 1756), pp. 59-60 (Kirkpatrick); XXIII (December, 1760), p. 449 (Ruffhead).
[381] *Monthly Review*, XXVIII (February, 1763), p. 148; XXVIII (April, 1763), pp. 281-282.
[382] *Monthly Review*, XXIII (September, 1760), pp. 204-205; XXVI (February, 1762), p. 140; XXVIII (February, 1763), p. 146; XXVIII (April, 1763), pp. 274-275.

senting primitive people without genuine knowledge on the part of the author, the reviewers, including Goldsmith and Ruffhead, thought it insulting to the readers' intelligence and demanded that historical truth be presented together with moral judgments in any honest depiction of the uncultivated society.[383]

Only the sublime, of all the pre-romantic aesthetic developments, truly appealed to the writers in the review. Griffiths himself noted that the response was not universal,[384] but regarded the sublime as natural. To be sure, it was inconsistent with concepts of regularity,[385] but it formed its model in nature itself. Just as "jarring elements are sometimes made to unite",[386] the sublime made use of nature "where nature, secure in her original majestic wildness, derides the subjection of art, inspires the mind with a congenial sublimity, and elevates the imagination by a kind of sympathetic power".[387] In his basic disagreement with Burke on the sublime, Goldsmith in the review made clear his own opinion that the power to terrify was also, because of its relation to the deity, the power to instruct,[388] thus placing it within the bounds of orthodox didactic criticism.

In all, then, it is apparent that if the aesthetic comments in the *Monthly* were more liberal than those in the *Critical*, the judgments of neither could escape the moral atmosphere in the climate of opinion during the Seven Years' War, and the didactic values of literature were the foremost manifestation of neoclassical theory.

---

[383] *Monthly Review*, XVII (August, 1757), pp. 150-151 (Goldsmith); XXII (February, 1760), p. 126 (Ruffhead); XXVI (June, 1762), p. 477.
[384] *Monthly Review*, XIV (April, 1756), p. 352.
[385] *Monthly Review*, XXV (August, 1761), p. 103 (Ruffhead).
[386] *Monthly Review*, XVI (February, 1757), p. 179.
[387] *Monthly Review*, XXVIII (May, 1763), p. 376 (Langhorne).
[388] *Monthly Review*, XVI (May, 1757), p. 475. See, also, XVI (March, 1757), p. 227 (Ward).

AFTERWORD

To summarize briefly the results of this investigation would seem as inappropriate as it would be difficult. The one fact that emerges most clearly is that too often scholars have oversimplified the complexities of both historical and literary subject matter. For example, in attempting to redress the excesses of Whig interpretations of the Seven Years' War, the Namier historians have provided a bias of their own, and, because of their partisan preoccupations, neither group has evaluated properly the role of John Wilkes as it appeared to his contemporaries. The subtleties in those early reactions to Wilkes have been obscured in the process of castigating his demagogy or defending his idealism. In the same way, literary analysts seeking the origin of romanticism in the eighteenth century too often have spoken about it from a point of view which has ignored the manner in which new aesthetic ideas were introduced and absorbed within the traditional framework. For just such reasons as these, therefore, an examination of the periodicals, which after all expressed popular contemporary opinion, should be valuable, but to reduce the results to capsule form would deny the evidence of an assortment of responses on the various topics investigated in this study.

Are there, then, no conclusions to be made at least about the relative liberalism and conservatism of the periodicals themselves? To be sure, it is possible to conclude that the *London* was generally more conservative than the *Gentleman's* or the *Grand* more liberal than the *British*, but to offer such flat statements has not been the main object of this analysis. What has been more particularly needed is some understanding of the range of conservative and liberal opinions in the periodicals as it is reflected by comments within specific, sensitive areas of judgment. This need becomes more apparent when even a single, important illustration is considered. It has for a long time – since Johnson's remarks, in fact – been common to suppose that comments in the *Monthly* were diametrically opposed to those in the *Critical*. Because they were political and religious antagonists, it has been assumed that the two reviews also reflected contrasting aesthetic views. Yet if this study has done nothing else, it has demonstrated the remarkable likeness in remarks on literature and the arts by the *Critical* and *Monthly*. This fact, together with the evidence from the other periodicals, should be ample warning against such easy generalizations as those that Samuel Kliger has made about the correspondence between political and literary opinions in the eighteenth century.

In more positive terms, what this study has attempted is an exploration of periodicals and their opinions during an important time in English history. By presenting an analysis of the contents of well-known periodicals, it has sought to set the record straight and to illuminate further areas for investigation. Moreover, by introducing hitherto unexamined periodical literature, this primary account has attempted to point out new paths for critical examination. Other studies already have demonstrated some of the possibilities. George Nobbe's careful consideration of the *North Briton* suggests the sort of analysis that should be made not only for other essay-journals but for magazines and reviews as well. While Carlson's important pioneering study of the *Gentleman's* was itself essential, the time now seems appropriate for a closer examination of such periodicals within a more limited area and a more restricted time period. The effect in this present work of Benjamin Nangle's discovery of the contributors to the *Monthly* sufficiently argues the need for seeking out more and more such information.

This, then, has been an attempt to mark out only one small area for further investigation. The needs for further studies even within this narrow compass are those that R.P. Bond has recently suggested for the full field of periodical literature:[1]

Short studies and sizable would be welcome of many individual periodicals and of editors, writers, and publishers of periodicals. Careful editions of the most meritorious and important journals would prove quite helpful. . . . The major and the minor types of periodicals, considered by form or by content, would repay thoughtful and scrupulous investigation. . . . Inquiries into influences from within and without the press can clarify its progression. Particular devices would prove appropriate for critical scrutiny, such as the eidolon, the club, correspondence, the motto, and serialization. Bibliographical explorations could make a collaboration of the history of the periodic press and the history of printing. The economic basis of journalistic society also would become clearer from specific investigations of circulation, the "taxes on knowledge', the profits of periodical publication, the wages of editor-and authorship, and especially . . . the finances of advertisements.

It is to be hoped that *English Literary Periodicals and the Climate of Opinion during the Seven Years' War* has contributed some light to help guide others in their journey through the darkness.

---

[1] Bond, pp. 47-48. Among recent work in the periodicals, Robert L. Haig's *The Gazetteer, 1735-1797* (Carbondale, 1960), which the author describes in his preface as "the first attempt ever made to record in detail the history of a single eighteenth-century daily newspaper", is evidence of both the accuracy of Bond's description of the situation and the fact that scholars are responding to the need.

BIBLIOGRAPHY

PERIODICALS COVERED IN THE STUDY

Unless otherwise noted, the edition of the periodical that was used for this study was the bound volume of the original or a microfilm copy of it. Dates outside parentheses refer to years in which the periodical appeared from 1756-1763.

Annual Register, 1758-1763.
Auditor, 1762-1763. The edition used was in *Political Controversy* (London, S. Williams, 1762-1763).
Bee, 1759. The edition used was the reprint in Oliver Goldsmith, *Essays and the Bee* (Boston, Wells and Lilly, 1820). Pagination for the *Bee* was kept separate from the other essays.
British Magazine, 1760-1763.
Briton, 1762-1763, in *Political Controversy*.
Busy Body, 1759.
Centinel, 1757.
Christian's Magazine, 1760-1763.
Connoisseur, 1756. The edition used was the *British Essayists* (London, Barnard and Farley, 1819). However, attributions of contributors is to the Boston, Little, Brown, 1866 edition.
Con-Test, 1756-1757.
Court Magazine, 1761-1763.
Crab Tree, 1757.
Critical Review, 1756-1763.
General Magazine of Arts and Sciences, 1756-1763.
Gentleman's Magazine, 1756-1763.
Grand Magazine, 1758-1760.
Grand Magazine of Magazines, 1758-1759.
Imperial Magazine, 1760-1762.
Lady's Museum, 1760-1761.
Literary Magazine, 1756-1758.
London Magazine, 1756-1763.
Monitor, 1756-1763. References which include volume numbers are to the London, J. Scott, 1757 and 1760 editions. Later references include those in *Political Controversy*.

Monthly Review, 1756-1763.
New Royal and Universal Magazine, 1759.
North Briton, 1762-1763, in *Political Controversy*.
Old Maid, 1756.
Patriot, 1762.
Philological Miscellany, 1761.
Prater, 1756.
Royal Female Magazine, 1760.
Royal Magazine, 1759-1763.
Spiritual Magazine, 1761-1762. The edition used was *Divine Moral, and Historical Miscellanies in Prose and Verse* (London, J. Fuller and T. Luckman, 1761-1762).
Test, 1756-1757.
Theatrical Review, 1763.
Universal Magazine, 1756-1763.
Universal Museum, 1762-1763.
Universal Visiter, 1756.
Weekly Magazine, 1758.
World, 1756. The edition used was the *British Essayists* (Boston, Little, Brown, 1866).

SECONDARY SOURCES

Abrams, Meyer H., *The Mirror and the Lamp* (New York, Norton, 1958).
Almon, John, *History of the Late Minority* (London, no pub., 1766).
——, *A Review of Lord Bute's Administration* (London, no pub., 1763).
——, *A Review of Mr. Pitt's Administration* (London, G. Kearsley, 1762).
Appleton, William W., *A Cycle of Cathay* (New York, Columbia University Press, 1951).
Aronson, A., "The Anatomy of Taste: a Note on Eighteenth-Century Periodical Literature", *MLN*, LXI (1946), pp. 228-236.
Atkins, John W. H., *English Literary Criticism: Seventeenth and Eighteenth Centuries* (London, Methuen, 1951).
Babcock, R. W., "The Idea of Taste in the Eighteenth Century", *PMLA*, L (1935), pp. 922-926.
Balderston, Katherine C., *A Census of the Manuscripts of Oliver Goldsmith* (New York, E. B. Hackett, 1926).
——, (ed.), *The Collected Letters of Oliver Goldsmith* (Cambridge, Cambridge University Press, 1928).
Barwick, G. F., "Some Magazines of the Eighteenth Century", *Transactions of the Bibliographical Society*, X (1908-1909), pp. 109-140.
Bateson, Frederick W., *Cambridge Bibliography of English Literature* (Cambridge, Cambridge University Press, 1940-1957), 5 volumes.
Becker, Carl L., *The Heavenly City of the Eighteenth-Century Philosophers* (New Haven, Yale University Press, 1932).
Beresford, John, (ed.), *The Diary of a Country Parson, the Reverend James Woodeforde, 1758-1781* (London, Oxford University Press, 1924).

Bissell, Benjamin H., *The American Indian in English Literature of the Eighteenth Century* (New Haven, Yale University Press, 1925).

Bleackley, Horace W., *Life of John Wilkes* (London, J. Lane, 1917).

Bloom, Edward A., *Samuel Johnson in Grub Street* (Providence, Brown University Press, 1957).

Bond, Donald F., "The *Gentleman's Magazine*", *MP*, XXXVIII 1940), pp. 85-100.

Bond, Richmond P., (ed.), *Studies in the Early English Periodical* (Chapel Hill, University of North Carolina Press, 1957).

Bosker, Aisso, *Literary Criticism in the Age of Johnson* (Groningen, J. B. Wolters, 1930).

Botting, R. B., "Johnson, Smart, and the *Universal Visiter*", *MP*, XXXVI (1939), pp. 293-300.

Bredvold, Louis I., *The Intellectual Milieu of John Dryden* (Ann Arbor, University of Michigan Press, 1956).

Brittain, Robert E., "Christopher Smart in the Magazines", *Library*, XXI (1941), pp. 320-336.

Brown, John, *An Estimate of the Manners and Principles of the Times*, Second Edition (London, L. Davis and C. Reymers, 1757-1758), 2 volumes.

Brown, W. C., *Charles Churchill: Poet, Rake, and Rebel* (Lawrence, University of Kansas Press, 1954).

Bryant, Donald C., "Edmund Burke and His Literary Friends", *Washington University Studies* (1939).

Burke, Edmund, *Works* (London, F. and J. Rivington, 1861), 8 volumes.

Butterfield, Herbert, *George the Third and the Historians* (London, Macmillan, 1957).

——, *George the Third, Lord North, and the People, 1779-1780* (London, Bell, 1949).

——, *Man on His Past: the Study of the History of Historical Scholarship* (Cambridge, Cambridge University Press, 1955).

——, *The Origins of Modern Science, 1300-1800* (New York, Macmillan, 1951).

Carlson, C. Lennart, *The First Magazine. A History of the Gentleman's Magazine* (Providence, Brown University Press, 1938).

Carlyle, Alexander, *Autobiography* (Edinburgh and London, Blackwood, 1861).

Caskey, John Homer, "The Life and Works of Edward Moore", *Yale Studies in English*, LXXV (1927).

Chapman, R. W., (ed.), *The Letters of Samuel Johnson* (Oxford, Clarendon Press, 1952), 3 volumes.

Christelow, Allan, "Economic Background of the Anglo-Spanish War of 1762", *JMH*, XVIII (1946), pp. 22-36.

Clark, Alexander F. B., *Boileau and the French Classical Critics in England, 1660-1830* (Paris, Champion, 1925).

Clifford, James L., (ed.), *Eighteenth-Century English Literature* (New York, Oxford University Press, 1959).

Collins, Arthur S., *Authorship in the Days of Johnson* (London, Holden, 1927).

Copeland, Thomas W., (ed.), *The Correspondence of Edmund Burke* (Chicago, University of Chicago Press, 1958).

——, *Our Eminent Friend Edmund Burke* (New Haven, Yale University Press, 1949).

Corbett, Julian S., *England in the Seven Years' War* (New York, London, Bombay, and Calcutta, Longmans, Green, 1907), 2 volumes.

Crane, Ronald S., (ed.), *Critics and Criticism, Ancient and Modern* (Chicago, University of Chicago Press, 1952).

——, (ed.), *New Essays by Oliver Goldsmith* (Chicago, University of Chicago Press, 1927).

——, "On Writing the History of English Criticism, 1650-1800", *University of Toronto Quarterly*, XXII (1953), pp. 376-391.

—— and F. B. Kaye, *A Census of British Newspapers and Periodicals, 1620-1800* (Chapel Hill, University of North Carolina Press, 1927).

Curtis, Lewis P., (ed.), *Letters of Laurence Sterne* (London, Oxford University Press, 1935).

Dampier, William C., *A History of Science*, Third Edition (Cambridge, Cambridge University Press, 1942).

Dobrée, Bonamy, (ed.), *The Letters of George the Third* (London, Cassell, 1935).

Dorn, Walter L., *Competition for Empire, 1740-1763* (New York, Harper and Brothers, 1940).

Drake, Nathan, *Essays, Biographical, Critical, and Historical, Illustrative of the Rambler, Adventurer, and Idler* (London, W. Suttaby, 1809-1810), 2 volumes.

Eldon, Carl W., *England's Subsidy Policy toward the Continent during the Seven Years' War* (Philadelphia, Times and News, 1938).

Eyck, Erich, *Pitt versus Fox, Father and Son, 1735-1806*, translated by Eric Northcott (London, G. Bell, 1950).

Fairchild, Hoxie Neale, *The Noble Savage* (New York, Columbia University Press, 1928).

——, *Religious Trends in English Poetry* (New York, Columbia University Press, 1939-1957), 4 volumes.

Feiling, Keith Grahame, *The Second Tory Party, 1714-1832* (London, Macmillan, 1938).

Fortesque, John W., (ed.), *Correspondence of King George the Third, from 1760 to December, 1783* (London, Macmillan, 1927-1928), 6 volumes.

Foster, James R., *History of the Pre-Romantic Novel in England* (New York, Modern Language Association of America, 1949).

——, "Smollett's Pamphleteering Foe Shebbeare", *PMLA*, LVII (1942), pp. 1053-1100.

Foster, Michael, *Lectures on the History of Physiology during the Sixteenth, Seventeenth, and Eighteenth Centuries* (Cambridge, Cambridge University Press, 1901).

Freeman, William, *Oliver Goldsmith* (London, H. Jenkins, 1951).

Friedman, Arthur, "Goldsmith's Contributions to the *Critical Review*", *MP*, XLIV (1946), pp. 23-52.

Frye, Northrup, *Anatomy of Criticism* (Princeton, Princeton University Press, 1957).

Gibbs, J. W. M., (ed.), *The Works of Oliver Goldsmith* (London, G. Bell, 1884-1886), 5 volumes.

Gipson, Lawrence H., *The British Empire before the American Revolution* (Caldwell, Idaho, Caxton, 1936-1956), 8 volumes.

Golden, Morris, "Goldsmith Attributions in the *Literary Magazine*", *Notes and Queries*, III (1956), pp. 432-435, 489-493.

——, "Goldsmith and 'The Distresses of a Hired Writer' ", *Notes and Queries*, II (1955), p. 200.

——, "Goldsmith and 'Natural Concord' ", *Notes and Queries*, II (1955), pp. 436-438.

——, "Goldsmith and 'The Present State of Russia and France' ", *Notes and Queries*, II (1955), pp. 393-394.

——, "Goldsmith and the *Universal Museum*", *Notes and Queries*, IV (1957), pp. 339-348.

——, "Three Goldsmith Attributions", *Notes and Queries*, V (1958), pp. 24-26.

Graham, Henry Grey, *Scottish Men of Letters in the Eighteenth Century* (London, A. and C. Black, 1901).

Graham, Walter, *The Beginnings of English Literary Periodicals* (New York and London, Oxford University Press, 1926).

——, *English Literary Periodicals* (New York, Thomas Nelson and Sons, 1930).

Grant, Douglas, (ed.), *The Poetical Works of Charles Churchill* (Oxford, Clarendon Press, 1956).

Grant, W. L., "Canada *versus* Guadeloupe, an Episode in the Seven Years' War", *American Historical Review*, XVII (1911-1912), pp. 735-743.

Gray, Charles Harold, *Theatrical Criticism in London to 1795* (New York, Columbia University Press, 1931).

Greene, Donald J., "Johnson's Contributions to the *Literary Magazine*", *RES*, VII (1956), pp. 367-392.

——, *The Politics of Samuel Johnson* (New Haven, Yale University Press, 1960).

Gregory, Winifred, *et al.*, *Union List of Serials in Libraries of the United States and Canada*, Second Edition (New York, H. W. Wilson, 1943), *Supplement* (1945).

Greig, J. Y. T., (ed.), *Letters of David Hume* (Oxford, Clarendon Press, 1932), 2 volumes.

Haber, Francis C., *The Age of the World: Moses to Darwin* (Baltimore, The Johns Hopkins Press, 1959).

Hagstrum, Jean H., *Samuel Johnson's Literary Criticism* (Minneapolis, University of Minnesota Press, 1952).

Haig, Robert L., *The Gazetteer: 1735-1797* (Carbondale, Southern Illinois University Press, 1960).

Hannay, David, *Life of Tobias George Smollett* (London, Walter Scott, 1887).

Hanson, Laurence, *Government and the Press, 1695-1763* (Oxford, Oxford University Press, 1936).

Hawkins, Aubrey, "Some Writers on the *Monthly Review*", *RES*, VII (1931), pp. 168-181.

Hazen, Allen T., (ed.), *Samuel Johnson's Prefaces and Dedications* (New Haven, Yale University Press, 1937).

Heidler, Joseph B., "History, from 1700-1800, of English Criticism of Prose Fiction", *University of Illinois Studies in Language and Literature*, XIII (1928).

Herrick, Marvin T., *The Poetics of Aristotle in England* (New Haven, Yale University Press, 1930).

Hill, George B. and L. F. Powell, (eds.), *Boswell's Life of Johnson* (Oxford, Clarendon Press, 1934-1950), 6 volumes.

Hogan, Charles B., *Shakespeare in the Theatre* (Oxford, Oxford University Press, 1957), 2 volumes.

Hooker, Edward N., "The Discussion of Taste, from 1750 to 1770, and the New Trends in Literary Criticism", *PMLA*, XLIX (1934), pp. 577-592.

——, "The Reviewers and the New Criticism, 1754-1770", *PQ*, XIII (1934), pp. 189-202.

——, "The Reviewers and the New Trends in Poetry, 1754-1770", *MLN*, LI (1936), pp. 207-214.

Ilchester, Mary Eleanor Anne Countess of and Lord Stavordale, (eds.), *The Life and Letters of Lady Sarah Lennox, 1745-1826* (London, J. Murray, 1902).

Joliat, Eugene, *Smollett et la France* (Paris, Librairie Ancienne Honore Champion, 1935).

Jones, Claude E., "Christopher Smart, Richard Rolt, and the *Universal Visiter*", *Library*, XVIII (1937), pp. 212-214.

——, "Contributors to the *Critical Review, 1756-1785*", *MLN*, LXI (1946), pp. 433-441.

——, "The *Critical Review's* First Thirty Years (1756-1785)", *Notes and Queries*, III (1956), pp. 78-80.

——, "The *Critical Review* and Some Major Poets", *Notes and Queries*, III (1956), p. 114.

——, "Dramatic Criticism in the *Critical Review*, 1756-1785", *MLQ*, XX (1959), pp. 18-26.

——, "The English Novel: a *Critical* View, 1756-1785", *MLR*, XIX (1958), pp. 147-159 and 213-224.

——, "Poetry and the *Critical Review*, 1756-1785", *MLQ*, IX (1948), pp. 17-36.

——, "Smollett Studies", *University of California Publications in English*, IX (1942).

Jones, Richard F., "Science and Criticism in the Neo-Classical Age of English Literature", *JHI*, I (1940), pp. 381-412.

Jones, W. P., "The Contemporary Reputation of Gray's *Odes*", *MP*, XXVIII (1930), pp. 61-82.

——, "The Vogue of Natural History in England, 1750-1770", *Annals of Science*, II (1937), pp. 345-352.

Jucker, Ninetta S., (ed.), *The Jenkinson Papers, 1760-1766* (London, Macmillan, 1949).

Kahrl, George M., *Tobias Smollett, Traveler-Novelist* (Chicago, University of Chicago Press, 1945).

Kent, Elizabeth E., *Goldsmith and His Booksellers* (Ithaca, Cornell University Press, 1933).

Kliger, Samuel, *The Goths in England: a Study in Seventeenth and Eighteenth-Century Thought* (Cambridge, Mass., Harvard University Press, 1952).

——, "Whig Aesthetics: a Phase of Eighteenth-Century Taste", *ELH*, XVI (1949), pp. 135-150.

Knapp, Lewis M., "Dr. John Armstrong, Litterateur, and Associate of Smollett, Thomson, Wilkes, and Other Celebrities", *PMLA*, LIX (1944), pp. 1019-1058.

——, "Ralph Griffiths, Author and Publisher, 1746-1750", *Library*, XX (1939), pp. 197-213.

——, "Rex *versus* Smollett: More Data on the Smollett-Knowles Libel Case", *MP*, XLI (1944), pp. 221-227.

——, "Smollett and the Elder Pitt', *MLN*, LIX (1944), pp. 250-257.

——, "Smollett's Works as Printed by William Strahan", *Library*, XIII (1932), pp. 282-291.

——, *Tobias Smollett, Doctor of Men and Manners* (Princeton, Princeton University Press, 1949).

Krutch, Joseph W., *Samuel Johnson* (New York, Henry Holt, 1944).

Laski, Harold J., *Political Thought in England: Locke to Bentham* (London, Oxford University Press, 1950).

Lewis, W. S., *et al.*, (eds.), *Horace Walpole's Correspondence* (New Haven, Yale University Press, 1937-   ).

Lovejoy, Arthur O., *Essays in the History of Ideas* (Baltimore, Johns Hopkins University Press, 1948).

Lynch, James J., *Box, Pit, and Gallery* (Berkeley and Los Angeles, University of California Press, 1953).

McAdam, Jr., Edward L., *Dr. Johnson and the English Law* (Syracuse, University of Syracuse Press, 1951).

MacClintock, William D., *Joseph Warton's Essay on Pope* (Chapel Hill, University of North Carolina Press, 1933).

Maccoby, Simon, *English Radicalism, 1762-1785* (London, Allen and Unwin, 1955).

McCutcheon, Roger P., "The Beginnings of Book-Reviewing in English Periodicals", *PMLA*, XXXVII (1922), pp. 691-706.

McKenzie, Gordon, "Critical Responsiveness: a Study of the Psychological Current in Later Eighteenth-Century Criticism", *University of California Publications in English*, XX (1949).

McKillop, Alan D., "Notes on Smollett", *PQ*, VII (1928), pp. 368-374.

Marlow, Louis, *Sackville of Drayton* (London, Home and Van Thal, 1948).

Marr, George S., *The Periodical Essayists of the Eighteenth Century* (London, James Clarke, 1923).

Martz, Louis L., "The Later Career of Tobias Smollett", *Yale University Studies in English*, XCVII (1942).

Mauduit, Israel, *Considerations on the Present German War*, Third Edition (London, no pub., 1760).

Mineka, Francis E., *The Dissidence of Dissent* (Chapel Hill, University of North Carolina Press, 1944).

Monk, Samuel, *The Sublime: a Study of Critical Theories in Eighteenth-Century England* (New York, Modern Language Association of America, 1935).

Moore, Cecil A., *Background of English Literature, 1700-1760* (Minneapolis, University of Minnesota Press, 1953).

Mossner, Ernest C., *The Forgotten Hume: le bon David* (New York, Columbia University Press, 1943).

——, *The Life of David Hume* (Austin, University of Texas Press, 1954).

—— and Raymond Klibansky, (eds.), *New Letters of David Hume* (London, Oxford University Press, 1955).

Namier, Lewis B., *Additions and Corrections to Sir John Fortesque's Edition of the Correspondence of King George the Third (Volume I)* (Manchester, Manchester University Press, 1937).

——, *The Structure of Politics at the Accession of George the Third* (London, Macmillan, 1929), 2 volumes.

Nangle, Benjamin C., *The Monthly Review, Indexes of Contributors and Articles* (Oxford, Oxford University Press, 1934).

Nichols, John, *Illustrations of the Literary History of the Eighteenth Century* (London, Nichols, son, and Bentley, 1817-1858), 8 volumes.

——, *Literary Anecdotes of the Eighteenth Century* (London, Nichols, son, and Bentley, 1812-1816), 9 volumes.

Nicolson, Marjorie, *Newton Demands the Muse* (Princeton, Princeton University Press, 1946).

Nobbe, George, *The North Briton* (New York, Columbia University Press, 1939).

Noyes, Edward S., (ed.), *The Letters of Tobias Smollett, M.D.* (Cambridge, Mass., Harvard University Press, 1926).

Oppenheimer, J. M., "John and William Hunter and Some Contemporaries in Literature and Art", *Bulletin of the History of Medicine*, XXIII (1949), pp. 21-47.

——, "A Note on William Hunter and Tobias Smollett", *Journal of the History of Medicine and Allied Sciences*, II (1947), pp. 481-486.

Page, Eugene R., *George Colman the Elder* (New York, Columbia University Press, 1935).

Pares, Richard, *King George the Third and the Politicians* (Oxford, Clarendon Press, 1953).

——, *War and Trade in the West Indies* (Oxford, Clarendon Press, 1936).

Parker, Alice, "Tobias Smollett and the Law", *SP*, XXXIX (1942), pp. 545-558.

Parkin, Charles, *The Moral Basis of Burke's Political Thought* (Cambridge, Cambridge University Press, 1957).

Paston, George [pseud.], *Sidelights on the Georgian Period* (London, Methuen, 1903).

Plomer, H. R., *A Dictionary of the Printers and Booksellers . . . in England, Scotland, and Ireland* (Oxford, Clarendon Press, 1932).

Plumb, John Harold, *England in the Eighteenth Century* (London, Penguin, 1950).

Plumb, John Harold, *The First Four Georges* (London, Batsford, 1956).
Pope, Dudley, *At Twelve Mr. Byng Was Shot* (Philadelphia and New York, J. B. Lippincott, 1962).
Postgate, Raymond W., *That Devil Wilkes* (New York, Vanguard, 1929).
Randall, John H., *The Making of the Modern Mind* (Boston and New York, Houghton Mifflin, 1926).
Raven, Charles E., *Natural Religion and Christian Theology* (Cambridge, Cambridge University Press, 1953).
Rea, Robert R., *The English Press in Politics, 1760-1774* (Lincoln, University of Nebraska Press, 1963).
Read, Allen Walker, "Suggestions for an Academy in England in the Latter Half of the Eighteenth Century", *MP*, XXXVI (1938), pp. 145-156.
Robbins, Caroline, *The Eighteenth-Century Commonwealthman* (Cambridge, Mass., Harvard University Press, 1959).
Roper, Derek, "Smollett's 'Four Gentemen': the First Contributors to the *Critical Review*", *RES*, X (1959), pp. 38-44.
Ross, John F., "Swift and Defoe, a Study in Relationship", *University of California Publications in English*, XI (1941).
Rudé, George, *Wilkes and Liberty* (Oxford, Clarendon Press, 1962).
Ryskamp, Charles, *William Cowper of the Inner Temple, Esquire* (Cambridge, Cambridge University Press, 1959).
Saintsbury, George, *A History of Criticism and Literary Taste in Europe* (New York, Humanities Press, 1950), 3 volumes.
Sarason, Bertram D., "Edmund Burke and the Two *Annual Registers*", *PMLA*, LXVIII (1953), pp. 496-508.
Schilling, Bernard N., *Conservative England and the Case against Voltaire* (New York, Columbia University Press (1950).
Sedgwick, Romney, (ed.), *Letters from George the Third to Lord Bute, 1756-1766* (London, Macmillan, 1939).
Seitz, R. W., "Goldsmith and the *Literary Magazine*", *RES*, V (1929), pp. 410-430.
Shebbeare, John, *A Fourth Letter to the People of England*, Second Edition (London, M. Collyer, 1756).
Sherbo, Arthur, "Christopher Smart and the *Universal Visiter*", *Library*, X (1955), pp. 203-205.
——, (ed.), *New Essays by Arthur Murphy* (East Lansing, Michigan State University Press, 1963).
Sherburn, George, *The Restoration and Eighteenth Century (1660-1789)* (New York, Appleton-Century-Crofts, 1949).
Sherrard, Oliver A., *Lord Chatham: Pitt and the Seven Years' War* (Fair Lawn, New Jersey, Essential Books, 1955).
Singer, Charles, *A Short History of Science to the Nineteenth Century* (Oxford, Clarendon Press, 1943).
Smelser, Marshall, *The Campaign for the Sugar Islands, 1759* (Chapel Hill, University of North Carolina Press, 1955).
Smollett, Tobias G., *The History of England from the Revolution in 1688 to the Death of George the Second* (Philadelphia, E. Littell, 1828), 2 volumes.

Spector, Robert D., "Additional Attacks on the *Critical Review*", *Notes and Queries*, III (1956), p. 425.

——, "Attacks on the *Critical Review*", *Periodical Post Boy* (1955), pp. 6-7.

——, "Further Attacks on the *Critical Review*", *Notes and Queries*, II (1955), p. 535.

——, "Language Control in the Eighteenth Century", *Word Study*, XXVII (1951), pp. 1-2.

——, "Late Neo-Classical Taste", *Notes and Queries*, CXCVI (1951), pp. 11-12.

——, "Smollett and Admiral Byng", *Notes and Queries*, III (1955), pp. 66-67.

Stearns, Bertha Monica, "Early English Periodicals for Ladies", *PMLA*, XLVIII (1933), pp. 38-60.

Stephen, Leslie, *History of English Thought in the Eighteenth Century*, Third Edition (New York, P. Smith, 1949), 2 volumes.

Straus, Ralph, *Robert Dodsley* (London, J. Lane, 1910).

Stromberg, Roland N., *Religious Liberalism in Eighteenth-Century England* (London, Oxford University Press, 1954).

Sutherland, Lucy S., *The East India Company in Eighteenth-Century Politics* (Oxford, Clarendon Press, 1952).

Sykes, Norman B., *Church and State in the Eighteenth Century* (Cambridge, Cambridge University Press, 1934).

Taylor, A. J. P. and Richard Pares, (eds.), *Essays Presented to Sir Lewis Namier* (London, Macmillan, 1956).

Tompkins, J. M. S., *The Popular Novel in England, 1770-1800* (London, Constable, 1932).

Trevelyan, G. M., *An Autobiography and Other Essays* (London, New York, and Toronto, Longmans, Green, 1949).

——, *English Social History* (London, New York, and Toronto, Longmans, Green, 1942).

——, *History of England* (London, Longmans, Green, 1937).

Tupper, Caroline F., "Essays Erroneously Attributed to Goldsmith", *PMLA*, XXXIX (1924), pp. 325-342.

——, "Goldsmith and 'The Gentleman Who Signs D' ", *MLN*, XLV (1930), pp. 71-77.

Turberville, A. S., *English Men and Manners in the Eighteenth Century* (Oxford, Clarendon Press, 1926).

——, (ed.), *Johnson's England* (Oxford, Clarendon Press, 1933), 2 volumes.

Tuveson, Ernest Lee, *Millennium and Utopia* (Berkeley and Los Angeles, University of California Press, 1949).

Underwood, Alfred C., *A History of the English Baptists* (London, Baptist Union, 1947).

Walpole, Horace, *Memoirs of the Reign of King George the Second* (London, H. Colburn, 1846-1847), 3 volumes.

——, *Memoirs of the Reign of King George the Third* (London, R. Bentley, 1845), 4 volumes.

Wardle, Ralph, *Oliver Goldsmith* (Lawrence, University of Kansas Press, 1957).

Warner, James H., "Eighteenth-Century English Reactions to the *Nouvelle Heloise*", *PMLA*, LII (1937), pp. 803-819.

Watson, J. Steven, *The Reign of George the Third, 1760-1815* (Oxford, Clarendon Press, 1960).

Watt, Ian, *The Rise of the Novel* (Berkeley and Los Angeles, University of California Press, 1957).

Weatherly, Edward H., (ed.), *The Correspondence of John Wilkes and Charles Churchill* (New York, Columbia University Press, 1954).

Weed, Katherine K. and R. P. Bond, *Studies of British Newspapers and Periodicals from the Beginnings to 1800: a Bibliography* (Chapel Hill, University of North Carolina Press, 1946).

Wellek, Rene, *A History of Modern Criticism, 1750-1950* (New Haven, Yale University Press, 1955), 2 volumes.

Weston, John Charles, "Burke's Authorship of the 'Historical Articles' in Dodsley's *Annual Register*", *PBSA*, LI (1957), pp. 244-249.

Whitridge, Arnold, *Tobias Smollett: a Study of His Miscellaneous Works* (New York, pub. by the author, 1925).

Wicheln, Herbert A., "Burke's *Essay on the Sublime* and Its Reviewers", *JEGP*, XXI (1922), pp. 645-661.

Wilkes, John, *A Complete Collection of the Genuine Papers, Letters, Etc., in the case of John Wilkes, Esq.* (Berlin [London?], no pub., 1769).

Wilkes, John W., "British Politics Preceding the American Revolution", *HLQ*, XX (1957), pp. 301-319.

Willey, Basil, *Seventeenth-Century Background* (New York, Doubleday, 1954).

Williams, Basil, *The Life of William Pitt, Earl of Chatham* (London, Longmans, Green, 1913), 2 volumes.

——, *The Whig Supremacy, 1714-1760* (Oxford, Clarendon Press, 1942).

Williams, Judith B., *A Guide to the Printed Materials for English Social and Economic History, 1750-1850* (New York, Columbia University Press, 1926).

Wimsatt, W. K. and Cleanth Brooks, *Literary Criticism, a Short History* (New York, Knopf, 1957).

Wolf, Abraham, *A History of Science, Technology, and Philosophy in the Eighteenth Century*, Second Edition (London, Allen and Unwin, 1952).

Wood, James P., *Magazines in the United States* (New York, Ronald Press, 1949).

INDEX